Beta Sigma Phi

Cook Light
Cookbook

Heritage
House INC.

COOK LIGHT
COOKBOOK

 Beta Sigma Phi

EDITORIAL STAFF

Managing Editor	Mary Jane Blount
Cookbook Editors	Georgia Brazil Mary Cummings Jane Hinshaw LaNita Stout
Typography	William Maul Sharon Whitehurst
Graphic Artist	John Robinson

PHOTOGRAPHY CREDITS

Mazola corn oil; American Spice Trade Association; Florida Celery Committee; Ocean Spray Cranberries, Inc.; Progresso Foods, Inc.; Florida Tomato Exchange; San Giorgio-Skinner Company; Minute rice.

© Favorite Recipes Press, A Division of Heritage House, Inc. MCMLXXXVI
P. O. Box 1408, Nashville, Tennessee 37202

Library of Congress Cataloging-in-Publication Data
Main entry under title:
The Beta Sigma Phi cook light cookbook.
    Includes index.
      1. Cookery. I. Beta Sigma Phi.
TX652.B477   1986   641.5   86-18408
ISBN 0-87197-213-1

Recipe for Cover on page 72.
Recipes for Page 1 on pages 166,169 and 184.
Recipes for Page 2 on page 79.

Contents

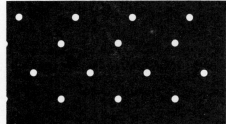  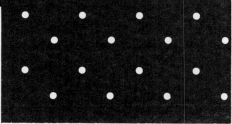

OFFICIAL PUBLICATION OF

BETA SIGMA PHI SORORITY

Dear Friends,

Beta Sigma Phi, the organization that has created this cookbook for you, is the largest sorority of its kind in the world. Members pursue social, cultural and service projects of all kinds. We are not a secret group; we are not connected with any school or college. We are non-political, and non-sectarian.

Our members are women of all ages, from all walks of life. We now have a membership of 250,000 in 34 countries around the world. Beta Sigma Phi is celebrating its 55th anniversary this year, and continues to offer the same opportunities it offered seven young women in Abilene, Kansas in 1931—that is, an intellectual and social experience that allows for self-growth and leadership opportunities; and a means for being of service to one's community, and to the world.

There is hardly a charitable or health foundation in existence that has not received, at some time, assistance from Beta Sigma Phi. Members give millions of dollars and hundreds of thousands of hours annually to service efforts around the globe. It is part of the Beta Sigma Phi philosophy— that is, to follow "only the good, only the true, only the beautiful."

Sincerely,

Linda Rostenberg, Vice President
Communications
Beta Sigma Phi International

6

Foreword

Your COOK LIGHT Cookbook is designed to help build an awareness of the nutritional value in your daily meals. It is not a substitute for a carefully planned weight loss program or a medically supervised special diet. It is a guide to cooking and serving foods that are the most nutritionally beneficial to your family.

The editors have attempted to present these tried-and-true family recipes in a form that allows approximate nutritional values to be computed. Persons with dietary or health problems or whose diets require close monitoring should not rely solely on the nutritional information provided. They should consult their physicians or a registered dietitian for specific information.

Abbreviations for Nutritional Analysis

Cal—Calories	Sod—Sodium
Prot—Protein	Potas—Potassium
Fat—Total Fat	gr—gram
Chol—Cholesterol	mg—milligram
Carbo—Carbohydrates	

Nutritional information for recipes is computed from values furnished by the United States Department of Agriculture Handbook. Many specialty items and new products now available on the market are not included in this handbook. However, producers of new products frequently publish nutritional information on each product's packaging and that information may be added, as applicable, for a more complete analysis.

Unless otherwise specified, the nutritional analysis is based on the following guidelines:

- All measurements are level.
- Artificial sweeteners vary in use. Some may be used as an equal substitution for sugar while others are more concentrated and require a lesser amount to equal sugar. Therefore, artificial sweeteners should be used "to taste," using the recipe ingredients as a guideline.
- Artificial sweeteners using aspartame (NutraSweet and Equal) should not be used as a sweetener in recipes involving prolonged heating, such as cakes, pies, casseroles, etc. Prolonged heating reduces the sweet taste. For further information on use of these sweeteners, refer to package information.
- Alcoholic ingredients have been analyzed for the basic ingredients, although cooking causes the evaporation of alcohol thus decreasing calories.
- Buttermilk, sour cream, and yogurt are commercial-type.
- Chicken, cooked for boning and chopping, has been roasted; this method yields the lowest caloric values.
- Cottage cheese is cream-style with 4.2% creaming mixture. Dry curd has no creaming mixture.
- Eggs are large.
- Evaporated milk is canned milk produced by the removal of approximately 60% of the water from whole milk.
- Flour is unsifted all-purpose flour.
- Garnishes, serving suggestions and other essentially optional additions and variations are not included in the analysis.
- Herbs, spices, seasoning mixes, flavoring extracts and artificial sweeteners are not included in the analysis.
- Low-fat milk is 1% butterfat.
- Margarine and butter are regular, not whipped or presoftened.
- Milk is whole milk, 3.5% butterfat.
- Oil is any cooking oil, usually a blend of oils from several sources.
- Salt to taste as noted in the method has not been included in the nutritional analysis.
- Shortening is hydrogenated vegetable shortening for all-purpose use.
- Soup referred to as "1 can" is the standard 10-ounce can of condensed soup.

If the nutritional analysis notes the exclusion of a particular ingredient, check the package information.

Cooking
on the
Light Side

Imagine having a gigantic covered dish dinner with Beta Sigma Phi sisters around the world! Or visiting in their homes where you would be served "the specialty of the house." What a great opportunity to sample each one's favorite nutritious dish!

The editors at Favorite Recipes Press have done the next best thing. We have asked you to send us your favorites to share with everyone. The result of this "covered dish dinner" is the BETA SIGMA PHI COOK LIGHT COOKBOOK—now you can try all these favorites—in your own home!

The Art of Menu Planning

As with any art, the first attempts at nutritious menu planning may be time-consuming and seem difficult, but practice leads to perfection. By learning the five basic food groups (see page 9), you have a foundation upon which you can create contrasting color and taste combinations for well balanced family meals. As your expertise grows, even your thoughts while shopping and planning will become nutrition conscious.

The nutritional analysis following the recipes in THE COOK LIGHT COOKBOOK provide information to take you one step further. The caloric content is a bonus that keeps your planning within a reasonable daily total. Total content listings for protein, fat, cholesterol, carbohydrates, sodium and potassium give you some of the necessary information to cater to special diets. Athletes are often on controlled intake of protein or carbohydrates. Persons with high blood pressure need to be very careful of sodium intake. And with the current concern about cholesterol and fat in the American diet, these values will be of primary concern for all.

There are lots of new products available that have been developed to make nutritious meals easier for YOU—the cook. Read the labels on foods you buy for accurate nutritional value. Many vegetables are processed with very little, if any, salt for low-sodium diets. "Packed in its own juice" appears on the labels of several brands of canned fruit. Wide use of artificial sweeteners is evident in desserts and cereals. Low-sugar cereals, especially the whole-grain varieties with their naturally sweet, nutty flavor, have gained popularity with cereal lovers of all ages.

Essentials for Good Nutrition

Meats

2 or more servings
Include meat, poultry, fish,
eggs, dried beans or peas,
and peanut butter.

Vegetables

3 or more servings
At least one dark green or
yellow vegetable every other
day; one choice each day
should be raw.

Fruits

2 servings
Have at least one citrus
fruit each day.

Milk

2 or more cups for adults and
4 or more cups for children
Includes cheeses and yogurt.

Breads & Cereals

4 servings
Include whole grain breads,
cereals and pasta.

For a well-balanced diet, 2 servings of fats and butter should also be included. Sweets and
extra servings of the basic groups provide additional food energy.

Basic Hints for Cooking Light

As you look through the recipes in THE COOK LIGHT COOKBOOK, you'll pick up special techniques that will carry over in all your cooking. The following list of general ideas will start you toward more nutritious meals for your whole family.

- When serving scrambled eggs, use only half the egg yolks, eliminating half the cholesterol.
- If a recipe calls for 2 eggs, leave out one of the yolks, substituting 1½ teaspoons polyunsaturated oil.
- Key words to look for on labels that will alert you to saturated fat—hydrogenated (hardened) oil, palm or palm-kernel oil, coconut oil, egg and egg-yolk solids, whole milk solids, imitation or milk chocolate, butter and any kind of animal fat. Avoid using these products.
- In most recipes, fats and oils can be reduced by ⅓ to ½ without a noticeable change in taste or texture. Experiment by gradually reducing the shortening or oil in your favorite recipes until you know exactly how much less you can use and still have satisfactory results.
- Use vegetable cooking spray for greasing pans or for sautéeing—saves the calories in shortening or margarine.
- Use brown rice in puddings and vegetable-rice combinations. It's higher in fiber and other nutrients than polished white rice.
- Cook in iron pots whenever possible—they add trace amounts of iron to your food.

Light Appetizers and Soups

Better nutrition starts every meal with a selection of finger foods so delicious that no one will suspect that they're actually good for you! Blend yogurt instead of sour cream with your favorite dip ingredients. Delicious! Mix equal parts yogurt and mayonnaise, to retain the taste of mayonnaise but appreciably less fat.

There are unending possibilities for healthy combinations of vegetables and low-calorie spreads or other toppings. Several possibilities are included in the photograph, Light Vegetable Canapés (see page 35 for photograph and page 37 for recipe).

The soups in COOK LIGHT are especially nutritious, whether you're in the mood for a hearty Chicken-Barley Soup or a summertime Creamy Garden Vegetable Soup. Keep in mind, also, that homemade soups and soup mixes are generally much lower in calories and sodium content than commercially canned soups.

Quick-Energy Beverages and Snacks

One sure way to save calories is to use nondairy creamer instead of cream in your coffee. Keep in mind, however, that creamers contain palm oil and other saturated fats. The best lightener for coffee is low-fat milk, or nonfat dry milk powder.

Stock up on low-sugar drink mixes or fruit juices to replace soft drinks. Children love the taste, and you'll love the nutritional value!

Snack on high-fiber foods to keep you from being hungry and still save calories. Whole-grain crackers, air-popped or unbuttered popcorn, raw vegetable sticks, apples and other fresh fruits—all are easy to keep on hand and good for you!

Your grocer's shelves are well-stocked with nutritious substitutes for candy bars and other high-calorie snacks. THE COOK LIGHT COOKBOOK includes many tasty treats that will satisfy your sweet tooth and your conscience at the same time.

Nutritious Main Dishes

To reduce the fat content when browning ground beef, drain in a colander. Blot with paper towels. Before returning ground beef to skillet, wipe the skillet with a paper towel.

Plan to use more recipes that call for minimal amounts of meat—each ounce of ground round in a casserole adds 90 calories!

Many casseroles call for cream of celery or mushroom soup. By using Soup and Casserole Sauce Mix (see page 44), not only will you save calories, you'll save money!

Baked or broiled fish retains about ⅓ more protein than when pan-fried, and also seals in more B vitamins and trace minerals.

Save calories by using sharp Cheddar cheese when the recipe calls for medium—it takes less sharp cheese for the same flavor result.

Legumes—lentils, dried peas and beans—combined with rice or other grains make an economical, complete protein substitute for meat. They are also a good source of vitamins, minerals and fiber.

Vitamin-Packed Breads

Whenever possible, bake your own breads for maximum nutritional value. Using the best whole-grain flours and ingredients will give you the best results. If you purchase dark bread, read the label carefully to make sure it is actually made with whole-grain flour—not with white flour and darkened with molasses or food coloring.

Versatile Vegetables

Scrub vegetables with a brush and cook with the skins on, whenever possible. The fiber in the skin seals in valuable nutrients during cooking. Prepare vegetables just before cooking. Rinse thoroughly in water, using a vegetable brush as needed. Do not soak vegetables in water as many of the vitamins and minerals are water-soluble, and these will be lost as the vegetables are drained.

Delightful Desserts

Dessert is the favorite part of any meal—even if you're cooking light! Serve sherbet, frozen yogurt, ice milk or frozen fruit bars. Although still comparatively high in calories and sugar, they're lower in fat. If fruit-flavored yogurt is your favorite, buy plain low-fat yogurt and add your own fresh fruit—the result is much lower in sugar.

Follow package directions for nonfat dry milk powder when making a delicious whipped topping. It has fewer calories and no palm oil or saturated fats that are abundant in commercial whipped toppings.

Light Menu Favorites

Low-Calorie Microwave Lunch

Kay Sandoz, Xi Beta Omega
Valentine, Nebraska

Low-Calorie Italian Pie
Tossed Salad
Strawberry Tapioca Parfait

Low-Calorie Italian Pie

1 pound lean ground beef	1 cup canned tomatoes
¼ cup chopped onion	¼ cup shredded Cheddar cheese substitute
½ teaspoon salt	2 tablespoons Parmesan cheese
¼ teaspoon pepper	
¼ teaspoon oregano	¼ teaspoon paprika
¼ teaspoon rosemary	½ 8-ounce package refrigerator crescent dinner rolls
1 4-ounce can mushrooms	

Combine crumbled ground beef, onion and seasonings in 2-quart glass casserole. Microwave, tightly covered, on High for 3 to 4 minutes or until ground beef is no longer pink, stirring once; drain. Stir in mushrooms, tomatoes and cheese substitute. Combine Parmesan cheese and paprika in shallow dish. Cut each crescent roll into 2 triangles. Roll and shape each into crescent. Coat with Parmesan mixture. Arrange over casserole. Microwave on High for 3 to 4 minutes or until rolls are cooked through. Yield: 6 servings.

Approx per serving: Cal 167, Prot 18.3 gr, Fat 8.7 gr, Chol 60.4 mg, Carbo 2.9 gr, Sod 320.4 mg, Potas 279.9 mg.
Nutritional information does not include refrigerator crescent rolls.

Strawberry Tapioca Parfait

1 cup low-fat milk	2 egg yolks, slightly beaten
1 tablespoon quick-cooking tapioca	1 teaspoon vanilla extract
Artificial sweetener to equal ¼ cup sugar	2 egg whites, stiffly beaten
⅛ teaspoon salt	2 cups strawberry halves

Combine milk, tapioca, sweetener and salt in 1-quart glass casserole. Let stand for 5 minutes. Stir in egg yolks. Microwave, covered, on High for 1½ to 2 minutes or until thickened, stirring several times. Stir in vanilla. Fold in egg whites gently. Alternate layers of strawberries and pudding in parfait glasses. Chill in refrigerator. Yield: 6 servings.

Approx per serving: Cal 66, Prot 3.8 gr, Fat 2.4 gr, Chol 85.5 mg, Carbo 7.5 gr, Sod 82.5 mg, Potas 166.0 mg.

Oriental Lunch

Sandra Claerhout, Omicron Omega
East Moline, Illinois

Sweet and Sour Chicken
Hot Fluffy Rice
Lettuce Salad
Fortune Cookies

Sweet and Sour Chicken

2 tablespoons oil	1 20-ounce can pineapple chunks
1½ pounds boned chicken	1 10-ounce jar sweet and sour sauce
3 stalks celery, sliced	
4 carrots, sliced	½ teaspoon salt
1 large green pepper, cut into squares	½ to 1 teaspoon coarsely ground pepper

Heat oil to 350 degrees in electric wok. Add chicken. Cook, covered, for 3 minutes. Turn chicken over. Cook, covered, for 3 minutes. Push to side of wok. Add vegetables, pineapple, sweet and sour sauce and seasonings. Cook for 2 minutes. Stir all ingredients together. Cook for 2 minutes longer or until vegetables are tender-crisp. Serve over rice. Yield: 4 servings.

Approx per serving: Cal 352, Prot 26.9 gr, Fat 9.9 gr, Chol 62.2 mg, Carbo 40.9 gr, Sod 395.0 mg, Potas 904.7 mg.
Nutritional information does not include sweet and sour sauce.

Cloud Lite Lunch

Jackie Vogler, Xi Sigma Pi
Hilltop Lakes, Texas

Crustless Mexican Quiche
Spinach and Mushroom Salad
Broiled Apple Slices

Crustless Mexican Quiche

1 small onion, chopped	10 ounces Monterey Jack cheese, shredded
1 red pepper, chopped	1¼ cups low-fat milk
1 green pepper, chopped	1 teaspoon basil
¼ cup broth	Dash of pepper
	Pinch of paprika

Sauté onion and peppers in broth in skillet until tender; drain. Layer sautéed vegetables and cheese in prepared pie plate. Pour mixture of milk and seasonings over cheese. Bake at 350 degrees for 35 minutes or until firm. Yield: 8 servings.

Approx per serving: Cal 168, Prot 10.7 gr, Fat 11.9 gr, Chol 36.7 mg, Carbo 5.1 gr, Sod 301.8 mg, Potas 164.9 mg.

Spinach and Mushroom Salad

4 cups crisp fresh spinach leaves	1 cup fresh mushrooms
2 tablespoons pine nuts	Tarragon vinegar to taste

Combine spinach, mushrooms and pine nuts in serving bowl. Season with salt substitute to taste. Sprinkle with tarragon vinegar; toss lightly. Yield: 8 servings.

Approx per serving: Cal 10, Prot 1.1 gr, Fat 0.1 gr, Chol 0.0 mg, Carbo 1.6 gr, Sod 20.8 mg, Potas 165.5 mg. Nutritional information does not include pine nuts.

Broiled Apple Slices

8 large apples	½ cup honey
½ cup butter, softened	Cinnamon to taste

Core apples. Cut crosswise into ½ inch thick slices. Spread 1 side with butter. Place buttered side down in baking dish. Spread with honey. Broil slowly until apples are tender. Sprinkle with cinnamon. Arrange in dessert dishes. Yield: 8 servings.

Approx per serving: Cal 288, Prot 0.6 gr, Fat 12.8 gr, Chol 35.5 mg, Carbo 48.0 gr, Sod 143.3 mg, Potas 246.7 mg.

Microwave Luncheon

Julie Gatsos, Zeta Chi
Monticello, Indiana

Microwave Tuna Wedges
Fresh Steamed Broccoli
Sliced Fresh Fruit
Ice Cold Milk

Microwave Tuna Wedges

1½ cups cooked rice	2 eggs, beaten
6 green onions, chopped	½ cup melted butter
2 cans water-pack tuna	¼ teaspoon thyme
	1 cup fine dry bread crumbs

Combine rice, onions, undrained tuna and eggs in bowl; mix well. Stir in butter, thyme and bread crumbs. Spread in lightly greased 9-inch pie plate. Cover with waxed paper. Microwave on High for 9 to 11 minutes or until set, turning dish once. Cut into wedges. Garnish with sliced tomato and grated cheese. Yield: 6 servings.

Approx per serving: Cal 369, Prot 22.7 gr, Fat 18.6 gr, Chol 171.1 mg, Carbo 26.4 gr, Sod 1059.0 mg, Potas 271.4 mg.

Bridge Luncheon

Ina M. Waldrop, Preceptor Omicron
Bethany, Oklahoma

Quiche
Fresh Fruit Salad
Crescent Rolls
Frozen Lemon Dessert
Tea or Coffee

Quiche

3 cups bread cubes	3 eggs, beaten
3 cups chopped ham	3 cups milk
8 ounces Cheddar cheese, grated	1 teaspoon dry mustard

Combine bread, ham, cheese, eggs, milk and mustard in bowl; mix well. Pour into large baking dish. Chill overnight. Let stand at room temperature for 1 hour. Bake at 350 degrees for 1 hour or until set. Yield: 6 servings.

Approx per serving: Cal 549, Prot 34.1 gr, Fat 35.7 gr, Chol 244.1 mg, Carbo 21.3 gr, Sod 1023.7 mg, Potas 432.7 mg.

Frozen Lemon Dessert

1 12-ounce can Milnot	½ to ¾ cup sugar
Juice and grated rind of 1 lemon	2 cups graham cracker crumbs
	¼ cup margarine

Chill Milnot in mixer bowl in freezer until ice crystals form around edge. Beat at high speed until stiff peaks form. Add lemon juice, lemon rind and sugar gradually, beating constantly. Combine graham cracker crumbs and margarine in bowl. Press into shallow rectangular dish. Spoon whipped mixture into prepared dish. Freeze until firm. Cut into squares. Yield: 6 servings.

Approx per serving: Cal 302, Prot 2.9 gr, Fat 11.0 gr, Chol 0.0 mg, Carbo 51.5 gr, Sod 328.3 mg, Potas 153.3 mg.
Nutritional information does not include Milnot.

Lunch à Deux

Mary Kay Simms, Preceptor Beta
Waukegan, Illinois

Barbecued Tuna
Cooked Cauliflower
Toast Points
Monster Cookies

Barbecued Tuna

1 6-ounce can water-pack tuna, drained	2 teaspoons prepared mustard
½ cup chopped celery	2 tablespoons Worcestershire sauce
¼ cup chopped onion	1 tablespoon vinegar
½ teaspoon oregano	½ cup tomato juice
2 packets artificial sweetener	

Combine tuna, celery, onion, seasonings and tomato juice in saucepan. Simmer for 45 minutes. Serve over cooked cauliflower with toast points. Yield: 2 servings.

Approx per serving: Cal 186, Prot 32.1 gr, Fat 1.1 gr, Chol 58.0 mg, Carbo 8.7 gr, Sod 2466.0 mg, Potas 656.7 mg.

Monster Cookies

6 eggs	4 teaspoons soda
2⅓ cups packed brown sugar	9 cups oats
2 cups sugar	1 24-ounce jar peanut butter
1 teaspoon vanilla extract	1 cup raisins
2 sticks butter, softened	1 cup chocolate chips
	1 cup pecans

Combine eggs and sugars in bowl. Add vanilla, butter and soda; mix well. Stir in oats, peanut butter, raisins, chocolate chips and pecans; mix well. Add a small amount of additional oats if dough is too sticky. Drop by ¼ cupfuls onto cookie sheet; flatten. Bake at 350 degrees for 10 to 12 minutes or until brown. Cool on wire rack. Yield: 60 cookies.

Approx per cookie: Cal 250, Prot 6.0 gr, Fat 13.4 gr, Chol 34.7 mg, Carbo 29.2 gr, Sod 179.2 mg, Potas 198.6 mg.

Light and Lively Dinner

Jean Udris, Xi Delta Xi
Lawrenceville, Georgia

★see Index for recipe

Gazpacho
Tossed Green Salad★
Marinated Chicken Drumettes
Strawberries with Strawberry Sauce

Gazpacho

1 large onion
2 large tomatoes
2 sweet red peppers, seeded
½ cup tomato paste
¼ cup olive oil
¼ cup lemon juice
2 cloves of garlic
¼ teaspoon cayenne pepper

2 cups chopped mushrooms
2 stalks celery, chopped
1 large cucumber, peeled, seeded, finely chopped
2 tablespoons chopped fresh parsley
2 teaspoons minced fresh chives

Combine onion, tomatoes, red peppers, tomato paste, olive oil, lemon juice, garlic, cayenne pepper and 3 cups water in blender container. Process at medium speed until smooth, scraping side occasionally. Pour into serving bowls. Sprinkle mushrooms, celery, cucumber, parsley and chives on top. Chill until serving time. Yield: 8 servings.

Approx per serving: Cal 108, Prot 2.4 gr, Fat 7.1 gr, Chol 0.0 mg, Carbo 10.5 gr, Sod 28.6 mg, Potas 455.4 mg.

Marinated Chicken Drumettes

24 chicken drumettes, skinned
⅔ cup Italian salad dressing
1½ teaspoons paprika

1½ teaspoons Italian seasoning
1½ tablespoons green chili salsa
1 tablespoon red wine vinegar

Place chicken in large saucepan. Add salad dressing, seasonings, salsa and vinegar. Bring to a boil over medium heat; reduce heat. Simmer, covered, for 20 to 30 minutes or until chicken is tender. Cool. Chill overnight. Arrange on serving plate lined with shredded lettuce. Garnish with parsley. Yield: 8 servings.
Note: Chicken may be reheated before serving.

Approx per serving: Cal 183, Prot 11.1 gr, Fat 14.7 gr, Chol 27.6 mg, Carbo 1.8 gr, Sod 493.9 mg, Potas 166.4 mg.

Strawberries with Strawberry Sauce

2 quarts fresh strawberries
Lemon juice to taste
1 tablespoon Kirsch

Frozen unsweetened apple juice concentrate to taste

Combine 2 cups strawberries, lemon juice, Kirsch and apple juice in blender container. Process until puréed. Combine with remaining strawberries in bowl; mix well. Chill until serving time. Spoon into stemmed dessert glasses. Garnish with whole stemmed strawberries and sprigs of mint. Yield: 8 servings.

Approx per serving: Cal 69, Prot 1.0 gr, Fat 0.7 gr, Chol 0.0 mg, Carbo 15.9 gr, Sod 1.3 mg, Potas 273.2 mg.

Gourmet Dinner For One

Gloria Smethers, Preceptor Laureate Kappa
Beatrice, Nebraska

★see Index for recipe

Lemon Chicken Breasts
Broccoli
Veggies with Low-Calorie Dressing
Fruit and Yogurt Dessert★

Lemon Chicken Breasts

4 chicken breast filets
½ cup lemon juice
Garlic powder to taste

Oregano to taste
Paprika to taste
16 ounces mushrooms

Place chicken breasts in Crock•Pot. Sprinkle with lemon juice and seasonings. Add mushrooms. Cook on High for 4 hours. Cook on Low until serving time. Yield: 4 servings.

Approx per serving: Cal 214, Prot 36.4 gr, Fat 4.0 gr, Chol 82.9 mg, Carbo 7.4 gr, Sod 84.5 mg, Potas 943.9 mg.

A Little Bit of Two Worlds

Beverly Oldaker, Laureate Alpha Delta
Pueblo, Colorado

Curry Beef Fried Rice
Chilled Asparagus Salad
Red-In-Snow Mousse

Curry Beef Fried Rice

¼ cup oil	4 cups cold cooked rice
½ onion, chopped	1 teaspoon salt
½ pound ground beef	1 scallion, finely chopped
1 tablespoon curry powder	

Heat oil in wok to 400 degrees. Add onion. Stir-fry until golden. Add ground beef. Stir-fry for 1 minute. Add curry powder. Reduce temperature to 375 degrees. Stir-fry until ground beef is cooked through. Add rice and salt. Stir-fry until heated through. Add scallion. Stir-fry for 1 minute longer. Spoon into serving dish. Yield: 4 servings.

Approx per serving: Cal 470, Prot 14.3 gr, Fat 22.1 gr, Chol 38.3 mg, Carbo 51.9 gr, Sod 1326.1 mg, Potas 209.9 mg.

Chilled Asparagus Salad

1 pound asparagus, sliced diagonally	2 tablespoons sesame oil
2 tablespoons reduced-sodium soy sauce	¼ teaspoon sugar
	1 clove of garlic, finely chopped

Bring 4 cups water to a boil in wok. Add asparagus. Cook for 1 minute; drain. Rinse in cold water. Combine soy sauce, sesame oil, sugar and garlic in bowl; mix well. Place asparagus in serving bowl. Add dressing. Chill in refrigerator. Yield: 4 servings.

Approx per serving: Cal 92, Prot 2.9 gr, Fat 7.0 gr, Chol 0.0 mg, Carbo 6.4 gr, Sod 2.4 mg, Potas 319.2 mg.
Nutritional information does not include reduced-sodium soy sauce.

Red-in-Snow Mousse

1 envelope unflavored gelatin	½ pint whipping cream
⅔ cup sugar	1 can whole cranberry sauce

Soften gelatin in ½ cup cold water for 5 minutes. Add sugar to 1½ cups boiling water in saucepan. Bring to a boil. Add softened gelatin. Boil for 1 minute. Chill until partially set. Fold in stiffly whipped cream. Pour into ring mold rinsed with cold water. Chill until set. Unmold onto serving plate. Spoon cranberry sauce into center of ring. Yield: 4 servings.

Approx per serving: Cal 546, Prot 2.9 gr, Fat 22.7 gr, Chol 79.1 mg, Carbo 87.1 gr, Sod 22.3 mg, Potas 95.9 mg.

Slim Chicken Dinner

Gail Lockridge, Xi Gamma Eta
Russell, Iowa

Baked Chicken Breasts
Baked Potato with Butter Buds
Tossed Salad with Low-Calorie Dressing
Ice Cream Soda
Tea

Baked Chicken Breasts

4 chicken breasts, skinned	½ cup low-calorie Italian salad dressing

Brush chicken breasts with salad dressing. Place in baking pan. Bake at 350 degrees for 1½ hours, basting with salad dressing every 20 minutes. Yield: 4 servings.

Approx per serving: Cal 189, Prot 33.2 gr, Fat 5.0 gr, Chol 82.9 mg, Carbo 0.8 gr, Sod 303.3 mg, Potas 436.0 mg.

Ice Cream Soda

12 scoops Weight Watchers' ice cream	2 cans Canfield's chocolate soda

Place 3 scoops ice cream in 4 tall glasses. Pour ½ can soda into each glass. Serve immediately. Yield: 4 servings.

Wiki Wiki Dinner

Nina Mischker, Preceptor Epsilon Chi
San Jose, California

Egg Drop Soup
Crispy Chicken Stir-Fry
Cooked Rice
Eight-Minute Cheesecake
Tea

Egg Drop Soup

2 cans chicken broth
1 egg, beaten
1 gingerroot

1 green scallion, sliced

Heat broth in saucepan to the simmering point. Add egg gradually, stirring once or twice. Place 1 thin slice gingerroot in each serving bowl. Pour in soup. Top with scallion slices. Yield: 4 servings.

Approx per serving: Cal 27, Prot 2.5 gr, Fat 1.6 gr, Chol 66.2 mg, Carbo 0.7 gr, Sod 975.1 mg, Potas 28.8 mg.

Crispy Chicken Stir-Fry

2 cups cubed chicken breast filets
2 eggs, slightly beaten
1 cup buttermilk baking mix
½ teaspoon pepper
¼ cup oil
3 carrots, sliced

1 green pepper, cut into strips
1 small onion, thinly sliced
1   20-ounce can pineapple chunks, drained

Dip chicken into eggs. Coat with mixture of baking mix and pepper. Stir-fry chicken in oil in skillet until brown. Add carrots, green pepper strips and onion slices. Stir-fry until tender-crisp. Add pineapple. Stir-fry until heated through. Serve over hot rice. Yield: 4 servings.

Approx per serving: Cal 562, Prot 29.5 gr, Fat 23.0 gr, Chol 181.7 mg, Carbo 60.6 gr, Sod 499.4 mg, Potas 794.7 mg.

Eight-Minute Cheesecake

1   8-ounce package cream cheese, softened
⅓ cup sugar
1 cup sour cream

2 teaspoons vanilla extract
1   8-ounce carton whipped topping
1 graham cracker pie shell

Beat cream cheese in bowl until light and fluffy. Add sugar gradually, beating constantly. Add sour cream and vanilla; mix well. Fold in whipped topping gently. Spoon into pie shell. Chill until set. Garnish with fresh strawberries. Yield: 6 servings.

Approx per serving: Cal 522, Prot 518.0 gr, Fat 40.6 gr, Chol 79.5 mg, Carbo 36.5 gr, Sod 287.3 mg, Potas 140.7 mg.

Early Summer Theater Dinner

Marilyn Kaston, Xi Eta
Lexington, Kentucky

Melon Chicken
Green-Fruit Salad
Biscuits with Honey-Butter

Melon Chicken

½ cup melon liqueur
¼ cup soy sauce
⅛ teaspoon garlic salt

1   3-pound broiler-fryer, cut up

Combine liqueur, soy sauce and garlic salt in bowl. Add chicken. Marinate in refrigerator, turning chicken occasionally. Place chicken skin side down in broiler pan. Bake at 325 degrees for 1¼ hours or until tender. Arrange on serving plate. Yield: 4 servings.

Approx per serving: Cal 188, Prot 35.8 gr, Fat 3.9 gr, Chol 89.6 mg, Carbo 0.0 gr, Sod 72.6 mg, Potas 466.1 mg. Nutritional information does not include marinade.

Green-Fruit Salad

½ medium head lettuce, torn
½ honeydew melon, sliced

½ cantaloupe, sliced
4 kiwifruit, sliced
8 ounces mild Cheddar cheese, cubed

Place lettuce in salad bowl. Arrange honeydew and cantaloupe on lettuce. Arrange kiwifruit over melon. Sprinkle with cheese. Serve with French dressing. Yield: 4 servings.

Approx per serving: Cal 317, Prot 16.8 gr, Fat 19.0 gr, Chol 56.1 mg, Carbo 22.7 gr, Sod 433.6 mg, Potas 805.4 mg.

Family Supper

Deborah Key, Xi Gamma Pi
Security, Colorado

Cantonese Chicken
Steamed Rice
Citrus Salad with Dressing
Whole Wheat Rolls
Iced Tea

Cantonese Chicken

1 whole chicken breast,
  boned, sliced
1½ tablespoons
  soy sauce
2 teaspoons cornstarch
1 teaspoon Sherry
Dash of pepper
2 tablespoons oil

3 green onions, cut into
  1-inch pieces
2 cups sliced celery
2 cups chopped broccoli
2 cups bean sprouts
1 teaspoon ginger
¼ cup chicken broth

Marinate chicken in mixture of soy sauce, cornstarch, Sherry and pepper for 30 minutes. Stir-fry chicken in oil with green onions in wok for 5 minutes. Add celery, broccoli, bean sprouts and ginger. Stir-fry for 10 minutes. Add broth. Cook for 2 minutes. Serve over rice. Yield: 4 servings.

Approx per serving: Cal 210, Prot 21.7 gr, Fat 9.0 gr, Chol 41.7 mg, Carbo 12.2 gr, Sod 675.4 mg, Potas 805.9 mg.

Citrus Salad with Dressing

1 cup grapefruit
  sections
1 cup orange sections
1 tablespoon grated
  orange rind
2 tablespoons honey

2 tablespoons sesame
  seed
⅛ teaspoon salt
1 cup yogurt
4 teaspoons toasted
  slivered almonds

Combine grapefruit and orange sections and orange rind in bowl. Chill in refrigerator. Mix honey, sesame seed, salt and yogurt in bowl. Chill, covered, for 1 hour. Add to fruit; mix gently. Spoon into serving dishes. Sprinkle with almonds. Yield: 4 servings.

Approx per serving: Cal 144, Prot 4.5 gr, Fat 4.7 gr, Chol 0.0 mg, Carbo 23.8 gr, Sod 188.7 mg, Potas 200.8 mg.

Sunday Supper

Tami S. Mason, Alpha Phi
Grandview, Washington

Baked Chicken
Green Beans
Bread Stuffing
Zucchini Muffins

Bread Stuffing

24 Wasa Brod
  crackers, crushed
½ cup minced
  mushrooms
2 tablespoons minced
  celery

1 tablespoon chopped
  parsley
¼ teaspoon poultry
  seasoning
Sage to taste

Combine cracker crumbs, mushrooms, celery, parsley and seasonings in bowl. Add enough water to moisten. Spoon into baking dish. Bake at 350 degrees for 35 minutes. Yield: 6 servings.

Zucchini Muffins

2 small eggs, beaten
1 cup shredded
  zucchini
1 tablespoon artificial
  sweetener
2½ teaspoons vanilla
  extract

1½ teaspoons
  cinnamon
¼ teaspoon nutmeg
¼ teaspoon ginger
1 teaspoon lemon juice
1 cup unprocessed bran

Combine eggs, zucchini, sweetener, vanilla and spices; mix well. Stir in lemon juice and bran. Let stand for 5 minutes. Stir mixture well. Spoon into 8 muffin cups sprayed with nonstick cooking spray. Bake in preheated 350-degree oven for 15 minutes or until muffins test done. Yield: 8 muffins.
Note: May substitute 1 cup shredded apple for zucchini or add ½ cup blueberries to original recipe.

Approx per muffin: Cal 25, Prot 1.9 gr, Fat 1.5 gr, Chol 63.2 mg, Carbo 1.0 gr, Sod 15.5 mg, Potas 65.4 mg.
Nutritional information does not include bran.

Soup Supper

Nancy Lamb, Omicron Omega
Rock Island, Illinois

Seafood Chowder
Fruit Salad
French Bread

Seafood Chowder

¾ cup chopped celery
¾ cup chopped onion
1 stick butter
6 tablespoons flour
2 cups tomato juice
1 cup chicken broth
2 cups half and half

1 cup shredded carrots
1 cup shredded potato
1 12-ounce can shrimp
1 12-ounce can clams
1 12-ounce can oysters
2 cups milk
Pinch of oregano

Sauté celery and onion in butter in saucepan. Stir in flour. Add tomato juice, broth, half and half, carrots and potato. Simmer until vegetables are tender. Cool slightly. Stir in shrimp, clams, oysters, milk, oregano and salt to taste. Yield: 6 servings.

Approx per serving: Cal 528, Prot 33.0 gr, Fat 30.2 gr, Chol 226.8 mg, Carbo 31.6 gr, Sod 1063.3 mg, Potas 886.7 mg.

Cool Summer Supper

Eugenia Bell, Preceptor Laureate
Louisville, Kentucky

Chicken Breasts Tarragon
Minted Peas
Frozen Fruit Salad
Rolls
Iced Tea

Chicken Breasts Tarragon

4 chicken breasts
1 cup dry white wine
¼ cup chopped fresh
  tarragon
1 cup half and half

1 egg
1 tablespoon flour
2 tablespoons butter
1 teaspoon salt
⅛ teaspoon pepper

Arrange chicken breasts with meaty side toward edge in glass baking dish. Microwave, covered, on High for 15 minutes or until tender, turning dish twice. Combine remaining ingredients in glass bowl; mix well. Microwave on Medium-High until thickened, stirring several times. Serve over chicken. Yield: 4 servings.

Approx per serving: Cal 358, Prot 37.0 gr, Fat 39.1 gr, Chol 187.9 mg, Carbo 5.6 gr, Sod 715.0 mg, Potas 558.8 mg.

Frozen Fruit Salad

2 cups yogurt
2 tablespoons lemon
  juice
¾ cup sugar
⅛ teaspoon salt
2 bananas, sliced

1 8-ounce can
  crushed pineapple
¼ cup chopped
  maraschino cherries
¼ cup chopped pecans

Combine yogurt, lemon juice, sugar and salt in bowl; mix well. Fold in bananas, pineapple, cherries and pecans. Spoon into paper-lined muffin cups. Freeze until firm. Store in freezer bag in freezer. Yield: 12 servings.

Approx per serving: Cal 133, Prot 1.8 gr, Fat 3.2 gr, Chol 3.3 mg, Carbo 26.0 gr, Sod 41.1 mg, Potas 166.5 mg.

Casserole Supper

Linda L. Colby, Xi Lambda Omega
Niceville, Florida

Chicken-Cheese Bake
Buttered Rice
Green Beans
Frozen Fruit Salad

Chicken-Cheese Bake

8 chicken breasts
8 ounces shredded
  mozzarella cheese

6 slices bacon, crisp-fried,
  crumbled

Cook chicken breasts in a small amount of water in saucepan until tender. Remove skin and bones. Place chicken in casserole. Sprinkle with cheese and bacon. Bake at 350 degrees for 20 minutes or until cheese melts. Yield: 8 servings.

Approx per serving: Cal 297, Prot 40.7 gr, Fat 13.4 gr, Chol 112.8 mg, Carbo 0.9 gr, Sod 240.8 mg, Potas 465.8 mg.

New Year's Brunch for-a-Bunch
A Brunch for Twelve

Anita Cofer, Preceptor Beta Alpha
Wynnewood, Oklahoma

★see Index for recipe

Sausage Brunch Casserole
Potatoes O'Brien Casserole
Super Coleslaw★
Orange Cake Delight

Sausage Brunch Casserole

1 pound lean sausage	10 slices bread
12 eggs, beaten	1 cup shredded
2 cups milk	Cheddar cheese

Brown sausage in skillet, stirring until crumbly; drain. Stir in eggs and mixture of milk and bread. Add ½ cup cheese; mix well. Pour into buttered 9x13-inch baking dish. Sprinkle with remaining cheese. Chill, covered with foil, overnight. Bake at 350 degrees for 30 minutes or until golden brown. Yield: 12 servings.

Approx per serving: Cal 294, Prot 15.5 gr, Fat 18.8 gr, Chol 284.3 mg, Carbo 14.6 gr, Sod 437.3 mg, Potas 203.5 mg.

Potatoes O'Brien Casserole

24 ounces frozen potatoes O'Brien	1 can cream of chicken soup
1½ cups grated Cheddar cheese	2 cups sour cream
1 can cream of mushroom soup	½ cup melted margarine
	3 cups crushed unsalted potato chips

Combine potatoes, cheese, soups and sour cream in bowl; mix well. Pour into buttered 9x13-inch baking dish. Sprinkle mixture of margarine and potato chips over top. Bake at 350 degrees for 1 hour. Yield: 12 servings.
Note: May substitute frozen hashed brown potatoes for potatoes O'Brien.

Approx per serving: Cal 456, Prot 8.1 gr, Fat 34.8 gr, Chol 34.8 mg, Carbo 29.8 gr, Sod 615.5 mg, Potas 522.4 mg.

Orange Cake Delight

1 can peach pie filling	1 small package vanilla instant pudding mix
1 2-layer package orange cake mix	1 20-ounce can crushed pineapple
½ cup sour cream	1 8-ounce carton whipped topping
2 eggs	
8 ounces cream cheese, softened	

Chop peaches into bite-sized pieces. Combine pie filling, cake mix, sour cream and eggs in bowl; mix well. Pour into greased and floured 9x13-inch cake pan. Bake at 350 degrees for 30 to 40 minutes or until cake tests done. Cool. Combine cream cheese and pudding mix in bowl. Beat until smooth. Add pineapple; mix well. Fold in whipped topping. Spread over cake. Yield: 12 servings.

Approx per serving: Cal 417, Prot 5.6 gr, Fat 18.1 gr, Chol 67.3 mg, Carbo 59.1 gr, Sod 513.7 mg, Potas 101.9 mg.

Valentine Candlelight Dinner
An Elegant Dinner for Six

Joan Stockman, Preceptor Pi
Gerring, Nebraska

Marinated Mushroom and Spinach Salad
Elegant Chicken Breasts
Brown Rice
Peas and Onions
Orange Cheesecake Dessert
Coffee

Marinated Mushroom and Spinach Salad

1 cup sliced fresh mushrooms	3 cups fresh spinach
⅓ cup low-calorie Italian salad dressing	3 cups torn lettuce
	1 hard-boiled egg, sliced

Combine mushrooms and salad dressing in bowl. Marinate in refrigerator for 1 hour. Mix spinach and lettuce in large salad bowl. Add mushrooms and dressing; toss lightly. Top with egg slices. Yield: 6 servings.

Approx per serving: Cal 34, Prot 2.5 gr, Fat 1.7 gr, Chol 42.1 mg, Carbo 2.9 gr, Sod 138.8 mg, Potas 238.5 mg.

Elegant Chicken Breasts

6 chicken breasts
¾ cup unsweetened
   pineapple juice
1½ teaspoons sugar

¼ teaspoon tarragon
2 teaspoons cornstarch
Paprika to taste

Arrange chicken breasts in 10-inch skillet. Combine pineapple juice, sugar, tarragon and salt to taste in bowl. Pour over chicken. Simmer, covered, for 25 minutes or until chicken is tender. Arrange chicken on serving platter; keep warm. Skim pan drippings. Blend cornstarch and 1 tablespoon cold water in small bowl. Stir into skillet. Cook until thickened, stirring constantly. Simmer for 2 minutes, stirring constantly. Drizzle sauce over chicken. Sprinkle with paprika. Garnish with parsley. Yield: 6 servings.

Approx per serving: Cal 199, Prot 33.3 gr, Fat 3.6 gr, Chol 82.9 mg, Carbo 6.0 gr, Sod 67.5 mg, Potas 478.1 mg.

Peas and Onions

4 green onions
1 16-ounce package
   frozen peas

2 tablespoons chopped
   pimento

Slice green onions diagonally into 1-inch pieces. Cook peas with green onions using package directions. Drain. Stir in pimento. Pour into serving bowl. Yield: 6 servings.

Approx per serving: Cal 61, Prot 4.7 gr, Fat 0.3 gr, Chol 0.0 mg, Carbo 11.0 gr, Sod 99.4 mg, Potas 147.4 mg.

Orange Cheesecake Dessert

1 envelope unflavored
   gelatin
2 tablespoons sugar
1 cup orange juice
3 ounces Neufchâtel
   cheese

1 teaspoon vanilla
   extract
½ teaspoon orange rind
1 1½-ounce envelope
   dessert topping mix
½ cup low-fat milk

Combine gelatin, sugar and orange juice in saucepan. Let stand until gelatin is softened. Heat over low heat until gelatin dissolves, stirring constantly. Combine with cheese and vanilla in blender container. Process until smooth. Mix with orange rind in bowl. Chill until partially set. Prepare topping mix according to package directions, using ½ cup low-fat milk. Fold in cheese mixture. Spoon into dessert glasses. Garnish with additional orange rind. Yield: 6 servings.

Approx per serving: Cal 88, Prot 4.0 gr, Fat 2.8 gr, Chol 0.8 mg, Carbo 10.0 gr, Sod 69.2 mg, Potas 115.8 mg.
Nutritional information does not include dessert topping mix.

St. Patrick's Day Supper
A Microwave Supper for Four

Ida May Humke, Preceptor Iota
Quincy, Illinois

Cut Green Salad
Potato Toppers
Baked Apples
Tea or Coffee

Potato Toppers

4 medium baking
   potatoes
½ pound extra lean
   ground beef
1 onion, chopped
¾ cup chopped
   green pepper

½ large tomato,
   chopped
2 tablespoons catsup
¼ teaspoon oregano
½ teaspoon basil
½ to ¾ cup shredded
   mozzarella cheese

Pierce potatoes several times with fork. Place on paper towel in microwave oven. Microwave on High for 10½ to 12 minutes, turning once. Wrap in foil. Let stand for 8 minutes. Crumble ground beef into 2-quart glass bowl. Add onion and green pepper. Microwave on High for 3 minutes or until ground beef is no longer pink; drain. Mix in tomato, catsup, oregano, basil and salt and pepper to taste. Cut potatoes in half lengthwise. Flake lightly in center with fork. Place on microwave-safe serving plate. Spoon ground beef mixture over potatoes. Sprinkle with cheese. Microwave on High for 1 minute or until cheese melts. Yield: 4 servings.

Approx per serving: Cal 339, Prot 21.6 gr, Fat 10.3 gr, Chol 58.6 gr, Carbo 41.0 gr, Sod 208.3 mg, Potas 1138.1 mg.

Baked Apples

4 cooking apples
4 teaspoons
   lemon juice

4 teaspoons honey
1 teaspoon cinnamon

Core apples. Place in glass baking dish. Place 1 teaspoon lemon juice and 1 teaspoon honey in center of each. Sprinkle with cinnamon. Microwave on High for 1½ minutes or until apples are tender. Yield: 4 servings.

Approx per serving: Cal 138, Prot 0.5 gr, Fat 1.3 gr, Chol 0.0 mg, Carbo 34.8 gr, Sod 2.4 mg, Potas 242.0 mg.

Friday without Fat
A Lenten Supper for Eight

Barbara Jensen, Laureate Phi
Texas City, Texas

Jen's Salmon Bake
Round and Round Vegetables
Eddie's Olé Corn
Mandarin Magic
Unsalted Crackers
Unsweetened Iced Tea

Jen's Salmon Bake

1 16-ounce can salmon	½ cup chopped onion
1 egg, beaten	1 cup bread crumbs
1 can cream of celery soup	1 tablespoon lemon juice
	1 teaspoon salt
	½ cup mayonnaise

Combine all ingredients in large bowl; mix well. Pack into greased loaf pan. Bake at 350 degrees for 1 hour. Remove to serving plate; slice. Serve with catsup or tartar sauce. Yield: 8 servings.

Approx per serving: Cal 241, Prot 13.9 gr, Fat 17.1 gr, Chol 63.7 mg, Carbo 7.8 gr, Sod 910.6 mg, Potas 277.9 mg.

Round and Round Vegetables

¼ cup peanut oil	2 zucchini, cut into wedges
2 cups cauliflowerets	1 cucumber, peeled, sliced
2 cups broccoli flowerets	1 onion, sliced

Heat peanut oil in skillet or wok. Add vegetables. Stir-fry until tender-crisp. Add celery salt, garlic salt, oregano and pepper to taste. Spoon into serving dish. Yield: 8 servings.

Approx per serving: Cal 96, Prot 3.2 gr, Fat 7.0 gr, Chol 0.0 mg, Carbo 7.7 gr, Sod 10.3 mg, Potas 360.5 mg.

Eddie's Olé Corn

6 cups fresh corn	1 teaspoon garlic salt
1 medium onion, chopped	1 teaspoon celery salt
3 tablespoons margarine	1 teaspoon salt
1 tablespoon parsley flakes	1 teaspoon pepper
1 teaspoon oregano	1 can Ro-Tel tomatoes
	1 16-ounce package Velveeta cheese, cubed

Sauté corn and onion in margarine in large skillet. Add seasonings; mix well. Mash tomatoes with fork. Stir into corn. Simmer for several minutes, adding a small amount of water if necessary to make of desired consistency. Add cheese. Simmer until cheese melts, stirring constantly. Spoon into serving dish. Yield: 8 servings.
Note: May substitute bacon drippings for margarine and frozen or canned corn for fresh corn.

Approx per serving: Cal 356, Prot 17.4 gr, Fat 22.0 gr, Chol 51.0 mg, Carbo 26.6 gr, Sod 1537.5 mg, Potas 356.4 mg.

Mandarin Magic

2 11-ounce cans mandarin oranges	1 cup flaked coconut
1 16-ounce can pineapple chunks	1 cup miniature marshmallows
2 cups seedless grapes	1 cup vanilla yogurt
½ cup pecans	1 tablespoon sugar
	1 apple, thinly sliced

Drain canned fruit. Combine with grapes, pecans, coconut and marshmallows in serving bowl. Mix yogurt and sugar in small bowl. Add to fruit; mix lightly. Arrange apple slices on top. Chill until serving time. Yield: 8 servings.

Approx per serving: Cal 209, Prot 2.1 gr, Fat 11.8 gr, Chol 1.0 mg, Carbo 32.3 gr, Sod 7.1 mg, Potas 254.7 mg.
Nutritional information does not include vanilla yogurt.

Mother's Day Brunch for Four
A Festive Brunch for Four

Joan Stockman, Preceptor Pi
Gering, Nebraska

Scrambled Egg-Filled Crêpes
Sliced Tomatoes
Rhubarb-Strawberry Cups
Mocha Cocoa

Low-Cal Crêpes

1 cup flour
1½ cups low-fat milk
1 egg
¼ teaspoon salt

Combine all ingredients in bowl; mix well. Pour 2 tablespoons at a time into crêpe pan, tilting to cover bottom. Cook until light brown. Stack between waxed paper. Yield: 18 crêpes.

Approx per crêpe: Cal 38, Prot 1.8 gr, Fat 0.6 gr, Chol 14.9 mg, Carbo 6.3 gr, Sod 43.3 mg, Potas 41.9 mg.

Scrambled Egg Crêpe Filling

8 eggs, beaten
¼ cup low-fat milk
1 tablespoon chopped chives
½ teaspoon salt
8 Low-Cal Crêpes
1 cup low-fat milk
1 tablespoon cornstarch
½ teaspoon dry mustard
¼ teaspoon salt
Dash of pepper
¼ cup shredded Monterey Jack cheese

Combine first 4 ingredients in bowl; mix well. Pour into nonstick skillet. Cook over low heat until set, stirring frequently. Spoon ¼ cup scrambled eggs into each crêpe. Roll to enclose filling. Place seam side down in 7x12-inch baking dish. Blend 1 cup milk, cornstarch, dry mustard, ¼ teaspoon salt and pepper in saucepan. Cook until thickened, stirring constantly. Simmer for 2 minutes longer, stirring constantly. Stir in cheese. Spoon over crêpes. Bake, covered, at 375 degrees for 15 minutes. Garnish with additional chopped chives. Yield: 8 crêpes.

Approx per crêpe: Cal 154, Prot 10.4 gr, Fat 7.9 gr, Chol 272.7 mg, Carbo 9.5 gr, Sod 347.8 mg, Potas 160.0 mg.

Rhubarb-Strawberry Cups

¼ cup sugar
2 cups chopped rhubarb
2 tablespoons orange juice
2 teaspoons cornstarch
1 cup sliced fresh strawberries

Bring sugar and ¼ cup water to a boil in saucepan. Add rhubarb; reduce heat. Simmer, covered, for 2 minutes or until tender-crisp. Drain, reserving syrup. Add enough water to reserved syrup to measure ¾ cup. Blend with orange juice and cornstarch in saucepan. Cook until thickened, stirring constantly. Simmer for 2 minutes longer, stirring constantly. Cool slightly. Add rhubarb and strawberries; mix gently. Chill until serving time. Spoon into dessert dishes. Yield: 4 servings.

Approx per serving: Cal 80, Prot 0.7 gr, Fat 0.3 gr, Chol 0.0 mg, Carbo 19.8 gr, Sod 1.8 mg, Potas 230.1 mg.

Mocha Cocoa

2 tablespoons cocoa
1 tablespoon sugar
2 teaspoons instant coffee powder
2¾ cups low-fat milk
1 3-inch cinnamon stick

Mix first 3 ingredients in saucepan. Blend in milk. Add cinnamon stick. Bring just to the simmering point; remove from heat. Discard cinnamon stick. Beat at high speed until frothy. Pour into mugs. Yield: 4 servings.

Approx per serving: Cal 89, Prot 6.0 gr, Fat 2.4 gr, Chol 6.7 mg, Carbo 12.4 gr, Sod 14.1 mg, Potas 302.9 mg.

Memorial Day Salad Luncheon
A Spring Luncheon for Eight

Merrilee Brown, Alpha Nu
Havre, Montana

Wild Rice Soup
Spaghetti Salad
Ham and Pineapple Salad
Chinese Noodle Salad
Icebox Bran Muffins

Wild Rice Soup

¾ cup wild rice
12 ounces bacon
1 large onion, chopped
2 cans cream of
  potato soup

2   4-ounce cans
    mushrooms
2 cups half and half
1 cup shredded
    Old English cheese

Cook rice according to package directions for 30 minutes. Fry bacon in saucepan until crisp; remove with slotted spoon. Sauté onion in bacon drippings in saucepan; drain. Add rice and remaining ingredients. Stir in 2 cups water. Cook until heated through. Spoon into serving bowl. Sprinkle with bacon. Yield: 8 servings.

Approx per serving: Cal 255, Prot 9.5 gr, Fat 13.8 gr, Chol 44.7 mg, Carbo 24.0 gr, Sod 766.3 mg, Potas 243.5 mg.

Spaghetti Salad

1   12-ounce package
    spaghetti, broken,
1 large cucumber,
    chopped
1 large green pepper,
    chopped
2 large tomatoes,
    chopped

1 medium red onion,
    chopped
2 ounces Salad Elegance
    seasoned salt
1   8-ounce bottle of
    Italian salad dressing
¼ cup red wine vinegar

Cook spaghetti using package directions; drain. Combine with next 5 ingredients in salad bowl; mix well. Mix salad dressing and wine vinegar in small bowl. Pour over salad; mix lightly. Chill for 24 hours. Yield: 8 servings.

Approx per serving: Cal 343, Prot 6.3 gr, Fat 18.6 gr, Chol 0.0 mg, Carbo 38.8 gr, Sod 1433.9 mg, Potas 264.8 mg.

Ham and Pineapple Salad

1   20-ounce can
    crushed pineapple
1 tablespoons sugar
1   8-ounce package
    cream cheese,
    softened
2½ cups mostaccioli
    noodles, cooked

1 teaspoon salt
1½ cups chopped
    cooked ham
1 cup sliced celery
1   6-ounce can mandarin
    oranges, drained
1   6-ounce package
    sliced almonds

Drain pineapple, reserving juice. Cream sugar, cream cheese and reserved juice in mixer bowl until smooth. Stir in noodles, salt, ham, pineapple, celery and oranges; mix well. Chill for 2 hours or longer. Sprinkle almonds over top. Yield: 8 servings.

Approx per serving: Cal 462, Prot 17.0 gr, Fat 26.0 gr, Chol 81.5 mg, Carbo 43.2 gr, Sod 600.1 mg, Potas 440.4 mg.

Chinese Noodle Salad

1 cup mayonnaise
2 tablespoons
    soy sauce
Dash of garlic powder
1   10-ounce package
    frozen peas, cooked

1 head lettuce, torn
4 stalks celery, sliced
2 cups chopped
    cooked chicken
1   5-ounce can Chinese
    noodles

Combine mayonnaise, soy sauce and garlic powder in small bowl. Mix peas, lettuce, celery and chicken in salad bowl. Add noodles just before serving. Pour dressing over salad; toss lightly. Yield: 8 servings.

Approx per serving: Cal 392, Prot 17.6 gr, Fat 28.1 gr, Chol 51.7 mg, Carbo 18.6 gr, Sod 775.7 mg, Potas 434.4 mg.

Icebox Bran Muffins

2 cups Bran Buds
½ cup margarine,
    softened
1½ cups sugar
2 eggs, beaten

2½ cups flour
2½ teaspoons soda
2 cups buttermilk
1 cup 100% bran cereal

Pour 1 cup boiling water over Bran Buds in bowl. Let stand until cool. Cream margarine and sugar in mixer bowl until light and fluffy. Blend in eggs. Add flour and soda alternately with buttermilk, mixing well after each addition. Stir in Bran Buds and 100% bran cereal. Spoon into greased muffin cups. Bake at 350 degrees for 20 minutes or until brown. Store unused batter in refrigerator for up to 2 weeks. Yield: 48 muffins.

Approx per muffin: Cal 83, Prot 1.8 gr, Fat 2.3 gr, Chol 10.7 mg, Carbo 15.4 gr, Sod 105.1 mg, Potas 46.1 mg.

Dad's Delight
A Father's Day Dinner for Six

Glenda C. Haas, Xi Delta Beta
Howard, Pennsylvania

Fresh Fruit Cup
Tossed Salad
Baked Haddock
Parmesan Potatoes
Fresh Steamed Broccoli
Warm French Bread
Cheese Torte

Baked Haddock

1 cup seasoned bread crumbs	Pepper and paprika to taste
6 4-ounce haddock fillets	4 ounces mild Cheddar cheese, shredded
2 tablespoons melted butter	¾ cup milk

Sprinkle half the bread crumbs in 2-quart baking dish. Place fillets over bread crumbs. Pour melted butter over fillets. Top with remaining bread crumbs and seasonings. Sprinkle cheese over top. Pour milk over layers. Bake at 350 degrees for 30 minutes. Yield: 6 servings.

Approx per serving: Cal 293, Prot 25.7 gr, Fat 11.9 gr, Chol 93.4 mg, Carbo 14.1 gr, Sod 386.7 mg, Potas 400.6 mg.

Parmesan Potatoes

¼ cup flour	6 medium potatoes, peeled, quartered
¼ cup Parmesan cheese	⅓ cup melted butter

Combine flour and Parmesan cheese with salt and pepper to taste in bowl. Coat potatoes with flour mixture. Place in baking pan. Pour melted butter over potatoes. Bake at 375 degrees for 1 hour. Yield: 6 servings.

Approx per serving: Cal 329, Prot 11.7 gr, Fat 15.5 gr, Chol 50.2 mg, Carbo 36.7 gr, Sod 274.5 mg, Potas 800.5 mg.

Cheese Torte

1 16-ounce package graham crackers, crushed	1 16-ounce carton small curd cream-style cottage cheese
½ cup sugar	1 cup sugar
½ cup softened butter	1 cup whipping cream
1 16-ounce carton dry-curd cottage cheese	¼ cup flour
	1 teaspoon vanilla extract
	½ teaspoon salt

Reserve ⅓ cup graham cracker crumbs for garnish. Combine crumbs, sugar and butter in bowl; mix well. Press into springform pan. Mix cottage cheese and remaining ingredients in bowl until smooth. Pour into prepared graham cracker crust. Sprinkle with reserved crumbs. Bake at 375 degrees for about 1 hour or until knife inserted in center comes out clean. Turn off oven. Let stand in closed oven until completely cooled.

Approx per serving: Cal 362, Prot 10.7 gr, Fat 16.4 gr, Chol 47.6 mg, Carbo 71.1 gr, Sod 484.4 mg, Potas 176.2 mg.

South-of-Any-Border Fiesta
A Fourth of July Dinner for Eight

Linda Miles, Xi Chi
Clinton, Utah

★see Index for recipe

Lyle's Margaritas★
Tortilla Chips and Salsa
Sour Cream Enchiladas
Garden Salad with Avocado
Carmel Custard

Sour Cream Enchiladas

1½ pounds ground beef	12 corn tortillas
1 onion, chopped	2 cups sour cream
1 green pepper, chopped	2 cans cream of chicken soup
2 cups grated Cheddar cheese	1 can chopped green chilies

Brown ground beef with onion and green pepper in skillet, stirring until crumbly; drain. Soften tortillas using package directions. Spoon ground beef mixture and cheese onto each tortilla; roll to enclose filling. Place seam side down in greased baking dish. Mix remaining ingredients in bowl. Pour over enchiladas. Bake at 325 degrees for 30 minutes or until bubbly. Yield: 8 servings.

Approx per serving: Cal 643, Prot 30.4 gr, Fat 39.0 gr, Chol 116.7 mg, Carbo 44.4 gr, Sod 871.7 mg, Potas 394.1 mg.

From-the-Garden Party
A Labor Day Feast for Six

Jennifer A. Welch, Alpha Omega Lambda
Corrigan, Texas

Ratatouille Pizza Pie
Microwave Bacon-Wrapped Bread Sticks
Sliced Tomato and Onion Salad
Fresh Melon Platter
Fruit Compote with Coconut and Yogurt
Sun Tea

Ratatouille Pizza Pie

1 clove of garlic, minced	½ cup chopped onion
2 cups chopped eggplant	1½ teaspoons Italian seasoning
1 cup thinly sliced zucchini	1 tablespoon oil
1 green pepper, cut into 1-inch squares	1 package refrigerator crescent rolls
1 tomato, peeled, chopped	¾ cup crushed croutons
	1½ cups shredded Swiss cheese

Sauté garlic, vegetables and Italian seasoning in oil in skillet until tender-crisp. Simmer for 5 minutes. Separate crescent rolls into triangles. Press over bottom and side of 12-inch pizza pan. Sprinkle with croutons and ½ cup cheese. Spoon sautéed vegetables evenly over top. Bake at 375 degrees for 20 to 25 minutes or until edge is brown. Sprinkle with remaining cheese. Bake for 3 to 5 minutes longer or until cheese is melted. Yield: 6 servings.

Approx per serving: Cal 191, Prot 10.6 gr, Fat 10.8 gr, Chol 28.7 mg, Carbo 14.0 gr, Sod 338.5 mg, Potas 283.4 mg. Nutritional information does not include refrigerator crescent rolls.

Microwave Bacon-Wrapped Bread Sticks

6 slices bacon, cut in half lengthwise	½ cup Parmesan cheese
	12 thin bread sticks

Coat 1 side of bacon strips with Parmesan cheese. Wrap bacon, cheese side out, around bread sticks. Place in paper towel-lined glass baking dish. Microwave on High for 4½ to 6 minutes or until bacon is nearly crisp. Roll in remaining cheese. Cool on paper towel. Yield: 12 breadsticks.

Trick or Treat
A Halloween Supper for Eight

Amy Beer, Laureate Pi
Mansfield, Ohio

★see Index for recipes

Devilish Brisket
Spooky Potato Casserole
Orange Delight Salad★
Goblin Bread Cookies★
Apple Cider

Devilish Brisket

1 3-pound beef brisket	Liquid smoke
	Barbecue sauce

Place brisket in foil-lined baking pan. Sprinkle with liquid smoke. Wrap in foil. Bake at 250 degrees for 4¼ hours. Add barbecue sauce to taste. Bake, covered, for 45 minutes longer. Yield: 8 servings.

Approx per serving: Cal 223, Prot 34.8 gr, Fat 8.3 gr, Chol 107.2 mg, Carbo 0.0 gr, Sod 60.9 mg, Potas 278.2 mg. Nutritional information includes only brisket.

Spooky Potato Casserole

8 potatoes, grated	1 stick butter
2 cups (about) half and half	

Soak potatoes in ice water to cover for several hours to overnight. Drain; rinse with cold water. Place in casserole. Season potatoes with salt and pepper to taste. Add enough half and half to almost cover potatoes. Place butter on top. Bake at 250 degrees for 3 hours. Stir to mix well. Bake for 2 hours longer. Yield: 8 servings.

Approx per serving: Cal 325, Prot 5.9 gr, Fat 18.7 gr, Chol 61.3 mg, Carbo 34.9 gr, Sod 173.4 mg, Potas 843.8 mg.

New-Fashioned Thanksgiving Dinner
A Festive Dinner for Eight

Carol A. Bruce, Xi Delta
Juneau, Alaska

★ see Index for recipes

Pumpkin Soup★
Relish Tray   Cranberry Sauce
Smoked Turkey
Infallible Rice
Pea and Carrot Medley
Orange Yamboree Bake★
Strawberry-Yogurt Pie
Cranberry Pudding

Smoked Turkey

2 quarts apple juice
2 cups dry white wine
½ cup noniodized salt
½ cup sugar
1 tablespoon rosemary
1 tablespoon thyme
1 small bay leaf

1 small Bermuda onion, chopped
6 to 10 whole peppercorns
2 to 4 large cloves of garlic, chopped
1   12-pound turkey

Combine first 10 ingredients in large stockpot. Bring to a boil. Stir until sugar and salt dissolve. Cool completely. Place large plastic bag in large bowl. Place turkey in bag. Pour marinade over turkey. Seal tightly. Refrigerate for 8 to 10 hours. Drain turkey; rinse with cold water. Pat dry inside and out with paper towel. Let stand on wire rack until dry. Place turkey in smoker. Smoke for 2½ to 3 hours. Pat dry inside. Bake turkey according to package directions, decreasing baking time by 10-percent for each hour of smoking time. Yield: 8 servings.

Infallible Rice

1 medium onion, chopped
2 tablespoons margarine

1 cup rice
2 cups hot chicken broth

Sauté onion in margarine in Dutch oven until tender. Stir in rice. Add hot chicken broth. Bring to a boil; cover. Bake in preheated 325 degree oven for 20 minutes. Yield: 8 servings.

Approx per serving: Cal 114, Prot 1.8 gr, Fat 3.0 gr, Chol 0.4 mg, Carbo 19.6 gr, Sod 157.3 mg, Potas 39.3 mg.

Strawberry-Yogurt Pie

2   8-ounce cartons strawberry yogurt
3½ cups whipped topping

½ cup mashed strawberries
1 graham cracker pie shell

Blend yogurt and whipped topping in bowl. Fold in strawberries. Spoon into pie shell. Freeze for 4 hours or until firm. Let stand at room temperature for 30 minutes before serving. Garnish with whole strawberries. Yield: 8 servings.

Approx per serving: Cal 202, Prot 1.3 gr, Fat 13.8 gr, Chol 15.5 mg, Carbo 19.7 gr, Sod 129.4 mg, Potas 73.5 mg.

Christmas Sweets
A Holiday Dessert Buffet

★ see Index for recipes

★
Date Roll
Praline Cookies
Snowball Dessert
Cranberry Pudding
Raspberry Jam Cake
Swiss Chocolate Roll
Cinnamon Cream Torte
Easy Rocky Road Candy
Magic Popcorn Macaroons
Low-Calorie Citrus Cheesecake

Christmas Dinner
A Holiday Family Dinner for Eight

Gini Gabower, Gamma Laureate
Wausau, Wisconsin

Creole Gumbo
Stuffed Flank Steak
Mashed Potatoes with Pan Gravy
Carrots with Honey
Sliced Cucumber and Onion Salad
Carrot Tea Cake

Creole Gumbo

3 tablespoons flour
4 tablespoons oil
½ pound round steak, cubed
1 medium onion, chopped
2 medium tomatoes

1 green pepper, chopped
4 cups okra, chopped
¾ teaspoon salt
Garlic powder to taste
½ teaspoon pepper

Blend flour and oil in skillet. Cook until smooth, stirring constantly. Stir in steak cubes and onion. Cook until onion is tender, stirring frequently. Add tomatoes and green pepper. Cook for several minutes, stirring constantly. Stir in okra, seasonings and 1 cup hot water. Simmer until vegetables are tender-crisp, stirring frequently. Serve over hot cooked rice. Yield: 8 servings.

Approx per serving: Cal 133, Prot 8.0 gr, Fat 7.2 gr, Chol 15.2 mg, Carbo 10.7 gr, Sod 289.4 mg, Potas 342.1 mg.

Stuffed Flank Steak

2 cups soft bread crumbs
1 onion, grated
1 tablespoon chopped parsley
1 tablespoon Worcestershire sauce

2 tablespoons oil
1 2-pound flank steak
2 onions, sliced
2 tablespoons oil
1 8-ounce can tomato sauce

Combine bread crumbs, grated onion, parsley, Worcestershire sauce and 2 tablespoons oil in bowl; mix well. Cut pocket in steak. Spoon stuffing into pocket. Sprinkle steak with salt and pepper to taste. Roll from open side. Fasten with skewers. Sauté sliced onions in 2 tablespoons oil in Dutch oven. Add steak. Brown on all sides. Add tomato sauce and 1 cup boiling water. Bake at 325 degrees for 1½ hours, basting frequently. Place on serving platter. Slice as desired. Serve with gravy. Yield: 8 servings.

Approx per serving: Cal 279, Prot 25.9 gr, Fat 12.4 gr, Chol 71.9 mg, Carbo 15.5 gr, Sod 301.4 mg, Potas 434.3 mg.

Carrots with Honey

1 pound carrots, sliced
2 tablespoons butter

½ teaspoon flour
1½ teaspoons sugar
1½ teaspoons honey

Combine carrots with cold water to cover in saucepan. Cook until tender-crisp; drain. Add butter and salt to taste. Heat until butter melts. Sprinkle with flour; mix gently. Add ½ cup water gradually, stirring gently. Stir in sugar and honey. Simmer until carrots are tender and sauce is thickened. Spoon into serving dish. Yield: 8 servings.

Approx per serving: Cal 55, Prot 0.6 gr, Fat 3.0 gr, Chol 8.9 mg, Carbo 6.9 gr, Sod 60.9 mg, Potas 189.0 mg.

Sliced Cucumber and Onion Salad

4 cucumbers, thinly sliced
2 onions, sliced
1 clove of garlic

¼ cup vinegar
½ teaspoon salt
½ teaspoon pepper
2 cups sour cream

Place cucumber and onion slices in bowl. Sprinkle with salt. Chill for 30 minutes; drain. Rub salad bowl with garlic. Place cucumber and onion slices in bowl. Pour mixture of vinegar, ½ teaspoon salt and pepper over top. Add sour cream; toss lightly. Yield: 8 servings.

Approx per serving: Cal 150, Prot 2.9 gr, Fat 12.2 gr, Chol 25.3 mg, Carbo 8.9 gr, Sod 172.3 mg, Potas 273.1 mg.

Carrot Tea Cake

¾ cup plus 2 tablespoons oil
2 cups sugar
4 eggs, beaten
2 cups finely grated carrots

2 cups flour
2 teaspoons soda
1 tablespoon cinnamon
1 teaspoon nutmeg
1 teaspoon salt

Mix oil, sugar, eggs and carrots in bowl. Add remaining ingredients; mix well. Pour into greased and floured bundt pan. Bake at 350 degrees for 1 hour. Cool in pan for 10 minutes. Invert onto serving plate. Cool completely. Dust with confectioners' sugar. Yield: 12 servings.

Approx per serving: Cal 379, Prot 4.5 gr, Fat 18.0 gr, Chol 84.3 mg, Carbo 50.9 gr, Sod 344.2 mg, Potas 104.9 mg.

Appetizers and Soups

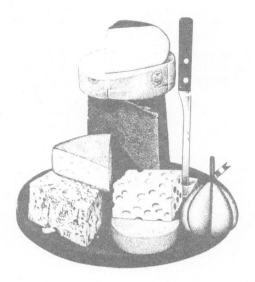

Tuna Garden Bites

2 cups buttermilk
   baking mix
1 8-ounce
   package
   Neufchâtel
   cheese, softened
½ cup reduced-
   calorie
   mayonnaise
½ cup sliced green
   onions
2 teaspoons
   horseradish
⅛ teaspoon hot
   sauce

1 7-ounce can
   water-pack tuna,
   drained
2 stalks celery,
   sliced diagonally
1 cup chopped
   tomatoes
½ cup chopped
   mushrooms
½ cup chopped
   green pepper
½ cup sliced
   radishes
2 cups shredded
   Cheddar cheese

Mix baking mix and ½ cup water into soft dough in bowl. Pat onto ungreased baking sheet, forming ½-inch rim. Bake at 450 degrees for 10 minutes. Cool for 10 minutes. Combine next 6 ingredients in bowl; mix well. Spread over crust. Top with vegetables and cheese. Chill, covered, for 1 hour. Cut into bite-sized squares to serve. Yield: 36 squares.

Approx per square: Cal 100, Prot 4.6 gr, Fat 5.7 gr, Chol 10.5 mg, Carbo 7.9 gr, Sod 206.8 mg, Potas 103.3 mg.

Pat Wullschleger, Preceptor
Home, Kansas

Broiled Grapefruit

½ grapefruit
2 tablespoons light
   brown sugar

1 teaspoon butter

Cut grapefruit sections free of membrane. Sprinkle with brown sugar. Dot with butter. Place on baking sheet. Broil until bubbly. Serve with breakfast or brunch or as appetizer. Yield: 1 serving.

Approx per serving: Cal 172, Prot 0.5 gr, Fat 3.9 gr, Chol 11.7 mg, Carbo 35.8 gr, Sod 55.1 mg, Potas 223.5 mg.

Dorothy A. Kramer, Laureate Theta
Omaha, Nebraska

Party Cheese Straws

1 pound Cheddar
   cheese, grated
2 sticks margarine,
   softened

2 cups sifted flour
¼ teaspoon
   cayenne pepper

Combine cheese and margarine in bowl; mix well. Sift in flour, salt and cayenne pepper. Pack into cookie press fitted with star tip. Press into S shapes on baking sheet. Bake at 375 degrees for 12 minutes or until very lightly browned. Cool on wire rack. Store in airtight container. Yield: 96 straws.

Approx per straw: Cal 45, Prot 1.4 gr, Fat 3.5 gr, Chol 4.7 mg, Carbo 1.9 gr, Sod 56.5 mg, Potas 6.7 mg.

Martha Musgrove, Laureate Zeta
Gardendale, Alabama

Crabby Eggs

6 hard-boiled eggs
½ cup crab meat
½ cup chopped
   celery

¼ cup reduced-
   calorie
   mayonnaise
Paprika to taste

Cut eggs in half lengthwise. Place yolks in bowl; mash. Add crab meat, celery, mayonnaise and salt to taste; mix well. Spoon into egg whites. Sprinkle with paprika. Arrange on serving plate. Yield: 12 servings.

Approx per serving: Cal 62, Prot 4.3 gr, Fat 4.6 gr, Chol 133.7 mg, Carbo 0.8 gr, Sod 93.1 mg, Potas 57.2 mg.

Nancy Jane Young, Xi Alpha Chi
Ripon, Wisconsin

Pineapple-Cheese Ball

¼ cup chopped
   green pepper
¼ cup shredded
   carrot
8 ounces Neufchâtel
   cheese, softened

1 8-ounce can
   juice-pack
   crushed
   pineapple
½ cup unsalted
   sunflower seed

Combine first 3 ingredients and drained pineapple in bowl; mix well. Chill, covered, for 1 hour or until firm. Shape into ball on waxed paper. Roll in sunflower seed, coating well. Chill, covered, until serving time. Place on serving plate. Serve with wheat crackers or Melba toast rounds. Yield: 48 tablespoons.

Approx per tablespoon: Cal 26, Prot 2.7 gr, Fat 1.9 gr, Chol 0.0 mg, Carbo 1.6 gr, Sod 20.0 mg, Potas 21.9 mg.

Shirley Melton, Xi Gamma Zeta
Garland, Texas

Gayle's Fruit Dip

1 7-ounce jar
   marshmallow
   creme

8-ounces cream
   cheese, softened
1 cup coconut

Combine marshmallow creme and cream cheese in serving bowl; mix well. Stir in coconut. Chill for 2 hours or longer. Serve with fresh fruit for dipping. Yield: 60 tablespoons.

Approx per tablespoon: Cal 31, Prot 0.4 gr, Fat 1.9 gr, Chol 4.2 mg, Carbo 3.3 gr, Sod 14.4 mg, Potas 8.4 mg.

Gayle Armstrong, Eta
Calgary, Alberta, Canada

Fruit-of-all-Kinds Dip

1 cup pineapple
   juice
¼ cup flour
3 tablespoons sugar
1 tablespoon
   margarine

2 eggs, beaten
1¾ cups whipped
   topping

Blend pineapple juice, flour and sugar in saucepan. Cook until thickened, stirring constantly. Add margarine. Stir small amount of hot mixture into eggs; stir eggs into hot mixture. Cook until mixture thickens, stirring constantly. Cool. Fold whipped topping in gently. Spoon into serving bowl. Serve with fresh fruit for dipping. Yield: 32 tablespoons.

Approx per tablespoon: Cal 32, Prot 0.5 gr, Fat 1.7 gr, Chol 15.8 mg, Carbo 3.1 gr, Sod 9.2 mg, Potas 17.5 mg.

Judy Ramer, Xi Alpha Mu
North Little Rock, Arkansas

Yogurt Fruit Dip

1 8-ounce package
  Neufchâtel
  cheese, softened
1 cup low-fat yogurt
1 teaspoon grated
  lemon rind

1 teaspoon vanilla
  extract
14 envelopes Equal

Blend Neufchâtel cheese and yogurt in bowl. Add remaining ingredients; mix well. Chill in refrigerator. Spoon into serving bowl. Serve with melon balls or other fresh fruit for dipping. Yield: 32 tablespoons.

Sarah Preston, Xi Beta Alpha
Bowling Green, Kentucky

Artichoke Dip

2 jars artichokes,
  drained,
  chopped
1 cup mayonnaise

1 cup Parmesan
  cheese
2 cloves of garlic,
  chopped

Combine all ingredients in serving bowl; mix well. Serve with crackers for spreading. Yield: 64 tablespoons.

Lori Brodhag, Zeta Eta
McKinleyville, California

Dill Dip

⅔ cup mayonnaise
1 teaspoon chopped
  parsley
1 teaspoon minced
  onion

1 teaspoon Beau
  Monde seasoning
1 teaspoon dillweed
1 teaspoon dillseed
⅔ cup sour cream

Combine all ingredients in serving bowl; mix well. Let stand for several hours. Serve with chips or fresh vegetables for dipping. Yield: 22 tablespoons.

Approx per tablespoon: Cal 64, Prot 0.3 gr, Fat 6.9 gr, Chol 7.8 mg, Carbo 0.5 gr, Sod 44.4 mg, Potas 13.0 mg.

Connie Young, Theta Delta
Endicott, Washington

Do-Little Dip

1 package dry
  Italian salad
  dressing mix

1 8-ounce
  carton
  sour cream

Combine salad dressing mix and sour cream in bowl; mix well. Spoon into serving bowl. Serve with raw vegetables or chips for dipping. Yield: 16 tablespoons.

Approx per tablespoon: Cal 34, Prot 0.5 gr, Fat 3.1 gr, Chol 6.3 mg, Carbo 1.2 gr, Sod 133.6 mg, Potas 24.2 mg.

Kandee Graham, Preceptor Beta Kappa
Hershey, Pennsylvania

Low-Calorie Hidden Valley Dip

2 cups cottage
  cheese
2 cups reduced-
  calorie
  mayonnaise

1 package low-calorie
  ranch-style salad
  dressing mix

Combine all ingredients in serving bowl; mix well. Chill in refrigerator. Serve with vegetables for dipping. Yield: 32 tablespoons.

Pam Sandy, Xi Gamma Eta
Russell, Iowa

Lori's Shrimp Dip

2 cans shrimp
9 radishes, grated
1 large carrot, grated
2 cups mayonnaise

3 green onions,
  chopped
1 teaspoon MSG

Combine all ingredients in serving bowl; mix well. Chill for 24 hours. Serve with water biscuits for spreading. Yield: 96 tablespoons.

Approx per tablespoon: Cal 37, Prot 0.7 gr, Fat 3.8 gr, Chol 7.3 mg, Carbo 0.3 gr, Sod 32.2 mg, Potas 11.2 mg.

Lori Brodhag, Zeta Eta
McKinleyville, California

Shrimp Dip

1 8-ounce
  package cream
  cheese, softened
1 green pepper,
  chopped
1 small red onion,
  chopped

1 6½-ounce can
  shrimp
1 8-ounce bottle
  of shrimp
  cocktail sauce

Spread cream cheese evenly on serving dish. Layer green pepper, onion and shrimp over cream cheese. Spread cocktail sauce over top. Serve with corn chips for dipping. Yield: 80 tablespoons.

Approx per tablespoon: Cal 18, Prot 0.9 gr, Fat 1.1 gr, Chol 6.6 mg, Carbo 1.1 gr, Sod 56.3 mg, Potas 23.2 mg.

Loretta Kerschen, Alpha Alpha
Anthony, Kansas

Spinach Dip

1 10-ounce
   package frozen
   chopped spinach
1 cup sour cream

1 cup mayonnaise
1 package Knorr's
   dry leek soup
   mix

Press spinach between paper towels to drain well. Combine with remaining ingredients in serving bowl; mix well. Let stand for 1 hour. Serve with chips for dipping. Yield: 48 tablespoons.

Approx per tablespoon: Cal 14, Prot 0.3 gr, Fat 1.3 gr, Chol 2.3 mg, Carbo 0.4 gr, Sod 7.7 mg, Potas 27.9 mg. Nutritional information does not include dry soup mix.

Susan Hutchinson, Zeta Eta
Eureka, California

Seven-Layer Taco Dip

1 20-ounce can
   spicy refried
   beans
1 cup sour cream
3 tablespoons
   mayonnaise
1 package taco
   seasoning mix
3 avocados, mashed
1 teaspoon garlic
   salt

3 tomatoes, seeded,
   chopped
3 green onions,
   chopped
2 cups grated
   Cheddar cheese
½ cup chopped green
   olives

Spread beans in 9x13-inch dish. Combine sour cream, mayonnaise and taco mix in bowl; mix well. Spread over beans. Layer avocado puree, garlic salt, tomatoes, green onions, cheese and olives over sour cream mixture. Chill until serving time. Serve with tortilla or corn chips for dipping. Yield: 12 servings.

Approx per serving: Cal 280, Prot 7.9 gr, Fat 25.8 gr, Chol 33.2 mg, Carbo 7.3 gr, Sod 560.6 mg, Potas 514.7 mg. Nutritional information does not include refried beans or seasoning mix.

Erin Haugh, Alpha Eta
Green River, Wyoming

Spinach Dip à la Linda

1 cup mayonnaise
4 green onions,
   finely chopped
1 package dry
   vegetable soup
   mix

1 can water
   chestnuts, chopped
1 10-ounce package
   frozen spinach,
   thawed, drained
1 cup yogurt

Combine all ingredients in serving bowl; mix well. Chill for 1 hour or longer. Spread on crackers or serve as topping for baked potatoes. Yield: 64 tablespoons.

Approx per tablespoon: Cal 32, Prot 0.4 gr, Fat 2.9 gr, Chol 2.8 mg, Carbo 1.3 gr, Sod 25.6 mg, Potas 29.1 mg. Nutritional information does not include vegetable soup mix.

Linda Miles, Xi Chi
Clinton, Utah

Dip for Veggies

1 cup cottage cheese
⅓ cup yogurt
1 tablespoon onion
   flakes
1 tablespoon parsley
   flakes

1 teaspoon dillweed
½ teaspoon celery
   seed
¼ teaspoon salt
⅓ cup mayonnaise

Combine all ingredients in serving bowl; mix well. Chill for 1 to 2 hours. Serve with assorted fresh vegetables for dipping. Yield: 28 tablespoons.

Approx per tablespoon: Cal 30, Prot 1.3 gr, Fat 2.6 gr, Chol 3.7 mg, Carbo 0.5 gr, Sod 56.2 mg, Potas 12.2 mg.

Deborah Key, Xi Gamma Pi
Security, Colorado

Toasted Party Sandwiches

½ cup salad
   dressing
2 tablespoons
   parsley flakes
1 2-ounce can
   chopped olives

½ cup minced onion
1 loaf cocktail
   rye bread
6 ounces Swiss cheese,
   thinly sliced

Combine first 4 ingredients in bowl; mix well. Spread on rye bread slices. Place on baking sheet. Top with cheese. Broil until brown and bubbly. Yield: 30 sandwiches.

Approx per sandwich: Cal 61, Prot 2.4 gr, Fat 3.7 gr, Chol 7.7 mg, Carbo 4.9 gr, Sod 168.0 mg, Potas 23.1 mg.

Connie Lohman, Iota Phi
Tracy, California

Chicken-Nut Puffs

1 cup chicken
   broth
½ cup oil
1 teaspoon celery
   seed
1 tablespoon
   parsley flakes
⅛ teaspoon
   cayenne pepper

2 tablespoons
   Worcestershire
   sauce
1 cup sifted flour
4 eggs
1 6-ounce can
   boned chicken
1 cup chopped
   toasted almonds

Combine first 6 ingredients with salt to taste in saucepan. Bring to a boil. Stir in flour. Cook over low heat until mixture forms smooth ball, stirring constantly. Remove from heat. Add eggs 1 at a time, beating until smooth after each addition. Stir in mixture of chicken and almonds. Drop by ½ teaspoonfuls onto greased baking sheet. Bake at 450 degrees for 10 minutes or until light brown. Arrange on serving plate. Yield: 48 puffs.

Approx per puff: Cal 57, Prot 2.0 gr, Fat 4.5 gr, Chol 23.7 mg, Carbo 2.4 gr, Sod 41.8 mg, Potas 32.4 mg.

Vam Erickson, Preceptor Gamma
Williston, North Dakota

Golden Chicken Nuggets

½ cup dry bread
  crumbs
¼ cup Parmesan
  cheese
1 teaspoon basil
1 teaspoon thyme

4 chicken breast
  filets, cut into
  bite-sized pieces
½ cup melted
  margarine

Combine bread crumbs, cheese and seasonings in bowl; mix well. Dip chicken pieces in margarine and then in crumb mixture. Place on foil-lined baking sheet. Bake at 400 degrees for 10 minutes. Arrange on serving plate. Yield: 20 nuggets.

Approx per nugget: Cal 91, Prot 7.5 gr, Fat 5.8 gr, Chol 18.1 mg, Carbo 1.9 gr, Sod 98.8 mg, Potas 93.6 mg.

Lisa Wallace, Epsilon Omega
Cullowhee, North Carolina

Chafing Dish Meatballs

2 pounds lean
  ground beef
1 egg, slightly
  beaten
1 large onion,
  grated

Salt to taste
1 12-ounce bottle
  of chili sauce
1 10-ounce jar grape
  jelly
Juice of 1 lemon

Combine ground beef, egg, onion and salt in bowl; mix well. Shape into small balls. Brown in skillet; drain. Combine chili sauce, jelly and lemon juice in saucepan. Heat to the simmering point. Add meatballs. Simmer for 30 minutes. Cool. Chill in refrigerator. Let stand until mixture reaches room temperature. Reheat in chafing dish. Serve with cocktail picks. Yield: 60 meatballs.

Heidi Bremer, Xi
Nepean, Ontario, Canada

Teriyaki Meatballs

1 pound ground
  chuck
¼ cup chopped
  onion
¼ cup flour
1 egg, beaten
1 tablespoon soy
  sauce
1 tablespoon oil
2 teaspoons Sherry

2 tablespoons
  brown sugar
⅛ teaspoon ginger
1 teaspoon minced
  garlic
2 teaspoons
  cornstarch
3 tablespoons soy
  sauce

Combine first 5 ingredients with salt and pepper to taste in bowl. Shape into 1-inch balls. Brown in oil in skillet; drain. Mix Sherry, brown sugar, ginger, garlic, cornstarch, 3 tablespoons soy sauce and ½ cup water in bowl. Combine with meatballs in skillet. Simmer for 30 minutes. Serve in chafing dish. Yield: 48 meatballs.

Approx per meatball: Cal 27, Prot 2.2 gr, Fat 1.2 gr, Chol 11.9 mg, Carbo 1.6 gr, Sod 116.2 mg, Potas 33.0 mg.

Esther Root, Tau Epsilon
New Richmond, Ohio

Crab Crescents

2 8-count cans
  refrigerator
  crescent rolls
1 6-ounce can
  crab meat
1 tablespoon
  chopped green
  onion
¼ cup mayonnaise

1 cup grated Swiss
  cheese
1 teaspoon lemon
  juice
¼ teaspoon curry
  powder
1 can sliced water
  chestnuts, drained

Separate crescent rolls. Cut each roll into 2 triangles. Combine next 6 ingredients in bowl; mix well. Place 1 tablespoonful on each triangle. Top with water chestnut slice. Bring up points of triangles to enclose filling; press to seal. Place on baking sheet. Bake at 400 degrees for 10 minutes or until light brown. Yield: 32 crescents.

Approx per crescent: Cal 38, Prot 2.1 gr, Fat 2.5 gr, Chol 10.4 mg, Carbo 1.6 gr, Sod 92.6 mg, Potas 21.0 mg. Nutritional information does not include refrigerator crescent rolls.

Verna Neitz, Mu
Yuma, Arizona

Microwave Crab-Stuffed Cherry Tomatoes

1 pint cherry tomatoes
1 can crab meat
2 green onions,
  finely chopped
½ teaspoon parsley
  flakes

1 teaspoon white wine
  vinegar
2 tablespoons dry bread
  crumbs
¼ teaspoon dillweed

Slice stem end from tomatoes; scoop out pulp. Combine crab meat, green onions, parsley flakes, vinegar, bread crumbs and dillweed in bowl; mix well. Stuff tomatoes with crab meat mixture. Arrange on paper towel-lined plate. Microwave on High for 2 to 4 minutes or until heated through, turning plate once or twice. Garnish with paprika. Yield: 5 servings.

Approx per serving: Cal 65, Prot 7.5 gr, Fat 1.2 gr, Chol 36.5 mg, Carbo 6.4 gr, Sod 380.9 mg, Potas 238.0 mg.

Oysters Rockefeller

Rock salt
36 fresh oysters on
  the half shell
¼ cup cream
4 medium onions,
  chopped
2 stalks celery,
  chopped

8 ounces spinach,
  chopped
3 sprigs of parsley
1 teaspoon salt
¼ teaspoon pepper
¼ teaspoon
  cayenne pepper

Spread rock salt in 2 shallow baking dishes. Arrange oysters in shells on rock salt. Place remaining ingredients in blender container. Process until puréed. Spoon purée onto oysters. Bake at 450 degrees for 4 minutes. Serve in bed of salt to retain heat. Yield: 36 oysters.

Approx per oyster: Cal 25, Prot 2.1 gr, Fat 0.9 gr, Chol 11.3 mg, Carbo 2.4 gr, Sod 82.7 mg, Potas 90.0 mg.

June Boehler, Preceptor Iota Omicron
Mertyon, Texas

Pink Salmon Pâté

1 16-ounce can
   pink salmon
2 envelopes
   unflavored gelatin
½ cup reduced-
   calorie
   mayonnaise
½ cup chili sauce
1 tablespoon
   Worcestershire
   sauce

2 tablespoons lemon
   juice
1 teaspoon dillweed
1 7-ounce can
   water-pack tuna,
   drained
4 hard-boiled eggs,
   chopped
¼ cup chopped onion
¼ cup chopped stuffed
   olives

Drain salmon, reserving liquid. Soften gelatin in reserved liquid in saucepan. Heat until gelatin dissolves, stirring constantly. Add next 5 ingredients; mix well. Stir in salmon, tuna, eggs, onion and olives. Pour into fish-shaped mold. Chill until set. Unmold on lettuce-lined serving plate. Serve with assorted crackers. Yield: 60 tablespoons.

Approx per tablespoon: Cal 30, Prot 3.1gr, Fat 1.5 gr,
Chol 22.0 mg, Carbo 0.8 gr, Sod 105.7 mg, Potas 51.8 mg.

Elizabeth B. Thompson, Preceptor Beta Eta
Bradenton, Florida

Sardine Bread

2 10-count cans
   refrigerator
   biscuits
2 small cans
   sardines

2 teaspoons
   mustard

Arrange biscuits in 9x13-inch baking pan. Flatten until edges touch. Mash sardines with mustard in bowl. Spread on biscuits. Bake at 375 degrees for 10 minutes or until golden brown. Cut into squares. Serve hot or cold. Yield: 20 squares.
Note: May add chopped onion and/or catsup.

Approx per square: Cal 116, Prot 4.8 gr, Fat 3.2 gr,
Chol 28.3 mg, Carbo 16.2 gr, Sod 386.0 mg, Potas 77.9 mg.

Joyce Ann Polite, Alpha Omega Lambda
Camden, Texas

Bill's Mock Shrimp Cocktail

1 6½-ounce can
   chopped clams,
   drained
2 tablespoons
   catsup
2 teaspoons
   horseradish

½ teaspoon lemon juice
¼ teaspoon
   Tabasco sauce
½ teaspoon
   Worcestershire
   sauce

Combine all ingredients in serving bowl; mix well. Serve with assorted crackers. Yield: 20 tablespoons.

Approx per tablespoon: Cal 8, Prot 0.9 gr, Fat 0.1 gr,
Chol 3.5 mg, Carbo 0.8 gr, Sod 79.9 mg, Potas 23.2 mg.

Edith Scott, Xi Lambda Psi
North Port, Florida

Shrimp Patties

1½ cups flour
½ teaspoon baking
   powder
3 eggs
3 stalks celery,
   chopped

1 medium onion,
   chopped
1½ pounds shrimp,
   chopped
2 tablespoons oil

Combine flour, baking powder and eggs in bowl with enough water to make thick batter. Stir in celery and onion. Let stand for several minutes. Cook shrimp in boiling water in saucepan for 1 minute; drain. Stir into batter. Drop by tablespoonfuls into hot oil in skillet. Cook until brown on both sides. Arrange on serving plate.
Yield: 30 patties.

Approx per patty: Cal 68, Prot 6.9 gr, Fat 1.8 gr,
Chol 59.3 mg, Carbo 5.5 gr, Sod 48.9 mg, Potas 60.5 mg.

Gerry Rainey, Pi Xi
Boca Raton, Florida

Party Shrimp Salad Mold

1 small package
   lemon gelatin
1⅓ cups tomato
   juice
⅔ cup reduced-
   calorie salad
   dressing
1 cup cottage cheese

½ cup chopped
   celery
2 tablespoons chopped
   green pepper
3 tablespoons grated
   onion
1 4-ounce can
   shrimp, drained

Dissolve gelatin in boiling tomato juice in bowl. Chill until partially set. Add salad dressing and cottage cheese. Beat until well mixed. Stir in remaining ingredients. Pour into 1-quart mold. Chill until set. Unmold on lettuce-lined serving plate. Serve with assorted crackers. Yield: 60 tablespoons.

Approx per tablespoon: Cal 14, Prot 1.3 gr, Fat 0.2 gr,
Chol 4.0 mg, Carbo 1.7 gr, Sod 28.7 mg, Potas 25.8 mg.

Carolyn Qualey, Xi Pi
Moscow, Indiana

Recipes for this photograph on pages 37 and 46. ◗

Artichoke Nibblers

2 6-ounce jars
  marinated
  artichoke hearts
1 small onion,
  finely chopped
1 clove of garlic,
  minced
4 eggs, beaten
¼ cup dry bread
  crumbs
¼ teaspoon salt
⅛ teaspoon pepper

⅛ teaspoon
  oregano
⅛ teaspoon
  Tabasco sauce
8 ounces sharp
  Cheddar cheese,
  shredded
1 4-ounce jar
  chopped pimento
2 tablespoons
  chopped parsley

Drain artichokes, reserving marinade from 1 jar. Cut artichokes into quarters. Sauté onion and garlic in reserved marinade in skillet. Add artichokes and next 8 ingredients; mix well. Pour into buttered 7x11-inch baking dish. Sprinkle with parsley. Bake at 325 degrees for 30 minutes or just until set. Cool. Cut into 1-inch squares. Arrange on serving plate. Yield: 77 squares.

Approx per square: Cal 18, Prot 1.1 gr, Fat 1.3 gr, Chol 16.1 mg, Carbo 0.5 gr, Sod 33.7 mg, Potas 12.2 mg. Nutritional information does not include artichokes.

Betty Ann Maylor, Eta
Calgary, Alberta, Canada

Hot Asparagus Canapés

3 ounces blue
  cheese, softened
1 8-ounce
  package
  Neufchâtel
  cheese, softened
1 egg, beaten

20 thin slices
  bread, trimmed
20 spears cooked
  asparagus
1 stick margarine,
  melted

Combine blue cheese, Neufchâtel cheese and egg in bowl; mix until smooth. Roll bread flat with rolling pin. Spread with cheese mixture. Place 1 asparagus spear on each slice. Roll to enclose spear; secure with toothpick. Dip in butter. Place seam side down on baking sheet. Freeze partially. Slice each roll into 3 pieces. Store in freezer. Place on baking sheet at serving time. Bake at 400 degrees for 15 minutes. Arrange on serving plate. Yield: 60 canapés.

Approx per canapé: Cal 45, Prot 1.3 gr, Fat 3.1 gr, Chol 5.6 mg, Carbo 2.7 gr, Sod 68.9 mg, Potas 17.2 mg.

Kaye Lewis, Xi Beta Upsilon
Wynnewood, Oklahoma

Marinated Brussels Sprouts

1 pound Brussels
  sprouts
½ cup Italian
  salad dressing
¾ teaspoon garlic
  powder

1 tablespoon
  minced onion
1 teaspoon parsley
  flakes
½ teaspoon
  dillweed

Combine Brussels sprouts with a small amount of water in saucepan. Steam, covered, until tender-crisp; drain. Combine remaining ingredients in bowl; mix well. Add Brussels sprouts. Chill, covered, overnight. Serve chilled on antipasto tray. Yield: 24 sprouts.

Approx per sprout: Cal 36, Prot 0.9 gr, Fat 3.1 gr, Chol 4.7 mg, Carbo 1.9 gr, Sod 56.5 mg, Potas 6.7 mg.

Donna Faxon, Preceptor Alpha Epsilon
Tucson, Arizona

Hawaiian Pupus

1 cup chopped
  ripe olives
½ cup chopped
  green onions
1½ cups shredded
  Cheddar cheese

½ cup mayonnaise
1 teaspoon curry
  powder
12 English muffins,
  split

Combine first 5 ingredients in bowl; mix well. Spread on muffin halves. Place on baking sheet. Broil until bubbly. Cut into quarters. Arrange on serving plate. Serve hot. Yield: 64 canapés.

Approx per canapé: Cal 52, Prot 1.5 gr, Fat 2.9 gr, Chol 3.8 mg, Carbo 5.1 gr, Sod 91.9 mg, Potas 5.1 mg.

Ilene L. Roswell, Preceptor Delta Beta
Lynwood, California

Light Vegetable Canapés

Cherry tomatoes
Cranberry sauce
Anchovies
Chopped chives
Cream cheese,
  softened
Snow peas, trimmed

Tiny cooked shrimp
Cucumber slices
Red caviar
Endive spears
Ratatouille (see Index)
Cranorange relish
Carrots, sliced

Cut cherry tomatoes in crisscross pattern to but not through bottom; open gently. Place cubed jellied cranberry sauce or rolled anchovies in centers. Garnish with chives. Mix chives with cream cheese. Pipe onto snow peas. Garnish with curry powder. Arrange shrimp on cucumber slices. Top with caviar. Fill endive spears with Ratatouille. Spread cranorange relish on carrot slices. Arrange canapés on serving plate as illustrated.

Photograph for this recipe on page 35.

♦ *Recipes for this photograph on pages 43, 59 and 129.*

Mushroom Delights

1 pound medium
  mushrooms
1 onion, finely
  chopped
1 clove of garlic,
  minced
¼ cup Parmesan
  cheese

1 teaspoon lemon
  juice
⅛ teaspoon
  seasoned salt
⅛ teaspoon pepper

Remove and chop mushroom stems. Sauté mushroom stems, onion and garlic in skillet. Add cheese, lemon juice, seasoned salt and pepper; mix well. Spoon into mushroom caps. Place in shallow 9-inch square baking pan. Pour in ¼ cup water gently. Bake at 350 degrees for 15 minutes. Arrange on serving plate.
Yield: 20 mushrooms.

Approx per mushroom: Cal 16, Prot 1.3 gr, Fat 0.5 gr,
Chol 1.4 mg, Carbo 1.8 gr, Sod 27.9 mg, Potas 110.6 mg.

Jackie Vogler, Xi Sigma Pi
Hilltop Lakes, Texas

Snow Peas With Crab

30 fresh snow peas
1 7-ounce can
  crab meat
2 tablespoons
  mayonnaise
½ teaspoon
  tarragon

1 tablespoon lemon
  juice
1 teaspoon
  Worcestershire
  sauce

Combine snow peas with boiling water to cover in bowl. Let stand for 1 minute. Drain well. Rinse in ice water. Drain well. Remove stems and strings from peapods. Open carefully with toothpick. Combine remaining ingredients in bowl; mix well. Spoon carefully into pea pods. Arrange on serving plate. Chill until serving time.
Yield: 30 canapés.

Kitty Whitehead, Eta
Calgary, Alberta, Canada

Italian Spinach Bites

1 16-ounce
  package frozen
  bread dough,
  thawed
2 ounces pepperoni,
  thinly sliced
1 pound spinach,
  cooked, drained

1 cup shredded
  mozzarella
  cheese
Italian seasoning
  to taste
½ cup Parmesan
  cheese

Roll bread dough on lightly greased baking sheet. Sauté pepperoni lightly in skillet. Layer spinach, pepperoni, mozzarella cheese, seasoning and Parmesan cheese in center of dough. Fold in edges, overlapping and pinching to seal. Bake at 350 degrees for 20 minutes or until brown. Cut into 1-inch slices. Arrange on serving plate.
Yield: 16 slices.

Approx per slice: Cal 137, Prot 7.0 gr, Fat 5.1 gr,
Chol 12.2 mg, Carbo 15.6 gr, Sod 264.6 mg, Potas 183.4 mg.

Jean Kask, Xi Alpha Epsilon
Enfield, Connecticut

Pita Bread Triangles

1 package dry
  vegetable soup
  mix
2 cups sour cream
1 8-ounce can
  water chestnuts,
  chopped

3 green onions,
  chopped
10-ounces frozen
  chopped spinach
10 pita bread rounds

Combine first 4 ingredients in bowl. Add thawed, drained spinach; mix well. Cut pita rounds into halves. Fill with spinach mixture. Cut each half into 4 wedges. Arrange on serving plate.
Yield: 80 triangles.
Note: May add a thin slice of Swiss cheese and/or ham to pita halves before cutting into triangles.

Pam Matlock, Preceptor Beta Gamma
Wichita, Kansas

Spinach Balls

1½ sticks
  margarine,
  softened
6 eggs
1 cup Parmesan
  cheese

2 10-ounce
  packages frozen
  chopped spinach,
  thawed
2 cups garlic-
  flavored croutons

Combine margarine, eggs and cheese in bowl; beat until smooth. Stir in spinach and croutons. Chill for 1 hour. Shape into 2-inch balls. Place on baking sheet. Bake at 375 degrees for 15 minutes. Arrange on serving plate. May be frozen. Yield: 24 canapés.

Approx per canapé: Cal 118, Prot 4.9 gr, Fat 8.8 gr,
Chol 68.1 mg, Carbo 5.4 gr, Sod 212.8 mg, Potas 119.0 mg.

Dora E. Benevides, Nu
Huntsville, Alabama

Zucchini Appetizers

3 cups thinly
  sliced zucchini
1 cup buttermilk
  baking mix
½ cup finely
  chopped onion
½ cup Parmesan
  cheese
4 eggs, beaten
2 tablespoons
  chopped parsley

1 clove of garlic,
  chopped
½ cup oil
½ teaspoon salt
½ teaspoon
  seasoned salt
½ teaspoon
  marjoram
½ teaspoon
  oregano
⅛ teaspoon pepper

Combine all ingredients in bowl; mix well. Spread in greased 9x13-inch baking pan. Bake at 350 degrees for 25 minutes or until golden brown. Cut into 1x2-inch pieces. Arrange on serving plate. Serve warm. Yield: 48 appetizers.

Approx per appetizer: Cal 45, Prot 1.3 gr, Fat 3.4 gr,
Chol 22.2 mg, Carbo 2.3 gr, Sod 91.4 mg, Potas 29.8 mg.

Julia Gatsos, Zeta Chi
Monticello, Indiana

Zucchini Slices

1 8-ounce
  package cream
  cheese, softened
1 medium tomato,
  seeded, chopped
2 tablespoons
  minced onion

¼ cup finely
  chopped walnuts
4 zucchini, 1½
  inches in
  diameter, sliced
  ¾ inch thick

Combine first 4 ingredients in bowl; mix well. Chill for up to 4 hours. Spread on zucchini slices. Arrange on serving plate. Yield: 32 slices.

Approx per slice: Cal 39, Prot 1.1 gr, Fat 3.3 gr, Chol 7.9 mg, Carbo 1.7 gr, Sod 18.2 mg, Potas 85.5 mg.

Marge Hefty, Preceptor Alpha Epsilon
Tucson, Arizona

Jenniffer's Veggie Pizza

2 8-count cans
  refrigerator
  crescent rolls
2 8-ounce
  packages cream
  cheese, softened
⅔ cup mayonnaise
1 teaspoon
  dillweed
¼ teaspoon garlic
  powder

1 tablespoon
  chopped onion
1½ cups chopped
  cauliflower
1½ cups chopped
  broccoli
1½ cups grated
  carrots
½ cup chopped
  radishes

Place roll dough on greased baking sheet; press edges to seal. Bake at 375 degrees for 15 minutes. Cool. Combine cream cheese, mayonnaise, dillweed, garlic powder and onion in bowl; mix well. Spread on crust. Top with remaining ingredients. Cut into 1x2-inch bars. Arrange on serving plate. Yield: 77 pieces.

Approx per piece: Cal 38, Prot 0.7 gr, Fat 3.8 gr, Chol 7.9 mg, Carbo 0.7 gr, Sod 28.1 mg, Potas 31.1 mg.
Nutritional information does not include refrigerator crescent rolls.

Jenniffer L. Anderson, Theta Delta
Endicott, Washington

Kimberly's Veggie Pizza

2 8-count cans
  refrigerator
  crescent rolls
2 8-ounce
  packages cream
  cheese, softened
⅔ cup mayonnaise
1 teaspoon
  dillweed
1 teaspoon onion
  flakes
¾ cup chopped
  tomatoes

¾ cup chopped
  cucumbers
¾ cup chopped
  radishes
¾ cup chopped
  green olives
¾ cup chopped
  green pepper
¾ cup chopped
  mushrooms
4 cups shredded
  Cheddar cheese

Place roll dough on lightly greased baking sheet; press edges to seal. Bake at 400 degrees for 10 minutes. Cool. Combine cream cheese, mayonnaise, dillweed and onion flakes in bowl; mix well. Spread on crust. Top with remaining ingredients. Cut into 2-inch squares. Arrange on serving plate. Yield: 40 squares.

Approx per square: Cal 120, Prot 4.0 gr, Fat 11.3 gr, Chol 26.4 mg, Carbo 1.1 gr, Sod 200.5 mg, Potas 50.7 mg.
Nutritional information does not include refrigerator crescent rolls.

Kimberly Wood, Delta Zeta
Madison, Wisconsin

Our Veggie Pizza

2 8-count cans
  refrigerator
  crescent rolls
1 8-ounce
  package cream
  cheese, softened
1 cup yogurt
1 package ranch
  dressing mix

1½ cups grated
  carrots
1½ cups chopped
  broccoli
1½ cups chopped
  cauliflower
2 cups grated
  Cheddar cheese

Place roll dough on 10x15-inch baking sheet; press edges to seal. Bake according to package directions. Cool. Combine cream cheese, yogurt and dressing mix in bowl; mix well. Spread on crust. Top with vegetables and cheese. Cut into bite-sized pieces. Yield: 40 squares.
Note: May substitute 1 cup mayonnaise for yogurt.

Approx per square: Cal 56, Prot 2.8 gr, Fat 4.2 gr, Chol 12.4 mg, Carbo 2.2 gr, Sod 63.5 mg, Potas 105.4 mg.
Nutritional information does not include refrigerator crescent rolls.

Cheryl Liebaert and Peggy Sislo, Xi Alpha Psi
Superior, Wisconsin

Special Bean Soup

1 pound dried navy
  beans
1 large onion,
  chopped
1 clove of garlic,
  minced
2 cups chopped
  celery

2 carrots, chopped
2 tablespoons oil
½ cup chopped ham
¾ teaspoon thyme
⅓ cup Parmesan
  cheese

Combine beans with 10 cups water in saucepan. Bring to a boil. Cook for 2 minutes. Let stand for 1 hour. Sauté onion, garlic, celery and carrots in oil in skillet. Add to beans. Simmer for 2 hours. Place 2 cups bean mixture in blender container. Process until smooth. Stir into soup. Add ham, thyme and cheese. Heat to serving temperature. Ladle into soup bowls to serve. Yield: 10 servings.

Approx per serving: Cal 230, Prot 13.5 gr, Fat 5.9 gr, Chol 9.6 mg, Carbo 31.8 gr, Sod 125.8 mg, Potas 723.4 mg.

Jane Friedman, Zeta Pi
Fulton, Missouri

Cheese Soup

1 envelope Butter
  Buds
1 cup chopped
  carrots
1 cup chopped
  celery
1 cup chopped
  onion

1 head cabbage
1½ pounds
  potatoes, peeled,
  chopped
8 chicken bouillon
  cubes
1 pound Velveeta
  cheese, chopped

Prepare Butter Buds with ½ cup water in saucepan. Add carrots, celery, onion and shredded cabbage. Cook until tender-crisp, stirring constantly. Add potatoes, bouillon cubes and 8 cups water. Simmer for 2 to 2½ hours. Add cheese. Cook for 30 minutes longer. Ladle into soup bowls. Yield: 8 servings.

Approx per serving: Cal 287, Prot 15.3 gr, Fat 14.0 gr, Chol 42.3 mg, Carbo 27.1 gr, Sod 1437.2 mg, Potas 836.9 mg. Nutritional information does not include Butter Buds.

Linda Patten, Xi Rho Zeta
Deer Park, Texas

Cauliflower-Broccoli Soup

1 cup chopped
  broccoli
1 cup chopped
  cauliflower
½ cup chopped celery
½ cup chopped onion
½ cup chopped
  green pepper

½ cup chopped carrot
3 chicken bouillon cubes
6 cups milk
1 stick margarine, melted
½ cup flour
1 cup chopped American
  cheese

Cook vegetables with bouillon in water to cover in saucepan until tender; drain. Add milk. Blend margarine and flour. Stir into soup. Bring to a boil, stirring constantly. Reduce heat. Add cheese. Cook until cheese melts. Do not boil. Yield: 8 servings.

Approx per serving: Cal 315, Prot 11.6 gr, Fat 21.5 gr, Chol 37.0 mg, Carbo 19.8 gr, Sod 836.5 mg, Potas 479.3 mg.

Jan Canby, Chi Omicron
Rancho Cordova, California

Fruit Soup

3 tablespoons
  Minute tapioca
½ cup sugar
½ orange
½ lemon
1 cup partially
  cooked prunes
½ cup raisins

1 apple, chopped
1 large cinnamon
  stick
2 canned pears,
  chopped
2 canned peaches,
  chopped

Combine first 8 ingredients and 5 cups cold water in saucepan. Cook for 30 minutes, stirring frequently. Remove orange, lemon and cinnamon stick. Stir in pears and peaches. Serve warm or chilled. Yield: 6 servings.

Approx per serving: Cal 294, Prot 1.5 gr, Fat 0.6 gr, Chol 0.0 mg, Carbo 76.3, Sod 7.9 mg, Potas 449.9 mg.

Joyce Ann Polite, Alpha Omega Lambda
Camden, Texas

Chicken-Barley Soup

4 chicken breasts
3 carrots, cut into
  thin sticks

¼ cup barley
2 cans cream of
  chicken soup

Cook chicken breasts in water to cover in saucepan until tender. Remove chicken with slotted spoon. Bone chicken; discard bones and skin. Cut chicken into small pieces. Add enough water to chicken broth to measure 4 cups. Add carrots and barley to broth. Simmer until barley is tender. Stir in chicken and cream of chicken soup. Heat to serving temperature, stirring frequently. Ladle into soup bowls. Yield: 4 servings.

Approx per serving: Cal 358, Prot 38.6 gr, Fat 11.0 gr, Chol 94.9 mg, Carbo 24.9 gr, Sod 1298.5 mg, Potas 751.3 mg.

Linda L. Colby, Xi Lambda Omega
Niceville, Florida

Ma's Frozen Chicken Soup

1 pound chicken
  wings
1 cup chopped
  carrots
1 cup chopped
  celery

1 cup chopped
  onion
5 tablespoons long
  grain rice
4 or 5 drops of hot
  pepper sauce

Combine chicken wings with water to cover in saucepan. Simmer for 1 hour. Remove chicken wings with slotted spoon. Bone chicken; discard bones and skin. Degrease cooled broth. Add remaining ingredients and 1 cup water to broth. Simmer for 30 minutes. Stir in chicken. Spoon into 6 freezer containers. Freeze until serving time. Combine 1 container frozen soup with 1 cup boiling water in saucepan for each serving. Cook until heated through. Ladle into soup bowls. Yield: 6 servings.

Approx per serving: Cal 105, Prot 8.4 gr, Fat 2.2 gr, Chol 20.3 mg, Carbo 12.7 gr, Sod 50.4 mg, Potas 247.5 mg.

Mary Ann Madar, Laureate Alpha Delta
Elizabeth Township, Pennsylvania

Chicken Nugget Soup

½ pound chicken
  breast filets,
  ground
½ cup dry bread
  crumbs
2 egg whites,
  slightly beaten
2 tablespoons
  chopped parsley
1 tablespoon
  Parmesan cheese
1 cup sliced
  mushrooms

1 cup sliced green
  onions
2 tablespoons olive
  oil
1 tablespoon lemon
  juice
¼ teaspoon
  oregano
8 cups chicken
  broth
1 cup broken
  spaghetti

Combine first 5 ingredients with salt and pepper to taste in bowl. Chill, covered, for 1 hour. Shape into 1-inch balls. Chill. Sauté mushrooms and green onions in oil in saucepan. Add lemon juice, oregano, chicken broth and salt and pepper to taste. Bring to a boil. Add chicken nuggets and spaghetti gradually. Cook for 10 minutes, stirring occasionally. Ladle into serving bowls. Garnish with additional parsley and Parmesan cheese. Yield: 10 servings.

Approx per serving: Cal 139, Prot 11.2 gr, Fat 4.2 gr, Chol 21.3 mg, Carbo 13.7 gr, Sod 836.3 mg, Potas 195.0 mg.

Betty Wells, Laureate Beta
Salt Lake City, Utah

Chicken Soup

1½ pounds
  chicken, boned,
  chopped
3 carrots, sliced
3 stalks celery,
  sliced
½ head cabbage,
  thinly sliced
1 16-ounce can
  cut green beans,
  drained

1 onion, chopped
1 teaspoon parsley
  flakes
2 tablespoons
  instant chicken
  bouillon
1 teaspoon salt
½ teaspoon
  coarsely ground
  pepper

Combine all ingredients with 8 cups water in saucepan. Bring to a boil. Simmer for 45 minutes, adding water if necessary for desired consistency. Ladle into soup bowls. Yield: 8 servings.

Approx per serving: Cal 118, Prot 15.8 gr, Fat 1.7 gr, Chol 34.7 mg, Carbo 10.5 gr, Sod 828.2 mg, Potas 536.2 mg.

Sandra Claerhout, Omicron Omega
East Moline, Illinois

Trimmer Boston Clam Chowder

1½ cups chicken
  broth
½ cup chopped
  onion
1 cup chopped
  potato
½ cup sliced
  carrots
½ cup chopped
  celery

1 tablespoon
  chopped parsley
½ teaspoon basil
1½ cups low-fat
  milk
1 14-ounce can
  baby clams,
  drained

Combine first 7 ingredients in saucepan. Simmer, covered, for 15 minutes or until vegetables are tender. Add milk slowly. Stir in clams. Bring just to the simmering point. Ladle into soup bowls. Yield: 4 servings.

Approx per serving: Cal 145, Prot 13.7 gr, Fat 2.0 gr, Chol 41.1 mg, Carbo 17.9 gr, Sod 1081.1 mg, Potas 593.4 mg.

Heather Robertson, Epsilon Rho
Harrison Hot Springs, British Columbia, Canada

Ground Beef Soup

1½ pounds ground
  beef, crumbled
2 potatoes,
  chopped
3 medium carrots,
  chopped
2 teaspoons
  chopped parsley
¾ cup chopped
  celery
2 cups canned
  tomatoes
2 medium onions,
  chopped

2 tablespoons
  chopped green
  pepper
¼ cup rice
1 teaspoon sugar
3½ teaspoons salt
1 clove of garlic,
  chopped
1 bay leaf
6 whole allspice,
  tied in
  cheesecloth
⅛ teaspoon pepper

Combine all ingredients and 6 cups water in stockpot. Bring to a boil. Simmer for several hours or to desired consistency. Remove bay leaf and allspice. Ladle into soup bowls. Yield: 8 servings.

Approx per serving: Cal 282, Prot 21.4 gr, Fat 8.9 gr, Chol 57.8 mg, Carbo 28.8 gr, Sod 1174.2 mg, Potas 918.8 mg.

Jenniffer L. Anderson, Theta Delta
Endicott, Washington

Hamburger Soup

1½ pounds ground
  chuck
1 28-ounce can
  tomatoes,
  chopped
3 medium onions,
  chopped
4 medium carrots,
  sliced
1 large green
  pepper, chopped
1 8-ounce can
  sliced
  mushrooms,
  drained
½ cup barley

1 medium potato,
  chopped
¼ cup instant beef
  bouillon
½ cup catsup
2 teaspoons basil
2 bay leaves
4 teaspoons
  seasoned salt
Garlic powder to
  taste
Thyme to taste
Sage to taste
Rosemary to taste
Marjoram to taste

Brown ground beef in stockpot; drain. Add remaining ingredients and 3 quarts water; mix well. Simmer for 1½ hours or to desired consistency. Remove bay leaf. Ladle into soup bowls.
Yield: 10 servings.
Note: Flavor improves if prepared the day before serving.

Approx per serving: Cal 226, Prot 18.1 gr, Fat 6.3 gr, Chol 49.8 mg, Carbo 24.8 gr, Sod 1711.6 mg, Potas 671.0 mg.

Renee Mathews, Zeta Eta
Eureka, California

Cabbage Soup

1 46-ounce can
  tomato juice
2 heads cabbage,
  shredded
1 green pepper,
  chopped
2 tablespoons onion
  flakes
⅛ teaspoon pepper

2 tablespoons lemon
  juice
8 packets artificial
  sweetener
½ cup chopped
  celery
½ cup bean sprouts
½ cup chopped
  mushrooms

Combine all ingredients in stockpot. Add salt to taste. Simmer for 45 minutes. Ladle into soup bowls. Yield: 6 servings.
Note: May be cooked in Crock•Pot for 2 hours.

Approx per serving: Cal 128, Prot 7.0 gr, Fat 0.9 gr, Chol 0.0 mg, Carbo 28.2 gr, Sod 522.3 mg, Potas 1349.6 mg.

Catherine Tait, Preceptor Alpha Psi
Golden, Colorado

Low-Calorie Minestrone Soup

1 large onion,
  chopped
6 large mushrooms,
  sliced
3 cloves of garlic,
  chopped
1½ teaspoons basil
½ teaspoon oregano
1 teaspoon Italian
  seasoning
3 tablespoons olive oil

1 20-ounce can
  mixed vegetable
  juice cocktail
½ cup elbow macaroni
½ small head
  cabbage, shredded
4 carrots, thinly
  sliced
2 zucchini, thinly
  sliced

Sauté onion, mushrooms, garlic, basil, oregano and Italian seasoning in olive oil in 6-quart saucepan. Add 5 cups water and vegetable juice cocktail. Bring to the boiling point. Add remaining ingredients. Cook just until macaroni and vegetables are tender. Ladle into soup bowls. Yield: 8 servings.

Approx per serving: Cal 138, Prot 4.3 gr, Fat 5.6 gr, Chol 0.0 mg, Carbo 19.9 gr, Sod 185.2 mg, Potas 678.1 mg.

Jeanette Azar, Preceptor Beta Zeta
Mt. Clemens, Michigan

Mushroom Soup

1 cup chicken
  broth
2 cups sliced fresh
  mushrooms

1 cup milk
1½ tablespoons
  flour

Bring chicken broth to a boil in saucepan. Add mushrooms. Simmer, covered, over low heat for 5 minutes. Blend milk and flour in small bowl. Stir into mushroom mixture. Cook for 3 minutes or until thickened, stirring frequently. Ladle into soup bowls.
Yield: 2 servings.

Approx per serving: Cal 122, Prot 7.2 gr, Fat 4.6 gr, Chol 18.6 mg, Carbo 13.4 gr, Sod 551.6 mg, Potas 472.8 mg.

Alice Galbraith, Laureate Beta
Waukegan, Illinois

Mushroom and Barley Soup

8 vegetable
　bouillon cubes
2 tablespoons
　chopped parsley
2 stalks celery
　with leaves,
　chopped

1 cup barley
1 onion, chopped
1 carrot, sliced
1 pound
　mushrooms,
　sliced

Bring vegetable bouillon and 8 cups water to a boil in saucepan. Add parsley, celery, barley and onion. Simmer, covered, for 1½ hours or until barley is tender. Add remaining ingredients. Cook until carrot is tender. Ladle into soup bowls. Yield: 8 servings. Note: May use homemade vegetable broth if desired.

Approx per serving: Cal 122, Prot 5.3 gr, Fat 0.6 gr, Chol 3.0 mg, Carbo 25.2 gr, Sod 988.9 mg, Potas 417.3 mg.

Anne Beirth, Kappa Omicron
Stroudsburg, Pennsylvania

Onion Soup

3 large onions,
　thinly sliced
3 tablespoons
　margarine
1 tablespoon flour
½ teaspoon salt
Pepper to taste

5 beef bouillon
　cubes
4 slices French
　bread, toasted
1 cup shredded
　mozzarella
　cheese

Sauté onions in margarine in saucepan. Sprinkle with flour. Cook for several minutes, stirring constantly. Season with salt and pepper. Add bouillon dissolved in 5 cups water. Bring to a boil, stirring constantly. Simmer for 30 minutes. Place 1 slice bread in each of 4 ovenproof bowls. Ladle soup over toast. Top with cheese. Broil until cheese is brown. Yield: 4 servings.

Approx per serving: Cal 329, Prot 12.4 gr, Fat 16.9 gr, Chol 29.8 mg, Carbo 32.9 gr, Sod 1903.6 mg, Potas 261.9 mg.

Sally Kees, Xi Eta Eta
Greensburg, Pennsylvania

Microwave Pumpkin Soup

5 green onions,
　chopped
2 tablespoons
　margarine
1　16-ounce can
　pumpkin
1 cup evaporated
　skim milk

1 cup low-fat milk
1 tablespoon sugar
2 teaspoons instant
　chicken bouillon
¼ teaspoon ginger
⅛ teaspoon
　turmeric

Combine green onions and margarine in 3-quart glass bowl. Microwave on High for 2½ minutes or until tender, stirring once. Add remaining ingredients; mix well. Microwave on High for 6 minutes or until heated through, stirring every 2 minutes. Ladle into soup bowls. Yield: 4 servings.

Approx per serving: Cal 236, Prot 3.5 gr, Fat 18.3 gr, Chol 26.1 mg, Carbo 17.2 gr, Sod 630.6 mg, Potas 422.8 mg. Nutritional information does not include evaporated skim milk.

Kathy Welch, Alpha Omega Lambda
Corrigan, Texas

Jill's Pumpkin Soup

½ cup sliced green
　onion
3 tablespoons
　reduced-calorie
　margarine
1 small tomato,
　peeled, chopped

1 cup chicken
　broth
2 cups mashed
　cooked pumpkin
1 cup half and
　half

Sauté green onion in margarine in saucepan. Stir in tomato, chicken broth and pumpkin. Season with salt and pepper to taste. Bring to a boil. Simmer for 15 minutes. Place ¼ of the mixture at a time in blender container. Process until smooth. Reheat to serving temperature in saucepan. Stir in half and half gradually. Ladle into soup bowls. Yield: 4 servings.

Approx per serving: Cal 186, Prot 3.9 gr, Fat 13.5 gr, Chol 26.6 mg, Carbo 14.9 gr, Sod 640.7 mg, Potas 475.1 mg.

Jill Kepler Campbell, Gamma Pi
Cleveland, Mississippi

Quick Italian Seafood Soup

2　20-ounce cans
　ready-to-serve
　minestrone
1 teaspoon Italian
　seasoning
2 tablespoons dry
　white wine

1　10-ounce can red
　clam spaghetti
　sauce
1 pound fish fillets,
　cut into 1-inch pieces

Bring soup and Italian seasoning to a boil in saucepan; reduce heat. Simmer, covered, for 5 minutes. Add remaining ingredients; mix well. Simmer, covered, for 2 minutes or until fish flakes easily. Ladle over toasted Italian bread slices in serving bowl. Yield: 6 servings.

Photograph for this recipe on page 36.

Anytime Vegetable Soup

1 46-ounce can
  tomato juice
1 stalk celery,
  chopped
1 cup sliced
  mushrooms
2 cups shredded
  cabbage
3 zucchini, sliced

1 cup canned cut
  green beans
4 carrots, cut into
  chunks
1 onion, finely
  chopped
6 teaspoons instant
  beef bouillon

Combine all ingredients and 6 cups water in saucepan. Season with salt and pepper to taste. Cook, covered, until vegetables are tender. Ladle into soup bowls. Yield: 6 servings.

Approx per serving: Cal 115, Prot 6.0 gr, Fat 0.7 gr, Chol 1.5 mg, Carbo 25.0 gr, Sod 1021.5 mg, Potas 1140.9 mg.

Becky Laverty, X5606
Kimberling City, Missouri

Cream Soup from Fresh Vegetables

1½ cups chicken
  broth
½ cup chopped
  onion
2 cups chopped
  broccoli
½ teaspoon thyme
1 small bay leaf

Garlic powder to
  taste
2 tablespoons
  margarine
2 tablespoons flour
½ teaspoon salt
Pepper to taste
1 cup milk

Combine first 6 ingredients in saucepan. Bring to a boil. Simmer, covered, for 10 minutes or until broccoli is tender. Remove bay leaf. Place in blender container. Process until smooth. Melt margarine in saucepan. Blend in flour, salt and pepper. Add milk. Cook until mixture thickens, stirring constantly. Stir in broccoli purée. Heat to serving temperature or chill, covered, for several hours. Ladle into soup bowls. Yield: 4 servings.
Note: For carrot soup, substitute 1 cup sliced carrots for broccoli and ½ teaspoon basil and 1 tablespoon chopped parsley for thyme and bay leaf.

Approx per serving: Cal 144, Prot 7.0 gr, Fat 8.2 gr, Chol 18.2 mg, Carbo 12.2 gr, Sod 826.2 mg, Potas 423.5 mg.

Sandra Matson, Xi Delta Sigma
Selah, Washington

Creamy Garden Vegetable Soup

1 10-ounce
  package frozen
  cauliflower
1 10-ounce
  package frozen
  broccoli
1 cup sliced
  carrots
¼ cup flour
¼ cup margarine

1 cup low-fat milk
1 medium onion,
  chopped
2 cups low-fat
  milk
1 teaspoon
  chopped parsley
Curry powder to
  taste

Combine cauliflower, broccoli and carrots with small amount of water in saucepan. Steam, covered, for 7 minutes; drain. Blend flour and melted margarine in saucepan. Cook until bubbly, stirring constantly. Add 1 cup milk gradually. Cook until mixture thickens, stirring constantly. Add onion, steamed vegetables and enough milk to make of desired consistency. Stir in parsley, curry powder and salt and pepper to taste. Simmer for several minutes. Ladle into soup bowls. Yield: 6 servings.

Approx per serving: Cal 178, Prot 7.6 gr, Fat 9.4 gr, Chol 4.9 mg, Carbo 18.0 gr. Sod 178.5 mg, Potas 513.9 mg.

Claudia Miller, Zeta Phi
Bryan, Ohio

Soup and Casserole Sauce Mix

2 cups nonfat dry
  milk powder
¾ cup cornstarch
¼ cup instant
  chicken bouillon

2 tablespoons
  onion flakes
1 teaspoon thyme
1 teaspoon basil
½ teaspoon pepper

Combine all ingredients in bowl; mix well. Store in airtight container. Mix ⅓ cup dry soup mix with 1¼ cups boiling water in saucepan for each serving or as substitute for 1 can soup in casserole recipes. Add cheese, mushrooms or celery to create flavor desired. Yield: 6 servings.

Approx per serving: Cal 150, Prot 9.2 gr, Fat 0.3 gr, Chol 8.0 mg, Carbo 27.1 gr, Sod 1080.6 mg, Potas 417.2 mg.

Gloria Smethers, Preceptor Laureate Kappa
Beatrice, Nebraska
Carol Cronester, Preceptor Upsilon
Cantrell, Illinois

Cream of Celery Soup Mix

2⅔ cups nonfat
  dry milk powder
½ cup celery
  powder
3 tablespoons
  cornstarch
3 tablespoons
  onion flakes

1 tablespoon
  parsley flakes
½ teaspoon
  paprika
1 teaspoon white
  pepper

Combine all ingredients in bowl; mix well. Divide into 7 portions in airtight plastic bags. Store until needed. Combine 1 cup boiling water with 1 package mix in saucepan for each serving. Simmer for 15 minutes. Ladle into soup bowl. Yield: 7 servings.

Approx per serving: Cal 112, Prot 9.6 gr, Fat 0.2 gr, Chol 5.8 mg, Carbo 17.7 gr, Sod 139.9 mg, Potas 482.4 mg.

Marie Skuffeeda, Xi Iota Mu
Crescent City, California

Beverages and Snacks

Twelve O'Clock Cocktails

2 cups orange juice
2 bananas
1 cup blueberries
½ cup strawberries
½ cup raspberries
2 tablespoons honey

Combine all ingredients in blender container. Process until smooth. Pour into frosted serving glasses. Garnish with orange twists. Yield: 10 servings.
Note: May pour into popsicle molds; freeze until firm.

Approx per serving: Cal 71, Prot 0.8 gr, Fat 0.3 gr, Chol 0.0 mg, Carbo 17.6 gr, Sod 1.2 mg, Potas 223.7 mg.

Kathleen Lacey, Xi Theta
Chubbock, Idaho

Orange Julius

½ cup sugar
1½ cups ice
1 cup orange juice
1 tablespoon vanilla instant pudding mix

Combine ½ cup sugar and ½ cup warm water. Let stand until sugar dissolves, stirring occasionally. Place 1½ to 2 cups ice in blender container. Add orange juice, pudding mix and sugar water. Process until smooth. Pour into glasses. Yield: 4 servings.

Approx per serving: Cal 136, Prot 0.5 gr, Fat 0.2 gr, Chol 0.0 mg, Carbo 34.2 gr, Sod 13.8 mg, Potas 127.5 mg.

Erin Haugh, Alpha Eta
Green River, Wyoming

Cranberry Light Punch

1 64-ounce bottle
of cranberry juice
1 2-liter bottle
of diet ginger ale

1 24-ounce bottle
of white grape
juice

Combine all ingredients in punch bowl; mix gently. Add ice ring. Garnish with lime slices. Yield: 40 servings.
Note: Make ice ring by placing lime slices in mold, filling with mixture of water and 2 tablespoons lime juice concentrate, and freezing overnight.

Approx per serving: Cal 38, Prot 0.1 gr, Fat 0.1 gr, Chol 0.0 mg, Carbo 9.6 gr, Sod 0.8 mg, Potas 22.6 mg.

Pamela Winans, Preceptor Zeta Iota
Abilene, Texas

Cranberry Spritzer

½ cup Ocean Spray
cranberry-apple
drink

¼ cup white grape
juice
2 tablespoons club soda

Pour mixture of cranberry-apple drink and grape juice over ice in tall glass. Add soda; stir gently. Garnish with twist of lemon. Yield: 1 serving.

Photograph for this recipe on page 35.

Low-Calorie Lemonade Syrup Base

Artificial sweetener
to equal 1 cup
plus 3 tablespoons
sugar
¼ cup sugar

2 teaspoons grated
lemon rind
1½ cups fresh
lemon juice

Dissolve artificial sweetener and sugar in ½ cup boiling water in pitcher. Add lemon rind and lemon juice; mix well. Store, covered, in refrigerator. Combine ¼ cup syrup and ⅔ cup cold water in glass; mix well. Add ice cubes to fill glass. Yield: 9 servings.

Approx per serving: Cal 23, Prot 0.0 gr, Fat 0.0 gr, Chol 0.0 mg, Carbo 5.9 gr, Sod 0.2 mg, Potas 5.4 mg.

Melody Dixon, Xi Delta Phi
Aurora, Indiana

Louisiana Punch

1 package lemon
instant drink mix,
prepared
1 6-ounce can
frozen lemonade
concentrate

1 46-ounce can
pineapple juice
1 46-ounce can
orange juice
2 1-liter bottles of
ginger ale

Combine first 4 ingredients in punch bowl; mix well. Add ginger ale slowly; mix gently. Ladle into punch cups. Yield: 48 servings.

Approx per serving: Cal 71, Prot 0.4 gr, Fat 0.1 gr, Chol 0.0 mg, Carbo 17.5 gr, Sod 0.7 mg, Potas 107.3 mg.

Maxine B. Mayer, Preceptor Omicron
Littleton, Colorado

Low-Calorie Sparkling Punch

2 cups strawberries
3 cups unsweetened
orange juice

1 liter caffeine-free
diet ginger ale

Combine strawberries and orange juice in blender container. Process until smooth. Pour over ice in punch bowl. Pour ginger ale gently down side of bowl. Mix gently. Yield: 10 servings.
Note: May substitute Perrier for ginger ale.

Approx per serving: Cal 48, Prot 0.7 gr, Fat 0.2 gr, Chol 0.0 mg, Carbo 11.2 gr, Sod 1.0 mg, Potas 199.8 mg.

Florence A. Kolb, Preceptor Chi
Alamogordo, New Mexico

Lyle's Margaritas

⅔ cup Tequila
⅓ cup Triple Sec
¼ cup sugar

⅔ cup freshly squeezed
lemon juice

Combine all ingredients in blender container. Add ⅓ cup water and enough ice to fill container. Process until smooth. Dip moistened rims of glasses in salt or sugar. Fill with Margaritas. Yield: 6 servings.

Linda Miles, Xi Chi
Clinton, Utah

Orange Smoothie

1 6-ounce can
frozen orange
juice concentrate
1 cup low-fat milk

¼ cup artificial
sweetener
½ teaspoon vanilla
extract

Combine all ingredients with 1 cup water and 10 ice cubes in blender container. Process until smooth. Pour into serving glasses. Yield: 6 servings.
Note: May be doubled but omit ice cubes.

Sandy Butcher, Xi Beta Lambda
Oshkosh, Wisconsin

Peachy Yogurt Sip

1 cup yogurt
¼ cup peach
  Brandy

1 10-ounce package
   frozen peaches,
   partially thawed

Combine all ingredients in blender container. Process until smooth. Pour into serving glasses. Garnish with sprinkle of ground nutmeg. Yield: 5 servings.

Approx per serving: Cal 97, Prot 1.7 gr, Fat 1.7 gr, Chol 3.9 mg, Carbo 16.1 gr, Sod 24.6 mg, Potas 144.0 mg.

Eloise Hood, Preceptor Epsilon Alpha
Winter Haven, Florida

Strawberry Punch

1 48-ounce can
   pineapple juice
1 6-ounce can
   frozen pink
   lemonade
   concentrate
1 750-milliliter
   bottle of
   strawberry wine

1 quart strawberry
  ice cream
1 10-ounce
   package frozen
   sliced
   strawberries
1 2-liter bottle
   of ginger ale

Combine pineapple juice, lemonade concentrate and wine in punch bowl. Add ice cream and strawberries; mix gently. Add ginger ale slowly. Ladle into punch cups. Yield: 46 servings.

Approx per serving: Cal 77, Prot 0.5 gr, Fat 2.1 gr, Chol 7.3 mg, Carbo 14.7 gr, Sod 4.7 mg, Potas 71.1 mg. Nutritional information does not include strawberry wine.

Nu Chapter
Thompson, Manitoba, Canada

Tomato Cocktail

1 24-ounce can
   mixed vegetable
   juice cocktail
1 10-ounce can
   condensed beef
   broth
1 tablespoon lemon
  juice

1 tablespoon
  Worcestershire
  sauce
⅛ teaspoon hot
  sauce
1 lemon, sliced

Combine all ingredients in saucepan. Bring to a boil, stirring constantly. Cool. Pour into pitcher. Chill, covered, in refrigerator. Pour over lemon slices in glasses. Yield: 8 servings.

Approx per serving: Cal 27, Prot 2.4 gr, Fat 0.1 gr, Chol 7.1 mg, Carbo 4.6 gr, Sod 443.1 mg, Potas 258.5 mg.

Louise Witte, Alpha Epsilon
Yoakum, Texas

Breakfast-in-a-Glass

⅓ cup orange
  juice concentrate
½ teaspoon vanilla
  extract

½ cup milk
1 egg
1 tablespoon honey

Combine all ingredients with ½ cup cold water and 6 ice cubes in blender container. Process for 2 minutes or until slushy. Pour into serving glass. Yield: 1 serving.

Approx per serving: Cal 344, Prot 12.6 gr, Fat 10.2 gr, Chol 269.9 mg, Carbo 52.3 gr, Sod 124.7 mg, Potas 745.9 mg.

Patty Kopp, Xi Kappa
Pasco, Washington

Hot Chocolate Mix

1 25-ounce
   package nonfat
   dry milk powder
1 9-ounce jar
   nondairy coffee
   creamer

1 16-ounce package
  instant chocolate
  drink mix
½ teaspoon salt
2 cups confectioners'
  sugar

Combine all ingredients in bowl; mix well. Store in airtight container. Combine ⅓ cup hot chocolate mix with 1 cup boiling water for each serving. Yield: 30 servings.

Approx per serving: Cal 212, Prot 9.2 gr, Fat 3.5 gr, Chol 5.0 mg, Carbo 38.0 gr, Sod 212.1 mg, Pot 540.4 mg.

Maxine B. Mayer, Preceptor Omicron
Littleton, Colorado

Cocoa Mix

1 24-ounce
   package nonfat
   dry milk powder
1 7-ounce jar
   nondairy
   creamer

1 cup sifted
  confectioners'
  sugar
1 16-ounce
   package instant
   cocoa mix

Combine all ingredients in bowl; mix well. Store in airtight container. Combine ⅓ cup cocoa mix with 1 cup hot water for each serving. Yield: 25 servings.

Approx per serving: Cal 224, Prot 10.9 gr, Fat 3.4 gr, Chol 6.0 mg, Carbo 39.6 gr, Sod 207.8 mg, Potas 630.1 mg.

Eloise Brandt, Preceptor Theta Zeta
Coleman, Texas

Fruit Milk Shake

3 cups chopped
  fresh fruit

½ cup nonfat dry milk
  powder

Combine fruit, dry milk, 1 cup water and 8 ice cubes in blender container. Process until smooth. Pour into glass. Yield: 1 serving.

Connie Jo Clapper, Alpha
Beatrice, Nebraska

Beverages and Snacks 47

Skinny Milk Shake

1 cup frozen
   strawberries
1½ cups low-fat
   milk

1 banana
½ teaspoon artificial
   sweetener

Combine all ingredients in blender container. Process until smooth. Pour into glass. Yield: 1 serving.

Approx per serving: Cal 283, Prot 14.7 gr, Fat 4.8 gr, Chol 14.6 mg, Carbo 49.9 gr, Sod 186.7 mg, Potas 1296.9 mg.

Doris Williams, Xi Iota Xi
Bosworth, Missouri

Fruity Iced Tea

5 tablespoons
   instant tea
   powder
½ cup orange juice

½ cup lime juice
Artificial sweetener
   to taste

Dissolve tea in 5 cups cold water in pitcher. Add remaining ingredients; mix well. Pour over ice in glasses. Garnish with orange or lime slices. Yield: 6 servings.

Approx per serving: Cal 27, Prot 0.2 gr, Fat 0.1 gr, Chol 0.0 mg, Carbo 6.4 gr, Sod 5.2 mg, Potas 212.7 mg.

Debby Duff, Xi Upsilon Sigma
Lubbock, Texas

Granola

3 cups oats
½ cup wheat germ
½ cup unprocessed
   bran
1 cup unsweetened
   coconut

½ cup sesame seed
½ cup chopped
   walnuts
1 cup raisins
⅔ cup oil
⅔ cup honey

Combine first 7 ingredients in large bowl; mix well. Combine oil, honey and ⅔ cup water in saucepan. Bring to a simmer, stirring to blend well. Pour over granola mixture, tossing to coat well. Spread in thin layer on 3 baking sheets. Bake at 300 degrees for 15 minutes or until dry, stirring frequently. Cool completely. Store in airtight container. Serve as snack or with low-fat milk or yogurt as breakfast cereal. Yield: 8 servings.
Note: May add other chopped dried fruits as desired.

Approx per serving: Cal 588, Prot 9.7 gr, Fat 34.2 gr, Chol 0.0 mg, Carbo 67.3 gr, Sod 34.8 mg, Potas 450.3 mg.
Nutritional information does not include unprocessed bran.

Neola Ivey, Preceptor Epsilon Kappa
Redding, California

Finger Jell-O

4 envelopes
   unflavored
   gelatin

3 small packages
   favorite flavor
   Jell-O

Soften gelatin in ½ cup water in saucepan. Add Jell-O and 3½ cups water. Bring to the boiling point, stirring until Jell-O and gelatin are dissolved. Pour into shallow dish. Chill until firm. Cut into small squares. Store in airtight container. Yield: 24 squares.

Approx per square: Cal 43, Prot 2.0 gr, Fat 0.0 gr, Chol 0.0 mg, Carbo 9.3 gr, Sod 34.8 mg, Potas 22.6 mg.

Judy Ramer, Xi Alpha Mu
North Little Rock, Arkansas
Sharon Evensen, Preceptor Gamma Epsilon
Aberdeen, Washington

Fruity Kabobs

1 8-ounce can
   pineapple
   chunks, drained
1 pear, cut into
   chunks
1 11-ounce can
   mandarin
   oranges, drained
1 peach, cut into
   chunks
1 8-ounce
   package dates,
   chopped
1 banana, sliced

1 cup cantaloupe balls
1 apple, cut into
   chunks
1 cup strawberries
1 cup seedless grapes
8 ounces Monterey
   Jack cheese, cut
   into cubes
1 4-ounce package
   pretzel sticks
1 cup yogurt
Grated rind of 1
   lemon

Place 3 pieces of fruit and/or cheese on each pretzel, varying combinations. Arrange on serving plate. Combine yogurt and lemon rind in serving bowl; mix well. Serve with fruit kabobs for dipping. Yield: 150 kabobs.

Janell Baird, Laureate Lambda
Carmen, Idaho

Hobo Pizza

1 tablespoon catsup
1 slice diet bread, toasted
Garlic powder to taste
Onion powder to taste
Oregano to taste

1 teaspoon chopped parsley
1 teaspoon Parmesan cheese
1 slice low-fat American cheese

Spread catsup on bread. Place on baking sheet. Sprinkle with seasonings, parsley and Parmesan cheese. Top with American cheese. Broil until bubbly. Yield: 1 serving.

Approx per serving: Cal 99, Prot 7.6 gr, Fat 5.1 gr, Chol 4.5 mg, Carbo 6.1 gr, Sod 588.9 mg, Potas 135.1 mg. Nutritional information does not include diet bread.

MaryAnn O'Sullivan, Xi Beta Alpha
Gretna, Louisiana

Oyster Cracker Snacks

1   16-ounce package oyster crackers
½ teaspoon lemon pepper

½ teaspoon dillweed
¼ teaspoon garlic powder
½ cup oil

Place crackers in plastic bag. Combine remaining ingredients in bowl; mix well. Pour over crackers, shaking to coat well. Spread on baking sheet. Let stand for several hours. Store in airtight container. Serve as snack or with soups and salads. Yield: 600 crackers.

Approx per cracker: Cal 5, Prot 0.1 gr, Fat 0.3 gr, Chol 0.0 mg, Carbo 0.5 gr, Sod 8.3 mg, Potas 0.9 mg.

Pat Moore, Xi Iota Kappa
St. Peters, Missouri

Good Snacks

1 cup honey
1 cup peanut butter
1 teaspoon cinnamon

3 cups oats
1 cup coconut
1 cup chopped walnuts
½ cup wheat germ
¼ teaspoon salt

Blend honey, peanut butter and cinnamon in bowl. Add remaining ingredients; mix well. Shape into small balls. Roll in additional coconut if desired. Store in airtight container in refrigerator. Yield: 99 snacks.

Approx per snack: Cal 48, Prot 1.4 gr, Fat 2.6 gr, Chol 0.0 mg, Carbo 5.7 gr, Sod 23.1 mg, Potas 39.2 mg.

Kate Williams, X5616
Oscoda, Michigan

Energy-Booster Snack

½ cup peanut butter
½ cup honey

1 cup confectioners' sugar

Combine all ingredients in bowl; mix well. Shape into log on waxed paper. Chill until firm. Slice to serve. Yield: 20 slices.

Approx per slice: Cal 86, Prot 1.6 gr, Fat 3.2 gr, Chol 0.0 mg, Carbo 14.1 gr, Sod 39.2 mg, Potas 44.6 mg.

Margaret Wilhelm, Preceptor Delta
Cheyenne, Wyoming

Breakfast Bars

⅓ cup nonfat dry milk powder
2 teaspoons baking powder
2 teaspoons cream of tartar
4 teaspoons cinnamon

¼ cup flour
2 packets artificial sweetener
⅛ teaspoon salt
2 cups crushed pineapple
1 cup oats

Combine first 8 ingredients in bowl; mix well. Let stand until bubbly. Stir in oats. Pour into greased 8x8-inch baking pan. Bake at 375 degrees for 25 minutes. Cool on wire rack. Cut into bars. Store in airtight container. Yield: 16 bars.

Approx per bar: Cal 56, Prot 1.5 gr, Fat 0.4 gr, Chol 0.3 mg, Carbo 11.9 gr, Sod 89.8 mg, Potas 85.9 mg.

Jan Clark, Xi Episilon Eta
Elkhart, Indiana

Carob Treat

8 ounces carob chips
6 tablespoons peanut butter
1 cup toasted wheat germ

1 teaspoon vanilla extract

Melt carob chips in double boiler over hot water. Add remaining ingredients; mix well. Spread on greased baking sheet. Bake at 350 degrees until set and brown. Cool on wire rack. Cut into squares. Store in airtight container. Yield: 36 squares.

Melody Behan, Xi Alpha Alpha
Kent, Washington

Banana Breakfast Bars

¾ cup margarine,
softened
1 cup packed dark
brown sugar
1 egg
½ teaspoon salt
½ teaspoon
cinnamon

1½ cups mashed
bananas
4 cups oats
½ cup chopped dried
apricots
½ cup chopped pecans
½ cup sunflower seed

Cream margarine and brown sugar in mixer bowl until light and fluffy. Beat in egg, salt, cinnamon and bananas. Stir in remaining ingredients. Spoon into greased 9x13-inch baking pan. Bake at 350 degrees for 45 minutes or until brown. Cool on wire rack. Cut into bars. Store in airtight container. Yield: 24 bars.

Approx per bar: Cal 193, Prot 3.4 gr, Fat 10.2 gr,
Chol 10.5 mg, Carbo 23.8 gr, Sod 121.8 mg, Potas 203.7 mg.

Edna Arp, Preceptor Psi
Custer, South Dakota

Chocolate-Peanut Butter Sticks

8 ounces semisweet
chocolate, melted
6 tablespoons
peanut butter

1 teaspoon vanilla
extract
1 cup toasted wheat
germ

Melt chocolate in double boiler over hot water. Blend in peanut butter and vanilla. Add wheat germ; mix well. Press into buttered 8x8-inch pan. Chill until firm. Cut into bars. Store in airtight container in refrigerator. Yield: 32 bars.

Approx per bar: Cal 65, Prot 2.0 gr, Fat 4.4 gr,
Chol 0.0 mg, Carbo 6.1 gr, Sod 18.4 mg, Potas 70.3 mg.

Patricia Thorpe, Xi Iota Mu
Crescent City, California

Microwave Granola Bars

½ cup margarine,
softened
¼ cup sugar
1 cup packed brown
sugar
2 tablespoons honey
1 egg
½ teaspoon vanilla
extract
1 cup flour

½ teaspoon baking
powder
1 teaspoon cinnamon
1½ cups quick-cooking
oats
1¼ cups crisp rice
cereal
1 cup chopped pecans
1 cup semisweet
chocolate chips

Cream margarine and sugars in mixer bowl until light and fluffy. Blend in honey, egg and vanilla. Add flour, baking powder, cinnamon and salt to taste gradually, mixing at low speed after each addition. Stir in remaining ingredients. Press into greased 9x13-inch glass dish. Microwave on Medium for 7 to 9 minutes or until set, rotating dish ½ turn every 3 minutes. Let stand until cool. Cut into bars. Store in airtight container. Yield: 24 bars.

Approx per bar: Cal 199, Prot 2.4 gr, Fat 10.5 gr,
Chol 10.5 mg, Carbo 25.9 gr, Sod 74.0 mg, Potas 113.1 mg.

Sally Finch, Xi Iota Zeta
Galesburg, Illinois

Oatmeal-Sesame Sticks

¾ cup butter
1½ cups packed
brown sugar
1½ teaspoons
vanilla extract

2¼ cups oats
¾ cup sesame seed
¾ teaspoon baking
powder

Melt butter in large saucepan. Blend in brown sugar and vanilla. Cook for 2 minutes or until bubbly. Remove from heat. Stir in remaining ingredients; mix well. Press into buttered 10x15-inch baking pan. Bake at 375 degrees for 7 minutes or until brown. Cool slightly. Cut into 1x2-inch bars. Chill in pan until firm. Remove to airtight container to store. Yield: 75 bars.

Approx per bar: Cal 36, Prot 0.6 gr, Fat 1.1 gr,
Chol 0.4 mg, Carbo 6.2 gr, Sod 7.0 mg, Potas 34.5 mg.

Brenda Miller, Epsilon Delta
Cambridge, Ontario, Canada

Summer Delight

1 carton yogurt
1 10-ounce can
applesauce

½ cup peanuts
Chopped apples
Raisins

Combine yogurt and applesauce in bowl; mix well. Stir in peanuts, apples and raisins. Spoon into salad bowls. Serve with cheese and whole wheat bread. Yield: 4 servings.

Sharon Tuck
Saskatchewan, Canada

Quick Energy Balls

1 cup confectioners'
sugar
½ cup nonfat dry
milk powder

1 cup peanut butter
1 cup chocolate chips
1 cup graham cracker
crumbs

Combine first 4 ingredients and ¼ cup water in bowl; mix well. Shape into small balls. Roll in cracker crumbs, coating well. Store in airtight container. Yield: 50 balls.

Approx per ball: Cal 67, Prot 1.8 gr, Fat 4.0 gr,
Chol 0.1 mg, Carbo 7.2 gr, Sod 48.7 mg, Potas 63.0 mg.

Kathleen Radcliffe, Preceptor Kappa
Lancaster, Pennsylvania

Salads

Italian Vegetable Toss

1½ cups shell
  macaroni,
  cooked
2 cups broccoli
  flowerets
1 cup
  cauliflowerets
1 cup sliced fresh
  mushrooms
1 cup sliced ripe
  olives
½ cup chopped
  green onions
⅔ cup reduced-
  calorie Italian
  salad dressing
1 medium
  avocado,
  chopped
1 medium tomato,
  seeded, chopped

Combine macaroni and next 6 ingredients in large bowl. Add salad dressing; toss to coat. Add avocado and tomato just before serving; toss gently. Yield: 12 servings.

Approx per serving: Cal 121, Prot 3.6 gr, Fat 6.6 gr, Chol 0.0 mg, Carbo 113.8 gr, Sod 212.3 mg, Potas 361.6 mg.

Eva Easley, Xi Omicron
Bluefield, West Virginia

Yogurt-Apple Salad

2 cups chopped
  apples
¾ cup sliced
  celery
⅓ cup chopped
  dates

½ cup vanilla-
  flavored yogurt
¼ teaspoon
  nutmeg

Combine apples, celery and dates in bowl. Add yogurt and nutmeg; mix well. Chill until serving time. Yield: 6 servings.

Approx per serving: Cal 49, Prot 0.4 gr, Fat 0.2 gr, Chol 0.0 mg, Carbo 12.9 gr, Sod 19.4 mg, Potas 154.9 mg.

Judy K. Neil, Xi Alpha Omega
Fairbank, Iowa

Waldorf Salad

5 red Delicious
  apples
¼ cup lemon juice
3 stalks celery,
  diced

⅓ cup coarsely
  chopped walnuts
5 tablespoons Dijon-
  Yogurt Mayonnaise

Cut each apple into 8 wedges. Combine with lemon juice and water to cover in bowl. Let stand for several minutes; drain. Add celery, nuts and mayonnaise; toss gently. Spoon into lettuce-lined salad bowl. Each serving has about 98 calories. Yield: 8 servings.

Dijon-Yogurt Mayonnaise

1 teaspoon Dijon
  mustard
1 teaspoon lemon
  juice
1 egg

½ clove of garlic
2 small shallots
2 hard-boiled eggs
½ cup low-fat yogurt

Combine first 6 ingredients with salt and pepper to taste in blender container. Add 1 tablespoon yogurt. Process until smooth. Fold into remaining yogurt in bowl. Store in airtight container in refrigerator. Each tablespoon has approximately 21 calories. Yield: ¾ cup.

Photograph for this recipe on page 103.

Glorified Apple Salad

½ cup sliced red
  apples
½ cup grated
  carrots
½ cup chopped
  celery

½ cup cream-style
  cottage cheese
2 tablespoons salad
  dressing

Combine apples, carrots and celery in bowl. Add cottage cheese and salad dressing; mix well. Chill for 1 hour or longer. Serve in lettuce cups. Yield: 4 servings.

Approx per serving: Cal 81, Prot 4.6 gr, Fat 4.5 gr, Chol 9.6 mg, Carbo 5.8 gr, Sod 139.9 mg, Potas 139.9 mg.

Josephine Monty, Xi Omicron
Greenville, Mississippi

Lemon Salad

2 small packages
  lemon gelatin
1 15-ounce can
  juice-pack
  crushed
  pineapple

2 12-ounce cans
  evaporated skim
  milk
½ cup chopped
  pecans

Dissolve gelatin in 1 cup boiling water in bowl. Stir in pineapple, evaporated milk and pecans; mix well. Pour into 8-inch square dish. Chill until firm. Cut into squares. Serve on lettuce leaves. Yield: 9 servings.

Approx per serving: Cal 157, Prot 2.5 gr, Fat 4.7 gr, Chol 0.0 mg, Carbo 28.6 gr, Sod 60.6 mg, Potas 133.6 mg.

Doris Blakeney, Preceptor Iota
Greenville, South Carolina

Lime Whip Salad

1 large package
  sugar-free lime
  gelatin
1½ tablespoons
  vinegar
½ cup low-fat
  yogurt

1 cup chopped
  grapefruit
1 cup chopped
  celery
2 tablespoons
  chopped onion

Dissolve gelatin in 2 cups boiling water in mixer bowl. Add 1 cup cold water, vinegar and yogurt. Beat until blended. Chill until partially set. Beat until smooth. Stir in remaining ingredients. Spoon into mold. Chill until set. Unmold on serving plate. Yield: 8 servings.

Approx per serving: Cal 37, Prot 1.3 gr, Fat 0.3 gr, Chol 1.1 mg, Carbo 7.4 gr, Sod 51.7 mg, Potas 120.9 mg.

Bunny Hyink, Xi Tau
Tacoma, Washington

Orange Delight

1⅓ cups cottage
  cheese
1 small package
  sugar-free orange
  gelatin
1 cup mandarin
  orange sections

1 cup drained
  unsweetened
  crushed
  pineapple
1 cup whipped
  topping

Combine cottage cheese and gelatin in bowl; mix well. Stir in fruit. Fold in whipped topping. Chill in refrigerator. Yield: 8 servings.

Approx per serving: Cal 106, Prot 6.4 gr, Fat 3.8 gr, Chol 7.7 mg, Carbo 11.7 gr, Sod 121.0 mg, Potas 93.7 mg.

Eloise Brandt, Preceptor Theta Zeta
Coleman, Texas

Mandarin Orange Salad

2 small packages
    orange gelatin
6 ounces frozen
    orange juice
    concentrate
1 11-ounce can
    mandarin
    oranges,drained

1 11-ounce can
    pineapple tidbits,
    drained
3 bananas, sliced
1 cup pecan halves
2 cups dry-curd
    cottage cheese

Dissolve gelatin in 2 cups boiling water in bowl. Cool. Stir in orange juice concentrate, oranges, pineapple, bananas and pecans. Pour into ring mold. Chill until set. Unmold on serving plate. Spoon cottage cheese into center. Yield: 10 servings.

Approx per serving: Cal 266, Prot 8.7 gr, Fat 8.7 gr, Chol 1.7 mg, Carbo 2.0 gr, Sod 139.6 mg, Potas 441.7 mg.

Helen Lacina, Preceptor Beta Omicron
Grinnell, Iowa

Jo's Pear And Seven-Up Salad

2 small packages
    sugar-free orange
    gelatin
1 12-ounce can
    7-Up
3 oranges, peeled

16 ounces juice-pack
    pears
1 8-ounce can
    juice-pack
    crushed
    pineapple

Dissolve gelatin in 1 cup boiling water in bowl. Add 7-Up; mix well. Chill until partially set. Chop oranges and pears. Fold fruit into gelatin. Pour into mold. Chill until set. Unmold on lettuce-lined serving plate. Yield: 8 servings.

Approx per serving: Cal 99, Prot 1.9 gr, Fat 6.2 gr, Chol 0.0 mg, Carbo 23.5 gr, Sod 51.5 mg, Potas 186.2 mg.

JoAnna Jones, Xi Pi Xi
Los Barros, California

Pineapple-Yogurt Salad

½ cup crushed
    pineapple
1 8-ounce carton
    low-fat yogurt
1 teaspoon coconut
    extract

½ teaspoon rum
    extract
2 packets Equal

Stir pineapple into yogurt in bowl. Add flavorings and Equal; mix well. Chill until serving time. Yield: 2 servings.

Approx per serving: Cal 104, Prot 4.0 gr, Fat 2.0 gr, Chol 9.0 mg, Carbo 18.2 gr, Sod 58.3 mg, Potas 222.8 mg.

Mildred Ruppert, Laureate Pi
Independence, Missouri

Pink Jell-O Salad

1 20-ounce can
    crushed
    pineapple
1 large package cherry
    sugar-free Jell-O

2 cups buttermilk
1 8-ounce carton
    whipped topping

Drain pineapple, reserving 1 cup juice. Microwave reserved juice in glass bowl for 1½ minutes. Stir in Jell-O until dissolved. Add pineapple, buttermilk and whipped topping; mix well. Chill for 2 hours. Yield: 12 servings.

Approx per serving: Cal 119, Prot 2.5 gr, Fat 4.8 gr, Chol 0.8 mg, Carbo 16.7 gr, Sod 91.6 mg, Potas 111.5 mg.

Linda Yee, Xi Upsilon Mu
Spring, Texas

Raspberry-Cranberry Salad

1 16-ounce can
    jellied cranberry
    sauce
1 large package
    raspberry gelatin
1 cup chopped
    peeled apples

1 cup chopped
    celery
½ cup chopped
    pecans

Heat cranberry sauce in saucepan over low heat until melted. Dissolve gelatin in 1 cup hot water in bowl. Add cranberry sauce. Cool. Stir in apples, celery and pecans. Pour into mold. Chill until set. Unmold on serving plate. Yield: 6 servings.

Approx per serving: Cal 319, Prot 3.8 gr, Fat 7.3 gr, Chol 0.0 mg, Carbo 64.0 gr, Sod 103.8 mg, Potas 200.8 mg.

Dorothy Droste, Laureate Alpha Kappa
Alton, Illinois

Diet Salad

1 small package
    sugar-free lemon
    gelatin
1 small package
    sugar-free lime
    gelatin
5 stalks celery,
    chopped
2 tablespoons
    grated onion

5 carrots, grated
1 cup reduced-
    calorie salad
    dressing
1 24-ounce carton
    low-fat cottage
    cheese
1 8-ounce carton
    whipped topping

Dissolve gelatins in 1 cup hot water in bowl. Cool. Add celery, onion and carrots; mix well. Fold in salad dressing, cottage cheese and whipped topping. Spoon into 9x13-inch dish. Chill until set. Yield: 8 servings.

Approx per serving: Cal 168, Prot 11.4 gr, Fat 7.4 gr, Chol 3.8 mg, Carbo 13.5 gr, Sod 267.6 mg, Potas 287.0 mg.

Katrina Shelton, Preceptor Kappa
Huron, South Dakota

Five-Cup Salad

1 11-ounce can
  mandarin oranges,
  drained, chopped
1 8-ounce can
  crushed
  pineapple,
  drained
1 3-ounce can
  coconut

10 maraschino
  cherries, chopped
2 cups miniature
  marshmallows
¼ cup chopped
  pecans
½ cup sugar
2 8-ounce cartons
  sour cream

Combine oranges, pineapple, coconut, cherries, marshmallows, pecans and sugar in bowl; mix well. Fold in sour cream. Chill until serving time. Yield: 6 servings.

Approx per serving: Cal 432, Prot 4.0 gr, Fat 24.0 gr, Chol 33.4 mg, Carbo 53.8 gr, Sod 77.2 mg, Potas 263.0 mg.

Mary Wright, Preceptor Iota Omicron
San Angelo, Texas

Kathy's Fruit Salad

1 cup cantaloupe
  balls
1 cup blueberries
1 cup green grape
  halves
1 cup strawberries

¾ cup orange juice
¼ cup white grape
  juice
2 tablespoons
  lemon juice
¼ cup white wine

Combine fruit in bowl; mix well. Mix orange juice, grape juice, lemon juice and wine in small bowl. Pour over fruit; mix gently. Chill for several hours. Yield: 4 servings.

Approx per serving: Cal 111, Prot 1.5 gr, Fat 0.8 gr, Chol 0.0 mg, Carbo 24.3 gr, Sod 7.9 mg, Potas 2 .2 .

Kath *.*

Judy's Fruit Salad

1 small package
  vanilla pudding
  and pie filling
  mix
2 cups pineapple
  juice
1 29-ounce can
  pineapple tidbits

1 29-ounce can
  sliced peaches
1 29-ounce can
  pear halves
1 large jar
  maraschino
  cherries

Prepare and cook pudding mix according package substituting pineapple juice for milk. Cool. Combine fruit in serving bowl. Add pudding; mix well serving time. Yield: 12 servings.

Approx per serving: Cal 218, Prot 1 gr, Fat 0.5 gr, Chol 0.0 mg, Carbo 68.4 gr, Sod 45 mg, Potas .

Judy Reeter, Xi
North Little Rock, Arkansas

Fruit Salad Spritzer

2 cups watermelon
  chunks
2 cups cantaloupe
  chunks
2 cups honeydew
  melon chunks

2 cups grapes
1 cup white wine
1 cup sugar-free
  lemon-lime soda

Combine fruit in bowl; mix well. Add gently. Chill refrigerator. Stir in soda just before servin .

Approx per serving: Cal 79, Prot 0.9 gr, Chol 0.0 mg, Carbo 14.0 gr, Sod 12.7 m Nutritional information does not include s

Sand

Microwave Tapioca Fruit Salad

1 20-ounce can
  juice-pack
  pineapple
  chunks
1 16-ounce can
  mandarin
  oranges

1 cup orange juice
½ cup minute
  tapioca
½ packet Equal
2 large bananas,
  sliced

Drain pineapple and oranges, reserving juice. Combine reserved juice, orange juice and enough water to make cups liquid in glass bowl. Stir in tapioca. Let stand for 5 minutes. Microwave on High for 12 to 15 minutes or until thickened, stirring 3 times. Let stand until cool. Stir in Equal and fruit; mix well. Chill, covered, for 4 hours or longer. Spoon into serving dishes. Garnish with maraschino cherries. Yield: 8 servings.

Approx per serving: Cal 109, Prot 1.0 mg, Fat 0.2 gr, Chol 0.0 mg, Carbo 27.4 gr, Sod 1.8 mg, Potas 2 .4 mg.

Jeanette Azua, Preceptor Beta Zeta
Mt. Clemens, Michigan

Mildred's Salad

1 cup low-fat
  cottage cheese
1 large package
  sugar-free orange
  gelatin
2 cups whipped
  topping

1 11-ounce can
  crushed
  pineapple,
  drained
1 11-ounce can
  mandarin
  oranges, drained

Combine cottage cheese, dry gelatin and whipped topping in bowl; mix well. Stir in pineapple and oranges. Chill until serving time. Yield: 6 servings.

Approx per serving: Cal 93, Prot 10.5 gr, Fat 0.3 gr, Chol 1.7 mg, Carbo 16.5 gr, Sod 137.9 mg, Potas 14.2 mg.

Mildred Ruppert, Laureate Pi
Independence, Missouri

2 3-ounce
packages cream
cheese, cut into
1-inch pieces
1 cup chopped carrot
⅔ cup crushed
pineapple

Combine gelatin and ⅔ cup very hot water in blender container. Process until gelatin is dissolved. Add pineapple juice, vinegar and evaporated milk. Process at low speed until well mixed. Add cream cheese, 1 piece at a time, processing until smooth after each addition. Add carrot and pineapple. Process just until carrot is grated. Pour into lightly oiled 1-quart mold. Chill until set. Unmold on lettuce-lined serving plate. Yield: 6 servings.

Approx per serving: Cal 242, Prot 6.0 gr, Fat 13.0 gr, Chol 40.2 mg, Carbo 27.2 gr, Sod 158.4 mg, Potas 272.4 mg.

Frances Panther, Xi Epsilon Omicron
Davenport, Iowa

Strawberry Whip Salad

1 10-ounce
package frozen
strawberries,
thawed
1 cup chopped
pecans
1 large package
strawberry
gelatin
1 pint whipping
cream, whipped

Combine strawberries, pecans and dry gelatin in bowl; mix well. Fold in whipped cream. Pour into 8-inch square dish. Chill until firm. Cut into squares. Yield: 8 servings.

Approx per serving: Cal 247, Prot 4.4 gr, Fat 10.6 gr, Chol 0.0 mg, Carbo 37.4 gr. Sod 120.1 mg, Potas 362.7 mg.

Dorothy Droste, Laureate Alpha Kappa
Alton, Illinois

Green Bean Salad

⅔ cup green beans
¼ cup grated carrot
2 teaspoons
chopped green
pepper
⅔ cup shredded
cabbage
4 teaspoons
reduced-calorie
salad dressing

Combine vegetables in bowl. Pour dressing over top; toss to coat. Serve immediately. Yield: 4 servings.

Approx per serving: Cal 12, Prot 0.6 gr, Fat 0.1 gr, Chol 0.0 mg, Carbo 2.7 gr, Sod 7.3 mg, Potas 93.4 mg. Nutritional information does not include reduced-calorie salad dressing.

Lucylle Doerr
Hettinger, North Dakota

Tex-Mex Bean Salad

1 19-ounce can
pinto beans,
drained
½ cup chopped
green pepper
½ cup chopped
seeded plum
tomatoes
4 teaspoons
chopped
scallions
2 teaspoons
chopped chili
pepper
½ teaspoon
chopped garlic
¼ teaspoon
coriander
⅛ teaspoon cumin
¼ teaspoon grated
lime rind
1 cup shredded
low-fat
mozzarella
cheese
1½ teaspoons fresh
lime juice

Combine first 9 ingredients in salad bowl; mix well. Chill, covered, until serving time, tossing once. Sprinkle cheese over top. Drizzle with lime juice. Serve with warm tostado chips. Yield: 2 servings.

Approx per serving: Cal 433, Prot 27.8 gr, Fat 15.0 gr, Chol 49.8 mg, Carbo 48.6 gr, Sod 323.7 mg, Potas 945.2 mg.

Jolyne M. Dunn, Preceptor Theta
Jefferson City, Missouri

Three-Bean Salad

1 16-ounce can
wax beans,
drained
1 16-ounce can
cut green beans,
drained
1 16-ounce can
red kidney
beans, drained
1 small green
pepper, chopped
1 small onion,
sliced into rings
1 cup sugar
½ cup oil
⅔ cup cider
vinegar
2 tablespoons
celery seed
1 teaspoon salt
½ teaspoon pepper

Combine beans, green pepper and onion in bowl; mix well. Mix remaining ingredients in saucepan. Heat to the boiling point. Pour over vegetables; mix well. Let stand, covered, until cool. Chill for 4 hours to overnight. Yield: 8 servings.

Approx per serving: Cal 299, Prot 4.9 gr, Fat 14.1 gr, Chol 0.0 mg, Carbo 41.4 gr, Sod 430.4 mg, Potas 289.7 mg.

Fran C. Naylor
Clendenin, West Virginia

Beet and Celery Salad

2 cups chopped
  cooked beets
½ cup chopped
  unpeeled
  cucumber
2 tablespoons
  chopped sweet
  pickle

½ cup chopped
  celery
2 tablespoons
  chopped onion
1 teaspoon sugar
⅓ cup reduced-
  calorie French
  dressing

Combine beets, cucumber, sweet pickle, celery, onion and salt and pepper to taste in bowl. Add mixture of sugar and French dressing. Chill for 30 minutes. Spoon onto lettuce-lined salad plates. Garnish with additional cucumber. Yield: 4 servings.

Approx per serving: Cal 69, Prot 1.3 gr, Fat 1.1 gr, Chol 0.0 mg, Carbo 15.1 gr, Sod 415.0 mg, Potas 254.9 mg.

Marilyn MacKay, Xi Beta Gamma
Woodstock, Ontario, Canada

Ruby's Beet Salad

1 8-ounce carton
  sour cream
1 tablespoon
  horseradish

1 16-ounce can
  julienne beets,
  drained

Mix sour cream, horseradish and salt to taste in bowl. Add beets; mix well. Chill until serving time. Serve on lettuce-lined salad plates. Yield: 6 servings.

Approx per serving: Cal 103, Prot 1.8 gr, Fat 8.1 gr, Chol 16.9 mg, Carbo 6.6 gr, Sod 154.0 mg, Potas 149.8 mg.

Patricia Cruger, Laureate Gamma Tau
North Hollywood, California

Broccoli-Cheddar Cheese Salad

1 bunch broccoli,
  chopped
2 tablespoons pine
  nuts
¼ cup olive oil
3 tablespoons
  lemon juice
2 tablespoons
  minced chives
⅛ teaspoon white
  pepper

¼ teaspoon garlic
  salt
¼ teaspoon dry
  mustard
4 ounces Cheddar
  cheese, slivered
4 ounces
  mushrooms,
  sliced

Cut flowerets from broccoli; slice stalks crosswise. Steam in a small amount of water in saucepan for 5 minutes or until tender-crisp; drain and rinse with cold water. Brown pine nuts in skillet over medium heat, stirring constantly. Combine olive oil, lemon juice, chives and seasonings in bowl; mix well. Pour over mixture of broccoli, cheese and mushrooms in serving bowl; toss to coat. Sprinkle with pine nuts. Garnish with radish roses. Yield: 6 servings.

Approx per serving: Cal 212, Prot 9.4 gr, Fat 17.7 gr, Chol 18.7 mg, Carbo 6.8 gr, Sod 235.2 mg, Potas 421.2 mg.

Violet Soper, Preceptor Theta
Selinsgrove, Pennsylvania

Marinated Broccoli Salad

Flowerets of 2 bunches
  broccoli
2 4-ounce cans
  sliced
  mushrooms,
  drained
1 8-ounce can
  black olives,
  drained

1 can sliced water
  chestnuts,
  drained
½ red onion,
  sliced
1 16-ounce bottle
  of Italian salad
  dressing
12 cherry tomatoes

Combine broccoli, mushrooms, olives, water chestnuts and onion in bowl. Add salad dressing; mix well. Chill, covered, for 2 days. Add tomatoes at serving time. Yield: 10 servings.

Approx per serving: Cal 231, Prot 4.6 gr, Fat 19.0 gr, Chol 0.0 mg, Carbo 14.3 gr, Sod 676.4 mg, Potas 430.8 mg.

Kathy Nelson, Lambda Chi
Dayton, Ohio

Melva's Broccoli-Cauliflower Salad

2 cups broccoli
  flowerets
2 cups cauliflowerets
2 green onions,
  chopped
⅓ cup raisins
1 cup sunflower
  seed

½ pound bacon,
  crisp-fried,
  crumbled
1 cup mayonnaise
3 tablespoons
  sugar
2 tablespoons
  vinegar

Combine broccoli, cauliflower, green onions, raisins, sunflower seed and bacon in bowl. Add mayonnaise, sugar and vinegar; mix well. Yield: 4 servings.

Approx per serving: Cal 836, Prot 19.8 gr, Fat 72.1 gr, Chol 55.9 mg, Carbo 36.9 gr, Sod 562.6 mg, Potas 1063.4 mg.

Melva M. Randolph, XP1932
Macomb, Illinois

Broccoli-Cauliflower Salad

2 stalks broccoli,
  chopped
1 small head
  cauliflower,
  chopped
1 small onion,
  chopped

1 2-ounce jar
  chopped pimento
½ cup mayonnaise
½ cup oil
¼ cup vinegar
½ cup sugar

Combine broccoli, cauliflower, onion and pimento in bowl; mix well. Blend remaining ingredients in small bowl. Add to vegetables; mix well. Chill overnight. Yield: 8 servings.

Approx per serving: Cal 323, Prot 5.3 gr, Fat 25.2 gr, Chol 9.8 mg, Carbo 23.5 gr, Sod 109.1 mg, Potas 579.1 mg.

Kathy Thompson, Delta Omega
Pleasant Shade, Tennessee

Cabbage Crunch Salad

1 cup slivered
  almonds
1 tablespoon
  sesame seed
1 medium head
  cabbage, finely
  chopped
4 green onions, minced
¼ cup sugar

1 cup oil
6 tablespoons red
  wine vinegar
1 teaspoon salt
1 teaspoon pepper
2 packages
  chicken-flavored
  Top Ramen
  noodles

Toast almonds and sesame seed in shallow baking pan in 350-degree oven. Mix cabbage and green onions in salad bowl. Combine sugar, oil, vinegar, salt, pepper and 1 flavor packet from noodles in small bowl; mix well. Pour over vegetables; mix well. Add noodles at serving time; mix gently. Sprinkle almonds and sesame seed over top. Yield: 10 servings.

Approx per serving: Cal 323, Prot 3.8 gr, Fat 29.8 gr, Chol 0.0 mg, Carbo 13.8 gr, Sod 232.1 mg, Potas 337.1 mg.
Nutritional information does not include Ramen noodles.

Debbi Lungi, Zeta Eta
Eureka, California

Margaret's Dietetic Coleslaw

½ large onion
1 large head
  cabbage
2 medium carrots
3 envelopes Sweet
  'N' Low

1 cup reduced-
  calorie
  mayonnaise
1 teaspoon salt

Place onion in food processor container. Process with knife blade. Remove onion. Combine cabbage and carrots in food processor container. Process with shredder disc. Combine processed vegetables in bowl. Add mixture of Sweet 'N' Low, mayonnaise and salt; mix well. Chill for several hours. Yield: 12 servings.

Approx per serving: Cal 76, Prot 0.7 gr, Fat 6.8 gr, Chol 6.7 mg, Carbo 5.0 gr, Sod 197.7 mg, Potas 133.7 mg.

Margaret Bell, Xi Psi
Oklahoma City, Oklahoma

Slaw

1 head cabbage,
  shredded
2 onions, sliced,
  separated into
  rings
¾ cup sugar
1 cup vinegar

¾ cup oil
2 teaspoons sugar
1 teaspoon dry
  mustard
1 teaspoon celery
  seed
1 teaspoon salt

Alternate layers of cabbage and onion rings in bowl. Sprinkle ¾ cup sugar over top. Combine remaining ingredients in saucepan. Bring to a boil, stirring to dissolve sugar. Pour over cabbage layers. Let stand for 4 to 6 hours. Yield: 8 servings.

Approx per serving: Cal 285, Prot 1.1 gr, Fat 20.5 gr, Chol 0.0 mg, Carbo 27.0 gr, Sod 278.2 mg, Potas 178.9 mg.

Karen Zahn, Alpha Phi
Moorcroft, Wyoming

Cabbage Patch Coleslaw

3 cups shredded
  cabbage, chilled
½ cup chopped
  parsley
½ cup sliced green
  onions

2 to 3 tablespoons
  sugar
3 tablespoons
  vinegar
2 tablespoons oil
1 teaspoon salt

Mix cabbage, parsley and green onions in salad bowl. Combine remaining ingredients in small bowl; stir until sugar is dissolved. Pour over vegetables. Toss lightly to coat well. Garnish with sprigs of parsley. Yield: 6 servings.
Note: To reduce calories, substitute an equivalent amount of Sweet-10 for sugar.

Approx per serving: Cal 81, Prot 0.9 gr, Fat 4.7 gr, Chol 0.0 mg, Carbo 10.3 gr, Sod 367.1 mg, Potas 167.4 mg.

Octavia Famuliner, Laureate Nu
Carrollton, Missouri

Super Coleslaw

1   3-pound head
  cabbage, shredded
1 large onion,
  shredded
1 large green pepper,
  shredded

¾ cup sugar
1 cup vinegar
¾ cup oil
1 tablespoon salt
1 tablespoon dry mustard
1 teaspoon celery seed

Layer cabbage, onion and green pepper in bowl. Sprinkle with sugar. Do not stir. Combine vinegar, oil, salt, mustard and celery seed in saucepan. Bring to a boil. Pour over cabbage. Do not stir. Chill overnight. Mix well before serving. Yield: 12 servings.

Approx per serving: Cal 207, Prot 1.8 gr, Fat 13.9 gr, Chol 0.0 mg, Carbo 21.6 gr, Sod 203.7 mg, Potas 333.5 mg.

Anita Cofer, Preceptor Alpha Beta
Wynnwood, Oklahoma

Carrot Salad

1 cup shredded
  carrots
½ cup pineapple
  chunks
½ cup chopped
  dates

¼ cup raisins
½ cup chopped
  walnuts
¾ cup orange
  juice

Combine carrots, pineapple, dates, raisins and walnuts in bowl; mix well. Stir in orange juice. Yield: 8 servings.

Approx per serving: Cal 120, Prot 1.8 gr, Fat 5.0 gr, Chol 0.0 mg, Carbo 19.6 gr, Sod 8.3 mg, Potas 249.1 mg.

Patricia Harmon, Iota Lambda
Auburn, California

Carrot-Raisin Salad

1½ cups shredded
  carrots
¼ cup raisins
⅓ cup mayonnaise

2 tablespoons
  French dressing
½ teaspoon salt

Combine carrots and raisins in bowl. Add mayonnaise, French dressing and salt; mix well. Chill in refrigerator. Yield: 6 servings.

Approx per serving: Cal 133, Prot 0.4 gr, Fat 12.0 gr, Chol 8.7 mg, Carbo 6.8 gr, Sod 330.9 mg, Potas 85.8 mg.

Patricia Thorpe, Xi Iota Mu
Crescent City, California

Marinated Carrots

3 pounds carrots
1 large onion,
  sliced into thin
  rings
1 large green
  pepper, sliced
  into thin rings
1 can tomato soup

½ cup oil
¾ cup white
  vinegar
1 teaspoon
  reduced-sodium
  salt
1 teaspoon pepper
12 envelopes Equal

Cut carrots in ¼ to ½-inch slices. Cook in water to cover in saucepan until tender-crisp. Drain and cool. Layer carrots, onion and green pepper in container with airtight seal. Combine soup, oil, vinegar, salt and pepper in saucepan. Bring to the boiling point; mix well. Cool for 5 minutes. Stir in Equal. Cool for 10 minutes. Pour over vegetable layers. Seal container. Chill for 8 to 24 hours, turning container frequently. Yield: 18 servings.

Approx per serving: Cal 83, Prot 0.8 gr, Fat 6.5 gr, Chol 0.0 mg, Carbo 6.5 gr, Sod 148.4 mg, Potas 162.0 mg.
Nutritional information does not include reduced-sodium salt.

Nelda G. Boyd, Epsilon Gamma
North Richland Hills, Texas

Minted Carrots

2 cups julienne
  carrots
½ teaspoon grated
  fresh gingerroot

1 cup orange juice
1 tablespoon
  chopped fresh
  mint

Combine carrots, ginger, orange juice and salt and pepper to taste in saucepan. Simmer for 7 minutes or until tender-crisp. Pour into serving dish. Chill, covered, overnight. Sprinkle with mint just before serving. Yield: 4 servings.

Approx per serving: Cal 51, Prot 1.0 gr, Fat 0.2 gr, Chol 0.0 mg, Carbo 11.8 gr, Sod 26.5 mg, Potas 311.5 mg.

Lee J. Beard, Preceptor Iota Omicron
San Angelo, Texas

Tropical Salad

4 cups grated
  carrots
1 8-ounce can
  unsweetened
  crushed pineapple,
  drained

1 envelope Equal
1 teaspoon coconut
  extract
2 tablespoons
  reduced-calorie
  salad dressing

Combine carrots and pineapple in bowl. Add remaining ingredients; mix well. Chill until serving time. Yield: 4 servings.

Approx per serving: Cal 116, Prot 1.4 gr, Fat 2.3 gr, Chol 2.5 mg, Carbo 24.0 gr, Sod 54.8 mg, Potas 436.3 mg.

LuAnne Hamilton, Xi Gamma Zeta
Bartlesville, Oklahoma

Creamy Cucumber Salad

1 cucumber, sliced
Rings of 2 onion
  slices
2 envelopes Equal

2 tablespoons cider
  vinegar
1 8-ounce carton
  low-fat yogurt

Combine cucumber and onion rings in bowl. Mix remaining ingredients with salt and pepper to taste in small bowl. Add to cucumber mixture; mix well. Chill, covered, overnight.
Yield: 2 servings.

Approx per serving: Cal 77, Prot 4.6 gr, Fat 2.0 gr, Chol 9.0 mg, Carbo 10.9 gr, Sod 64.3 mg, Potas 326.0 mg.

Anita Prescott, Preceptor Theta Beta
Dallas, Texas

Seven-Layer Salad

1½ heads lettuce,
  torn
½ cup sliced
  mushrooms
¾ cup chopped
  tomatoes
½ cup chopped
  green pepper
½ cup green peas
½ cup chopped
  cauliflower

2 hard-boiled eggs,
  chopped
½ cup sliced
  radishes
½ cup chopped
  broccoli
1½ cups
  mayonnaise
1 cup grated
  Cheddar cheese

Layer first 9 ingredients in order listed in large glass serving bowl. Spread mayonnaise over top, sealing to side of bowl. Sprinkle with Cheddar cheese. Chill, covered with plastic wrap, overnight. Garnish with crumbled bacon. Yield: 10 servings.

Approx per serving: Cal 327, Prot 6.3 gr, Fat 31.8 gr, Chol 85.3 mg, Carbo 62.0 gr, Sod 312.4 mg, Potas 293.9 mg.

Kristi Mealey, Alpha Sigma
Kindersley, Saskatchewan, Canada

Layered Salad

1 avocado, sliced
1 teaspoon lemon
  juice
1 head lettuce,
  torn
1 bunch green
  onions, chopped
1 stalk celery,
  chopped
1 10-ounce
  package frozen
  peas
2 cups mayonnaise

½ cup Parmesan
  cheese
2 teaspoons sugar
¼ teaspoon garlic
  powder
1 teaspoon salt
3 hard-boiled eggs,
  chopped
1 pound bacon,
  crisp-fried,
  crumbled
2 tomatoes, cut
  into wedges

Dip avocado slices in lemon juice. Layer lettuce, green onions, avocado, celery and peas in glass salad bowl. Spread mayonnaise over top, sealing to side of bowl. Combine cheese, sugar, garlic powder and salt in small bowl. Sprinkle cheese mixture, egg and bacon over top. Chill, covered, for 3 to 4 hours. Arrange tomatoes over top. Dip through all layers to serve. Yield: 12 servings.

Aileen Bennett, Phi
Gulfport, Mississippi

Alabama Stack Salad

1 head lettuce, torn
1 head cauliflower,
  chopped
1 bunch broccoli,
  chopped
2 tomatoes, chopped
1 cup reduced-calorie
  mayonnaise

1 package reduced-
  calorie Italian
  salad dressing
  mix
1 cup shredded
  mozzarella
  cheese

Layer lettuce, cauliflower, broccoli and tomatoes in glass salad bowl. Spread mayonnaise over top, sealing to side of bowl. Sprinkle salad dressing mix and cheese over mayonnaise. Chill, covered, overnight. Toss to serve. Yield: 6 servings.

Carolyn Blackwell, Xi Beta Alpha
Huntsville, Alabama

Overnight Salad

1 medium head
  lettuce, torn
1 head cauliflower,
  chopped
1 pound bacon,
  crisp-fried,
  crumbled

2 cups salad
  dressing
¼ cup (or less)
  sugar
½ cup Parmesan
  cheese

Layer lettuce, cauliflower and bacon in glass salad bowl. Spread salad dressing over top, sealing to side of bowl. Sprinkle with sugar and cheese. Chill, covered, overnight. Toss to serve. Yield: 8 servings.

Approx per serving: Cal 463, Prot 11.7 gr, Fat 37.3 gr, Chol 53.7 mg, Carbo 23.2 gr, Sod 617.5 mg, Potas 495.9 mg.

Carolyn Howland, Preceptor Gamma Theta
Bloomington, Illinois

Chick-Pea Salad

⅔ cup olive oil
⅓ cup red wine
  vinegar
1 teaspoon oregano,
  crushed
½ teaspoon garlic
  powder
1 teaspoon salt

Ground pepper
  to taste
2 20-ounce cans
  chick-peas, drained
½ cup diced roasted
  red peppers
3 or 4 tomatoes, cut
  into wedges

Combine olive oil, wine vinegar and seasonings in medium bowl; mix well. Add chick-peas and red peppers; toss to coat. Chill, covered, overnight. Let stand until at room temperature. Spoon into lettuce-lined salad bowl. Arrange tomato wedges around edge. Garnish with chopped scallions. Yield: 4 servings.

Photograph for this recipe on page 36.

Marinated Mushrooms

3 green onions
  with tops, sliced
⅔ cup olive oil
¼ cup lemon juice
1 teaspoon
  Worcestershire
  sauce
½ teaspoon dry
  mustard

½ teaspoon salt
⅛ teaspoon pepper
1 pound
  mushrooms,
  sliced
12 slices bacon,
  crisp-fried,
  crumbled

Combine green onions, oil, lemon juice, Worcestershire sauce, dry mustard, salt and pepper in bowl; mix well. Add mushrooms; mix gently. Chill, covered, for 4 hours to overnight. Spoon into lettuce-lined serving bowl. Sprinkle with bacon. Drizzle with remaining marinade. Yield: 6 servings.

Approx per serving: Cal 330, Prot 6.1 gr, Fat 32.2 gr, Chol 13.3 mg, Carbo 5.6 gr, Sod 350.8 mg, Potas 387.6 mg.

Reggie Smith, Pi Epsilon
Morton, Illinois

Mandarin Orange Toss

⅓ cup sliced
  almonds
2 tablespoons
  sugar
½ head lettuce,
  torn
1 head romaine
  lettuce, torn
1 cup thinly sliced
  celery
1 11-ounce can
  mandarin
  oranges, drained

2 green onions,
  thinly sliced
3 tablespoons
  sugar
⅓ cup oil
3 tablespoons
  vinegar
1 tablespoon
  chopped parsley
½ teaspoon salt
Pepper to taste
Tabasco sauce to
  taste

Combine almonds and 2 tablespoons sugar in heavy saucepan. Heat until sugar is melted, stirring constantly to coat almonds well. Pour onto waxed paper; separate almonds with forks. Cool. Combine lettuce, celery, oranges, onions and almonds in bowl; mix well. Mix 3 tablespoons sugar and remaining ingredients in small bowl. Pour over salad; toss to coat well. Yield: 8 servings.

Approx per serving: Cal 160, Prot 1.7 gr, Fat 11.8 gr, Chol 0.0 mg, Carbo 13.9 gr, Sod 157.5 mg, Potas 227.8 mg.

Nu Chapter
Thompson, Manitoba, Canada

Spanish Orange Salad

3 medium oranges
½ cup thinly
  sliced red onion
2 tablespoons wine
  vinegar
½ teaspoon
  coriander

¼ cup oil
¾ teaspoon salt
⅛ teaspoon pepper
4 cups torn lettuce
4 cups torn
  spinach
½ cup ripe olives

Peel oranges and cut into thin slices. Mix with onion in bowl. Combine vinegar, coriander, oil, salt and pepper in small bowl. Add to oranges; mix well. Let stand for 30 minutes. Add lettuce and spinach; toss well. Sprinkle with olives. Yield: 6 servings.

Approx per serving: Cal 148, Prot 2.7 gr, Fat 10.6 gr, Chol 0.0 mg, Carbo 13.3 gr, Sod 347.4 mg, Potas 401.4 mg.

Maureen Dwyer, Omicron Tau
Kimberling City, Missouri

Sweet and Sour Lettuce Salad

1 medium head
  lettuce, torn
6 green onions,
  chopped
½ cup sliced
  almonds
2 tablespoons
  sugar
⅓ cup oil

3 tablespoons
  sugar
3 tablespoons
  white vinegar
¾ teaspoon salt
Dash of pepper
4 medium oranges,
  peeled, sectioned

Combine lettuce and green onions in plastic bag. Chill in refrigerator. Spread almonds in shallow glass dish. Sprinkle with mixture of 2 teaspoons water and 2 tablespoons sugar. Microwave on High for 3 minutes, stirring once. Cool. Combine oil, 3 tablespoons sugar, vinegar, salt and pepper in mixer bowl. Beat until well mixed. Chill until serving time. Combine lettuce, almonds and oranges in salad bowl. Add dressing; toss lightly to coat well. Serve immediately. Yield: 6 servings.
Note: May substitute one 15-ounce can mandarin oranges for fresh oranges.

Approx per serving: Cal 269, Prot 4.0 gr, Fat 17.4 gr, Chol 0.0 mg, Carbo 28.3 gr, Sod 276.8 mg, Potas 454.8 mg.

Helen Heath, Preceptor Upsilon
Muncie, Indiana

Tossed Green Salad

1 clove of garlic
1 large head lettuce
2 cups cherry tomatoes
1 cup sliced
  mushrooms
1 cup chopped green
  onions
1 cup chopped
  zucchini

½ cup chopped celery
½ cup grated carrots
Freshly chopped dillweed
  to taste
2 hard-boiled eggs, sliced
1 cup crumbled feta
  cheese

Rub salad bowl with garlic clove. Combine lettuce, tomatoes, mushrooms, green onions, zucchini, celery, carrots and dillweed in prepared bowl; toss to mix. Arrange egg slices on top. Sprinkle with cheese. Yield: 8 servings.

Approx per serving: Cal 49, Prot 3.3 gr, Fat 1.7 gr, Chol 63.2 mg, Carbo 6.2 gr, Sod 27.7 mg, Potas 331.1 mg.

Jean Udries, Xi Delta Xi
Lawrenceville, Georgia

Caesar Potato Salad Special

4 potatoes, peeled,
  cooked, chopped
4 pitted ripe
  olives, sliced
¼ cup reduced-
  calorie Italian
  salad dressing
1 egg, beaten

1 tablespoon
  Worcestershire
  sauce
2 teaspoons
  mustard
8 teaspoons
  Parmesan cheese

Combine potatoes and olives in bowl. Mix remaining ingredients and garlic salt to taste in small bowl until smooth. Add to potatoes; mix well. Chill, covered, in refrigerator. Yield: 8 servings.

Approx per serving: Cal 101, Prot 3.8 gr, Fat 2.2 gr, Chol 33.9 mg, Carbo 16.8 gr, Sod 135.7 mg, Potas 411.5 mg.

Lisa Martiny, Delta Delta
May, Idaho

German Potato Salad

6 strips bacon,
  chopped
1½ teaspoons flour
½ teaspoon parsley
  flakes
2 tablespoons
  onion flakes
1 tablespoon sugar

½ teaspoon salt
⅛ teaspoon white
  pepper
⅓ cup cider
  vinegar
6 medium
  potatoes,
  cooked, sliced

Cook bacon in skillet until crisp. Add next 7 ingredients and ⅔ cup water. Simmer for 5 minutes, stirring constantly. Pour over potatoes in serving bowl; toss to coat. Yield: 6 servings.

Peggy Raschke, Preceptor Iota Omicron
San Angelo, Texas

Pueblo Herbed Potato Salad

½ cup low-fat
  yogurt
¼ cup reduced-
  calorie
  mayonnaise
2 tablespoons
  chopped parsley
1 tablespoon
  chopped fresh
  basil

1 tablespoon
  chopped green
  onion
3 medium
  potatoes,
  cooked, chopped
½ cup frozen
  green peas,
  thawed

Combine yogurt, mayonnaise, parsley, basil and green onion in bowl; mix well. Add potatoes and peas; mix lightly. Chill, covered, for several hours. Yield: 4 servings.

Approx per serving: Cal 329, Prot 5.6 gr, Fat 6.2 gr, Chol 7.3 mg, Carbo 71.0 gr, Sod 58.6 mg, Potas 999.0 mg.

Beverly Oldaker, Laureate Alpha Delta
Pueblo, Colorado

Andrea's Spinach Salad

1 small head
  romaine, torn
5 ounces spinach,
  torn
1 cup sliced
  radishes
½ cup chopped
  celery
½ cup sliced green
  onions
1 cup sliced
  mushrooms

½ cup oil
¼ cup cider
  vinegar
2 cloves of garlic,
  crushed
1 teaspoon
  seasoned salt
2 hard-boiled eggs,
  sliced
4 slices bacon,
  crisp-fried,
  crumbled

Combine vegetables in salad bowl. Mix oil, vinegar, garlic and seasoned salt in jar with lid; shake well. Pour over salad; toss gently. Top with egg slices, bacon and freshly ground pepper to taste. Yield: 6 servings.

Approx per serving: Cal 245, Prot 5.6 gr, Fat 22.9 gr, Chol 88.7 mg, Carbo 5.9 gr, Sod 466.7 mg, Potas 450.7 mg.

Andrea E. Kessler, Preceptor Beta
Waukegan, Illinois

Fresh Spinach Salad

1 pound fresh
  spinach, torn
1 medium red
  onion, sliced
  into rings
4 stalks celery,
  chopped
8 mushrooms,
  sliced
4 green onions,
  chopped
¼ cup raisins
4 teaspoons
  chopped parsley

¼ cup chopped
  walnuts
4 slices bacon,
  crisp-fried,
  crumbled
¼ cup reduced-
  calorie Italian
  salad dressing
½ cup orange
  juice
4 hard-boiled eggs,
  cut into quarters
½ cup garlic-
  flavored croutons

Combine spinach, red onion, celery, nushrooms, green onions, raisins, parsley, walnuts and bacon in bowl; mix well. Mix salad dressing and orange juice in small bowl. Pour over salad; toss lightly. Top with egg quarters and croutons. Yield: 8 servings.

Approx per serving: Cal 147, Prot 8.1 gr, Fat 8.2 gr, Chol 132.1 mg, Carbo 12.3 gr, Sod 220.6 mg, Potas 525.9 mg.

Mary Ann O'Sullivan, Xi Beta Alpha
Gretna, Louisiana

Fire and Ice Tomatoes

6 large tomatoes,
  peeled, quartered
2 large green peppers,
  cut into strips
1 large red onion,
  sliced
1½ teaspoons
  celery salt

¾ cup vinegar
1½ teaspoons
  mustard seed
⅛ teaspoon pepper
⅛ teaspoon
  cayenne pepper
4½ tablespoons
  sugar

Layer tomatoes, green peppers and onion in bowl. Combine remaining ingredients in saucepan. Bring to a boil. Pour over vegetables. Marinate, covered, for 12 to 72 hours. Yield: 12 servings.

Approx per serving: Cal 42, Prot 1.0 gr, Fat 0.2 gr, Chol 0.0 mg, Carbo 10.0 gr, Sod 270.0 mg, Potas 213.0 mg.

Tomatoes Vinaigrette

4 large tomatoes,
  sliced
6 tablespoons
  chopped fresh
  parsley
6 tablespoons olive
  oil
2 tablespoons
  vinegar

1 clove of garlic,
  crushed
1½ teaspoons
  chopped fresh
  basil
1 teaspoon salt
⅛ teaspoon pepper

Place tomatoes in serving bowl. Sprinkle with parsley. Combine remaining ingredients in jar with lid; shake well. Pour over tomatoes. Chill for 3 hours. Garnish with additional parsley. Yield: 8 servings.

Approx per serving: Cal 106, Prot 0.8 gr, Fat 10.3 gr, Chol 0.0 mg, Carbo 3.4 gr, Sod 269.6 mg, Potas 174.7 mg.

Ellen R. Wilkinson, Preceptor Upsilon
Chesapeake, Virginia

Light Salad

1 bunch broccoli,
  chopped
1 small head
  cauliflower,
  chopped
1 onion, chopped
1 cup raisins
½ pound bacon,
  crisp-fried,
  crumbled

6 ounces
  sunflower seed
1½ cups reduced-
  calorie
  mayonnaise
3 tablespoons
  honey
4 ounces cream
  cheese, softened

Combine broccoli, cauliflower, onion, raisins, bacon and sunflower seed in bowl. Blend remaining ingredients in small bowl. Beat until smooth. Add to vegetable mixture; mix well. Yield: 10 servings.

Approx per serving: Cal 398, Prot 4.6 gr, Fat 28.8 gr, Chol 31.3 mg, Carbo 31.0 gr, Sod 146.0 mg, Potas 430.8 mg.

Lois Leach, Preceptor Delta
Belle Fourche, South Dakota

Marinated Garden Salad

1 small head
  cauliflower
3 stalks celery
4 stalks broccoli
2 zucchini
1 small onion
1 green pepper
½ pound
  mushrooms

3 tomatoes
½ cup vinegar
1½ cups oil
½ cup sugar
1 teaspoon salt
2 teaspoons dry
  mustard
2 tablespoons
  poppy seed

Cut vegetables into bite-sized pieces. Combine in bowl; mix well. Mix vinegar, oil, sugar, salt, dry mustard and poppy seed in small bowl. Add to vegetables; mix well. Chill, covered, for 3 hours to 1 week. Yield: 8 servings.

Approx per serving: Cal 490, Prot 7.1 gr, Fat 41.5 gr, Chol 0.0 mg, Carbo 28.3 gr, Sod 317.1 mg, Potas 929.6 mg.

Val Jean Beugli, Preceptor Laureate Chi
Salem, Oregon

Diana's Marinated Vegetables

1 cup chopped
  carrots
1 zucchini,
  chopped
1 cup chopped
  cauliflower
1 cup chopped
  broccoli
¼ cup chopped
  green pepper

3 radishes,
  chopped
12 cherry tomatoes
1 cup low-fat
  yogurt
¼ cup white wine
1 clove of garlic,
  crushed
Oregano and basil
  to taste

Mix vegetables in bowl. Combine yogurt, wine, garlic and seasonings in small bowl; mix well. Pour over vegetables; mix well. Chill, covered, for several hours to overnight. Yield: 6 servings.

Approx per serving: Cal 55, Prot 3.2 gr, Fat 0.9 gr, Chol 3.0 mg, Carbo 8.1 gr, Sod 34.5 mg, Potas 345.9 mg.

Diana Allen, Preceptor Alpha Zeta
Grand Prairie, Texas

Katrina's Marinated Vegetable Salad

2 cups chopped
  cauliflower
1 16-ounce can
  cut green beans,
  drained
4 ounces fresh
  mushrooms,
  sliced
1 cup pitted olives
1 medium onion,
  sliced, separated
  into rings

½ cup chopped
  sweet pickles
½ cup oil
¼ cup lemon juice
2 tablespoons
  sugar
1 teaspoon salt
⅛ teaspoon pepper
1 teaspoon
  dillweed
2 cups torn lettuce

Combine cauliflower, beans, mushrooms, olives, onion and pickles in 2½-quart bowl. Combine next 6 ingredients in small bowl; mix well. Pour over vegetables; toss to coat well. Chill, covered, for 24 to 48 hours, stirring occasionally. Add lettuce at serving time. Toss gently to mix well. Yield: 6 servings.

Approx per serving: Cal 257, Prot 3.8 gr, Fat 21.8 gr, Chol 0.0 mg, Carbo 15.1 gr, Sod 1097.6 mg, Potas 449.5 mg.

Katrina Shelton, Preceptor Kappa
Huron, South Dakota

Shirley's Vegetable Salad

2 small packages
  lemon gelatin
½ cup grated
  carrot
2 cups chopped
  celery
½ cup chopped
  green pepper
1 cucumber,
  chopped

2 tablespoons
  grated onion
1 cup reduced-
  calorie salad
  dressing
1½ cups cottage
  cheese
1 cup whipped
  topping

Dissolve gelatin in 1 cup boiling water. Stir in vegetables. Fold in mixture of remaining ingredients. Spoon into serving dish. Chill for several hours. Yield: 8 servings.

Approx per serving: Cal 257, Prot 9.0 gr, Fat 14.0 gr, Chol 18.7 mg, Carbo 27.0 gr, Sod 228.4 mg, Potas 264.0 mg.

Shirley Miller, Laureate Theta
Lodgepole, South Dakota

Rebecca's Vegetable Salad

1 cup chopped
  cauliflower
1 cup chopped
  broccoli
1 bunch green
  onions, chopped
1 green pepper,
  chopped
1 tomato, chopped
1 cup chopped
  carrots

1 cup chopped
  celery
1 cup chopped
  cucumber
½ cup olives
1 envelope Good
  Seasons Italian
  salad dressing
  mix
Lemon juice

Combine vegetables and olives in bowl. Prepare salad dressing mix according to package directions, substituting lemon juice for vinegar and omitting water. Add to vegetables; mix well. Let stand for 30 minutes. Yield: 4 servings.

Approx per serving: Cal 140, Prot 7.4 gr, Fat 3.4 gr, Chol 0.0 mg, Carbo 24.9 gr, Sod 1049.0 mg, Potas 1067.8 mg.

Rebecca Davis, Xi Gamma Theta
Casa Grande, Arizona

Health Salad

2 cups chopped
  broccoli
2 cups chopped
  cauliflower
1 10-ounce
  package frozen
  green peas,
  thawed
1 cup chopped apple

½ cup raisins
1 cup cubed
  American cheese
½ cup salted
  peanuts
1 cup ranch-style
  salad dressing

Combine vegetables, apple, raisins, cheese and peanuts in bowl. Add salad dressing; toss to mix well. Chill, covered, in refrigerator. Yield: 8 servings.

Approx per serving: Cal 285, Prot 10.2 gr, Fat 20.0 gr, Chol 22.6 mg, Carbo 19.5 gr, Sod 360.9 mg, Potas 406.6 mg.

Lois Jean Patrick, Xi Delta Iota
Oklahoma City, Oklahoma

Brenda's Chicken Salad with Grapes

3 cups chopped
  cooked chicken
1 cup chopped
  celery
1 13-ounce can
  juice-pack
  pineapple tidbits,
  drained
3 tablespoons
  lemon juice

¾ cup chopped
  pecans
1½ cups seedless
  green grapes
1 cup mayonnaise
¼ cup pineapple
  juice
1 teaspoon curry
  powder

Combine chicken, celery, pineapple and lemon juice in bowl; mix well. Chill for several hours or overnight. Add pecans and grapes. Combine remaining ingredients with salt and pepper to taste in bowl. Add to salad, tossing gently to mix well. Chill for 1 hour or longer. Serve in lettuce cups. Garnish with tomato wedges. Yield: 8 servings.

Approx per serving: Cal 424, Prot 19.8 gr, Fat 32.4 gr, Chol 64.4 mg, Carbo 15.5 gr, Sod 223.5 mg, Potas 444.3 mg.

Brenda Inman, Delta Rho
Hayti, Missouri

Chicken-Rotini Salad

1 8-ounce
  package rotini,
  cooked
2 cups chopped
  cooked chicken
2 cups cherry
  tomato halves

2 cups slivered
  green pepper
2 cups fresh broccoli
  flowerets
1 8-ounce bottle of
  reduced-calorie zesty
  Italian salad dressing

Combine rotini, chicken, tomatoes, green pepper and broccoli in salad bowl; mix well. Add salad dressing and salt and pepper to taste; toss lightly. Chill until serving time. Yield: 6 servings.

Photograph for this recipe on page 70.

Fancy Chicken Salad

12 cups chopped
cooked chicken
1½ onions, chopped
1½ pounds
seedless grapes
1½ stalks celery,
chopped
1 16-ounce
package shell
macaroni, cooked

1½ quarts salad
dressing
1½ cups ranch-
style dressing
6 tablespoons
sugar
3 tablespoons
mustard

Combine chicken, onions, grapes, celery and macaroni in large bowl; mix well. Blend remaining ingredients in bowl. Add to chicken mixture; mix well. Chill, covered, for several hours.
Yield: 25 servings.

Approx per serving: Cal 544, Prot 23.8 gr, Fat 36.0 gr, Chol 92.0 mg, Carbo 31.4 gr, Sod 456.6 mg, Potas 317.8 mg.

Beta Delta Chapter
Fort Atkinson, Iowa

Nutritional Chicken Salad

4 cups chopped
cooked chicken
2 cups
unsweetened
pineapple
tidbits
2 cups seedless
grapes
1 cup mandarin
oranges

1 cup chopped
celery
¾ cup peanuts
1 cup reduced-
calorie
mayonnaise
2 tablespoons
lemon juice
2 tablespoons
pineapple juice

Combine chicken, pineapple, grapes, oranges, celery and peanuts in bowl; mix well. Blend remaining ingredients in small bowl. Add to chicken mixture; mix well. Chill, covered, in refrigerator.
Yield: 8 servings.

Approx per serving: Cal 390, Prot 25.3 gr, Fat 18.5 gr, Chol 65.9 mg, Carbo 22.5 gr, Sod 120.5 mg, Potas 458.3 mg.

Chris L. Mayer, Theta Delta
Endicott, Washington

Chicken-Pineapple Salad

2 cups chicken broth
1 small package
sugar-free lemon
gelatin
½ teaspoon salt
1 8-ounce can
unsweetened
crushed
pineapple

1⅔ cups chopped
cooked chicken
¼ cup green grape
halves
2 tablespoons
minced onion
2 tablespoons
chopped
pimento

Bring broth to a boil in saucepan. Add gelatin and salt; stir until gelatin is dissolved. Chill until partially set. Add remaining ingredients; mix well. Spoon into 4-cup mold. Chill for 3 hours or until set. Unmold on lettuce-lined serving plate. Garnish with green pepper rings, parsley, radish roses or carrot curls. Yields: 4 servings.

Approx per serving: Cal 201, Prot 21.5 gr, Fat 5.4 gr, Chol 62.9 mg, Carbo 15.5 gr, Sod 742.9 mg, Potas 318.9 mg.

Juanita Lunn, Alpha Kappa
Mount Vernon, Ohio

Turkey Salad

2 cups chopped
cooked turkey
breast
½ cup chopped
celery
¼ cup chopped
onion

¼ cup chopped
red pepper
1 cup low-fat
yogurt
¼ teaspoon curry
powder

Combine turkey with celery, onion and red pepper in bowl; mix well. Add yogurt; mix well. Blend in curry powder. Chill for several hours. Spoon onto lettuce-lined serving plates. Sprinkle with paprika. Garnish with sliced ripe olives. Yield: 4 servings.

Approx per serving: Cal 112, Prot 16.3 gr, Fat 2.7 gr, Chol 37.2 mg, Carbo 4.9 gr, Sod 84.8 mg, Potas 343.3 mg.

Peggy Simpson, Gamma Phi
Snohomish, Washington

Ham and Asparagus Salad

1 pound fresh or
frozen asparagus
2 cups chopped
ham
8 mushrooms,
sliced
½ cup shredded
Swiss cheese

1 small onion,
chopped
2 tablespoons
sesame seed
¾ cup Italian
salad dressing
1 tomato, cut into
wedges

Cut asparagus into bite-sized pieces. Cook in water to cover in saucepan until tender-crisp. Drain and chill. Combine with ham, mushrooms, cheese, onion and sesame seed in bowl. Add salad dressing; mix lightly. Spoon into lettuce cups. Top with tomato wedges. Yield: 6 servings.

Approx per serving: Cal 385, Prot 15.7 gr, Fat 32.9 gr, Chol 51.0 mg, Carbo 8.7 gr, Sod 1049.6 mg, Potas 419.5 mg.

Bettie Wilson, Preceptor Beta Mu
Hatfield, Pennsylvania

Crab Meat Salad

4 crabstix,
  chopped
1 teaspoon onion
  flakes
1 tablespoon
  chopped green
  pepper

1 tablespoon
  chopped celery
1 teaspoon Old
  Bay seasoning
3 tablespoons
  reduced-calorie
  mayonnaise

Combine crabstix, onion flakes, green pepper, celery and seasoning in bowl. Add mayonnaise; toss gently. Serve on wheat bread or croissants. Yield: 2 servings.

Sherry Murray, Xi Gamma Sigma
Marion, Iowa

Asparagus-Shrimp Salad

1½ cups torn
  spinach
½ cup sliced
  mushrooms
16 fresh asparagus
  spears
12 peeled raw
  shrimp

¼ cup unsalted
  butter
1 red pepper, cut
  into strips
1 tablespoon olive
  oil
2 teaspoons lemon
  juice

Arrange spinach on 4 salad plates. Sprinkle mushrooms over spinach. Cut asparagus into ½-inch pieces. Combine with ¾ cup water in saucepan. Cook until tender-crisp. Drain, reserving ½ cup liquid. Cut shrimp into thirds. Stir-fry in butter in skillet just until cooked through. Add red pepper. Stir-fry until tender-crisp. Add asparagus. Cook just until heated through. Remove to salad plates with slotted spoon. Stir reserved asparagus liquid into pan juices. Add olive oil. Cook until reduced to ⅓ cup liquid. Remove from heat. Whisk in lemon juice and salt and freshly ground pepper to taste. Spoon over salads. Yield: 4 servings.

Approx per serving: Cal 182, Prot 7.6 gr, Fat 15.4 gr, Chol 61.5 mg, Carbo 5.7 gr, Sod 187.3 mg, Potas 383.9 mg.

Nancy F. Otte, Preceptor Alpha Kappa
Freeport, Illinois

Camille's Shrimp-Pea Salad

8 ounces peeled
  small shrimp,
  cooked
1 16-ounce
  package frozen
  tiny peas,
  thawed
½ cup finely
  chopped red
  onion

½ cup finely
  chopped celery
4 teaspoons lemon
  juice
½ cup mayonnaise
1 teaspoon soy
  sauce
½ teaspoon curry
  powder

Combine shrimp, peas, onion, celery and 2 teaspoons lemon juice in bowl. Chill, covered, for 2 hours. Blend 2 teaspoons lemon juice with remaining ingredients and salt and pepper to taste in small bowl. Add to shrimp mixture; toss gently to mix well. Serve immediately. Yield: 6 servings.

Approx per serving: Cal 228, Prot 12.7 gr, Fat 15.5 gr, Chol 69.8 mg, Carbo 10.2 gr, Sod 307.1 mg, Potas 211.0 mg.

Camille Nielsen, Psi Omicron
El Cajon, California

Shrimp and Melon Salad

3 cantaloupes
2 cups cooked
  shrimp, chilled
1 cup chopped
  celery

¼ cup mayonnaise
1 tablespoon lemon
  juice
¼ teaspoon salt
⅛ teaspoon pepper

Cut cantaloupes in half; discard seed. Combine shrimp with remaining ingredients in bowl; mix lightly. Place cantaloupe halves on lettuce-lined plates. Spoon shrimp mixture into cantaloupes. Yield: 6 servings.

Approx per serving: Cal 216, Prot 15.9 gr, Fat 8.4 gr, Chol 41.6 mg, Carbo 21.5 gr, Sod 280.9 mg, Potas 809.3 mg.

Julie Ann Prahler, Preceptor Omega
Pontiac, Michigan

Shrimp-Macaroni Salad

8 ounces shell
  macaroni, cooked
1 tablespoon
  chopped green
  pepper
1 tablespoon
  chopped celery
1 tablespoon
  chopped onion

1 tablespoon
  chopped pimento
2 6-ounce cans
  shrimp
½ teaspoon milk
1 cup salad
  dressing

Combine macaroni, green pepper, celery, onion, pimento and shrimp in bowl; mix well. Blend milk into salad dressing. Add to macaroni mixture; mix well. Chill, covered, in refrigerator. Yield: 8 servings.

Approx per serving: Cal 292, Prot 14.3 gr, Fat 14.5 gr, Chol 105.5 mg, Carbo 25.5 gr, Sod 239.2 mg, Potas 108.3 mg.

Bonnie Arrigoni, Alpha Phi
Moorcroft, Wyoming

Shrimp-Pasta Salad

8 ounces shell pasta, cooked
¼ cup chopped green olives
½ cup chopped broccoli
¼ cup chopped red onion
¼ cup chopped celery
½ cup chopped zucchini
¼ cup chopped green pepper
1 cup shrimp
¾ cup red wine vinegar
¾ cup olive oil
½ teaspoon basil
½ teaspoon garlic salt
¼ teaspoon pepper

Combine pasta, olives, vegetables and shrimp in salad bowl; mix well. Mix vinegar, oil and seasonings in bowl. Pour over salad, tossing lightly to mix well. Yield: 6 servings.
Note: May use pasta, vegetables and meat of your choice.

Approx per serving: Cal 430, Prot 11.1 gr, Fat 28.8 gr, Chol 32.0 mg, Carbo 33.1 gr, Sod 373.6 mg, Potas 266.5 mg.

Renee Mathews, Zeta Eta
Eureka, California

Tomatoes Stuffed with Shrimp

2 large firm tomatoes
½ head lettuce, shredded
2 canned artichoke hearts
1 cup cooked small shrimp
½ cup chopped celery
1 green onion, chopped
1 tablespoon lemon juice
½ cup mayonnaise
1 cup Thousand Island dressing
4 ripe olives
8 asparagus spears, cooked
2 hard-boiled eggs, cut into quarters

Peel tomatoes and slice off stem end. Scoop out center. Invert shells on paper towel to drain. Place tomato shells on lettuce-lined salad plates. Sprinkle inside with salt to taste. Place 1 artichoke heart in each tomato. Combine shrimp, celery, onion, lemon juice and mayonnaise in bowl; mix well. Spoon into tomato shells. Top with dressing and olives. Arrange asparagus spears and egg quarters around tomato. Yield: 2 servings.

Approx per serving: Cal 1284, Prot 28.6 gr, Fat 117.6 gr, Chol 452.0 mg, Carbo 36.6 gr, Sod 1636.7 mg, Potas 1117.2 mg.
Nutritional information does not include artichoke hearts.

Margie G. Hendricks, Xi Beta Tau
Little Rock, Arkansas

Shrimp Salad

1½ cups sugar
1 tablespoon cornstarch
¾ cup vinegar
1 tablespoon flour
3 egg yolks, beaten
3 cups shell macaroni, cooked
1 onion, chopped
1 green pepper, chopped
2 cups chopped celery
½ cup stuffed olive halves
2 6½-ounce cans shrimp

Blend sugar, cornstarch, vinegar, flour, egg yolks and ¾ cup water in saucepan. Cook until thickened, stirring constantly. Cool. Combine macaroni and remaining ingredients in bowl. Add dressing; mix well. Chill, covered, for 24 hours. Yield: 12 servings.
Note: May substitute 4½ tablespoons Egg Beaters for egg yolks to reduce cholesterol.

Approx per serving: Cal 258, Prot 11.3 gr, Fat 3.3 gr, Chol 109.0 mg, Carbo 46.6 gr, Sod 124.7 mg, Potas 230.6 mg.

Diane R. Korf, Preceptor Kappa
Valley City, North Dakota

Tuna Salad Vinaigrette

½ cup olive oil
3 tablespoons lemon juice
2 cloves of garlic, crushed
Freshly ground black pepper to taste
1 teaspoon basil
1 bunch scallions, minced
1 8-ounce package spiral pasta, cooked
2 7-ounce cans water-pack tuna, drained
1 16-ounce can green beans, drained
4 large tomatoes, sliced

Combine olive oil, lemon juice, garlic, black pepper and basil in bowl; mix well. Combine scallions, pasta, tuna and green beans in bowl. Pour dressing over top; toss to coat. Place overlapping tomato slices on each serving. Sprinkle with additional freshly ground black pepper. Yield: 4 servings.

Approx per serving: Cal 522, Prot 36.0 gr, Fat 15.5 gr, Chol 58.0 mg, Carbo 59.6 gr, Sod 972.5 mg, Potas 895.0 mg.

Irene Lozar, Xi Gamma Iota
Yuma, Arizona

Apple-Tuna Salad

1 small package
   sugar-free lemon
   gelatin
½ teaspoon salt
2 tablespoons
   lemon juice
Pepper to taste
1 7-ounce can
   water-pack tuna

½ cup chopped
   unpeeled apple
¼ cup minced
   onion
1 tablespoon
   chopped parsley

Dissolve gelatin and salt in 1 cup boiling water in bowl. Add 1 cup cold water, lemon juice and pepper to taste. Chill until partially set. Fold in tuna, apple, onion and parsley. Pour into 4-cup mold. Chill until set. Unmold on lettuce-lined serving plate. Yield: 3 servings.

Approx per serving: Cal 112, Prot 19.0 gr, Fat 0.6 gr, Chol 38.6 mg, Carbo 6.0 gr, Sod 962.3 mg, Potas 258.6 mg.

Juanita Lunn, Alpha Kappa
Mount Vernon, Ohio

Chow Mein Salad

½ cup oil
½ cup vinegar
½ cup soy sauce
2 tablespoons
   chopped parsley
2 teaspoons dried
   celery leaves
½ teaspoon pepper
1 head lettuce,
   shredded
½ cup bean
   sprouts
½ cup bamboo
   shoots
½ cup sliced water
   chestnuts

½ cup chopped
   celery
½ cup sliced
   mushrooms
¼ cup chopped
   onion
½ cup chopped
   green pepper
¼ cup sliced olives
1 7-ounce can
   water-pack tuna
2 hard-boiled eggs,
   sliced
1 can chow mein
   noodles

Combine oil, vinegar, soy sauce, parsley, celery leaves and pepper in bowl; mix well. Pour into small pitcher. Combine vegetables in bowl. Add olives, tuna, eggs, and noodles; toss to mix well. Serve with dressing. Yield: 15 servings.

Approx per serving: Cal 154, Prot 6.8 gr, Fat 10.0 gr, Chol 42.1 mg, Carbo 10.3 gr, Sod 949.0 mg, Potas 252.6 mg.

Tish Naprstek, Xi Beta Omega
Valentine, Nebraska

Tuna and Red Bean Salad

2 tablespoons
   soybean oil
2 teaspoons lemon
   juice
⅛ teaspoon
   crushed basil
½ teaspoon salt
Pepper to taste
1 16-ounce can
   red kidney
   beans, drained

3 hard-boiled eggs,
   chopped
1 7-ounce can
   water-pack
   albacore tuna
1 cup chopped
   celery
2 tablespoons
   chopped parsley
1 hard-boiled egg,
   sliced

Mix oil, lemon juice, basil, salt and pepper in bowl. Add beans; mix well. Chill for 1 hour. Combine 3 chopped eggs with tuna, celery and parsley in bowl; mix well. Add to bean mixture; toss gently to mix. Spoon onto lettuce-lined salad plates. Top with hard-boiled egg slices. Yield: 5 servings.

Approx per serving: Cal 257, Prot 21.6 gr, Fat 10.8 gr, Chol 225.4 mg, Carbo 18.3 gr, Sod 618.1 mg, Potas 518.6 mg.

Jill Kepler Campbell, Gamma Pi
Cleveland, Mississippi

Linda's Tuna Salad

2 6½-ounce cans
   water-pack tuna,
   drained
2 hard-boiled eggs,
   chopped
¾ cup chopped
   bread and butter
   pickles

¼ cup chopped
   onion
1 pint reduced-
   calorie salad
   dressing
1 head lettuce,
   torn

Combine tuna, eggs, pickles and onion in bowl. Add salad dressing, pepper and light seasoned salt to taste; mix well. Chill for 1 hour or longer. Place lettuce on salad plates. Spoon tuna mixture onto lettuce. Yield: 6 servings.

Approx per serving: Cal 667, Prot 33.8 gr, Fat 26.9 gr, Chol 281.4 mg, Carbo 75.8 gr, Sod 1480.9 mg, Potas 535.8 mg.

Linda Cheshier, Epsilon Rho
Bethany, Missouri

Tuna Salad

4 ounces water-
   pack tuna,
   drained
½ teaspoon onion
   flakes
¼ cup chopped
   celery

3 ounces peas
1 medium dill
   pickle, chopped
⅔ cup cooked
   macaroni
1 tablespoon
   mayonnaise

Combine tuna, onion flakes, celery, peas, pickle and macaroni in bowl. Add mayonnaise; mix well. Chill, covered, for 1 hour to overnight. Yield: 1 serving.

Approx per serving: Cal 405, Prot 45.2 gr, Fat 14.0 gr, Chol 96.9 mg, Carbo 30.1 gr, Sod 2313.6 mg, Potas 749.3 mg.

Lori Murray, Theta Rho
New Hampton, Iowa

Salads   67

Low-Calorie Tuna Salad

1 6-ounce can
    water-pack tuna,
    drained
½ cup low-fat
    yogurt
½ cucumber,
    chopped

½ teaspoon dillweed
¼ teaspoon garlic
    powder
2 lettuce leaves
1 tomato, sliced

Combine tuna, yogurt, cucumber, dillweed and garlic powder in bowl. Serve in pita bread pockets with lettuce and tomato. Yield: 2 servings.

Approx per serving: Cal 181, Prot 31.2 gr, Fat 2.0 gr, Chol 66.9 mg, Carbo 8.8 gr, Sod 77.1 mg, Potas 666.8 mg.

Jeanette Azar, Preceptor Beta Zeta
Mt. Clemens, Michigan

Tuna-Pasta Salad

2½ cups shell
    macaroni, cooked
1 6-ounce can
    water-pack tuna,
    drained
1 cup thinly sliced
    celery
½ cup sliced carrots

½ cup sliced sweet
    pickles
¼ cup finely chopped
    onion
1 cup reduced-calorie
    creamy cucumber
    salad dressing

Combine macaroni, tuna, celery, carrots, pickles and onion in bowl; mix well. Add salad dressing and salt and pepper to taste; toss lightly. Chill until serving time. Spoon into lettuce-lined bowl. Yield: 6 servings.

Photograph for this recipe on page 70.

Tuna-Stuffed Tomatoes

6 medium Florida
    tomatoes
1 teaspoon salt
2 6-ounce cans
    water-pack tuna,
    drained, flaked
½ cup sliced water
    chestnuts

½ cup diced green
    pepper
½ cup bean sprouts
4 teaspoons cider
    vinegar
⅛ teaspoon pepper

Cut thin slice from stem end of each tomato. Cut slice in half, removing stem; set aside. Scoop out tomato pulp; chop and reserve ½ cup pulp. Sprinkle tomato shells with salt; invert to drain. Combine reserved tomato pulp with remaining ingredients. Spoon into shells. Arrange 2 reserved slices on each tomato to resemble butterfly. Serve on lettuce-lined plate. Garnish with radish roses and carrot curls. Yield: 6 servings.

Photograph for this recipe on page 69.

Tuna Waldorf Salad

1 medium apple,
    chopped
1 tablespoon lemon
    juice
4 ounces water-
    pack canned
    tuna

½ medium dill
    pickle, chopped
1 tablespoon
    chopped pimento
¼ cup chopped
    cabbage

Sprinkle apple with lemon juice. Combine with remaining ingredients in bowl; mix lightly. Chill until serving time. Spoon onto lettuce-lined plate.Yield: 1 serving.

Approx per serving: Cal 296, Prot 35.7 gr, Fat 2.5 gr, Chol 77.7 mg, Carbo 34.7 gr, Sod 1553.1 gr, Potas 747.6 mg.

Jannette Bennett, Preceptor Iota Omicron
San Angelo, Texas

Tuna-Yogurt Salad

2 hard-boiled eggs
½ cup low-fat
    yogurt
½ teaspoon mustard
¼ teaspoon pepper
½ teaspoon Old
    Bay spice
1 7-ounce can
    water-pack tuna

½ cup sliced apple
½ cup chopped
    celery
¼ cup chopped
    green onions
1 tablespoon
    minced onion
1 tablespoon
    chopped parsley

Mash egg yolks in bowl. Blend in yogurt, mustard, and spices. Add chopped egg whites and remaining ingredients; mix well. Chill for 1 hour. Garnish with parsley sprigs. Serve with crackers, bagels or toast. Yield: 6 servings.

Approx per serving: Cal 114, Prot 12.3 gr, Fat 2.7 gr, Chol 105.1 mg, Carbo 10.0 gr, Sod 320.0 mg, Potas 339.6 mg.

Mareke Campbell, Theta Kappa
Belleville, Illinois

Tuna Salad Mold

1 9-ounce can tuna
1 cup chopped celery
1½ tablespoons
    chopped green
    pepper
2 tablespoons
    pickle relish

½ teaspoon salt
4 hard-boiled eggs,
    chopped
1 tablespoon vinegar
2 cups mayonnaise
2 envelopes unflavored
    gelatin

Combine first 8 ingredients in bowl; mix well. Soften gelatin in ¾ cup cold water in double boiler. Heat over boiling water until gelatin dissolves, stirring constantly. Stir into tuna mixture; mix well. Spoon into 1½-quart mold. Chill until firm. Unmold onto lettuce-lined serving plate. Yield:L 8 servings.

Approx per serving: Cal 557, Prot 13.9 gr, Fat 54.7 gr, Chol 184.6 mg, Carbo 3.5 gr, Sod 821.6 mg, Potas 219.8 mg.

Recipe for this photograph on page 68. ◗

Brown Rice Salad

1 cup brown rice
1 cup frozen peas
1   8-ounce can
    sliced mushrooms
¾ cup sliced ripe
    olives
2 green onions,
    chopped
¾ cup Cheddar
    cheese cubes

3 tablespoons
    chopped parsley
1 tomato, chopped
¼ cup safflower
    oil
Juice of 2 lemons
1   2-ounce jar
    chopped pimento

Cook rice according to package directions. Add peas; stir to thaw peas. Let stand for several minutes. Add remaining ingredients; mix well. Serve at room temperature. Yield: 4 servings.

Approx per serving: Cal 509, Prot 12.8 gr, Fat 27.9 gr, Chol 21.0 mg, Carbo 56.1 gr, Sod 405.6 mg, Potas 484.1 mg.

Kathryn L. Johnson, Preceptor Beta
Park City, Illinois

Saffron Rice Salad

½ teaspoon saffron
1½ cups long
    grain rice
6 tablespoons olive
    oil
2 tablespoons
    safflower oil
¼ cup red wine
    vinegar
½ cup chopped
    green pepper
1 tomato, chopped

½ cup chopped
    red pepper
1 cup cooked
    chick peas
1 cup cooked
    green peas
⅓ cup sliced ripe
    olives
⅓ cup whole
    almonds with
    skins

Dissolve saffron in ½ teaspoon boiling water. Combine rice, saffron and 3 cups boiling water in saucepan. Simmer, covered, for 30 minutes or until rice is tender. Whisk oils gradually into vinegar in bowl. Add salt and pepper to taste. Add rice, vegetables, olives and almonds; mix well. Serve on lettuce-lined plate. Yield: 8 servings.

Approx per serving: Cal 402, Prot 10.0 gr, Fat 19.2 gr, Chol 0.0 mg, Carbo 48.9 gr, Sod 71.5 mg, Potas 389.7 mg.

Constance M. Orell, Xi Eta Eta
North Huntingdon, Pennsylvania

Rice and Lentil Salad

2 cups rice,
    cooked
1 cup lentils,
    cooked
½ cup chopped
    tomato
½ cup chopped
    green pepper
½ cup chopped
    chives
½ cup chopped
    celery
½ cup chopped
    carrots

½ cup chopped
    broccoli
½ cup chopped
    cauliflower
½ cup chopped
    mushrooms
½ cup chopped
    radishes
½ cup chopped
    avocado
1   8-ounce bottle
    Italian dressing

Mix cooled rice and lentils in bowl. Add tomato, green pepper, chives, celery, carrots, broccoli, cauliflower, mushrooms, radishes and avocado. Pour dressing over top. Chill for 1 to 2 hours. Yield: 8 servings.

Approx per serving: Cal 455, Prot 10.5 gr, Fat 20.9 gr, Chol 0.0 mg, Carbo 58.0 gr, Sod 657.3 mg, Potas 532.5 mg.

Lana Livingston, Xi Eta
West Lebanon, New Hampshire

Audrey's Spaghetti Salad

16 ounces vermicelli,
    broken
1 large green
    pepper, chopped
1 medium red
    onion, chopped
1   4-ounce jar
    chopped pimento

1   16-ounce bottle
    zesty Italian
    salad dressing
2 tablespoons
    Salad Supreme
    spice mix
½ cup red wine
    vinegar

Cook vermicelli according to package directions. Rinse and drain. Combine with remaining ingredients in bowl; mix well. Chill, covered, for 24 hours or longer. Yield: 20 servings.

Approx per serving: Cal 225, Prot 3.2 gr, Fat 14.7 gr, Chol 0.0 mg, Carbo 20.9 gr, Sod 506.3 mg, Potas 103.1 mg.

Audrey O. Greever, Preceptor Nu
Annandale, Virginia

◆ Recipes for this photograph on pages 63 and 68.

Fisherman's Italian Salad

2 packages dry
  Italian salad
  dressing mix
2 cups low-fat milk
2 cups reduced-
  calorie mayonnaise
16 ounces vermicelli,
  broken

2 cups chopped
  celery
½ cup chopped
  onion
3 hard-boiled eggs,
  chopped

Combine dressing mix, milk and mayonnaise in bowl; mix well. Cook vermicelli according to package directions; drain. Add to dressing; mix well. Fold in remaining ingredients. Chill, covered, for 48 to 76 hours. Yield: 10 servings.

Approx per serving: Cal 364, Prot 9.6 gr, Fat 18.8 gr, Chol 93.8 mg, Carbo 41.2 gr, Sod 90.8 mg, Potas 280.2 mg.
Nutritional information does not include Italian salad dressing mix.

Stacy Zugar, Theta Delta
Endicott, Washington

South-of-the Border Salad Dressing

1 cup corn oil
⅓ cup white vinegar
¼ cup orange juice
1 tablespoon minced
  onion
1 small clove of garlic,
  crushed

2 teaspoons sugar
1½ teaspoons salt
1 teaspoon cumin
1 teaspoon dried
  oregano leaves
¼ teaspoon crushed
  red pepper flakes

Combine all ingredients in covered 1-pint jar; shake vigorously. Chill until serving time. Remove garlic. Shake vigorously. Pour over assorted salad greens in salad bowl, using 2 teaspoons dressing for each cup greens. For lower-calorie salad dressing: Decrease oil to ¾ cup, add ¼ cup water, omit sugar and cumin, decrease salt to 1 teaspoon and add ½ teaspoon chili powder. Yield: 1½ cups.

Photograph for this recipe on Cover.

Vegetable Pasta Salad

8 ounces
  vegetable pasta,
  cooked
2 medium apples,
  chopped

1 cup raisins
1 cup chopped
  black walnuts
1 cup mayonnaise

Mix pasta, apples, raisins and walnuts in bowl. Add mayonnaise; toss to coat. Chill for several hours. Yield: 6 servings.

Approx per serving: Cal 594, Prot 10.1 gr, Fat 37.4 gr, Chol 21.6 mg, Carbo 69.5 gr, Sod 190.3 mg, Potas 438.8 mg.

Loretta Hunt, Delta Upsilon
Angel Fire, New Mexico

Summer Salad Dressing

1 cup corn oil
½ cup lime juice
1 tablespoon minced
  fresh dillweed
1½ teaspoon salt

1 teaspoon sugar
1 teaspoon minced onion
½ teaspoon celery seed

Combine all ingredients in covered 1-pint jar; shake vigorously. Chill until serving time. Shake vigorously. Pour over assorted salad greens in salad bowl, using 2 teaspoons dressing for each cup greens. For lower-calorie salad dressing: Decrease oil to ¾ cup, add ¼ cup water, omit sugar and decrease salt to 1 teaspoon. Yield: 1½ cups.

Photograph for this recipe on Cover.

Stay-Trim Dressing

1 teaspoon
  cornstarch
½ teaspoon dry
  mustard
¼ cup catsup
½ teaspoon
  Worcestershire
  sauce

2 tablespoons
  vinegar
½ teaspoon
  horseradish
½ teaspoon
  paprika
1 small clove of
  garlic, crushed

Mix cornstarch and mustard in small saucepan. Stir in 1 cup cold water gradually. Cook over medium heat until thickened, stirring constantly. Cool. Add remaining ingredients; mix well. Pour into jar with lid. Store in refrigerator. Shake well before using. Yield: 21 tablespoons.

Approx per tablespoon: Cal 4, Prot 0.1 gr, Fat 0.0 gr, Chol 0.0 mg, Carbo 1.0 gr, Sod 31.0 mg, Potas 13.5 mg.

Harriett Flournoy
DeQueen, Arkansas

French Herbed Salad Dressing

1 cup corn oil
⅓ cup lemon juice
1 tablespoon sugar
1 teaspoon salt
1 teaspoon dried fine
  herbs

½ teaspoon paprika
¼ teaspoon dry
  mustard
1 clove of garlic,
  crushed

Combine all ingredients in covered 1-pint jar; shake vigorously. Chill until serving time. Remove garlic. Shake vigorously. Pour over assorted salad greens in salad bowl, using 2 teaspoons dressing for each cup greens. For lower-calorie salad dressing: reduce oil to ¾ cup, add ¼ cup water, omit sugar and decrease salt to ½ teaspoon. Yield: 1⅓ cups.

Photograph for this recipe on Cover.

Main Dishes

Roast Turkey with Apple-Sage Stuffing

6 medium yellow onions	1 teaspoon poultry seasoning
12 cups dry bread crumbs	4 cups chopped tart apples
3 tablespoons sage	1 12 to 15-pound turkey
Salt to taste	½ cup butter

Parboil onions in water to cover in saucepan for 15 minutes. Drain and chop. Combine onions, bread crumbs, apples and seasonings in bowl; toss lightly. Spoon into turkey cavity; truss turkey. Place breast side up on rack in roasting pan. Brush with a small amount of butter. Cover with foil tent. Bake at 325 degrees for 4 to 5 hours or to 175 degrees on meat thermometer, basting with butter, occasionally. Remove foil. Bake for 15 minutes longer or to 185 degrees. Remove to serving platter. Let stand for 15 minutes before slicing. Skim and thicken pan juices if desired. Garnish turkey platter with artichoke hearts, small whole potatoes and whole pickled green beans.

Jean Sheriff, Xi Beta Kappa
Santa Rosa, New Mexico

Beef and Green Beans

1   4-ounce can
   mushrooms
½ pound lean beef,
   cut into strips
2 tablespoons oil
1 medium onion,
   chopped

1 cup cut fresh
   green beans
1 medium green
   pepper, sliced
1 cup sliced celery
4 teaspoons cornstarch
1 tablespoon soy sauce

Drain mushrooms reserving liquid. Add enough water to liquid to measure ¾ cup. Brown beef strips in hot oil in skillet, stirring frequently. Add vegetables. Cook for 3 to 5 minutes longer or until tender-crisp, stirring constantly. Add mixture of reserved liquid, cornstarch, soy sauce and salt and pepper to taste; mix well. Add mushrooms. Cook until thickened, stirring constantly. Garnish with pimento strips. Yield: 4 servings.

Approx per serving: Cal 219, Prot 13.5 gr, Fat 14.0 gr, Chol 38.6 mg. Carbo 10.1 gr, Sod 415.0 mg, Potas 458.2 mg.

Frances Simmins, Preceptor Epsilon
Hot Springs, Arkansas

Beef and Noodles

1 pound beef
   tenderloin, cut
   into cubes
¼ cup instant onion
   flakes
¼ cup margarine
1½ teaspoons garlic
   powder

1 can beefy
   mushroom soup
1 can beef broth
⅓ cup flour
1   8-ounce package
   wide noodles,
   cooked

Brown beef cubes and onion flakes in margarine in skillet. Season with garlic powder and salt and pepper to taste. Add soup and ⅔ cup beef broth. Bring to a simmer. Blend flour with reserved broth. Stir into beef mixture. Simmer until mixture thickens, stirring constantly. Stir in noodles. Simmer until heated through. Spoon into serving dish. Yield: 6 servings.

Approx per serving: Cal 539, Prot 21.1 gr, Fat 32.6 gr, Chol 100.8 mg, Carbo 39.0 gr, Sod 845.6 mg, Potas 313.9 mg.

Shirley Strunk, Epsilon Mu
Carbondale, Kansas

Beef Chaufleur

1 pound round
   steak, cut into ½-
   inch cubes
2 tablespoons oil
1 medium head
   cauliflower,
   broken into
   flowerets
1 green pepper, cut
   into ¾-inch
   pieces
1 clove of garlic,
   minced

¼ cup soy sauce
2 tablespoons
   cornstarch
½ teaspoon sugar
1½ cups beef broth
1 cup sliced green
   onions
8 ounces mushrooms,
   sliced
3 cups hot cooked rice

Brown steak cubes in oil in skillet. Add cauliflower, green pepper and garlic. Add soy sauce; mix well. Simmer, covered, for 8 to 10 minutes. Blend cornstarch, sugar and broth in bowl. Stir into beef mixture with green onions and mushrooms. Cook until thickened, stirring constantly. Serve over rice. Yield: 6 servings.

Approx per serving: Cal 372, Prot 24.3 gr, Fat 13.3 gr, Chol 55.2 mg, Carbo 40.0 gr, Sod 1521.5 mg, Potas 918.3 mg.

Lois Sherpitis, Xi Eta Beta
Aurora, Illinois

Beef Sandwich Spread

2 cups ground
   cooked roast beef
1 cup shredded
   Swiss cheese
½ cup sweet pickle
   relish

2 tablespoons
   finely chopped
   onion
¾ cup mayonnaise
¼ teaspoon salt

Combine all ingredients in bowl; mix well. Chill in refrigerator. Spread on bread, toasted buns or spoon into pita rounds. Yield: 8 servings.
Note: May also serve in tomato shells or celery sticks.

Approx per serving: Cal 293, Prot 12.2 gr, Fat 24.7 gr, Chol 53.9 mg, Carbo 6.0 gr, Sod 413.6 mg, Potas 119.5 mg.

Lori Laures, Theta Rho
New Hampton, Iowa

Brisket

1   9 to 10-pound
   brisket
Garlic powder
Onion powder
Celery salt
½ bottle liquid
   smoke

2 tablespoons
   Worcestershire sauce
Open Pit barbecue
   sauce
Curley's barbecue
   sauce

Place brisket in shallow baking pan. Sprinkle with garlic powder, onion powder, celery salt and liquid smoke. Marinate, covered, in refrigerator overnight. Sprinkle Worcestershire sauce over brisket. Bake, covered, at 250 degrees for 5 hours. Cool. Chill, wrapped in foil, overnight. Trim and slice thin. Arrange brisket slices in baking dish. Pour barbecue sauces over top. Heat at 250 degrees for 1 hour. Yield: 16 servings.

Marilyn Cleveland, Laureate Rho
Hutchinsen, Kansas

Cheesy Sirloin Steak

¼ cup flour
¼ teaspoon garlic
  powder
1 pound boneless
  sirloin steak,
  ½-inch thick
3 tablespoons oil

¼ cup chopped
  onion
¼ cup chopped
  green pepper
½ cup shredded
  Cheddar cheese

Mix flour with garlic powder and salt and pepper to taste. Pound flour mixture into steak with meat mallet. Cut steak into 4 pieces. Brown slowly on both sides in oil in skillet. Add 1½ cups hot water. Sprinkle with onion and green pepper. Simmer, covered, for 1 hour. Sprinkle with cheese. Cook, covered, for 5 minutes or until cheese melts. Remove steak to serving plate. Serve with pan gravy and rice or mashed potatoes. Yield: 4 servings.

Approx per serving: Cal 501, Prot 23.6 gr, Fat 41.3 gr, Chol 91.8 mg, Carbo 7.5 gr, Sod 147.5 mg, Potas 261.4 mg.

Cynthia Hanselman, Xi Omicron Lambda
Del Rio, Texas

Donna's Chinese Beef

1½ pounds flank
  steak, cut into
  thin strips
1 tablespoon oil
½ cup chopped
  onion
1½ cups beef broth
2 tablespoons soy
  sauce
½ teaspoon ginger

1 cup thinly sliced
  carrots
½ cup thinly sliced
  celery
1 small green pepper,
  sliced
1 16-ounce can bean
  sprouts, drained
1 tablespoon cornstarch

Stir-fry steak strips in 325-degree oil in skillet or wok. Remove steak with slotted spoon. Reduce heat to 225 degrees. Add onion. Stir-fry until tender. Add steak, broth, soy sauce, ginger and carrots. Cook, covered, for 5 minutes. Add celery, green pepper and bean sprouts. Cook, covered, for 5 minutes. Stir in mixture of cornstarch and 1 tablespoon water. Cook for 5 minutes or until thickened. Serve with rice. Yield: 6 servings.

Approx per serving: Cal 208, Prot 25.7 gr, Fat 8.1 gr, Chol 72.2 mg, Carbo 7.9 gr, Sod 746.0 mg, Potas 418.5 mg.

Donna McDonald, Xi Gamma Nu
Waverly, Iowa

Finger Steaks

2 tablespoons
  margarine
1 egg, beaten
⅓ cup dry bread
  crumbs
2 tablespoons
  Parmesan cheese

Onion salt to taste
1 pound round
  steak, ½ inch.
  thick, cut into strips
2 tablespoons flour

Melt margarine in 9x13-inch baking dish. Beat egg with 1 teaspoon water in bowl. Mix bread crumbs and Parmesan cheese with onion salt to taste in bowl. Dip steak strips in flour, egg and crumb mixture. Arrange in prepared baking dish. Bake for 30 minutes, turning strips once. Place on serving plate. Yield: 4 servings.

Approx per serving: Cal 336, Prot 26.8 gr, Fat 20.6 gr, Chol 140.8 mg, Carbo 9.2 gr, Sod 227.3 mg, Potas 290.7 mg.

Patricia Reynolds, Alpha Chi
Pope AFB, North Carolina

Fajitas

1 pound top round
  steak, cut into
  thin strips
3 tablespoons red
  wine vinegar
3 tablespoons oil

1 teaspoon garlic
  salt
½ teaspoon cumin
12 6-inch flour
  tortillas
Juice of ½ lime

Combine steak strips with vinegar, oil, garlic salt and cumin in bowl; mix well. Marinate for 20 minutes or longer. Wrap tortillas in damp cloth. Warm in 350-degree oven for 10 to 15 minutes. Drain steak strips. Stir-fry in skillet for 1 to 2 minutes or until tender. Sprinkle with lime juice. Spoon onto warm tortillas. Top with Guacamole and Picante Sauce. Roll to enclose filling. Yield: 12 servings.

Approx per serving: Cal 201, Prot 10.1 gr, Fat 9.9 gr, Chol 25.7 mg, Carbo 17.8 gr, Sod 204.4 mg, Potas 128.6 mg.

Guacamole

2 medium avocados,
  mashed
1 tablespoon
  mayonnaise

Juice of ½ lemon
¾ teaspoon
  seasoned salt

Combine avocados, mayonnaise, lemon juice and seasoned salt in bowl; mix until smooth. Yield: 32 tablespoons.

Approx per tablespoon: Cal 27, Prot 0.3 gr, Fat 2.7 gr, Chol 0.3 mg, Carbo 1.0 gr, Sod 53.1 mg, Potas 87.0 mg.

Picante Sauce

1 16-ounce can
  stewed tomatoes
1 small onion,
  chopped
1 tablespoon
  chopped jalapeño
  peppers

1 tablespoon garlic
  powder
1 teaspoon salt
½ teaspoon sugar
6 cilantro leaves
1 tablespoon cider
  vinegar

Combine all ingredients in blender container. Process for 30 seconds or until smooth. Store in covered container in refrigerator. Yield: 50 tablespoons.

Approx per tablespoon: Cal 3, Prot 0.1 gr, Fat 0.0 gr, Chol 0.0 mg, Carbo 0.6 gr, Sod 54.6 mg, Potas 23.0 mg.

Carole Temple, Xi Delta Gamma
Princeton, Oregon

Flank Steak Florentine

2 1-pound flank
　steaks
1 egg, beaten
1 10-ounce
　package frozen
　chopped spinach,
　cooked, drained
½ cup shredded
　sharp American
　cheese
½ teaspoon sage

¾ cup soft bread
　crumbs
2 tablespoons oil
1 8-ounce can tomato
　sauce
½ cup dry red wine
½ cup chopped onion
1 clove of garlic,
　minced
2 tablespoons flour

Pound steaks to ¼-inch thickness with meat mallet. Combine egg, spinach, cheese and sage with salt and pepper to taste in bowl. Stir in bread crumbs. Spread on steaks. Roll from narrow side to enclose filling; secure with string. Brown steak rolls in oil in skillet. Place in shallow baking dish. Combine tomato sauce, wine, onion and garlic in bowl. Pour over steak. Bake at 350 degrees for 1½ hours. Remove rolls to serving plate. Stir in mixture of flour and ¼ cup water. Cook over low heat until thickened, stirring constantly. Serve with steak rolls. Yield: 8 servings.

Approx per serving: Cal 263, Prot 27.8 gr, Fat 11.7 gr, Chol 108.3 mg, Carbo 9.9 gr, Sod 374.1 mg, Potas 484.0 mg.

Ann Clapper, Kappa Omicron
Shawnee on Delaware, Pennsylvania

Grilled Flank Steak

1½ pounds flank
　steak
½ cup oil
¼ cup soy sauce
1 green onion,
　chopped

3 tablespoons honey
2 tablespoons red
　wine vinegar
1 clove of garlic,
　crushed
1½ teaspoons ginger

Place steak in shallow dish. Combine remaining ingredients in bowl; mix well. Pour over steak. Marinate, covered, in refrigerator for 5 hours, turning steak several times. Place on grill 2 inches from hot coals. Grill to desired degree of doneness. Slice diagonally cross grain into thin strips. Arrange slices on serving plate.
Yield: 4 servings.

Approx per serving: Cal 528, Prot 35.9 gr, Fat 35.8 gr, Chol 107.2 mg, Carbo 15.7 gr, Sod 1380.6 mg, Potas 372.2 mg.

Anita Karl, Xi Gamma
Cheyenne, Wyoming

Italian Rolled Beef

6 tablespoons
　Parmesan cheese
1 small onion,
　chopped
2 pounds round
　steak, cut into 6
　pieces
3 tablespoons oil
1 tablespoon
　oregano

1 tablespoon garlic
　powder
1 tablespoon sugar
1 28-ounce can
　tomato sauce
1 12-ounce can
　tomato paste
½ cup chopped
　onion

Place 1 tablespoon Parmesan cheese and about 3 tablespoons onion in center of each steak piece. Sprinkle with pepper to taste. Roll to enclose filling; secure with toothpicks. Brown on all sides in oil in skillet. Combine remaining ingredients with 1½ cups water in saucepan. Bring to a boil. Add steak rolls. Simmer for 2 hours or until steak is tender. Arrange on serving plate. Spoon sauce over top. Yield: 6 servings.
Note: Serve on bed of hot pasta.

Approx per serving: Cal 477, Prot 37.1 gr, Fat 25.4 gr, Chol 105.4 mg, Carbo 26.6 gr, Sod 917.5 mg, Potas 1434.2 mg.

Anna Rose Kerr, Alpha Pi
Tacoma, Washington

Beef Kabobs

¾ cup oil-free
　Italian salad
　dressing
3 tablespoons soy
　sauce
2 pounds lean
　sirloin, cut into
　1½-inch cubes

¼ teaspoon garlic
　powder
16 large mushrooms
16 cherry tomatoes
1 large onion, cut into
　wedges
1 large green pepper,
　cut into chunks

Combine salad dressing and soy sauce in bowl; mix well. Add steak cubes. Sprinkle with garlic powder. Marinate for 30 minutes. Drain, reserving marinade. Alternate steak cubes and vegetables on skewers. Brush with marinade. Place on broiler pan. Broil to desired degree of doneness, turning and basting with marinade once. Serve on rice. Yield: 6 servings.

Approx per serving: Cal 475, Prot 27.5 gr, Fat 37.0 gr, Chol 103.7 mg, Carbo 7.1 gr, Sod 966.4 mg, Potas 563.0 mg.

Teresa Hartman, Alpha Psi Epsilon
McAllen, Texas

Corn and Sirloin Kabobs

½ cup red wine
⅓ cup oil
1 tablespoon chili
　powder
⅛ teaspoon salt
½ teaspoon dry
　mustard
1 clove of garlic,
　crushed

1½ pounds sirloin,
　cubed
4 ears of corn, cut into
　1-inch pieces
2 green peppers, cut
　into bite-sized pieces
2 sweet red peppers,
　cut into bite-sized
　pieces

Combine first 6 ingredients in bowl; mix well. Add steak and vegetables, tossing to coat well. Marinate, covered, in refrigerator for 2 hours or longer, turning occasionally. Drain, reserving marinade. Alternate steak cubes and vegetables on skewers. Grill over hot coals to desired degree of doneness, basting frequently with reserved marinade. Place on serving plate. Yield: 6 servings.

Approx per serving: Cal 543, Prot 21.4 gr, Fat 39.2 gr, Chol 77.8 mg, Carbo 16.2 gr, Sod 101.0 mg, Potas 483.8 mg.

Gale Vrtiak, Alpha Alpha
Worms, Germany

Dilly-Bobs

¾ cup pineapple
  juice
1 cup lemon juice
¼ cup oil
2 tablespoons
  Worcestershire
  sauce
½ cup packed
  brown sugar
1 tablespoon
  dillweed

½ teaspoon salt
1½ pounds round
  steak, cut into
  thin strips
1 green pepper,
  cut into pieces
8 cherry tomatoes
8 large mushrooms
1½ cups pineapple
  chunks

Combine first 7 ingredients in saucepan; mix well. Bring to a simmer. Pour over steak strips in bowl. Marinate, covered, in refrigerator overnight. Drain, reserving marinade. Alternate steak strips with vegetables and pineapple chunks on skewers. Grill for 10 minutes or to desired degree of doneness, basting frequently with reserved marinade. Place on serving plate. Yield: 4 servings.

Approx per serving: Cal 674, Prot 31.3 gr, Fat 35.2 gr, Chol 116.7 mg, Carbo 60.7 gr, Sod 427.9 mg, Potas 916.7 mg.

Susan Rada, Theta Lambda
Colorado Springs, Colorado

Shish Kabob

2 tablespoons oil
2 tablespoons catsup
1 teaspoon sugar
1 tablespoon vinegar
⅛ teaspoon salt

½ teaspoon marjoram
½ teaspoon rosemary
1 pound sirloin, cut
  into 2-inch cubes
12 large mushrooms

Combine first 7 ingredients in bowl; mix well. Add steak and mushrooms. Marinate at room temperature for 2 hours. Alternate steak cubes and mushrooms on skewers. Grill over hot coals to desired degree of doneness, basting frequently with marinade. Place on serving plate. Yield: 4 servings.

Approx per serving: Cal 403, Prot 20.1 gr, Fat 33.4 gr, Chol 77.8 mg, Carbo 4.7 gr, Sod 194.1 mg, Potas 389.1 mg.

Sydnee Paul, Xi Delta Eta
Plymouth, Michigan

Steak on-a-Stick

1 tablespoon soy
  sauce
1½ teaspoons wine
  vinegar
1½ teaspoons
  catsup
¼ cup Sherry

1½ teaspoons honey
⅛ teaspoon garlic
  salt
1 pound sirloin
  steak, cut
  into 1-inch
  pieces

Combine first 6 ingredients in bowl; mix well. Add steak. Marinate, covered, in refrigerator for 2 hours, stirring occasionally. Drain, reserving marinade. Thread steak strips on skewers. Grill over medium-hot coals for 5 minutes on each side or to desired degree of doneness, basting frequently with reserved marinade. Remove from skewers to serving plate. Yield: 4 servings.

Approx per serving: Cal 374, Prot 19.4 gr, Fat 26.5 gr, Chol 77.8 mg, Carbo 5.4 gr, Sod 463.8 mg, Potas 261.8 mg.

Connie Burgess, Xi Gamma Sigma
Concord, Tennessee

Lemony Beef Steak

3 tablespoons fresh
  lemon juice
1 tablespoon oil
1 teaspoon salt
¼ teaspoon dillweed

1 pound top round
  steak, 1¼ inches
  thick
¼ teaspoon freshly
  ground pepper

Combine first 4 ingredients and ¼ cup water in shallow dish. Add steak, turning to coat well. Marinate, covered, in refrigerator for 6 hours to overnight, turning steak several times. Drain, reserving marinade. Press pepper into both sides of steak. Place on broiler pan. Broil 4 to 5 inches from heat source to desired degree of doneness, turning and brushing with reserved marinade once. Slice thin. Arrange steak slices on serving plate. Yield: 4 servings.

Approx per serving: Cal 238, Prot 22.5 gr, Fat 15.5 gr, Chol 73.8 mg, Carbo 0.9 gr, Sod 588.1 mg, Potas 267.6 mg.

Carole Temple, Xi Delta Gamma
Princeton, Oregon

Oriental Beef and Broccoli

1½ pounds flank
  steak
3 tablespoons
  soy sauce
2 tablespoons
  cornstarch
½ teaspoon minced
  garlic
⅛ teaspoon ground
  pepper

⅛ teaspoon red pepper
1 small green or red
  pepper, thinly sliced
2 tablespoons oil
2 cups broccoli
  flowerets
1 can sliced water
  chestnuts, drained

Cut steak in half lengthwise. Slice diagonally cross grain into thin slices. Mix next 5 ingredients and ¾ cup water in bowl. Stir-fry steak and peppers in hot oil in wok. Add broccoli and water chestnuts. Stir-fry for 2 minutes. Add cornstarch mixture. Cook until mixture thickens, stirring constantly. Serve over rice.
Yield: 6 servings.

Approx per serving: Cal 266, Prot 27.4 gr, Fat 10.5 gr, Chol 71.4 mg, Carbo 15.9 gr, Sod 716.0 mg, Potas 578.8 mg.

Judy Bryant, Xi Delta Iota
Oklahoma City, Oklahoma

Carol's Pepper Steak

1 pound round steak
2 tablespoons paprika
1 onion, chopped
2 tablespoons oil
2 to 3 tablespoons garlic powder
2 beef bouillon cubes
1   4-ounce can mushrooms, drained
1 medium green pepper, chopped
1 tablespoon cornstarch
2 tablespoons soy sauce

Slice steak diagonally cross grain into thin strips. Sprinkle with paprika. Brown steak and onion in oil in skillet. Add garlic powder, bouillon cubes and 2 to 3 cups water. Simmer for 30 to 45 minutes or until of desired consistency. Add mushrooms and green pepper. Simmer for 10 minutes. Blend cornstarch and soy sauce in small bowl. Add to steak mixture. Cook until mixture thickens, stirring constantly. Serve over rice. Yield: 6 servings.

Approx per serving: Cal 204, Prot 16.3 gr, Fat 12.8 gr, Chol 50.2 mg, Carbo 5.3 gr, Sod 800.6 mg, Potas 261.6 mg.

Carol Terpstra, Alpha
Billings, Montana

Chinese Pepper Steak

1 pound round steak, partially frozen
1/4 cup reduced-sodium soy sauce
1 tablespoon cornstarch
1/2 teaspoon sugar
1/4 teaspoon ginger
2 tablespoons oil
3 medium green peppers, cut into 1-inch pieces
1 clove of garlic, minced
2 small tomatoes, cut into wedges

Slice steak diagonally cross grain into thin strips. Place in shallow bowl. Blend soy sauce into mixture of cornstarch, sugar and ginger in bowl. Pour over steak; mix well. Stir-fry steak 1/3 at a time in hot oil in skillet until brown. Remove with slotted spoon when brown. Reduce heat. Add green peppers, garlic and 1/4 cup water. Cook for 5 minutes or until peppers are tender-crisp. Add steak and tomatoes. Cook until heated through, stirring constantly. Spoon onto serving plate. Yield: 4 servings.

Approx per serving: Cal 314, Prot 24.5 gr, Fat 19.2 gr, Chol 73.8 mg, Carbo 10.8 gr, Sod 71.6 mg, Potas 644.9 mg. Nutritional information does not include reduced-sodium soy sauce.

Melva M. Randolph, XP1932
Macomb, Illinois

Peppers and Steak

2 pounds lean round steak, partially frozen
1 cup beef broth
1/4 cup soy sauce
1/2 teaspoon garlic powder
1/2 teaspoon ginger
3 large green peppers, cut into thin strips
1   2-ounce jar chopped pimentos, drained
3 tablespoons cornstarch
4 cups hot cooked rice

Slice steak diagonally cross grain into 1/4x2-inch strips. Combine with next 4 ingredients in shallow dish; mix well. Marinate, covered, in refrigerator overnight. Drain, reserving 1/2 cup marinade. Spray skillet with nonstick cooking spray, using manufacturers directions. Heat over medium-high heat. Add steak. Stir-fry until light brown. Add mixture of reserved marinade and 1 cup water. Simmer, covered, for 45 minutes. Add green peppers and pimentos. Cook for 15 minutes. Blend cornstarch with 1/4 cup water. Stir into steak mixture. Cook until thickened, stirring constantly. Serve over rice. Yield: 8 servings.

Approx per serving: Cal 346, Prot 26.0 gr, Fat 12.4 gr, Chol 76.8 mg, Carbo 30.4 gr, Sod 1200.8 mg, Potas 404.3 mg.

Marlene Mallon, Mu Theta
Salina, Kansas

Rita's Pepper Steak

12 ounces boneless chuck steak
1 medium sweet red pepper, cut into strips
1 tablespoon oil
3/4 cup canned beef broth
1 teaspoon soy sauce
2 tablespoons cornstarch
1/8 teaspoon pepper

Place steak on broiler pan. Broil until rare. Cut into thin strips. Sauté steak strips and red pepper in oil in skillet. Add beef broth and soy sauce. Cook for 3 minutes. Blend cornstarch with 1 tablespoon water. Stir into steak mixture. Cook until mixture thickens, stirring constantly. Season with pepper. Spoon into serving bowl. Yield: 2 servings.

Approx per serving: Cal 328, Prot 28.1 gr, Fat 17.9 gr, Chol 92.9 mg, Carbo 12.3 gr, Sod 971.0 mg, Potas 391.2 mg.

Rita Elms, Preceptor Iota Omicron
San Angelo, Texas

Penny's Beef and Broccoli Stir-Fry

½ pound beef
  round steak
1 tablespoon
  cornstarch
1 tablespoon soy
  sauce
1 teaspoon sugar
2 teaspoons minced
  gingerroot
1 clove of garlic,
  minced
1 tablespoon peanut
  oil

1 pound broccoli,
  chopped
1 onion, chopped
2 carrots, cut
  diagonally into
  ⅛-inch slices
2 tablespoons
  peanut oil
¾ ounce cashews
1 tablespoon
  cornstarch
3 tablespoons soy
  sauce

Slice beef cross grain into thin slices. Marinate in mixture of 1 tablespoon cornstarch, 1 tablespoon soy sauce, sugar, gingerroot and garlic for 15 minutes. Stir-fry beef in 1 tablespoon hot oil in wok for 1 minute; remove beef. Stir-fry broccoli, onion and carrots in 2 tablespoons oil for 4 minutes or until tender-crisp. Add beef, cashews and mixture of 1 tablespoon cornstarch, 3 tablespoons soy sauce and ½ cup water. Cook until thickened, stirring constantly. Serve over rice. Yield: 4 servings.

Approx per serving: Cal 314, Prot 17.5 gr, Fat 19.2 gr, Chol 36.9 mg, Carbo 20.8 gr, Sod 676.0 mg, Potas 793.4 mg.

Penny Taylor, Pi
Hockessin, Delaware

Beef and Broccoli Stir-Fry

1 pound round
  steak, partially
  frozen
⅓ cup soy sauce
2 tablespoons
  brown sugar
1 clove of garlic,
  crushed

1 tablespoon
  cornstarch
3 tablespoons oil
4 cups broccoli
  flowerets
1 large onion, sliced

Slice steak cross grain into ¼x3-inch strips. Add to mixture of soy sauce, brown sugar, garlic, cornstarch and ¼ cup water. Marinate, covered, in refrigerator for 1 hour. Drain, reserving marinade. Stir-fry steak in hot oil in wok over medium heat for 2 to 3 minutes; remove steak. Stir-fry broccoli and onion in wok for 3 to 5 minutes. Add steak and reserved marinade. Cook for 1 minute, stirring constantly. Yield: 4 servings.

Approx per serving: Cal 398, Prot 28.5 gr, Fat 22.9 gr, Chol 73.8 mg, Carbo 21.4 gr, Sod 1825.3 mg, Potas 866.3 mg.

Marcia Sierotowicz, Xi Eta Psi
Collensville, Illinois

Best Ever Stir-Fry

1½ pounds rib
  steaks, cut into
  thin strips
½ cup sukiyaki
  sauce
2 cloves of garlic,
  thinly sliced
¼ cup peanut oil

8 stalks celery,
  thinly sliced
2 cups thinly sliced
  mushrooms
1 bunch green
  onions, sliced
3 tablespoons oyster
  sauce

Marinate steak strips in sukiyaki sauce for 1 hour, stirring occasionally; drain. Stir-fry steak and garlic in hot oil in wok until brown. Add vegetables. Stir-fry for 2 to 3 minutes or until tender-crisp. Add oyster sauce. Heat to serving temperature. Serve over rice. Yield: 4 servings.

Approx per serving: Cal 364, Prot 24.8 gr, Fat 24.6 gr, Chol 72.3 mg, Carbo 11.4 gr, Sod 164.3 mg, Potas 815.3 mg.

Linda Miles, Xi Chi
Clinton, Utah

Chinese Beef

1 2-pound flank
  steak
¼ cup soy sauce
2½ tablespoons
  cornstarch
1 beef bouillon cube
2 tablespoons oil
1 clove of garlic,
  minced

½ cup sliced scallions
6 cups diagonally sliced
  celery
1 16-ounce can bean
  sprouts, drained
1 cup diagonally sliced
  carrots
½ teaspoon sugar
½ teaspoon ginger

Freeze steak for 30 minutes. Slice diagonally cross grain into thin slices. Blend soy sauce and cornstarch in small bowl. Dissolve bouillon cube in ½ cup boiling water. Stir-fry steak slices several at a time in hot oil in wok. Add garlic, scallions, celery and browned steak. Stir-fry for 2 minutes. Stir in cornstarch mixture, bouillon and remaining ingredients. Bring to a boil; reduce heat. Simmer, covered, for 3 to 5 minutes or until carrots are tender-crisp. Serve over hot steamed rice. Yield: 6 servings.

Photograph for this recipe on page 2.

Stir-Fry Beef and Broccoli

1 pound round
  steak, thinly
  sliced
¼ cup soy sauce
¼ cup peanut oil
Flowerets of 1
  stalk broccoli
1 carrot, thinly
  sliced
1 medium onion,
  cut into quarters

1 cup sliced
  mushrooms
1 green pepper, cut
  into 8 strips
1 can chicken broth
3 tablespoons
  cornstarch
2 tablespoons soy
  sauce

Marinate steak in ¼ cup soy sauce overnight. Heat oil in wok. Add steak. Cook, covered, for 5 minutes; stir. Cook for 20 minutes longer. Remove steak. Add vegetables. Stir-fry for 10 minutes. Remove vegetables. Add mixture of broth, cornstarch and 2 tablespoons soy sauce. Cook until clear and thickened, stirring constantly. Stir in steak and vegetables. Heat to serving temperature. Serve on steamed rice. Yield: 6 servings.

Approx per serving: Cal 284, Prot 18.7 gr, Fat 18.8 gr, Chol 53.6 mg, Carbo 9.3 gr, Sod 1714.8 mg, Potas 605.1 mg.

Carol Beth Grounds, Laureate Rho
Hutchinson, Kansas

Tavern Beef Puff

⅔ cup flour
¼ teaspoon salt
⅔ cup milk
2 eggs
1 tablespoon
  margarine
1 pound flank steak
2 tablespoons flour
2 tablespoons
  margarine

¼ cup soy sauce
1½ cups sliced
  zucchini
1½ cups sliced yellow
  squash
1 cup sliced fresh
  mushrooms
3 small tomatoes,
  cut into wedges
½ cup chopped onion

Combine first 4 ingredients in bowl; mix well. Heat 1 tablespoon margarine in 9-inch skillet until very hot. Pour in batter. Bake at 450 degrees for 10 minutes. Remove to serving plate. Slice steak thinly. Coat with flour. Sauté in 2 tablespoons margarine and soy sauce for 7 to 10 minutes. Add vegetables. Sauté for 5 minutes. Spoon into puff shell. Yield: 6 servings.

Approx per serving: Cal 298, Prot 23.0 gr, Fat 12.9 gr, Chol 135.7 mg, Carbo 22.4 gr, Sod 1105.0 mg, Potas 597.4 mg.

Rebecca Howell, Alpha Psi Epsilon
Pharr, Texas

Steak and Veggies

2 pounds round
  steak, cut into
  1-inch strips
3 tablespoons
  sunflower oil
2 cups sliced
  onions

2 cups chopped celery
1 8-ounce can
  mushrooms
2 green peppers, sliced
¼ cup soy sauce

Brown steak strips in hot oil in skillet. Reduce heat. Simmer, covered, for 20 minutes. Increase heat to medium-high. Add vegetables. Stir-fry for several minutes. Stir in mixture of soy sauce and ½ cup water. Simmer, covered, for 10 minutes or until vegetables are tender-crisp. Serve over Chinese noodles. Yield: 4 servings.

Approx per serving: Cal 571, Prot 48.7 gr, Fat 34.9 gr, Chol 147.6 mg, Carbo 14.4 gr, Sod 1517.5 mg, Potas 985.4 mg.

Dorothy M. Yates, Xi Lambda Beta
Panama City, Florida

Black Kettle Stew

3 pounds stew beef
Parsley to taste
2 onions, sliced
3 carrots, sliced
3 stalks celery,
  sliced

1 4-ounce can
  mushrooms
3 tablespoons Minute
  tapioca
2 cans golden
  mushroom soup

Layer beef, salt, pepper and parsley to taste in Dutch oven. Layer remaining ingredients in order given over beef. Bake, covered, at 275 degrees for 4 hours. Do not uncover during baking. Serve over noodles, rice or mashed potatoes. Yield: 8 servings.

Approx per serving: Cal 461, Prot 37.0 gr, Fat 27.0 gr, Chol 121.6 mg, Carbo 16.2 gr, Sod 748.5 mg, Potas 821.5 mg.

Merelda Gough, Laureate Lambda
Salmon, Idaho

Five-Hour Stew

1 pound lean stew
  beef
2 cups sliced carrots
2 cups chopped
  potatoes

1 cup sliced celery
½ tablespoon salt
2 tablespoons tapioca
1½ cups tomato juice

Combine all ingredients in casserole; mix well. Bake, covered, at 250 degrees for 5 hours. Do not uncover during baking. Serve with fresh bread, salad and fruit. Yield: 4 servings.

Approx per serving: Cal 369, Prot 27.0 gr, Fat 14.3 gr, Chol 77.1 mg, Carbo 33.3 gr, Sod 596.0 mg, Potas 1321.9 mg.

Jan Britson, Kappa Beta
Ames, Iowa

Low-Calorie Beef Stroganoff

1 pound round steak
1 tablespoon oil
8 ounces
  mushrooms,
  sliced

1 envelope dry onion
  soup mix
1 teaspoon dillweed
1 cup yogurt
2 tablespoons flour

Slice steak diagonally cross grain into ⅛-inch strips. Stir-fry steak in hot oil in skillet over medium-high heat. Do not overcook. Remove steak and pan juices. Stir-fry mushrooms for 2 to 3 minutes. Add soup mix, dillweed and ⅔ cup water. Simmer for 3 minutes. Add steak with juices. Stir in mixture of yogurt and flour. Cook until thickened, stirring constantly. Serve over noodles or rice. Yield: 4 servings.

Approx per serving: Cal 341, Prot 27.7 gr, Fat 18.9 gr, Chol 94.6 mg, Carbo 14.3 gr, Sod 810.1 mg, Potas 630.9 mg.

Shirley Fryatt, Laureate Alpha Sigma
Federal Way, Washington

Teriyaki Stir-Fry

1 pound lean
  ground beef
5 green peppers,
  sliced
3 large onions,
  sliced
¼ cup oil

¾ cup soy sauce
1 tablespoon flour
⅛ teaspoon garlic
  powder
1 teaspoon Sherry
2 envelopes
  Sweet 'N' Low

Brown ground beef in skillet, stirring frequently; drain. Stir-fry green peppers and onions in hot oil in skillet over high heat until tender-crisp. Blend soy sauce, flour, garlic powder and Sherry in saucepan. Cook until slightly thickened, stirring constantly. Stir in sweetener. Mix ground beef and vegetables on serving plates. Top with sauce. Yield: 4 servings.

Approx per serving: Cal 420, Prot 29.5 gr, Fat 24.2 gr, Chol 79.9 mg, Carbo 22.2 gr, Sod 4037.4 mg, Potas 857.8 mg. Nutritional information does not include Sweet 'N' Low.

Diane James, Beta Eta
Longview, Washington

Beef Casserole

2 pounds ground
  beef
2 medium onions,
  chopped
1 4-ounce can
  chopped
  mushrooms
1 can cream of
  celery soup

1 can cream of
  chicken soup
1 teaspoon thyme
1 8-ounce
  package noodles,
  cooked
3 cups shredded
  Cheddar cheese
5 eggs, beaten

Brown ground beef in skillet, stirring frequently; drain. Add onions. Cook until onions are transparent. Drain mushrooms, reserving liquid. Combine soups, thyme and salt and pepper to taste in saucepan. Add reserved liquid and enough water to make of desired consistency. Stir in mushrooms. Cook until heated through. Combine with ground beef. Layer noodles, ground beef mixture and cheese in 9x13-inch baking pan. Pour eggs over top. Bake at 350 degrees for 30 minutes or until bubbly. Yield: 8 servings.

Approx per serving: Cal 638, Prot 40.2 gr, Fat 38.5 gr, Chol 308.5 mg, Carbo 30.8 gr, Sod 986.7 mg, Potas 459.5 mg.

Virginia S. Tyler, Delta Tau
Thomaston, Georgia

Beef-Broccoli Wellington

1 pound ground beef
1 10-ounce
  package frozen
  broccoli, thawed,
  drained
1 cup shredded low-
  fat mozzarella
  cheese
½ cup chopped
  onion

½ cup sour cream
¼ teaspoon salt
¼ teaspoon pepper
2 8-count cans
  refrigerator crescent
  rolls
1 egg, beaten
1 tablespoon poppy
  seed

Brown ground beef in skillet, stirring frequently; drain. Stir in broccoli, cheese, onion, sour cream and salt and pepper. Simmer for 10 minutes. Separate crescent rolls into rectangles. Place 2 rectangles on baking sheet, overlapping long sides. Press into 7x13-inch rectangle. Spoon half the ground beef mixture onto center. Fold long edges to enclose filling; seal edges. Repeat with remaining ingredients. Brush rolls with egg; sprinkle with poppy seed. Bake at 375 degrees for 18 to 22 minutes or until golden brown. Yield: 8 servings.

Approx per serving: Cal 216, Prot 15.4 gr, Fat 15.6 gr, Chol 88.7 mg, Carbo 3.8 gr, Sod 171.2 mg, Potas 252.0 mg. Nutritional information does not include refrigerator crescent rolls.

Rachelle M. Young, Lambda
Walla Walla, Washington

Beefy-Vegetable Supper

½ pound lean
  ground beef
½ cup chopped
  onion
1 clove of garlic,
  minced
1 medium zucchini,
  cut into thin
  strips
6 medium
  mushrooms, cut
  into quarters

1 cup fresh bean
  sprouts
1 cup shredded Chinese
  cabbage
⅓ cup diagonally sliced
  celery
1 teaspoon basil
¼ teaspoon oregano
¼ teaspoon salt
⅛ teaspoon pepper
1 large tomato,
  coarsely chopped

Brown ground beef, onion and garlic in heated skillet sprayed with nonstick cooking spray for 7 minutes, stirring frequently; drain well. Pat with paper towel. Wipe pan drippings from skillet. Combine zucchini, mushrooms, bean sprouts, cabbage, celery and seasonings with ground beef in skillet. Cook, covered, over medium heat for 5 minutes or until vegetables are tender-crisp, stirring frequently. Stir in tomato. Cook for 2 minutes longer, stirring frequently. Spoon into serving dish. Yield: 4 servings.

Approx per serving: Cal 162, Prot 13.1 gr, Fat 8.6 gr, Chol 38.3 mg, Carbo 9.3 gr, Sod 180.8 mg, Potas 563.1 mg.

Margaret L. Browning, Preceptor Alpha Delta
South Daytona, Florida

Broiled Ground Round Steak

1 pound ground round
1 tablespoon
  grated onion
1 clove of garlic,
  minced
½ teaspoon mustard

1 teaspoon tomato
  paste
½ teaspoon minced
  dill pickle
½ teaspoon
  Worcestershire sauce

Combine all ingredients in bowl; mix well. Shape into 6 patties. Place on rack in broiler pan. Broil to desired degree of doneness. Yield: 6 servings.

Approx per serving: Cal 128, Prot 15.6 gr, Fat 6.4 gr, Chol 53.3 mg, Carbo 0.7 gr, Sod 56.2 mg, Potas 190.6 mg.

Clady L. Beher, Precepter Gamma
Memphis, Tennessee

Calico Beans

½ pound ground
  beef
1 large onion,
  chopped
½ pound bacon,
  chopped
2 tablespoons vinegar
1   29-ounce can
  pork and beans

1   16-ounce can
  kidney beans,
  drained
2   16-ounce cans
  lima beans,
  drained
½ cup catsup
½ cup packed
  brown sugar

Brown ground beef and onion in skillet, stirring frequently; drain. Cook bacon in skillet until crisp. Add ground beef and remaining ingredients; mix well. Pour into casserole. Bake at 350 degrees for 45 minutes. Yield: 6 servings.

Approx per serving: Cal 620, Prot 30.7 gr, Fat 16.7 gr, Chol 42.6 mg, Carbo 88.9 gr, Sod 1319.2 mg, Potas 1076.6 mg.

Carol Terpstra, Alpha
Billings, Montana

Chili

2 cups sliced
  mushrooms
1 cup chopped celery
1 cup chopped onion
2 tablespoons
  margarine
1 pound lean
  ground beef
2 tablespoons
  chili powder

¼ teaspoon salt
½ teaspoon pepper
2   28-ounce cans
  tomatoes
1 tablespoon sugar
1 teaspoon
  Worcestershire
  sauce
2 cups kidney beans

Sauté mushrooms, celery and onion in margarine in skillet until onion is tender. Add ground beef and about ¼ of the mixture of chili powder, salt and pepper. Cook until ground beef is brown, stirring frequently. Stir in remaining seasoning mixture, tomatoes, sugar, Worcestershire sauce and ¼ cup water. Simmer, covered, for 15 minutes. Add kidney beans. Simmer for 10 minutes longer. Spoon into serving bowls. Garnish with shredded Cheddar cheese and sour cream. Yield: 6 servings.

Approx per serving: Cal 292, Prot 23.0 gr, Fat 11.0 gr, Chol 53.3 mg, Carbo 26.1 gr, Sod 387.9 mg, Potas 902.6 mg.

Debbie Schlegel, Kappa
Bozeman, Montana

Chili Con Carne

½ pound ground
  round
¼ pound ground
  fresh turkey
1   28-ounce can
  tomatoes
1   8-ounce can
  tomato sauce
¾ cup chopped
  carrots
¾ cup chopped
  onion

½ cup chopped
  green pepper
1 teaspoon minced
  garlic
1 tablespoon
  chili powder
1 bay leaf
1 cup drained red
  kidney beans
2 cups cooked long
  grain rice

Brown ground beef and ground turkey in skillet, stirring frequently; drain. Add tomatoes, tomato sauce, carrots, onion, green pepper and seasonings. Simmer, loosely covered, for 1 hour. Stir in beans. Simmer for 15 minutes longer. Remove bay leaf. Spoon over hot rice in serving bowls. Yield: 4 servings.

Approx per serving: Cal 366, Prot 23.6 gr, Fat 6.4 gr, Chol 46.1 mg, Carbo 54.9 gr, Sod 1047.3 mg, Potas 1183.1 mg.

Faye Williams, Xi Delta Pi
Kennett, Missouri

Chili-Stuffed Potatoes

1 pound ground
  beef
1 medium onion,
  chopped
1 medium green
  pepper, chopped
1 can tomato soup
1   4-ounce can
  sliced
  mushrooms,
  drained

1   20-ounce can
  kidney beans
⅛ teaspoon Tabasco
  sauce
½ teaspoon Italian
  seasoning
1 tablespoon maple
  syrup
Chili powder to taste
8 potatoes, baked

Brown ground beef and onion in skillet, stirring frequently; drain. Combine green pepper, soup, mushrooms, kidney beans and seasonings in large saucepan. Add ground beef and onion. Simmer for 2 hours. Scoop out potato pulp to form shells; place shells on serving plates. Spoon in chili. Garnish with grated Cheddar cheese and sour cream. Yield: 8 servings.

Approx per serving: Cal 369, Prot 19.0 gr, Fat 9.6 gr, Chol 38.3 mg, Carbo 52.9 gr, Sod 337.6 mg, Potas 1196.9 mg.

Marianne Morrison, Eta
Calgary, Alberta, Canada

Honey Chili

1 pound ground
  beef
1 cup chopped
  celery
2 teaspoons salt
1   20-ounce can
  red kidney beans,
  drained

½ cup chopped
  onion
2 teaspoons chili
  powder
2 teaspoons wine
  vinegar
½ cup honey

Brown ground beef in skillet, stirring frequently; drain. Add celery, salt, kidney beans, onion, chili powder and 1 cup water; mix well. Simmer, covered, for 1 hour. Stir in vinegar and honey. Yield: 6 servings.

Approx per serving: Cal 337, Prot 19.1 gr, Fat 11.5 gr, Chol 51.1 mg, Carbo 41.0 gr, Sod 784.1 mg, Potas 509.9 mg.

Lynn Cannon, Delta Omega
Carthage, Tennessee

One-Pot Chili

1 pound ground
  beef
1 medium onion,
  chopped
1 20-ounce can
  kidney beans

1 20-ounce can
  chili beans
2 cans tomato soup
Hot sauce to taste
Chili pepper to taste

Brown ground beef and onion in large saucepan, stirring frequently; drain. Stir in remaining ingredients. Simmer, covered, for 1 hour. Yield: 6 servings.

Approx per serving: Cal 407, Prot 25.9 gr, Fat 13.9 gr, Chol 51.1 mg, Carbo 45.8 gr, Sod 845.2 mg, Potas 870.7 mg.

Shirley Welander, Alpha
Billings, Montana

Company Casserole

1 pound ground beef
2 8-ounce cans
  tomato sauce
1 8-ounce package
  cream cheese,
  softened
1 cup cottage cheese
¼ cup sour cream

⅓ cup snipped green
  onions
1 tablespoon chopped
  green pepper
1 8-ounce package
  noodles, cooked
2 tablespoons melted
  margarine

Brown ground beef in skillet, stirring until crumbly; drain. Stir in tomato sauce; set aside. Combine cream cheese, cottage cheese, sour cream, green onions and green pepper in bowl; mix well. Place half the noodles in 8x12-inch baking dish. Layer cream cheese mixture, remaining noodles, margarine and ground beef mixture over top. Bake at 350 degrees for 30 minutes. Yield: 6 servings.

Approx per serving: Cal 572, Prot 28.3 gr, Fat 34.8 gr, Chol 140.6 mg, Carbo 36.7 gr, Sod 711.7 mg, Potas 600.4 mg.

Michele Elsbernd, Beta Delta
Fort Atkinson, Iowa

Italian-Style Macaroni Casserole

2 pounds ground
  beef
1 32-ounce jar
  spaghetti sauce
  with mushrooms
1½ teaspoons
  Italian seasoning
2 10-ounce
  packages frozen
  chopped spinach,
  thawed, drained
2 cups soft bread
  crumbs
½ cup oil

½ cup chopped
  parsley
1 8-ounce package
  shredded
  mozzarella
  cheese
1 teaspoon sage
1½ teaspoons salt
1 16-ounce
  package shell
  macaroni, cooked
½ cup Parmesan
  cheese

Brown ground beef in skillet, stirring frequently; drain. Stir in spaghetti sauce and Italian seasoning; set aside. Combine spinach, bread crumbs, oil, parsley, mozzarella cheese, sage and salt in bowl; mix well. Layer macaroni, ground beef mixture and spinach mixture ½ at a time in greased 9x13-inch baking pan. Sprinkle with Parmesan cheese. Bake at 350 degrees for 30 minutes. Yield: 8 servings.

Approx per serving: Cal 494, Prot 26.2 gr, Fat 27.0 gr, Chol 73.0 mg, Carbo 36.0 gr, Sod 49.4 mg, Potas 441.1 mg.

Alma Lynch, Preceptor Theta Sigma
Woodland Hills, California

Ground Beef-Tater Tot Casserole

2 pounds ground
  chuck
½ green pepper,
  chopped
1 medium onion,
  chopped

1 can cream of
  celery soup
2 soup cans milk
1 16-ounce
  package Tater Tots

Brown ground chuck with green pepper and onion in skillet. Drain. Add soup and milk; mix well. Stir in Tater Tots gently. Spoon into greased baking dish. Bake at 350 degrees for 1 hour or until brown and bubbly. Yield: 5 servings.

Approx per serving: Cal 466, Prot 42.2 gr, Fat 20.5 gr, Chol 141.7 mg, Carbo 26.4 gr, Sod 613.0 mg, Potas 786.4 mg.

Julie Ann M. Prahler, Preceptor Omega
Pontiac, Michigan

Stuffed Green Peppers

½ pound lean
  ground beef
1 large onion,
  chopped
6 medium tomatoes,
  chopped
8 large green
  peppers, seeded
3 cups grated
  Monterey Jack
  cheese

3 cups kidney beans
2 tablespoons chopped
  parsley
1 clove of garlic,
  minced
¼ teaspoon basil
¼ teaspoon oregano
¼ teaspoon salt
¼ teaspoon pepper

Brown ground beef in skillet, stirring frequently; drain. Sauté onion and tomatoes in skillet; drain. Parboil green peppers in salted water in saucepan for 3 minutes; drain. Mix ground beef, tomato mixture and remaining ingredients in bowl. Spoon into green peppers. Arrange in baking pan. Bake, covered, at 325 degrees for 30 minutes. Yield: 8 servings.

Approx per serving: Cal 346, Prot 24.1 gr, Fat 16.8 gr, Chol 61.9 mg, Carbo 26.4 gr, Sod 394.9 mg, Potas 769.8 mg.

Sarah Barton, Alpha Kappa
Pascagoula, Mississippi

Light Lasagna

½ pound lean
  ground beef
½ teaspoon basil
1 teaspoon oregano
8 ounces tomato
  paste
6 tablespoons
  grated mozzarella
  cheese
⅔ cup cottage
  cheese

¼ cup Parmesan
  cheese
1 cup low-fat milk
¼ cup flour
2 teaspoons baking
  powder
2 eggs
Pinch of pepper
6 tablespoons grated
  mozzarella cheese

Brown ground beef in skillet, stirring frequently; drain. Add basil, oregano, tomato paste and 6 tablespoons mozzarella cheese; mix well. Layer cottage cheese, Parmesan cheese and ground beef mixture in 8-inch square baking pan sprayed with nonstick cooking spray. Combine milk, flour, baking powder, eggs, pepper and salt to taste in blender container. Process for 30 seconds. Pour over layers. Sprinkle with 6 tablespoons mozzarella cheese. Bake at 400 degrees for 30 to 35 minutes or until golden. Yield: 4 servings.

Approx per serving: Cal 496, Prot 30.4 gr, Fat 32.3 gr, Chol 223.6 mg, Carbo 21.3 gr, Sod 506.2 mg, Potas 787.6 mg.

Susan Mary Spindler
Paris, Ontario, Canada

Zucchini Lasagna

½ pound lean
  ground beef
½ cup chopped
  onion
1 15-ounce can
  tomato sauce
½ teaspoon oregano
¼ teaspoon basil
½ teaspoon salt

⅛ teaspoon pepper
4 medium zucchini
1 8-ounce carton
  cottage cheese
1 egg
2 tablespoons flour
1 cup shredded low-fat
  mozzarella cheese

Brown ground beef with onion in skillet, stirring frequently; drain. Stir in tomato sauce, oregano, basil, salt and pepper. Simmer for 5 minutes. Slice zucchini lengthwise into ¼-inch slices. Combine cottage cheese and egg in bowl; mix well. Layer half the zucchini, half the flour, all the cottage cheese mixture, half the ground beef mixture, remaining zucchini and flour, mozzarella cheese and remaining ground beef mixture in 8x12-inch baking dish. Bake at 375 degrees for 40 minutes. Let stand for 10 minutes before cutting. Yield: 6 servings.

Approx per serving: Cal 251, Prot 22.2 gr, Fat 10.8 gr, Chol 93.1 mg, Carbo 17.6 gr, Sod 818.4 mg, Potas 829.9 mg.

Carole Pipetti, Xi Xi
Altoona, Pennsylvania

Delicious Low-Calorie Meat Loaf

1 pound ground
  beef
3 tablespoons onion
  juice
½ teaspoon oregano
½ teaspoon paprika

½ cup finely
  chopped green
  pepper
½ cup finely
  chopped green
  beans

Combine all ingredients, salt and pepper to taste and enough water to moisten in bowl; mix well. Shape into loaf in baking dish. Bake at 375 degrees for 1 hour. Yield: 2 servings.

Approx per serving: Cal 489, Prot 40.6 gr, Fat 33.2 gr, Chol 153.2 mg, Carbo 5.0 gr, Sod 182.8 mg, Potas 579.0 mg.

Georgia M. Cuneo, Laureate Alpha
Winston-Salem, North Carolina

Family Meat Loaf

1½ pounds ground
  beef
½ cup nonfat dry
  milk powder
2 slices bread,
  crumbled
1 onion, chopped
1 egg, beaten
¾ cup catsup
1 teaspoon salt

¼ teaspoon pepper
¼ teaspoon dry
  mustard
¼ teaspoon garlic
  salt
¼ teaspoon celery salt
¼ teaspoon sage
1 tablespoon
  Worcestershire
  sauce

Mix ground beef and dry milk powder in bowl. Add remaining ingredients; mix well. Shape into loaf in greased 5x9-inch loaf pan. Bake at 350 degrees for 1 to 1½ hours or until brown. Yield: 6 servings.

Approx per serving: Cal 337, Prot 24.7 gr, Fat 18.0 gr, Chol 120.3 mg, Carbo 18.3 gr, Sod 1009.1 mg, Potas 512.8 mg.

Martha B. Horsman, Alpha Eta
Sulphur, Oklahoma

Meat Loaf

2 pounds lean
  ground beef
½ cup oats
1 onion, chopped
½ cup tomato juice

2 teaspoons salt
Pepper to taste
3 slices onion
1 cup tomato juice

Combine ground beef, oats, chopped onion, ½ cup tomato juice and salt and pepper in bowl; mix well. Shape gently into loaf in baking dish. Top with onion slices. Pour tomato juice over loaf. Bake at 325 degrees for 1½ hours, basting occasionally with pan juices. Skim juices before serving. Yield: 8 servings.

Approx per serving: Cal 273, Prot 21.3 gr, Fat 17.0 gr, Chol 76.6 mg, Carbo 8.1 gr, Sod 675.7 mg, Potas 392.0 mg.

Ann Titus, Xi Gamma Zeta
Dallas, Texas

Old-Fashioned Meat Loaf

1 pound lean
   ground beef
1 large onion,
   finely chopped
¼ cup natural bran
1 slice whole wheat
   bread, crumbled
½ teaspoon thyme
½ teaspoon salt

Freshly ground
   pepper to taste
Dash of Worcestershire
   sauce
1 cup tomato juice
1 egg, lightly beaten
1 tablespoon chopped
   fresh thyme, savory,
   rosemary and sage

Combine all ingredients in bowl; mix well. Shape into loaf in loaf pan. Bake at 350 degrees for 45 minutes or until brown and firm. Drain. Place on serving plate. Yield 6 servings.

Helen Stokaluk, Laureate Eta
Thunder Bay, Ontario, Canada

Microwave Mexican Beef and Rice

½ pound ground
   beef
½ cup chopped
   onion
1 8-ounce can
   tomato sauce
2 tablespoons sliced
   ripe olives

¾ cup minute rice
1½ teaspoons chili
   powder
½ cup crushed tortilla
   chips
½ cup shredded
   Cheddar cheese

Crumble ground beef into 1½-quart glass dish. Add onion. Microwave, covered, on High for 2 minutes; drain. Add tomato sauce, olives, rice, chili powder and ½ cup water; mix well. Microwave, covered, for 5 minutes. Let stand, covered, for 5 minutes; fluff with fork. Sprinkle with crushed tortilla chips and cheese. Let stand, covered, for 1 minute or until cheese melts. Yield: 2 servings.

Photograph for this recipe on page 104.

Microwave Chop Suey Casserole

1 pound lean
   ground beef
1 large onion,
   chopped
1½ cups chopped
   celery
1 can mushroom
   soup

1 20-ounce can
   bean sprouts,
   drained
1 4-ounce can
   mushrooms,
   drained
½ cup rice

Microwave crumbled ground beef with onion in glass casserole on High until no longer pink, stirring frequently; drain. Add celery and 1 cup water. Microwave until celery is tender. Add soup, bean sprouts, mushrooms, rice and 1 soup can water. Microwave for 20 minutes. Serve with soy sauce. Yield: 6 servings.

Approx per serving: Cal 269, Prot 20.0 gr, Fat 10.6 gr,
Chol 57.2 mg, Carbo 23.3 gr, Sod 476.4 mg, Potas 456.9 mg.

Brita Reams, Theta Rho
New Hampton, Iowa

Microwave Pizza Potatoes

4 medium baking
   potatoes
½ pound lean
   ground beef
1 small onion,
   chopped
½ cup chopped
   green pepper
2 tablespoons
   catsup

1 large tomato, chopped
⅛ teaspoon pepper
¼ teaspoon oregano
¼ teaspoon basil
¼ teaspoon parsley
   flakes
½ cup shredded
   mozzarella cheese

Microwave potatoes according to microwave manufacturer's instructions. Wrap in foil; set aside. Microwave ground beef, onion and green pepper in glass casserole on High for 3 to 4 minutes, stirring once; drain. Stir in catsup, tomato and seasonings. Split potatoes lengthwise. Place on serving plate; fluff centers with fork. Spoon ground beef mixture over potatoes. Sprinkle with cheese. Microwave on High for 1 minute or until cheese melts. Yield: 4 servings.

Approx per serving: Cal 333, Prot 18.0 gr, Fat 12.0 gr,
Chol 50.8 mg, Carbo 39.3 gr, Sod 172.1 mg, Potas 1078.8 mg.

Karen Fitch, Preceptor Delta Beta
Chesterfield, Missouri

Microwave Stir-Fry Cabbage

½ pound ground
   beef
½ pound sausage
3 tablespoons soy
   sauce
8 cups shredded
   cabbage
2 carrots, thinly
   sliced

4 green onions,
   thinly sliced
⅛ teaspoon garlic
   powder
3 tablespoons sesame
   oil
⅛ teaspoon ginger

Microwave ground beef and sausage in glass dish on High for 6 minutes; drain. Combine remaining ingredients except ginger in glass casserole; mix well. Microwave on High for 5 minutes or until tender-crisp. Stir in meat mixture and ginger. Microwave, covered, on High for 2 minutes. Yield: 6 servings.

Approx per serving: Cal 272, Prot 12.2 gr, Fat 20.6 gr,
Chol 41.3 mg, Carbo 10.7 gr, Sod 881.2 mg, Potas 539.0 mg.

Jane Dieter, Xi Delta
Baltimore, Maryland

Moussaka

2 medium eggplant,
 sliced ½ inch
 thick
5 medium potatoes,
 thinly sliced
¼ cup olive oil
1 large onion,
 chopped
1 clove of garlic,
 minced
1½ pounds ground
 beef

1 tablespoon olive
 oil
1 6-ounce can
 tomato paste
1 tablespoon oregano
2 eggs, beaten
1 cup Italian bread
 crumbs
¾ cup Parmesan
 cheese
1 recipe Béchamel
 Sauce

Béchamel Sauce

¼ cup butter,
 melted
¼ cup flour

2 cups milk
4 eggs, lightly beaten
Turmeric to taste

Sprinkle eggplant slices with salt. Let stand for 30 minutes or longer. Cook potatoes in water to cover in saucepan for 5 minutes; drain. Press liquid from eggplant. Sauté in ¼ cup olive oil in skillet until light brown on both sides. Drain on paper towels. Sauté onion, garlic and ground beef in 1 tablespoon olive oil in skillet, stirring until ground beef is crumbly; drain. Add tomato paste, 1 tomato paste can water and oregano; mix well. Simmer to desired consistency. Season with salt to taste. Remove from heat. Add eggs and bread crumbs; mix well. Layer half the potatoes, ⅓ of the Béchamel Sauce, ¼ cup Parmesan cheese, all the eggplant, ⅓ of the Béchamel Sauce, ¼ cup cheese, remaining potatoes, remaining sauce and remaining cheese in 3-quart baking dish. Bake at 375 degrees for 30 minutes or until light brown. Yield: 6 servings.

Blend butter and flour in saucepan. Cook over low heat for 3 to 5 minutes, stirring constantly. Add milk gradually, stirring constantly. Cook until thickened, stirring constantly. Stir a small amount of hot mixture into eggs; stir eggs into hot mixture. Cook until thickened, stirring constantly. Season with turmeric to taste.

Approx per serving: Cal 857, Prot 43.2 gr, Fat 49.4 gr, Chol 379.4 mg, Carbo 61.2 gr, Sod 494.9 mg, Potas 1591.9 mg. Nutritional information does not include salt used to draw liquid from eggplant.

Vicky Jager, Zeta Eta
Eureka, California

Hamburger Pie

1¼ pounds ground
 beef
⅓ cup chopped
 onion
1 8-ounce can
 tomato sauce
¼ cup chopped
 green pepper
1 8-ounce can
 mushrooms,
 drained
¼ teaspoon cumin

¼ teaspoon garlic
 salt
¼ teaspoon salt
1 8-count can
 refrigerator crescent
 dinner rolls
1 egg, beaten
1 cup shredded
 Cheddar cheese
Paprika to taste
1 cup shredded
 Cheddar cheese

Brown ground beef and onion in skillet; drain. Stir in tomato sauce, green pepper, mushrooms and seasonings. Simmer for several minutes. Separate roll dough into 8 triangles. Press into ungreased 9-inch pie plate, sealing edges. Mix egg and 1 cup cheese in bowl. Pour into crust. Spoon ground beef mixture into prepared plate. Sprinkle paprika and remaining cheese over top. Bake at 375 degrees for 20 minutes. Let stand for 5 minutes. Cut into wedges. Yield: 6 servings.

Approx per serving: Cal 383, Prot 28.1 gr, Fat 27.0 gr, Chol 143.3 mg, Carbo 6.0 gr, Sod 712.2 mg, Potas 408.1 mg. Nutritional information does not include refrigerator crescent rolls.

Renee Mathews, Zeta Eta
Eureka, California

Mexican Tamale Pie

3 cups chicken stock
1½ cups yellow
 cornmeal
1 clove of garlic,
 minced
1 medium onion,
 chopped
½ cup chopped
 green pepper
2 tablespoons oil
1 pound ground beef

3 tomatoes, chopped
1 cup cooked corn
1 tablespoon chili
 powder
¼ teaspoon pepper
¼ teaspoon cumin
¼ teaspoon oregano
2 cups shredded
 Monterey Jack
 cheese

Bring chicken stock to the boiling point in saucepan. Stir in cornmeal gradually. Cook until thick and smooth, stirring constantly. Cool. Press over bottom and side of greased 9-inch casserole with wet fingertips. Sauté garlic, onion and green pepper in oil in skillet. Add ground beef. Cook until no longer pink, stirring frequently. Add tomatoes, corn and seasonings. Simmer for 10 minutes, stirring occasionally. Pour into prepared casserole. Sprinkle with cheese. Bake at 350 degrees for 30 minutes. Yield: 6 servings.

Approx per serving: Cal 523, Prot 27.3 gr, Fat 28.6 gr, Chol 88.4 mg, Carbo 39.3 gr, Sod 382.6 mg. Potas 468.7 mg.

Debbie Crockett, Zeta Upsilon
Garden City, Kansas

Pizza Bundt

2 cups pizza crust
  mix
1 egg
½ pound lean
  ground beef
3 tablespoons oil-
  free salad
  dressing
½ cup pizza sauce
¼ cup cottage cheese

½ cup sliced canned
  mushrooms,
  drained
10 to 15 slices
  pepperoni
1 cup shredded
  mozzarella cheese
¼ cup Parmesan
  cheese

Combine crust mix, egg and ⅓ to ½ cup water in bowl; mix well. Knead on floured surface for several minutes. Place in greased bowl, turning to coat surface. Let rise for 30 minutes. Brown ground beef in salad dressing in skillet; drain. Stir in 2 tablespoons pizza sauce. Press half the dough over bottom and as far up side of bundt pan as possible. Spread dough with half the remaining sauce. Alternate layers of ground beef and remaining ingredients in prepared pan. Top with remaining dough, sealing edge. Bake at 375 degrees for 30 to 40 minutes or until golden brown. Cool for 5 minutes. Invert onto serving plate. Yield: 12 servings.

Paula Lipko, Beta Pi
Ellsworth Air Force Base, South Dakota

Pumpkin Dinner

2 pounds lean
  ground beef
1 green pepper,
  chopped
1 onion, chopped
2 cloves of garlic,
  chopped
½ cup raisins

½ teaspoon vinegar
3 eggs, beaten
2½ teaspoons oregano
1 15-ounce can
  tomato sauce
1 teaspoon pepper
1 10-inch pumpkin,
  seeded

Brown ground beef with green pepper, onion and garlic in skillet, stirring frequently; drain. Stir in remaining ingredients except pumpkin. Spoon into pumpkin shell. Bake, covered, at 350 degrees for 1 hour or until pumpkin is tender. Spoon ground beef mixture and pumpkin onto plates. Yield: 10 servings.

Approx per serving: Cal 220, Prot 21.9 gr, Fat 9.6 gr, Chol 139.8 mg, Carbo 11.7 gr, Sod 331.1 mg, Potas 514.5 mg. Nutritional information does not include pumpkin.

Cherllyn McAndrew, Lambda
Boise, Idaho

Roly Polys

1 pound ground beef
1 small onion,
  chopped
½ green pepper,
  chopped
½ cup chopped
  mushrooms
2 tablespoons
  chopped ripe
  olives
1 tablespoon oil
½ cup picante salsa

1 15-ounce can
  stewed tomatoes
1 15-ounce can
  tomato sauce
1 tablespoon chopped
  jalapeño peppers
4 12-inch flour
  tortillas
1 cup shredded
  mozzarella cheese
1 cup chopped lettuce
1 tomato, chopped

Brown ground beef with onion, green pepper, mushrooms and olives in oil in skillet, stirring frequently; drain. Mix salsa, tomatoes, tomato sauce and peppers in saucepan. Heat to serving temperature. Soften tortillas 1 at a time in skillet over low heat. Top with cheese, ground beef mixture, lettuce and tomato. Heat until cheese melts. Roll tortilla to enclose filling. Place on serving plates. Serve with salsa and additional cheese. Yield: 4 servings.

Approx per serving: Cal 543, Prot 32.5 gr, Fat 30.5 gr, Chol 101.5 mg, Carbo 37.4 gr, Sod 1005.4 mg, Potas 1145.1 mg.

Rita J. Miller, Xi Lambda Beta
Lynn Haven, Florida

Hamburger Stroganoff

1½ pounds lean
  ground beef
¼ cup butter
1 cup chopped onion
1 clove of garlic,
  chopped
8 ounces
  mushrooms,
  sliced
3 tablespoons flour

2 teaspoons instant
  beef bouillon
1 tablespoon catsup
1 tablespoon steak
  sauce
½ teaspoon salt
⅛ teaspoon pepper
½ cup white wine
¼ teaspoon dillweed
1½ cups sour cream

Brown ground beef in 1 tablespoon butter in skillet; drain. Add 3 tablespoons butter and vegetables. Sauté for 3 to 4 minutes. Remove ground beef and vegetables with slotted spoon. Mix flour, bouillon, catsup, steak sauce, salt and pepper in skillet. Add 1½ cups water gradually. Cook until thickened, stirring constantly. Add ground beef and vegetables. Simmer for 5 minutes. Stir in wine, dillweed and sour cream. Serve over noodles or rice. Yield: 6 servings.

Approx per serving: Cal 349, Prot 26.5 gr, Fat 21.7 gr, Chol 109.1 mg, Carbo 9.8 gr, Sod 496.2 mg, Potas 521.9 mg.

Renee Mathews, Zeta Eta
Eureka, California

Saturday Lunch Taco Spread

1 pound ground beef
1 6-ounce can
  tomato paste
1 envelope taco
  seasoning mix
1 3-ounce
  package cream
  cheese, softened
1 cup sour cream

2 green onions,
  chopped
⅓ head lettuce,
  chopped
3 tomatoes, chopped,
  drained
½ cup grated Cheddar
  cheese

Brown ground beef in skillet, stirring frequently; drain. Stir in tomato paste and seasoning mix. Layer cream cheese, sour cream, ground beef mixture and remaining ingredients in order given on serving plate. Serve with tortilla chips. Yield: 4 servings.

Approx per serving: Cal 556, Prot 29.7 gr, Fat 41.6 gr, Chol 139.5 mg, Carbo 17.4 gr, Sod 253.8 mg, Potas 1021.2 mg. Nutritional information does not include taco seasoning mix.

Carolynne Russell, Eta
Calgary, Alberta, Canada

Low-Sodium Spaghetti Sauce

1 pound ground
  chuck
1 tablespoon olive
  oil
1½ cups chopped
  onion
1 tablespoon
  chopped garlic
Pepper to taste
½ cup dry red wine

2 14-ounce cans
  salt-free tomatoes
1 6-ounce can salt-
  free tomato paste
1 teaspoon marjoram
1 teaspoon rosemary
2 teaspoons oregano
⅛ teaspoon hot red
  pepper flakes

Brown ground beef in olive oil in large saucepan, stirring frequently; drain. Add onion, garlic and pepper. Cook for 1 minute, stirring constantly. Add wine. Cook for 2 minutes. Stir in remaining ingredients. Simmer for 45 minutes. Serve over hot cooked pasta. Yield: 4 servings.

Approx per serving: Cal 342, Prot 28.3 gr, Fat 13.7 gr, Chol 79.9 mg, Carbo 25.5 gr, Sod 90.0 mg, Potas 1314.6 mg.

Ivy Alexander, Kappa Kappa
Baytown, Texas

Cauliflower-Ham Casserole

2 tablespoons butter
2 tablespoons flour
1 cup milk
4 slices sharp
  American cheese
½ cup sour cream
1 medium head
  cauliflower,
  chopped, cooked

2 cups chopped
  cooked ham
1 3-ounce can
  mushrooms,
  drained
½ cup dry bread
  crumbs

Melt butter in saucepan. Blend in flour. Stir in milk gradually. Cook until thickened, stirring constantly. Add cheese. Cook until melted, stirring constantly. Remove from heat. Add sour cream; blend well. Pour over mixture of drained cauliflower, ham and mushrooms in 1½-quart casserole. Sprinkle crumbs over top. Bake at 350 degrees for 30 minutes or until bubbly. Yield: 6 servings.

Approx per serving: Cal 380, Prot 20.9 gr, Fat 24.9 gr, Chol 81.5 mg, Carbo 20.0 gr, Sod 807.8 mg, Potas 672.7 mg.

Cindy Burns, Beta Pi
Rapid City, South Dakota

Ham Fried Rice

½ cup chopped
  onion
3 tablespoons oil
½ cup chopped
  mushrooms
½ cup bean sprouts
1½ cups sliced
  celery

1½ cups chopped
  cooked ham
6 cups cooked rice
3 tablespoons soy sauce
2 eggs, scrambled
½ cup chopped green
  onion

Stir-fry onion in hot oil in skillet over high heat until brown. Reduce heat to medium. Add mushrooms, bean sprouts and celery. Stir-fry until tender. Add ham, rice, MSG and salt and pepper to taste and enough soy sauce to make of desired color; mix well. Spoon into serving bowl. Cut eggs into strips. Arrange over top. Sprinkle with green onion. Serve immediately. Yield: 6 servings.

Approx per serving: Cal 436, Prot 15.2 gr, Fat 16.9 gr, Chol 115.4 mg, Carbo 54.5 gr, Sod 1749.1 mg, Potas 380.5 mg.

Norie Mitchell, Xi Iota Mu
Crescent City, California

Yuki's Fried Rice

4 cups cold cooked
  rice
2 tablespoons oil
1½ cups chopped
  cooked ham
1 cup chopped green
  onion bulbs
1 tablespoon oil
3 eggs, beaten

1 tablespoon oil
1 teaspoon garlic
  powder
2 tablespoons soy
  sauce
½ teaspoon MSG
½ cup chopped
  green onion tops

Stir-fry rice in 2 tablespoons hot oil in skillet for 3 minutes. Set rice aside. Stir-fry ham and green onion bulbs in 1 tablespoon hot oil for 1 minute. Set aside. Scramble eggs very lightly in 1 tablespoon hot oil in skillet. Set aside. Clean skillet. Stir-fry rice and ham mixture in 1 tablespoon hot oil in skillet for 1 to 2 minutes. Add garlic powder, soy sauce, MSG, and salt and pepper to taste. Add egg and green onion tops; toss to mix. Serve immediately. Yield: 5 servings.
Note: May add leftover cooked vegetables, nuts, mushrooms and bean sprouts. If chopping vegetables and scrambling eggs is done in advance, the cooking requires only 7 minutes.

Approx per serving: Cal 463, Prot 17.1 gr, Fat 23.9 gr, Chol 189.1 mg, Carbo 43.0 gr, Sod 1580.9 mg, Potas 275.9 mg.

Yukiko Henderson, Xi Omicron
Harlingen, Texas

Ham and Broccoli Bake

1 10-ounce
   package frozen
   chopped broccoli
12 slices white bread
1 cup shredded
   Cheddar cheese
2 cups chopped
   cooked ham

2 teaspoons
   chopped onion
6 eggs, beaten
3½ cups milk
½ teaspoon salt
¼ to ½ teaspoon
   dry mustard

Cook broccoli according to package directions until partially cooked; drain. Trim and discard crusts from bread. Cut each slice with doughnut cutter. Place scraps in greased 9x13-inch baking dish. Layer cheese, broccoli and ham in prepared dish. Sprinkle with onion. Arrange bread doughnuts over top. Beat eggs, milk, salt and dry mustard. Pour over layers. Refrigerate, covered, for 6 hours or longer. Bake at 325 degrees for 1 hour. Let stand for 10 minutes. Cut into 12 squares. Yield: 12 servings.

Approx per serving: Cal 276, Prot 16.2 gr, Fat 14.5 gr, Chol 167.3 mg, Carbo 19.5 gr, Sod 543.3 mg, Potas 284.9 mg.

Michele Elsbernd, Beta Delta
Fort Atkinson, Iowa

Ham Turnovers

1 cup minced
   baked ham
⅓ cup chopped
   celery
¼ cup chopped
   walnuts
1 teaspoon minced
   onion
3 tablespoons sweet
   pickle relish

½ teaspoon mustard
¼ cup salad
   dressing
¼ cup butter,
   softened
12 slices (or more)
   whole wheat
   bread, crusts
   trimmed
½ cup Cheez Whiz

Combine ham, celery, walnuts, onion, relish, mustard and salad dressing in bowl; mix well. Butter bread lightly; spread with Cheez Whiz. Place about 1 tablespoon ham mixture on center of each. Fold over to form triangle, enclosing filling; secure with toothpick. Store in tightly covered container in refrigerator for several hours if desired. Place folded side down on baking sheet. Bake at 450 degrees for 5 to 6 minutes or until toasted. Yield: 12 servings.

Approx per serving: Cal 188, Prot 6.5 gr, Fat 12.0 gr, Chol 28.9 mg, Carbo 14.8 gr, Sod 404.0 mg, Potas 138.6 mg.

Margaret M. Berry, Preceptor Alpha Kappa
Trenton, Ontario, Canada

Ham and Bacon Quiche

1 unbaked deep-
   dish pie shell
1 egg white, beaten
1 cup shredded
   Cheddar cheese
1 cup chopped
   cooked ham
1 cup crumbled
   crisp-fried bacon
¼ cup Parmesan
   cheese

¼ cup chopped
   onion
1 cup shredded
   Swiss cheese
5 eggs
1 cup milk
½ teaspoon white
   pepper

Bake pie shell at 400 degrees until golden. Cool for 3 minutes. Brush pie shell including edge with beaten egg white. Bake for several seconds longer to seal pie shell. Layer Cheddar cheese, ham, bacon, Parmesan cheese, onion and Swiss cheese in pie shell. Beat eggs until frothy. Add milk and pepper; beat well. Pour over layers. Place on baking sheet. Bake at 350 degrees for 1 hour or until set. Let stand for 15 minutes before cutting. Yield: 8 servings.

Approx per serving: Cal 441, Prot 20.9 gr, Fat 32.2 gr, Chol 212.3 mg, Carbo 16.0 gr, Sod 667.7 mg, Potas 218.0 mg.

Erin Haugh, Alpha Eta
Green River, Wyoming

Quick Quiche

3 eggs
½ cup melted butter
1½ cups milk
½ cup buttermilk
   baking mix
½ teaspoon salt

⅛ teaspoon pepper
1 cup grated Swiss
   cheese
1 cup chopped ham
1 cup sliced onion

Combine first 6 ingredients in blender container. Process until smooth. Pour into bowl. Stir in cheese, ham and onion. Pour into greased pie plate. Bake at 350 degrees for 45 minutes or until set. Yield: 6 servings.
Note: May substitute meat, cheese and vegetables of your choice.

Approx per serving: Cal 366, Prot 15.5 gr, Fat 28.2 gr, Chol 213.6 mg, Carbo 12.9 gr, Sod 820.9 mg, Potas 236.9 mg.

Chris Booth, Zeta Eta
Eureka, California

Polynesian Sandwich

½ teaspoon butter
1 slice bread
1 1-ounce slice
   ham

1 pineapple ring
1 1-ounce slice
   Cheddar cheese

Spread butter on 1 side of bread. Place on rack in broiler pan. Broil until lightly toasted. Add ham and pineapple ring. Broil until heated through. Top with cheese. Broil until cheese melts. Yield: 1 serving.

Approx per serving: Cal 365, Prot 15.7 gr, Fat 18.3 gr, Chol 59.9 mg, Carbo 35.3 gr, Sod 576.9 mg. Potas 220.0 mg.

Martha B. Horsman, Alpha Eta
Sulphur, Oklahoma

Victoria's Ham and Noodle Casserole

2 cups low-fat milk
2 tablespoons flour
1 teaspoon mustard
Paprika to taste
Nutmeg to taste
2 cups noodles,
  cooked
1½ cups chopped
  cooked lean ham
1 cup thinly sliced
  carrots

1 tablespoon chopped
  onion
1 tablespoon chopped
  parsley
6 tablespoons grated
  low-fat Swiss cheese
6 tablespoons seasoned
  bread crumbs

Blend milk and flour in saucepan. Bring to the boiling point over medium heat, stirring constantly. Cook until thickened, stirring constantly. Add mustard and seasonings; mix well. Layer noodles, ham and vegetables in 1½-quart casserole. Pour sauce over layers. Top with mixture of cheese and bread crumbs. Bake at 350 degrees for 30 minutes or until bubbly. Yield: 6 servings.

Approx per serving: Cal 271, Prot 15.5 gr, Fat 11.8 gr, Chol 58.3 mg, Carbo 25.0 gr, Sod 420.1 mg, Potas 322.2 mg.

Mary Ann Madar, Laureate Alpha Delta
Elizabeth Township, Pennsylvania

Herbed Lamb Stew

1 pound lean lamb,
  cut into bite-sized
  pieces
½ cup chopped
  onion
1 tablespoon oil
¼ cup dry white
  wine
1½ teaspoons
  instant chicken
  bouillon
½ teaspoon basil
¼ teaspoon dry
  mustard

½ teaspoon thyme
3 carrots, cut into
  1-inch pieces
2 potatoes, peeled,
  chopped
2 stalks celery, cut into
  1-inch pieces
1 cup cut fresh green
  beans
1 green pepper, cut
  into 1-inch pieces
1 to 2 tablespoons
  cornstarch

Sauté lamb and onion in oil in skillet until brown; drain. Add wine, bouillon, seasonings and 1 cup water. Simmer for 30 minutes or until lamb is tender. Add vegetables. Simmer, covered, for 20 minutes or until vegetables are tender. Dissolve cornstarch in 5 tablespoons cold water. Stir half the cornstarch mixture into stew. Cook until clear and thickened, stirring constantly. Add enough remaining cornstarch mixture to make of desired consistency. Cook until thickened, stirring constantly. Yield: 4 servings.

Approx per serving: Cal 422, Prot 24.2 gr, Fat 22.1 gr, Chol 81.1 mg, Carbo 30.6 gr, Sod 310.9 mg, Potas 1104.0 mg.

Sandra Miller, Preceptor Beta Lambda
Lakewood, Colorado

Moussaka

2 large eggplant,
  peeled, cut into
  ½-inch slices
2 tablespoons oil
2 pounds ground
  lamb
1½ cups chopped
  onions
1 clove of garlic,
  chopped
1 8-ounce can
  tomato sauce
¾ cup red wine

2 tablespoons
  chopped parsley
1 teaspoon salt
¼ teaspoon oregano
¼ teaspoon cinnamon
1 egg, beaten
¼ cup melted
  margarine
¼ cup flour
2 cups low-fat milk
3 eggs
½ cup Parmesan
  cheese

Sprinkle eggplant slices lightly with salt; brush with oil. Brown on both sides in skillet; drain and set aside. Brown lamb with onions in skillet, stirring until crumbly; drain. Add garlic, tomato sauce, wine and seasonings. Simmer for 10 minutes. Stir into 1 beaten egg in bowl gradually. Blend margarine, flour and salt and pepper to taste in saucepan. Stir in milk gradually. Cook until thickened, stirring constantly. Stir a small amount of hot mixture into 3 beaten eggs; stir eggs into hot mixture. Layer half the eggplant, all the lamb mixture, remaining eggplant and all the milk mixture in 9x13-inch baking pan. Top with cheese and additional cinnamon. Bake at 325 degrees for 45 minutes. Yield: 8 servings.

Approx per serving: Cal 504, Prot 31.1 gr, Fat 33.4 gr, Chol 216.4 mg, Carbo 18.4 gr, Sod 1046.4 mg, Potas 876.1 mg.

Sandra Miller, Preceptor Beta Lambda
Lakewood, Colorado

Chili Verde

1½ to 2 pounds
  lean pork,
  chopped
2 cloves of garlic,
  chopped
2 tablespoons oil
1 10-ounce jar
  green chili salsa

1 15-ounce can
  stewed tomatoes
½ teaspoon minced
  jalapeño pepper
1 6-ounce can
  whole green
  chilies

Brown pork and garlic in oil in saucepan. Add salsa and tomatoes. Simmer for 30 minutes. Add jalapeño pepper. Simmer for 15 minutes. Add chili peppers. Simmer for 15 minutes longer or to desired consistency. Serve with warm flour tortillas. Yield: 8 servings.

Approx per serving: Cal 395, Prot 20.6 gr, Fat 31.8 gr, Chol 70.3 mg, Carbo 5.9 gr, Sod 155.4 mg, Potas 734.1 mg.

Debbie Lungi, Zeta Eta
Eureka, California

Oriental Casserole Stir-Fry

2 tablespoons oil
1½ cups thinly
   sliced cauliflower
1½ cups thinly
   sliced broccoli
1 cup thinly sliced
   carrots
1 cup thinly sliced
   celery
1 cup thinly sliced
   green pepper
¼ cup chopped
   onion
1 tablespoon oil
1 pound thinly
   sliced pork
1½ tablespoons
   cornstarch
1 teaspoon instant
   chicken bouillon
1 teaspoon sugar
2 tablespoons soy sauce

Heat 2 tablespoons oil in electric skillet at 375 degrees. Add sliced vegetables; stir lightly. Cook, covered, for 3 minutes, stirring occasionally. Remove vegetables. Add 1 tablespoon oil to skillet. Stir-fry pork in hot oil for several minutes. Add mixture of remaining ingredients. Simmer until thickened, stirring constantly. Add vegetables. Heat to serving temperature. Serve on hot cooked brown rice. Yield: 4 servings.

Approx per serving: Cal 453, Prot 37.8 gr, Fat 26.7 gr,
Chol 99.5 mg, Carbo 16.1 gr, Sod 929.7 mg, Potas 1007.6 mg.

Gertrude Dux
Hebron, Nebraska

Pork and Cabbage

1 tablespoon oil
2 cups shredded
   cabbage
1 onion, thinly
   sliced
2 stalks celery,
   thinly sliced
1 clove of garlic,
   chopped
¼ teaspoon ginger
1 cup thin cooked
   pork strips
1 tablespoon
   cornstarch
1 tablespoon soy sauce
2 chicken bouillon
   cubes

Heat oil in skillet or wok over medium heat. Add cabbage, onion, celery, garlic and ginger. Stir-fry for 3 to 5 minutes. Add pork. Stir-fry for 1 to 2 minutes. Blend cornstarch with ¼ cup cold water in bowl. Stir in soy sauce and bouillon cubes dissolved in ¾ cup boiling water. Add to pork and vegetables. Cook until sauce thickens, stirring constantly. Serve over steamed rice with additional soy sauce. Yield: 2 servings.

Approx per serving: Cal 326, Prot 24.8 gr, Fat 17.3 gr,
Chol 64.6 mg, Carbo 18.8 gr, Sod 1746.8 mg, Potas 754.9 mg.

Octavia Famuliner, Laureate Nu
Carrollton, Missouri

Pork Chop Dinner

4 ½-inch thick
   pork chops,
   trimmed
¼ cup chopped
   onion
¼ cup chopped
   green pepper
1½ cups canned
   tomatoes
½ cup rice
¼ teaspoon dry
   mustard
⅛ teaspoon allspice
⅛ teaspoon pepper

Brown pork chops on both sides in skillet; drain. Remove pork chops. Sauté onion and green pepper in skillet until tender. Add mixture of remaining ingredients and salt to taste; mix well. Arrange pork chops on top. Simmer, covered, for 30 minutes or until rice is tender. Yield: 4 servings.

Approx per serving: Cal 565, Prot 31.0 gr, Fat 42.6 gr,
Chol 105.5 mg, Carbo 12.5 gr, Sod 347.3 mg, Potas 755.3 mg.

Barbara Eberle, Mu Tau
Lombard, Illinois

Pork Chops in Cider

4 ½-inch thick
   loin pork chops
2 tablespoons
   margarine
2 red cooking
   apples, cut into
   quarters
1 medium onion,
   sliced
½ cup apple cider
½ teaspoon instant
   chicken bouillon
¼ teaspoon sage
½ teaspoon salt
½ cup half and half

Brown pork chops in margarine in skillet over medium-high heat; remove pork chops. Cook apples and onion in pan drippings until tender, stirring occasionally; remove apples and onion. Arrange pork chops in skillet. Add cider, bouillon, sage and salt. Bring to a boil; reduce heat. Simmer, covered, for 15 minutes. Arrange apples and onion around pork chops. Simmer for 5 minutes longer or until pork chops are tender. Remove to serving platter. Cook pan juices until reduced to about ½ cup. Stir in half and half. Cook until slightly thickened, stirring constantly. Spoon over pork chops. Garnish with parsley sprigs. Serve with corn muffins. Yield: 4 servings.

Approx per serving: Cal 687, Prot 30.9 gr, Fat 52.3 gr,
Chol 118.6 mg, Carbo 23.2 gr, Sod 516.6 mg, Potas 703.7 mg.

Helen Heath, Preceptor Upsilon
Muncie, Indiana

Pork Chops with Sauerkraut

6 lean pork chops,
   trimmed
1 large onion,
   sliced
1 29-ounce can
   sauerkraut
2 apples, sliced
4 potatoes, sliced

Brown pork chops in heavy skillet. Layer onion, sauerkraut, apples and potatoes over pork chops. Add ½ cup water and salt and pepper to taste. Cook, covered, over medium heat until potatoes are tender, adding a small amount of water if necessary. Yield: 6 servings.

Approx per serving: Cal 622, Prot 30.4 gr, Fat 38.5 gr,
Chol 93.7 mg, Carbo 39.6 gr, Sod 1121.7 mg, Potas 1236.4 mg.

Norma Jean Lane, Xi Alpha
Makakilo, Hawaii

Microwave Sausage and Peppers

6 brown and serve
 sausages, sliced
1 cup green pepper
 strips
1 medium onion,
 sliced

2 tablespoons oil
1 8-ounce can
 tomatoes
¾ cup minute rice
1 teaspoon basil
¼ teaspoon salt

Combine sausages, green pepper, onion and oil in 1½-quart glass dish. Microwave, covered, on High for 3 minutes. Add remaining ingredients and ½ cup water; mix well. Microwave, covered, for 5 minutes. Let stand, covered, for 5 minutes; fluff with fork. Yield: 2 servings.

Photograph for this recipe on page 104.

Szechwan Pork

2 teaspoons
 cornstarch
½ teaspoon salt
⅛ teaspoon white
 pepper
2 tablespoons dry
 Sherry
1½ pounds lean
 boneless pork,
 slivered
1½ teaspoons oil
2 tablespoons sugar
2 tablespoons
 vinegar
2 tablespoons dry
 Sherry
¼ cup soy sauce
6 tablespoons
 chicken broth

4 teaspoons
 cornstarch
2 tablespoons oil
2 cloves of garlic,
 minced
1 teaspoon minced
 fresh gingerroot
3 or 4 dried hot chili
 peppers
1 8-ounce can
 bamboo shoots,
 drained
8 to 10 green onions,
 cut into 1-inch pieces
1 carrot, cut into thin
 strips
1 tablespoon oil

Combine first 4 ingredients in bowl. Add pork; stir until coated. Add 1½ teaspoons oil; mix well. Let stand for 15 minutes. Combine sugar and next 5 ingredients in bowl; mix well. Set aside. Heat 2 tablespoons oil in skillet. Add garlic, gingerroot and chili peppers. Add pork. Stir-fry until brown. Remove pork. Stir-fry bamboo shoots, green onions and carrot in 1 tablespoon oil for 1 minute. Add pork and sugar mixture. Cook for 2 minutes or until thickened. Serve over rice. Yield: 4 servings.

Approx per serving: Cal 735, Prot 32.4 gr, Fat 54.8 gr, Chol 105.7 mg, Carbo 24.2 gr, Sod 1772.9 mg, Pot 1008.6 mg.

Rosemary Pareja, Epsilon Omega
Denver, Colorado

French Veal Stew

3 pounds lean veal,
 cut into 1-inch
 cubes
¼ cup Cognac
2 bay leaves
¼ teaspoon thyme
 leaves
¼ teaspoon cloves
1 onion, thinly
 sliced
2 carrots, thinly
 sliced
2 cups dry red wine

2 tablespoons oil
2 cups beef bouillon
1 teaspoon salt
2 tablespoons
 Worcestershire sauce
1 teaspoon soy sauce
2 teaspoons sugar
1 pound mushrooms,
 quartered
6 green onions,
 chopped
6 carrots, sliced
4 onions, sliced

Combine first 7 ingredients in large bowl. Add enough wine to cover. Marinate, covered, for 12 to 36 hours. Strain, reserving liquid; discard onion, carrots and bay leaves. Sauté veal in oil in Dutch oven until brown. Add reserved marinade, bouillon and next 4 ingredients. Bake, covered, at 350 degrees for 1½ to 2 hours or until veal is tender. Sauté remaining vegetables in skillet. Add to Dutch oven. Bake for 30 to 45 minutes longer. Serve with rice or noodles and fresh green salad. Yield: 8 servings.

Approx per serving: Cal 454, Prot 36.3 gr, Fat 18.1 gr, Chol 119.2 mg, Carbo 22.3 gr, Sod 654.4 mg, Potas 959.1 mg.

Nu Chapter
Thompson, Manitoba, Canada

Microwave Wheat-Crusted Quiche

¾ cup wheat germ
¾ cup flour
¼ teaspoon salt
½ cup shortening
10 slices crisp-
 fried bacon,
 crumbled
¼ cup minced onion

¾ cup shredded
 Swiss cheese
3 eggs
½ cup evaporated
 milk
½ teaspoon salt
⅛ teaspoon cayenne
 pepper

Mix wheat germ, flour and salt in bowl. Cut in shortening until crumbly. Press over bottom and side of 9-inch glass pie plate. Prick with fork. Microwave on High for 1½ to 2 minutes or until firm but not dry. Sprinkle bacon, onion and cheese over crust. Beat remaining ingredients in bowl until smooth. Pour into prepared dish. Microwave on Medium for 6 to 8 minutes or until set, turning once. Let stand for several minutes. Yield: 6 servings.

Approx per serving: Cal 468, Prot 17.2 gr, Fat 35.2 gr, Chol 158.2 mg, Carbo 21.4 gr, Sod 551.4 mg, Potas 279.9 mg.

Tina Steffen, Mu Zeta
Big Spring, Texas

Slim Baked Chicken

4 chicken breasts,
   skinned
½ teaspoon garlic
   salt
1 teaspoon
   paprika
½ cup lemon juice
2 teaspoons soy
   sauce
1 teaspoon basil
8 green olives,
   thinly sliced

Sprinkle both sides of chicken with garlic salt and paprika. Arrange rib side up in baking pan. Pour mixture of lemon juice, soy sauce and basil over chicken. Bake at 400 degrees for 20 minutes. Turn chicken; baste. Arrange olives on top. Bake for 20 minutes longer or until chicken is tender. Yield: 4 servings.

Approx per serving: Cal 195, Prot 33.6 gr, Fat 4.9 gr, Chol 82.9 mg, Carbo 2.8 gr, Sod 786.7 mg, Potas 490.8 mg.

Lisa Martiny, Delta Delta
May, Idaho

Microwave Barbecued Chicken

2 chicken breasts
Barbecue spice
Soy sauce
Thick and rich
   100% natural
   barbecue sauce

Place chicken in glass baking dish. Sprinkle with barbecue spice and soy sauce. Spoon barbecue sauce over each piece. Microwave, covered with waxed paper, on High for 22 minutes, turning chicken once. Let stand for 5 minutes before serving. Yield: 2 servings.

Barbara Fettinger, Xi Lambda Beta
Panama City, Florida

Skinny Week Chicken Barbecue

½ cup vinegar
2 medium onions,
   sliced
2 tablespoons
   Worcestershire
   sauce
1 teaspoon dry
   mustard
1 cup catsup
5 envelopes
   artificial sweetener
½ teaspoon pepper
6 chicken breasts,
   skinned
2 lemons, thinly
   sliced

Combine first 7 ingredients and 1 cup water in saucepan. Cook over medium heat for 5 minutes. Place chicken in greased 9x13-inch baking pan. Top with lemon slices. Pour prepared sauce over chicken. Bake, covered, at 350 degrees for 25 minutes. Turn chicken; baste with sauce. Bake, uncovered, for 15 minutes longer or until chicken is tender. Place chicken on serving plate. Serve with sauce. Yield: 6 servings.

Approx per serving: Cal 249, Prot 35.1 gr, Fat 3.9 gr, Chol 82.9 mg, Carbo 18.8 gr, Sod 538.2 mg, Potas 752.2 mg.

Carol McLennan, Preceptor Alpha Tau
Lawton, Oklahoma

Chicken Curry

4 chicken breasts
2 tablespoons
   butter
½ teaspoon (about)
   curry powder
1 can cream of
   mushroom soup
Juice of 1 lemon

Brown chicken in butter in skillet. Sprinkle with curry powder. Add mixture of soup and lemon juice. Simmer, covered, until chicken is tender. Thin sauce with a small amount of milk if necessary. Serve over hot rice. Garnish with chutney sauce, chopped peanuts and coconut. Yield: 4 servings.

Approx per serving: Cal 311, Prot 34.7 gr, Fat 15.3 gr, Chol 106.7 mg, Carbo 7.4 gr, Sod 729.7 mg, Potas 515.8 mg.

Edith J. Howell, Preceptor Theta Sigma
Glendale, California

Easy Chicken

6 chicken breasts
¼ cup soy sauce

1 can sodium-free
   diet orange drink

Arrange chicken in baking dish. Pour soy sauce and orange drink over chicken. Bake at 350 degrees until tender and brown, turning once. Yield: 6 servings.

Approx per serving: Cal 163, Prot 30.2 gr, Fat 3.3 gr, Chol 73.7 mg, Carbo 1.1 gr, Sod 938.7 mg, Potas 427.5 mg.

Margaret Mahoney, Laureate Phi
LaMarque, Texas

Chicken Italiano

1   14-ounce can
   tomatoes
½ teaspoon basil
½ teaspoon
   tarragon
¼ teaspoon pepper
1 clove of garlic,
   chopped
2 teaspoons oil
4 chicken breasts,
   skinned
2 tablespoons
   parsley flakes
½ cup shredded
   mozzarella
   cheese

Combine tomatoes, basil, tarragon and pepper in blender container. Process until smooth. Sauté garlic in oil in skillet for 1 minute. Add chicken, rib side up. Pour tomato sauce over top. Bring to a boil; reduce heat. Simmer for 15 minutes or until chicken is tender. Place chicken rib side up in baking dish. Stir parsley into tomato sauce in skillet. Pour over chicken. Sprinkle with mozzarella cheese. Broil for 1 minute or until cheese melts. Yield: 4 servings.

Approx per serving: Cal 264, Prot 37.4 gr, Fat 9.5 gr, Chol 95.4 mg, Carbo 5.5 gr, Sod 272.9 mg, Potas 692.1 mg.

Carolynne Russell, Eta
Calgary, Alberta, Canada

Main Dishes   93

Lemon Chicken

2 tablespoons oil
1 clove of garlic, minced
Grated rind and juice of 1 lemon
½ teaspoon thyme
2 tablespoons finely chopped parsley
6 chicken breasts

Sprinkle mixture of first 5 ingredients over chicken in large bowl. Marinate in refrigerator for 2 hours or longer, turning occasionally. Arrange chicken in greased baking dish. Pour marinade over chicken. Bake at 350 degrees for 1 hour or until chicken is tender, basting frequently. Sprinkle with parsley. Yield: 6 servings.

Approx per serving: Cal 218, Prot 33.3 gr, Fat 8.1 gr, Chol 82.9 mg, Carbo 1.1 gr, Sod 67.5 mg, Potas 450.1 mg.

Jerri Balsam, Beta
Miles City, Montana

Chicken with Mushrooms and Grapes

4 chicken breasts
4 chicken thighs
4 chicken legs
½ cup flour
3 tablespoons margarine
¼ cup minced onion
¼ cup chicken broth
¼ cup vermouth
8 ounces mushrooms, sliced
2 cups seedless grapes

Coat chicken with mixture of flour and salt and pepper to taste. Brown in margarine in skillet. Arrange chicken in shallow baking dish. Sauté onion in pan drippings. Add broth and vermouth. Bring to a boil. Pour over chicken. Bake, covered, for 40 minutes. Sauté mushrooms in skillet. Arrange mushrooms and grapes over chicken. Bake for 8 minutes longer. Yield: 12 servings.

Approx per serving: Cal 269, Prot 33.6 gr, Fat 9.0 gr, Chol 96.5 mg, Carbo 10.5 gr, Sod 146.8 mg, Potas 530.3 mg.

Nu Chapter
Thompson, Manitoba, Canada

Chicken à L'Orange

1½ cups tomato juice
¼ cup dried onion flakes
½ cup chopped green pepper
½ cup chopped celery
¼ cup frozen orange juice concentrate
1 teaspoon mustard
2 tablespoons soy sauce
2 tablespoons Worcestershire sauce
½ teaspoon Tabasco sauce
Garlic powder to taste
Pinch of sugar
2 chicken breasts

Combine tomato juice, onion, green pepper, celery, orange juice concentrate and seasonings in saucepan. Cook until thickened, stirring frequently. Place chicken breasts in baking dish. Pour sauce over chicken. Bake at 350 degrees for 1½ hours. Yield: 1 serving.

Approx per serving: Cal 266, Prot 27.5 gr, Fat 3.1 gr, Chol 55.3 mg, Carbo 33.4 gr, Sod 1956.0 mg, Potas 1387.7 mg.

Marsha Jordan, Xi Eta Upsilon
Steubenville, Ohio

Oriental Chicken with Peaches

1 16-ounce can sliced peaches
1 4-ounce can mushrooms
6 chicken breasts
½ cup flour
¼ cup oil
1 green pepper, chopped
2 tablespoons chopped onion
2 tablespoons soy sauce
2 tablespoons vinegar
1 tablespoon cornstarch
⅓ cup blanched slivered almonds

Drain peaches and mushrooms, reserving ½ cup liquid. Coat chicken with flour. Brown in oil in skillet; remove chicken and set aside. Sauté mushrooms and green pepper in pan drippings for 1 minute. Add chicken. Pour mixture of onion, soy sauce, vinegar and reserved liquid over chicken. Simmer, covered, for 40 minutes or until tender. Add peaches. Cook for 5 minutes longer. Remove chicken to serving tray. Stir mixture of cornstarch and 1 tablespoon water into pan drippings. Cook until thickened, stirring constantly. Pour over chicken. Sprinkle with almonds. Yield: 6 servings.

Approx per serving: Cal 413, Prot 36.5 gr, Fat 16.4 gr, Chol 82.9 mg, Carbo 29.6 gr, Sod 510.9 mg, Potas 659.8 mg.

Carol Ann Robinson, Xi Psi
North Vancouver, British Columbia, Canada

Peachy Chicken

6 chicken breasts
3 chicken drumsticks
3 chicken thighs
1 16-ounce can diet-pack cling peaches
2 tablespoons lemon juice
1 teaspoon soy sauce

Arrange chicken in single layer in 8x12-inch baking pan. Drain peaches, reserving juice. Combine peach juice, lemon juice and soy sauce. Brush half the mixture over chicken. Bake at 400 degrees for 1 hour, basting frequently with remaining juice and pan juices. Arrange peach halves around chicken. Brush with pan juices. Bake for 5 minutes longer. Yield: 9 servings.

Approx per serving: Cal 266, Prot 43.5 gr, Fat 7.2 gr, Chol 124.1 mg, Carbo 4.4 gr, Sod 159.2 mg, Potas 606.7 mg.

Sharon Driver, Gamma Iota
Sidney, British Columbia, Canada

Oriental Chicken Light

4 chicken breasts,
  skinned
1 small onion, cut
  into quarters
1 stalk celery,
  chopped
¼ teaspoon salt
1 tablespoon oil
1 pound Chinese
  cabbage, chopped

8 ounces snow
  peas, trimmed
¼ cup soy sauce
¼ cup chopped
  roasted red
  pepper
5 green onions,
  chopped
4 cups cooked rice

Cook chicken with onion, celery and salt in water to cover in saucepan for 15 minutes or until tender; cool. Cut chicken into bite-sized pieces. Remove vegetables; discard. Reserve ¼ cup chicken broth. Heat wok or skillet over high heat for 30 seconds. Add oil. Heat for 30 seconds longer. Reduce heat to medium. Add cabbage. Stir-fry for 2 minutes. Add snow peas, chicken stock and soy sauce. Stir-fry for 2 minutes. Add chicken, red peppers and green onions. Stir-fry for 1 minute. Spoon over hot rice on serving plates. Yield: 4 servings.

Approx per serving: Cal 470, Prot 40.1 gr, Fat 7.6 gr, Chol 82.9 mg, Carbo 58.0 gr, Sod 2315.0 mg, Potas 924.4 mg. Nutritional information does not include snow peas.

Gloria M. Giovelli
Winter Haven, Florida

Poppy Seed Chicken

6 chicken breasts,
  cooked, chopped
2 cans mushroom
  soup
1 cup sour cream

½ cup melted butter
1 stack butter crackers,
  crushed
Poppy seed to taste

Place chicken in 9x13-inch baking dish. Combine soup, sour cream and butter in bowl; mix well. Pour over chicken. Sprinkle cracker crumbs and poppy seed over top. Bake at 350 degrees for 45 minutes. Yield: 4 servings.

Approx per serving: Cal 842, Prot 50.9 gr, Fat 56.3 gr, Chol 218.8 mg, Carbo 32.4 gr, Sod 1866.0 mg, Potas 816.0 mg.

Kay Suddarth
Hayti, Missouri

Microwave Chicken Tetrazzini

2 chicken breasts
¼ cup flour
¼ cup corn oil
  margarine,
  melted
2 cups evaporated
  skim milk
1 cup shredded
  mozzarella
  cheese

1 4-ounce can
  mushrooms,
  drained
1 8-ounce
  package
  spaghetti,
  cooked
¼ cup Parmesan
  cheese

Spray 2-quart casserole with vegetable cooking spray. Place chicken in prepared casserole. Microwave, covered, on High for 10 minutes; cool. Shred chicken. Blend flour into margarine in glass dish. Stir in milk. Microwave on Medium until bubbly and thickened. Stir in cheese. Microwave until cheese melts. Stir in mushrooms, chicken and spaghetti. Spoon into glass baking dish. Microwave, covered, on High for 15 minutes. Sprinkle with Parmesan cheese. Let stand for 5 minutes before serving. Yield: 6 servings.

Approx per serving: Cal 378, Prot 22.3 gr, Fat 16.7 gr, Chol 49.0 mg, Carbo 33.4 gr, Sod 137.0 mg, Potas 244.7 mg.

Susan Crewe, Laureate Alpha Theta
Springfield, Ohio

Chicken Breasts Veronique

8 chicken breasts,
  skinned
1 cup cracker
  crumbs
½ teaspoon tarragon
½ teaspoon salt
¼ teaspoon pepper
3 tablespoons (or
  less) margarine
¼ cup chopped
  onion

½ cup chicken
  broth
½ cup dry white
  wine
2 cups sliced fresh
  mushrooms
2 tablespoons
  margarine
2 cups green
  grapes

Coat chicken with mixture of cracker crumbs, tarragon and salt and pepper. Brown in 3 tablespoons margarine in skillet. Place chicken in shallow baking pan. Sauté onion in pan drippings; drain. Add broth and wine. Bring to a boil. Pour over chicken. Bake at 375 degrees for 30 minutes. Sauté mushrooms in 2 tablespoons margarine in skillet. Arrange sautéed mushrooms and grapes around chicken. Bake for 10 minutes longer. Yield: 8 servings.

Approx per serving: Cal 319, Prot 34.9 gr, Fat 12.0 gr, Chol 83.1 mg, Carbo 15.4 gr, Sod 449.1 mg. Potas 607.5 mg.

Betty Kelly
Fort Dodge, Iowa

Chicken with Wild Rice

1 large green
  pepper, coarsely
  chopped
4 stalks celery,
  coarsely chopped
1½ cups chicken
  broth

⅔ cup wild rice
4 chicken breasts
2 tablespoons soy
  sauce
2 green onions,
  chopped

Combine green pepper, celery, broth and rice in large casserole. Brush chicken with soy sauce. Place on rice mixture. Bake, covered, at 350 degrees for 1½ hours. Sprinkle with green onions. Yield: 4 servings.

Approx per serving: Cal 291, Prot 38.4 gr, Fat 4.0 gr, Chol 84.1 mg, Carbo 24.3 gr, Sod 1141.5 mg, Potas 718.0 mg.

Lucille Burkett, Laureate Alpha Epsilon
Effingham, Illinois

Microwave Chicken and Broccoli

4 chicken breast
  filets, cut into
  strips
3 cups broccoli
  flowerets
3 green onions,
  sliced
4 ounces
  mushrooms,
  sliced

3 tablespoons
  chicken stock
1 tablespoon soy
  sauce
1 tablespoon
  cornstarch
1 tablespoon sugar
¼ teaspoon garlic
  powder

Place chicken in 2½-quart casserole. Microwave, covered with waxed paper, on Medium-High for 10 minutes or until tender, stirring once. Add broccoli and green onions. Microwave, covered, on High for 4 to 5 minutes or until broccoli is tender-crisp. Stir in mushrooms. Add mixture of remaining ingredients; toss to coat. Microwave on High for 2 to 3 minutes or until sauce thickens, stirring several times. Yield: 4 servings.

Approx per serving: Cal 246, Prot 38.4 gr, Fat 4.1 gr, Chol 83.1 mg, Carbo 14.3 gr, Sod 466.7 mg, Potas 1024.9 mg.

Alexis Koester, Xi Alpha Alpha
Kent, Washington

Barbecued Chicken

2 envelopes
  unflavored
  gelatin
1 tablespoon
  paprika
½ teaspoon dry
  mustard
½ teaspoon garlic
  powder

½ teaspoon onion
  powder
Artificial sweetener
  to taste
4 chicken breast
  filets
Juice of 1 lemon
¼ teaspoon cider
  vinegar

Combine gelatin, seasonings and artificial sweetener to taste in bowl. Dip chicken in mixture of lemon juice and vinegar. Roll in dry mixture to coat. Place in 9x13-inch baking pan. Bake at 350 degrees for 45 minutes or until tender. Yield: 4 servings.

Approx per serving: Cal 190, Prot 36.2 gr, Fat 3.6 gr, Chol 82.9 mg, Carbo 1.2 gr, Sod 70.5 mg, Potas 453.9 mg.

Mildred Ormiston
Kismet, Kansas

Chicken Cacciatore

2 cups canned
  tomatoes
½ cup tomato sauce
½ cup finely
  chopped onion
1 teaspoon
  chopped parsley

¼ teaspoon garlic
  powder
¼ teaspoon pepper
4 chicken breast
  filets

Combine tomatoes, tomato sauce, onion and seasonings in saucepan. Simmer for 10 to 15 minutes or until onion is tender. Place filets in baking pan. Top with tomato sauce. Bake, covered, at 350 degrees for 1 hour or until chicken is tender. Serve with hot rice. Yield: 4 servings.

Approx per serving: Cal 217, Prot 35.1 gr, Fat 3.9 gr, Chol 82.9 mg, Carbo 9.2 gr, Sod 380.7 mg, Potas 826.7 mg.

Yvonne Sorge, Xi Kappa Theta
Lebanon, Ohio

Slim Chicken Cacciatore

¾ cup sliced fresh
  mushrooms
½ cup canned
  tomatoes
½ cup chopped
  green pepper
¼ cup chopped
  onion
3 tablespoons dry
  red wine

1 clove of garlic,
  minced
½ teaspoon
  oregano
4 chicken breast
  filets
Paprika to taste
2 teaspoons
  cornstarch

Combine first 7 ingredients with salt and pepper to taste in skillet. Place chicken on top. Bring to a boil; reduce heat. Simmer, covered, for 25 minutes. Remove chicken to serving plate; sprinkle with paprika. Stir cornstarch dissolved in 2 tablespoons cold water into pan drippings. Cook until thickened, stirring constantly. Cook for 1 minute longer. Spoon over chicken. Yield: 4 servings.

Approx per serving: Cal 229, Prot 34.3 gr, Fat 3.7 gr, Chol 82.9 mg, Carbo 6.8 gr, Sod 112.9 mg, Potas 628.4 mg.

Karen Jones, Xi Eta Psi
Akron, Ohio

Microwave California Chicken

4 chicken breast
  filets
2 teaspoons lemon
  juice
1 teaspoon dried
  onion flakes
Basil and pepper
  to taste

⅔ cup shredded
  sharp Cheddar
  cheese
½ avocado, thinly
  sliced
4 thin tomato
  slices

Arrange chicken breasts in glass baking dish. Sprinkle with lemon juice, onion flakes, basil and pepper. Microwave, covered, with waxed paper, on High for 7½ minutes or until chicken is tender, turning dish twice. Sprinkle with half the cheese. Arrange avocado and tomato on top. Microwave, covered, for 2½ minutes. Sprinkle with remaining cheese. Let stand, covered, for 5 minutes. Yield: 4 servings.

Approx per serving: Cal 338, Prot 40.5 gr, Fat 15.9 gr, Chol 101.7 mg, Carbo 8.0 gr, Sod 188.1 mg, Potas 803.3 mg.

Dijon Chicken

16 ounces
mushrooms,
sliced
2 pounds chicken
breast filets

1½ cups white
wine
1 8-ounce jar
Dijon mustard

Layer mushrooms and chicken in 9x13-inch baking dish. Pour mixture of wine and mustard over chicken. Marinate for 15 minutes. Bake at 350 degrees for 35 minutes. Serve with wild rice. Yield: 8 servings.

Approx per serving: Cal 219, Prot 36.1 gr, Fat 5.1 gr, Chol 82.9 mg, Carbo 4.7 gr, Sod 451.7 mg, Potas 712.0 mg.

Susan Emsiek, Tri Alpha
Long Beach, California

Chicken Divan

¾ pound chicken
breast filets,
cut into strips
2 teaspoons oil
1 tablespoon dry
Sherry
1 can cream of
chicken soup

1 10-ounce
package broccoli
spears
1½ cups minute
rice
1 tablespoon
Parmesan cheese

Brown chicken in oil in skillet, stirring frequently. Add Sherry, soup, broccoli and 1 cup water. Bring to a full boil. Stir in rice; remove from heat. Let stand, covered, for 5 minutes. Spoon into serving bowl. Sprinkle with Parmesan cheese. Yield: 4 servings.

Approx per serving: Cal 376, Prot 32.3 gr, Fat 9.3 gr, Chol 69.9 mg, Carbo 38.4 gr, Sod 678.7 mg, Potas 549.4 mg.

Angie Cyr, Xi Delta Tau
Stillwater, Oklahoma

Best Dressed Chicken

1 1-pound loaf
bread, cubed
½ teaspoon salt
½ teaspoon pepper
1 teaspoon sage
1 teaspoon celery
salt

½ cup melted
butter
8 chicken breast
filets
¼ cup melted
butter

Combine bread cubes, seasonings, ½ cup melted butter and 1½ cups hot water in bowl; mix well. Dip chicken into ¼ cup melted butter. Layer dressing mixture and chicken in greased 9x13-inch baking pan. Add salt and pepper to taste. Bake at 350 degrees for 1 hour. Turn chicken. Bake for 1 hour longer. Yield: 8 servings.

Approx per serving: Cal 480, Prot 38.2 gr, Fat 22.6 gr, Chol 137.9 mg, Carbo 28.7 gr, Sod 964.6 mg, Potas 496.0 mg.

Nelsa Mullin, Preceptor Alpha Kappa
Loveland, Colorado

Swiss Chicken Breasts

8 chicken breast
filets
2 cans cream of
mushroom soup
8 ounces Swiss
cheese slices

1 package chicken-
flavored stove-
top stuffing mix,
prepared

Layer chicken, soup, cheese and stuffing in 9x13-inch baking pan. Bake, covered, at 350 degrees for 1 hour. Remove cover. Bake for 30 minutes longer. Yield: 8 servings.

Approx per serving: Cal 613, Prot 46.9 gr, Fat 32.7 gr, Chol 162.1 mg, Carbo 31.7 gr, Sod 1488.0 mg, Potas 585.1 mg.

Shirley I. Welander, Alpha
Billings, Montana

Grilled Chicken with Vegetables

4 chicken breast
filets
4 sprigs of thyme
2 small zucchini,
thickly sliced
4 large mushrooms,
thickly sliced

1 sweet red pepper,
cut into 8 strips
2 onions,
thinly sliced
2 tablespoons oil

Place chicken in shallow glass dish. Sprinkle with thyme. Add vegetables. Drizzle oil over top. Sprinkle with salt and pepper to taste. Marinate for 1 hour, turning and basting occasionally. Drain, reserving oil. Place chicken in broiler pan. Arrange vegetables around chicken. Broil until chicken is tender, basting occasionally. Season with salt and pepper to taste. Yield: 4 servings.

Vicky Jager, Zeta Eta
Eureka, California

Chicken-Beef Kabobs

4 chicken breast
filets, cubed
1½ pounds cubed
beef chuck
2 green peppers,
cut into chunks
16 mushrooms
½ cup soy sauce
6 tablespoons
white wine

¼ cup oil
1½ teaspoons
mixed herb
seasoning
1 teaspoon grated
gingerroot
2 cloves of garlic,
minced
½ teaspoon onion
powder

Thread chicken, beef, green peppers and mushrooms onto skewers. Marinate in mixture of remaining ingredients for several hours or overnight. Grill over hot coals for 3 to 4 minutes on each side. Yield: 8 servings.

Approx per serving: Cal 237, Prot 23.5 gr, Fat 9.4 gr, Chol 41.5 mg, Carbo 12.8 gr, Sod 729.9 mg, Potas 1239.2 mg.

Kathy Nelson, Lambda Chi
Dayton, Ohio

Microwave Chicken Mandarin

4 chicken breast
  filets
½ teaspoon garlic
  powder
¼ teaspoon
  paprika
½ cup orange
  juice
2 tablespoons
  white wine
1 teaspoon
  tarragon
1 teaspoon
  cornstarch

¼ teaspoon grated
  orange rind
1   9-ounce
  package frozen
  broccoli spears,
  thawed
1   11-ounce can
  mandarin
  oranges, drained
2 tablespoons
  toasted sliced
  almonds

Flatten chicken breasts. Place in 2-quart glass baking dish. Sprinkle with garlic powder and paprika. Microwave, covered with waxed paper, on High for 4 minutes. Combine orange juice, wine, tarragon, cornstarch and orange rind in glass bowl. Microwave on High for 2 to 3 minutes or until thickened. Pour over chicken. Arrange broccoli on top of chicken. Top with mandarin oranges and almonds. Microwave for 2 to 3 minutes or until chicken is tender. Yield: 4 servings.

Approx per serving: Cal 258, Prot 36.9 gr, Fat 6.1 gr, Chol 82.9 mg, Carbo 12.3 gr, Sod 81.3 mg, Potas 724.8 mg.

Shirley Melton, Xi Gamma Zeta
Garland, Texas

Mock Abalone

4 chicken breast
  filets
1 teaspoon garlic
  powder
¼ cup chopped
  green onion tops

1   8-ounce bottle
  of clam juice
¼ cup flour
2 tablespoons oil

Flatten chicken breasts. Place in glass baking dish. Sprinkle with garlic powder and green onions. Pour clam juice over top. Chill, covered with foil, for 24 hours. Drain; remove green onions. Dip chicken in flour. Brown in oil in skillet, turning once. Yield: 4 servings.

Approx per serving: Cal 276, Prot 35.5 gr, Fat 10.5 gr, Chol 88.3 mg, Carbo 7.7 gr, Sod 307.7 mg, Potas 452.8 mg.

Cameron Stimson, Xi Theta
Mayfield, Kentucky

Microwave Chicken Breasts in Mushroom Sauce

4 chicken breast
  filets
Pepper to taste
½ cup sliced
  mushrooms

3 medium carrots,
  thinly sliced
¼ cup milk
1 can cream of
  chicken soup

Place chicken in 1½-quart glass baking dish. Sprinkle with pepper. Top with mushrooms and carrots. Pour in milk. Spoon soup over top. Microwave, covered with waxed paper, on High for 15 minutes or until carrots and chicken are tender. Serve over rice or noodles. Yield: 4 servings.

Approx per serving: Cal 268, Prot 36.3 gr, Fat 7.8 gr, Chol 91.0 mg, Carbo 11.4 gr, Sod 704.3 mg, Potas 723.3 mg.

Sandra Crosby, Xi Epsilon Sigma
Oscoda, Michigan

Chicken Nuggets

3 chicken breast
  filets
½ cup diet
  margarine
½ cup dry bread
  crumbs

¼ cup Parmesan
  cheese
2 teaspoons MSG
1 teaspoon salt
1 teaspoon thyme
1 teaspoon basil

Cut chicken into bite-sized pieces. Dip in melted margarine. Roll in mixture of crumbs, Parmesan cheese and spices. Place on baking sheet. Bake at 400 degrees for 20 minutes. Yield: 2 servings.

Approx per serving: Cal 437, Prot 61.4 gr, Fat 10.4 gr, Chol 139.8 mg, Carbo 18.8 gr, Sod 2323.7 mg, Potas 707.6 mg.

Vickie Stonestreet, Beta Psi
Albemarle, North Carolina

Orange Chicken

1¼ pounds chicken
  breast filets
8 teaspoons
  reduced-calorie
  margarine
2 cups sliced
  mushrooms
2 teaspoons flour
¼ cup frozen orange
  juice concentrate

2 chicken bouillon
  cubes
½ cup thinly
  sliced green
  onions
1 cup mandarin
  orange sections

Brown chicken in margarine in skillet; remove chicken. Sauté mushrooms in pan drippings until liquid evaporates. Sprinkle with flour; stir quickly. Stir in ⅔ cup water gradually. Add orange juice concentrate and bouillon, stirring constantly. Bring to a boil; reduce heat. Add chicken. Simmer for 3 minutes. Spoon onto serving platter. Sprinkle with green onions. Arrange oranges over top. Yield: 4 servings.

Approx per serving: Cal 201, Prot 27.3 gr, Fat 3.0 gr, Chol 63.7 mg, Carbo 15.7 gr, Sod 537.5 mg, Potas 677.3 mg.

Becky Laverty, Omicron Tau
Kimberling City, Missouri

Chicken Parmesan

6 chicken breast
  filets
2 eggs, beaten
½ cup flour
¾ cup fine bread
  crumbs
¼ cup oil
2 cups tomato
  sauce
Pinch of basil

¼ teaspoon
  oregano
⅛ teaspoon garlic
  powder
½ cup Parmesan
  cheese
8 ounces
  mozzarella
  cheese, sliced

Flatten filets to ¼-inch thickness. Cut into finger-sized pieces. Beat eggs with salt and pepper to taste. Coat filets with flour, dip into egg mixture and roll in crumbs. Brown in oil in skillet; drain. Place in baking dish. Combine tomato sauce and seasonings in skillet. Simmer for 10 minutes. Spoon around filets. Sprinkle with Parmesan cheese. Bake, covered, at 350 degrees for 30 minutes. Top with mozzarella cheese. Bake, uncovered, for 10 minutes longer. Yield: 8 servings.

Approx per serving: Cal 416, Prot 38.2 gr, Fat 15.0 gr, Chol 157.9 mg, Carbo 18.8 gr, Sod 633.4 mg, Potas 625.1 mg.

Patricia Andersen, Xi Gamma Lambda
Cobourg, Ontario, Canada

Chicken Breasts with Grape Sauce

8 chicken breast
  filets
¼ cup melted
  margarine
1½ cups wild rice,
  cooked
8 1-ounce slices
  ham
3 tablespoons melted
  margarine

3 tablespoons flour
1½ cups chicken
  broth
2 tablespoons
  lemon juice
2 tablespoons
  sugar
1 cup seedless
  grape halves

Sprinkle filets with salt and pepper to taste. Place in foil-lined broiler pan. Brush with melted margarine. Broil 3 to 4 inches from heat source for 15 minutes. Turn filets. Brush with remaining melted margarine. Broil for 10 minutes or until tender. Layer wild rice, ham and broiled filets on serving plate. Blend 3 tablespoons margarine, flour and salt to taste in saucepan. Stir in broth gradually. Cook until thickened, stirring constantly. Stir in lemon juice and sugar. Fold in grapes. Spoon over filets. Yield: 8 servings.

Approx per serving: Cal 491, Prot 44.1 gr, Fat 20.3 gr, Chol 109.1 mg, Carbo 32.0 gr, Sod 587.4 mg, Potas 614.4 mg.

Ruth Neumann, Preceptor Gamma Epsilon
DeKalb, Illinois

Microwave Arroz con Pollo

½ pound chicken
  breast filets,
  slivered
½ cup chopped
  onion
1 clove of garlic,
  minced

1 tablespoon oil
¾ cup minute rice
¾ cup frozen green
  peas, thawed
1 16-ounce can
  stewed tomatoes
¼ teaspoon salt

Combine chicken, onion, garlic and oil in glass dish. Microwave, covered, on High for 2 minutes. Stir in remaining ingredients. Microwave, covered, for 5 minutes. Let stand, covered, for 5 minutes; fluff with fork. Spoon into serving dish. Garnish with orange sections and avocado slices. Yield: 2 servings.

Photograph for this recipe on page 104.

Anne's Chicken and Rice

1 package long
  grain and wild
  rice mix
2 chicken bouillon
  cubes

4 chicken breast
  filets
1 cup seasoned
  bread crumbs

Cook rice according to package directions. Remove from heat before all water is absorbed. Spread rice in bottom of 9x13-inch baking pan. Dissolve bouillon cubes in 1 cup boiling water. Pour over rice. Roll chicken in bread crumbs. Arrange over rice. Bake at 350 degrees for 1 hour. Yield: 4 servings.

Anne Garrison-Ross, Xi Kappa Eta
Troy, Ohio

Chicken Cordon Bleu

8 chicken breast filets
8 teaspoons
  chopped parsley
8 thin slices
  mozzarella cheese
4 thin slices boiled
  ham, cut into
  halves

1 tablespoon
  reduced-calorie
  mayonnaise
¼ cup seasoned
  bread crumbs

Flatten chicken breasts. Sprinkle with parsley. Top each with slice of cheese and slice of ham. Roll tightly to enclose filling. Dip each roll in mixture of mayonnaise and 1 tablespoon warm water. Coat with bread crumbs. Place seam side down on greased baking sheet. Bake at 425 degrees for 15 to 20 minutes or until brown. Serve with white sauce. Yield: 8 servings.

Approx per serving: Cal 276, Prot 39.6 gr, Fat 10.6 gr, Chol 108.0 mg, Carbo 3.0 gr, Sod 206.4 mg, Potas 457.3 mg.

Lisa Martiny, Delta Delta
May, Idaho

Main Dishes 99

Chicken Hmmmmmmm

4 chicken breast
  filets
4 teaspoons
  parsley flakes
⅛ teaspoon garlic
  salt
¼ cup melted
  margarine
1 cup herb-seasoned
  stuffing mix

Season filets with parsley and garlic salt. Roll up; secure with toothpicks. Dip in margarine. Coat with stuffing mix. Place in greased baking dish. Sprinkle with remaining stuffing mix. Moisten lightly with water. Bake at 325 degrees for 30 to 40 minutes or until chicken is tender. Yield: 4 servings.

Approx per serving: Cal 342, Prot 35.5 gr, Fat 15.7 gr, Chol 83.6 mg, Carbo 12.7 gr, Sod 504.2 mg, Potas 464.9 mg.

Margie Gugino Hendricks, Xi Beta Tau
Little Rock, Arkansas

Crab-Stuffed Chicken Breasts

8 6-ounce chicken
  breast filets
½ cup thinly sliced
  green onions
4 ounces
  mushrooms,
  thinly sliced
¼ cup margarine
3 tablespoons flour
½ cup chicken
  broth
½ cup milk
½ cup dry white
  wine
1 6-ounce can
  crab meat,
  drained
1⅓ cups fine dry
  bread crumbs
1⅓ cups finely
  chopped parsley
1 cup shredded
  Swiss cheese

Flatten filets to ¼-inch thickness. Sauté green onions and mushrooms in margarine in skillet until tender. Stir in flour. Stir in broth, milk and wine gradually. Cook until thickened, stirring constantly. Add salt and pepper to taste. Mix ¼ cup mushroom sauce with crab meat, bread crumbs and parsley in bowl. Spoon onto filets. Roll to enclose filling. Place seam side down in 8x12-inch baking dish. Pour remaining mushroom sauce over top. Sprinkle with cheese. Bake, covered, at 400 degrees for 40 minutes or until tender. Yield: 8 servings.

Approx per serving: Cal 401, Prot 44.8 gr, Fat 15.3 gr, Chol 123.0 mg, Carbo 17.6 gr, Sod 657.4 mg, Potas 672.4 mg.

Joan R. McDonald, Xi Beta Rho
Bellevue, Washington

Microwave Chicken Roll-Ups

4 chicken breast
  filets
¼ teaspoon garlic
  powder
2 slices mozzarella
  cheese, cut into
  halves
12 asparagus
  spears
¼ cup Parmesan
  cheese
¼ teaspoon
  paprika

Flatten chicken breasts. Sprinkle with garlic powder. Top with cheese and asparagus spears. Roll to enclose filling. Secure with toothpicks. Place seam side down in glass casserole. Microwave, loosely covered, on High for 3 minutes. Sprinkle with Parmesan cheese and paprika. Let stand for 5 minutes. Yield: 4 servings.

Approx per serving: Cal 257, Prot 39.9 gr, Fat 9.0 gr, Chol 102.5 mg, Carbo 2.2 gr, Sod 180.1 mg, Potas 535.5 mg.

Jane Dieter, Xi Delta
Baltimore, Maryland

Stuffed Chicken Breasts

6 chicken breast
  filets
1 package stove-
  top stuffing mix,
  prepared
¼ cup flour
2 eggs, beaten
¼ cup milk
2 cups fine cracker
  crumbs
½ cup oil

Slit each chicken breast filet to make pocket. Fill with stuffing. Fold to enclose filling. Roll in flour. Dip in mixture of eggs and milk. Roll in cracker crumbs. Cook in oil in skillet over low heat for about 1 hour or until tender, turning frequently. Drain on paper towel. Place on serving plate. Yield: 6 servings.

Approx per serving: Cal 823, Prot 44.4 gr, Fat 47.2 gr, Chol 228.4 mg, Carbo 54.5 gr, Sod 1185.7 mg, Potas 584.7 mg.

Shirley I. Welander, Alpha
Billings, Montana

Chicken Roma

1 pound chicken
  breast filets
½ cup reduced-
  calorie Italian
  dressing
¼ cup chopped
  onion
2 tablespoons
  reduced-calorie
  margarine
1 medium
  zucchini, sliced
1 cup sliced
  mushrooms
1 large tomato, cut
  into wedges
6 1-ounce slices
  reduced-calorie
  process cheese,
  cut into strips

Cut chicken into strips. Marinate in Italian dressing in bowl for 30 minutes. Drain, reserving marinade. Sauté onion in margarine until tender. Add chicken. Cook, covered, over medium heat for 5 minutes. Add vegetables and reserved marinade. Cook until zucchini is tender, stirring constantly; remove from heat. Arrange cheese on top. Let stand, covered, for 2 minutes or until cheese melts. Garnish with parsley. Serve over hot rice or noodles. Yield: 4 servings.

Approx per serving: Cal 363, Prot 44.6 gr, Fat 15.8 gr, Chol 86.4 mg, Carbo 9.4 gr, Sod 985.6 mg, Potas 885.1 mg.

Bobbie Bishop, XP940
Lovington, New Mexico

Microwave Marinated Chicken Sandwich

2 chicken breast filets
⅓ cup reduced-calorie Italian salad dressing
2 whole wheat sandwich buns
2 teaspoons reduced-calorie mayonnaise
2 teaspoons mustard
2 lettuce leaves

Combine chicken and salad dressing in shallow dish. Marinate, covered, for 6 to 8 hours in refrigerator. Drain. Preheat browning dish in microwave on High for 5 minutes. Place chicken in dish. Microwave on High for 2 minutes. Turn chicken over; turn dish ½ turn. Microwave on High for 2 to 3 minutes or until brown. Spread buns with mayonnaise and mustard. Place chicken filet and lettuce leaf on each bun. Yield: 2 servings.

Approx per serving: Cal 414, Prot 38.8 gr, Fat 17.3 gr, Chol 87.1 mg, Carbo 23.0 gr, Sod 407.0 mg, Potas 614.1 mg. Nutritional information does not include reduced-calorie salad dressing used as marinade.

Kathy Gabbard
DeQueen, Arkansas

Chicken Scallopini

2 tablespoons Parmesan cheese
2 tablespoons seasoned bread crumbs
4 chicken breast filets
½ cup dry Sherry

Combine cheese and bread crumbs in bowl; mix well. Moisten chicken; coat with cheese mixture. Place in greased skillet. Cook over medium-low heat for 8 minutes or until golden, turning once. Remove to serving plate. Pour Sherry into skillet. Cook over high heat until reduced by ½. Pour over chicken. Garnish with parsley and additional Parmesan cheese. Yield: 4 servings.

Approx per serving: Cal 243, Prot 35.0 gr, Fat 4.7 gr, Chol 86.8 mg, Carbo 4.8 gr, Sod 120.6 mg, Potas 464.4 mg.

Lynn Collins, Xi Gamma
Winston-Salem, North Carolina

Chicken Breast Schnitzel

6 chicken breast filets
2 tablespoons flour
1½ teaspoons salt
¼ teaspoon pepper
2 eggs, beaten
2 cups cracker meal
2 tablespoons margarine
2 tablespoons oil
½ cup dry white wine
¼ cup chicken broth
2 tablespoons chopped parsley
2 tablespoons chopped chives

Flatten chicken breasts. Mix flour, salt and pepper in bowl. Add eggs; beat until smooth. Dip chicken into batter; coat with cracker meal. Place on baking sheet. Chill for 15 minutes. Sauté in margarine and oil in skillet for 8 minutes or until golden brown, turning once. Drain, reserving 2 tablespoons drippings. Place on warm platter. Blend wine and broth into reserved pan drippings. Deglaze skillet. Add parsley and chives. Simmer for 1 minute. Pour over warm chicken. Yield: 4 servings.

Approx per serving: Cal 393, Prot 37.9 gr, Fat 17 gr, Chol 167.0 mg, Carbo 19.3 gr, Sod 965.3 mg, Potas 404.9 mg.

Diane Elizabeth Linden, Delta Nu
Waupaca, Wisconsin

Chicken-Sour Cream Casserole

3 ounces dried beef
6 chicken breast filets
6 slices bacon, crisp-fried
1 cup sour cream
1 can cream of chicken soup
6 large mushrooms, sliced
6 green onions, chopped

Layer dried beef, chicken and bacon in casserole. Heat mixture of sour cream and soup in saucepan over low heat. Pour over chicken. Sauté mushrooms and green onions in skillet. Sprinkle over top. Bake at 350 degrees for 1 hour. Yield: 6 servings.

Approx per serving: Cal 372, Prot 39.2 gr, Fat 19.4 gr, Chol 116.0 mg, Carbo 8.3 gr, Sod 667.8 mg, Potas 641.4 mg.

Loretta Kirchen, Alpha Alpha
Anthony, Kansas

Chicken and Cashews

¼ cup dry Sherry
¼ cup soy sauce
2 tablespoons dark corn syrup
1 tablespoon vinegar
4 teaspoons cornstarch
¼ cup peanut oil
4 chicken breast filets, cut into pieces
½ cup chopped green pepper
½ cup cashews
3 green onions, chopped
2 cloves of garlic, minced
½ teaspoon ginger

Mix first 5 ingredients and ¼ cup water in bowl; set aside. Heat oil in wok for 2 minutes. Add chicken. Stir-fry for 30 seconds. Push to side. Add green pepper and cashews. Stir-fry for 30 seconds. Add green onions, garlic and ginger. Stir-fry for 1 minute. Add soy sauce mixture. Cook until sauce is thickened, stirring constantly. Serve over hot rice. Yield: 4 servings.

Approx per serving: Cal 478, Prot 37.5 gr, Fat 25.4 gr, Chol 82.9 mg, Carbo 20.9 gr, Sod 1391.9 mg, Potas 695.8 mg.

Kathy Nelson, Lambda Chi
Dayton, Ohio

Cora's Chicken-Vegetable Stir Fry

1 pound chicken
    breast filets,
    thinly sliced
3 tablespoons dry
    Sherry
¼ cup chicken
    broth
1 tablespoon
    cornstarch
1 tablespoon soy
    sauce

½ teaspoon sugar
⅛ teaspoon red
    pepper
½ cup thinly
    sliced carrots
½ cup thinly
    sliced cauliflower
½ cup chopped
    fresh asparagus
1 tablespoon oil

Cut chicken into 1-inch pieces. Marinate in mixture of Sherry and 3 tablespoons water in refrigerator for 2 hours, stirring occasionally. Drain, reserving marinade. Combine reserved marinade, broth, cornstarch, soy sauce, sugar and red pepper in bowl; set aside. Stir-fry vegetables in oil in heated wok for 2 minutes. Remove vegetables. Add half the chicken. Stir-fry for 3 minutes. Push to side of wok. Repeat with remaining chicken. Add reserved marinade mixture. Cook until thickened, stirring constantly. Cook for 30 seconds longer, stirring constantly. Add vegetables. Cook for 1 minute longer, stirring constantly. Spoon onto serving plates. Yield: 4 servings.

Approx per serving: Cal 250, Prot 34.8 gr, Fat 7.2 gr, Chol 83.1 mg, Carbo 7.1 gr, Sod 465.8 mg, Potas 628.6 mg.

Cora L. Campbell, Preceptor Pi
Loyall, Kentucky

Oriental Barbecue

2 chicken breast filets,
    cut into strips
1 green pepper,
    cut into strips
2 medium carrots,
    grated
4 stalks celery,
    sliced
1 onion, thinly
    sliced into rings

1 medium head
    cabbage,
    shredded
2 pounds fresh
    bean sprouts
1 cup peanut oil
1 cup blackstrap
    molasses
½ cup vinegar

Divide chicken and vegetables into 4 equal portions. Add ¼ cup oil and ½ cup of a mixture of molasses, vinegar and ½ cup water to each portion. Stir-fry each portion in wok until vegetables are tender-crisp, adding 1 tablespoon water if necessary. Spoon into serving bowls. Serve with hot rice, soy sauce, egg rolls and tea. Yield: 4 servings.

Approx per serving: Cal 465, Prot 26.1 gr, Fat 6.4 gr, Chol 41.5 mg, Carbo 83.9 gr, Sod 127.3 mg, Potas 2913.3 mg.

Nancy L. McAtee, Preceptor Delta Gamma
Port Hueneme, California

Chicken with Snow Peas and Cashews

2 chicken breast
    filets, cut into
    strips
1 clove of garlic,
    chopped
1 teaspoon ginger
1 tablespoon
    sesame oil

1 tablespoon soy
    sauce
½ cup cashews
3 tablespoons
    safflower oil
½ pound snow
    peas

Marinate chicken in mixture of garlic, ginger, sesame oil and soy sauce in bowl. Stir-fry cashews in safflower oil in wok until golden brown. Remove cashews. Add snow peas. Stir-fry for 2 minutes or until bright green. Remove snow peas. Add chicken. Stir-fry for 5 minutes. Add cashews and snow peas. Heat to serving temperature. Serve with rice. Yield: 2 servings.

Approx per serving: Cal 619, Prot 39.8 gr, Fat 46.9 gr, Chol 82.9 mg, Carbo 11.6 gr, Sod 732.0 mg, Potas 634.8 mg.

Andrea E. Kessler, Preceptor Beta
Waukegan, Illinois

Teriyaki Chicken and Vegetables

2 teaspoons
    teriyaki sauce
½ teaspoon
    chopped chives
⅛ teaspoon ginger
⅛ teaspoon garlic
    powder

5 ounces chicken
    breast filets
1 medium zucchini,
    sliced
1 cup sliced
    mushrooms

Mix teriyaki sauce, chives, ginger and garlic powder with 2 teaspoons water in saucepan. Bring to a boil. Pour over chicken and vegetables in bowl; toss to coat. Let stand for 20 minutes; drain, reserving marinade. Spray skillet with vegetable cooking spray. Sauté chicken in prepared skillet for 1 minute. Add vegetables and marinade. Simmer, covered, for about 3 minutes or until vegetables are tender-crisp. Yield: 1 serving.

Approx per serving: Cal 217, Prot 17.9 gr, Fat 1.2 gr, Chol 82.9 mg, Carbo 10.6 gr, Sod 57.0 mg, Potas 1162.0 mg.

Constance J. Yost, Xi Gamma Epsilon
Indian Harbour Beach, Florida

Chicken Breasts in Wine Sauce

6 chicken breast
    filets
2 tablespoons
    margarine
3 medium carrots,
    thinly sliced

¼ cup white wine
1 can cream of
    chicken soup
½ teaspoon salt
Pepper to taste

Brown chicken in margarine in skillet. Add remaining ingredients. Simmer, covered, for 25 to 35 minutes or until chicken and carrots are tender. Serve with rice or noodles. Yield: 6 servings.

Approx per serving: Cal 267, Prot 34.8 gr, Fat 9.9 gr, Chol 86.9 mg, Carbo 7.0 gr, Sod 710.5 mg, Potas 592.8 mg.

Diane Olivarri, Xi Epsilon Omicron
Des Peres, Missouri

Recipes for this photograph on pages 52, 162 and 181. ◗

Broccoli Casserole

2 10-ounce packages frozen broccoli, cooked
2 cups chopped cooked chicken breasts
1 can cream of chicken soup
½ cup reduced-calorie salad dressing
½ cup bread crumbs
2 tablespoons reduced-calorie margarine, melted
½ teaspoon lemon juice
¼ teaspoon reduced-sodium vegetable seasoning
¼ cup grated sharp Cheddar cheese

Layer half the broccoli and all of the chicken in greased 1½-quart baking dish. Mix soup and salad dressing in small bowl. Layer half the soup mixture, remaining broccoli and remaining soup over chicken. Mix bread crumbs and margarine in bowl. Sprinkle over top. Bake at 350 degrees for 25 minutes. Sprinkle with remaining ingredients. Bake for 5 minutes longer or until cheese melts. Yield: 6 servings.

Approx per serving: Cal 279, Prot 21.2 gr, Fat 14.2 gr, Chol 52.6 mg, Carbo 16.5 gr, Sod 705.3 mg, Potas 469.8 mg.

Helen Lacina, Preceptor Beta Omicron
Grinnell, Iowa

Divine Chicken

2 10-ounce packages frozen broccoli, cooked
4 chicken breasts, cooked, sliced
2 cans cream of chicken soup
1 teaspoon lemon juice
1 teaspoon curry powder
¾ cup reduced-calorie salad dressing
4 ounces sliced mushrooms,
1 cup seasoned stuffing mix
¾ cup shredded sharp Cheddar cheese

Arrange broccoli in 9x13-inch baking pan. Top with chicken. Combine next 5 ingredients in bowl; mix well. Pour over chicken. Sprinkle dry stuffing mix and cheese over top. Bake at 350 degrees for 20 to 30 minutes. Yield: 6 servings.

Approx per serving: Cal 325, Prot 32.8 gr, Fat 12.5 gr, Chol 77.7 mg, Carbo 20.8 gr, Sod 1118.7 mg, Potas 614.2 mg.

Sherry Meyer, Xi Gamma Tau
Rancho Cordova, California

Low-Calorie Chicken Oriental

3 chicken breasts, cooked, chopped
2 green peppers, cut into strips
3 tablespoons wine vinegar
1 tablespoon soy sauce
1 16-ounce can pineapple chunks, drained
½ teaspoon dry mustard
1 teaspoon salt
1 tablespoon cornstarch

Combine first 7 ingredients in bowl; mix well. Spoon into shallow baking dish. Bake at 325 degrees for 40 minutes. Stir in cornstarch dissolved in 2 tablespoons water. Bake for 15 minutes longer or until thickened and bubbly. Serve with rice. Each serving has approximately 248 calories. Yield: 6 servings.

Claudia Dunlap, Preceptor Epsilon Kappa
Central Valley, California

Seven-Minute Corn and Chicken

1 can mushroom soup
⅓ cup milk
2 eggs, beaten
3 tablespoons chopped pimento
2 cans boned chicken
1 16-ounce can whole kernel corn

Combine soup and milk in saucepan. Cook over low heat for several minutes. Stir a small amount of hot mixture into eggs; stir eggs into hot mixture. Cook until thickened, stirring constantly. Add pimento and salt and pepper to taste. Stir in chicken and corn. Cook, covered, over low heat for 7 minutes. Pour into serving dish. Yield: 4 servings.

Approx per serving: Cal 375, Prot 24.7 gr, Fat 19.4 gr, Chol 196.5 mg, Carbo 27.5 gr, Sod 1269.6 mg, Potas 392.4 mg.

Gayla Smith, Preceptor Iota Omicron
San Angelo, Texas

Curry Chicken

3 pounds chicken, boned
¼ cup butter
2 onions, chopped
1 clove of garlic, chopped
1 teaspoon cinnamon
3 tablespoons curry powder
8 cloves
3 bay leaves
2 cups canned tomatoes
2½ cups chicken stock

Sauté chicken in butter in skillet until light brown. Remove chicken. Sauté onions and garlic in pan drippings until onions are brown. Add cinnamon, curry powder, cloves and bay leaves tied in cheesecloth bag. Cook for 2 minutes. Add tomatoes and 1 cup stock. Cook until thickened. Add chicken and remaining stock. Simmer for 30 minutes. Remove cheesecloth bag. Pour into serving dish. Yield: 4 servings.

Approx per serving: Cal 350, Prot 38.9 gr, Fat 15.7 gr, Chol 127.0 mg, Carbo 12.7 gr, Sod 968.8 mg, Potas 855.3 mg.

Patricia Doyle, Xi Beta Mu
DeRidder, Louisiana

◀ *Recipes for this photograph on pages 85, 92 and 99.*

Crispy Baked Chicken

1 2½ to 3-pound
   chicken, cut up,
   skinned
1 cup low-fat milk
1 cup cornflake
   crumbs

Dip chicken in milk; shake off excess liquid. Coat with cornflake crumbs. Let stand for several minutes. Place in baking pan lined with greased foil. Bake at 400 degrees for 45 minutes or until tender. Yield: 4 servings.

Approx per serving: Cal 296, Prot 39.5 gr, Fat 4.6 gr, Chol 92.0 mg, Carbo 21.1 gr, Sod 316.6 mg, Potas 586.7 mg.

Mary Hildebrand, Omicron Tau
Elgin, Illinois

Baked Chicken Parmesan

¼ cup Parmesan
   cheese
1 tablespoon
   minced parsley
⅛ teaspoon ground
   pepper
¼ teaspoon garlic
   powder
¼ teaspoon paprika
⅛ teaspoon thyme
⅓ cup bread
   crumbs
1 3-pound
   chicken, cut up
1 tablespoon oil
¼ cup melted
   margarine
⅓ cup Marsala

Combine first 7 ingredients in bag. Add chicken several pieces at a time, shaking to coat well. Pour ⅓ cup water into shallow roasting pan. Arrange chicken in prepared pan. Drizzle with oil and margarine. Bake at 350 degrees for 30 minutes. Add wine. Cover with foil. Reduce temperature to 325 degrees. Bake for 15 minutes. Remove foil. Increase temperature to 350 degrees. Bake for 10 minutes longer. Yield: 4 servings.

Approx per serving: Cal 400, Prot 39.2 gr, Fat 20.9 gr, Chol 96.9 mg, Carbo 5.6 gr, Sod 303.9 mg, Potas 504.4 mg.

Penny Taylor, Pi
Newark, Delaware

Sue's Barbecue Chicken

1 chicken, cut up
½ cup chopped
   celery
½ cup chopped
   onion
1 cup barbecue sauce
1 cup catsup
¼ to ½ cup packed
   brown sugar

Arrange chicken in baking dish. Sprinkle with celery and onion. Combine remaining ingredients in bowl; mix well. Pour over chicken. Bake at 325 degrees for 1½ to 2 hours. Yield: 4 servings.

Approx per serving: Cal 365, Prot 37.5 gr, Fat 4.1 gr, Chol 89.6 mg, Carbo 44.2 gr, Sod 727.1 mg, Potas 863.0 mg. Nutritional information does not include barbecue sauce.

Susan Hutchinson, Zeta Eta
Eureka, California

Baked Chicken

1 cup oats
⅓ cup Parmesan
   cheese
½ teaspoon
   paprika
½ teaspoon salt
⅛ teaspoon pepper
1 3-pound
   chicken, cut up
1 egg
¼ cup milk

Process oats in blender for 1 minute. Combine with Parmesan cheese, paprika, salt and pepper. Dip chicken into mixture of egg and milk; coat with oat mixture. Place in greased baking pan. Bake at 375 degrees for 1 hour. Yield: 6 servings.
Note: Oat mixture may be used to coat pork chops or fish.

Approx per serving: Cal 268, Prot 35.5 gr, Fat 7.9 gr, Chol 131.4 mg, Carbo 11.8 gr, Sod 347.3 mg, Potas 471.4 mg.

Joann Kikel, Xi Gamma Epsilon
Corvallis, Oregon

Lemon Chicken

1 chicken, cut up
2 teaspoons garlic
   powder
Rind and juice of
   1 lemon
1 unsalted bouillon
   cube, crushed
1 teaspoon oregano
½ teaspoon thyme

Season chicken with garlic powder. Place chicken skin side down in single layer in baking dish. Sprinkle with lemon rind. Pour mixture of lemon juice and ¼ cup water over chicken. Sprinkle crushed bouillon over chicken. Sprinkle with oregano and thyme. Bake in preheated 400-degree oven for 30 minutes. Turn chicken pieces. Bake for 30 minutes longer. Garnish with parsley. Yield: 4 servings.

Approx per serving: Cal 193, Prot 35.9 gr, Fat 3.9 gr, Chol 84.6 mg, Carbo 1.4 gr, Sod 72.8 mg, Potas 490.0 mg.

Ivy Alexander, Kappa Kappa
Baytown, Texas

Ellen's Country Captain

1¼ pounds chicken pieces
½ teaspoon garlic salt
½ teaspoon paprika
8 ounces onions, chopped
2 medium green peppers, chopped
¾ teaspoon garlic powder
2 cups canned tomatoes
½ cup tomato paste
1 tablespoon parsley flakes
Artificial sweetener to equal 2 teaspoons sugar
1 teaspoon thyme
1 teaspoon curry powder
1 teaspoon Sherry extract
½ teaspoon seasoned salt
¼ teaspoon pepper
3 chicken bouillon cubes
1 cup cooked rice

Season chicken with garlic salt and paprika. Brown in nonstick skillet over medium heat. Remove chicken. Add onions, green peppers and garlic powder. Stir-fry for 4 minutes. Add tomatoes, tomato paste, parsley and seasonings; mix well. Add bouillon cubes dissolved in ¼ cup boiling water and chicken. Cook, covered, for 40 minutes or until chicken is tender. Serve over hot rice. Yield: 2 servings.

Approx per serving: Cal 433, Prot 33.8 gr, Fat 4.0 gr, Chol 58.3 mg, Carbo 68.6 gr, Sod 3565.0 mg, Potas 2139.7 mg.

Ellen Schwien, Delta Mu
Russell, Kansas

Poached Chicken

4 chicken thighs, skinned
2 cups canned tomatoes
1 onion, chopped
4 carrots, cut into quarters
½ cup wine
¼ cup reduced-calorie Italian salad dressing

Arrange chicken in skillet. Add tomatoes, onion and carrots. Simmer for 25 minutes. Remove chicken; drain and discard vegetables. Return chicken to skillet. Add wine and salad dressing. Simmer for 5 minutes. Yield: 4 servings.

Approx per serving: Cal 342, Prot 35.5 gr, Fat 8.5 gr, Chol 103.2 mg, Carbo 23.1 gr, Sod 549.7 mg, Potas 1193.1 mg.

Patricia Doyle, Xi Beta Mu
DeRidder, Louisiana

Chicken and Rice

1¼ pounds chicken pieces, skinned
½ teaspoon paprika
½ teaspoon garlic salt
8 ounces onions, chopped
2 medium green peppers, chopped
¾ teaspoon garlic powder
2 cups canned tomatoes
½ cup tomato paste
2 teaspoons artificial sweetener
1 teaspoon parsley flakes
1 teaspoon thyme
1 teaspoon curry powder
½ teaspoon seasoned salt
¼ teaspoon pepper
1 4-ounce can mushrooms, drained
3 chicken bouillon cubes

Sprinkle chicken with paprika and garlic salt. Brown in nonstick skillet. Remove chicken. Add onions, green peppers and garlic powder. Cook until vegetables wilt. Add remaining ingredients and ¼ cup water. Cook for 40 minutes. Bone chicken. Add to sauce. Cook for 30 minutes longer. Serve with hot rice. Yield: 4 servings.

Approx per serving: Cal 165, Prot 16.1 gr, Fat 2.0 gr, Chol 29.2 mg, Carbo 22.5 gr, Sod 1590.8 mg, Potas 1055.5 mg.

Matha L. Koch, Xi Alpha Omicron
Forrest Park, Georgia

Carol Ann's Chicken and Rice

2 cups long grain rice
1 envelope dry onion soup mix
1 can cream of mushroom soup
1 can cream of chicken soup
1 chicken, cut up

Layer rice and soup mix in greased 9x13-inch baking dish. Pour mixture of soups and 2 soup cans water over top. Arrange chicken in prepared dish. Bake, uncovered, at 325 degrees for 1½ hours. Yield: 8 servings.

Approx per serving: Cal 352, Prot 23.4 gr, Fat 7.5 gr, Chol 58.7 mg, Carbo 45.7 gr, Sod 994.9 mg, Potas 360.4 mg.

Carol Ann Cochran, Omega
Spokane, Washington

Chicken-Rice-Spice Dinner

1 tablespoon flour
1 cup rice
1 16-ounce can tomatoes
½ cup chopped onion
½ teaspoon basil

Garlic powder to taste
1 2½-pound chicken, cut up
1 tablespoon oil
6 ounces smoked sausage links, cut into thirds

Shake flour in 14x20-inch oven cooking bag. Place in 9x13-inch baking pan. Add rice, tomatoes, onion, basil, garlic powder and salt and pepper to taste. Brush chicken with oil. Place chicken and sausage in bag. Close with twist tie. Cut 6 half-inch slits in bag. Bake at 350 degrees for 50 minutes or until chicken is tender. Arrange chicken and sausage on serving plate. Spoon rice around chicken. Yield: 6 servings.

Approx per serving: Cal 283, Prot 27.1 gr, Fat 5.1 gr, Chol 59.7 mg, Carbo 30.2 gr, Sod 149.6 mg, Potas 526.6 mg.

Patti Dutton, Zeta Eta
Eureka, California

Microwave Sweet and Sour Chicken

1¼ pounds chicken pieces
1 20-ounce can pineapple chunks
2 tablespoons cornstarch
¼ cup vinegar
1 tablespoon soy sauce

¼ cup catsup
2 tablespoons brown sugar substitute
½ teaspoon salt
¼ teaspoon ginger
1 medium green pepper, sliced
1 medium tomato, cut into wedges

Brown chicken in nonstick skillet. Place in 2-quart casserole. Drain pineapple, reserving juice. Add cornstarch, vinegar, soy sauce, catsup, brown sugar, salt and ginger; mix well. Pour over chicken. Microwave on High for 8 minutes or until chicken is tender. Top with green pepper and tomatoes. Serve over hot rice. Yield: 4 servings.

Approx per serving: Cal 221, Prot 12.4 gr, Fat 1.5 gr, Chol 26.9 mg, Carbo 41.9 gr, Sod 779.2 mg, Potas 493.0 mg.

Sylvia McCowan, Preceptor Tau
Anderson, Indiana

Chicken and Vegetables

1 2½-pound chicken, cut up
1 chicken bouillon cube
1 cup 1-inch carrot chunks
¼ cup chopped onion
1 pound mushrooms, sliced

½ pound green beans, cut into 1-inch pieces
1 teaspoon bay leaves
1¼ teaspoons salt
⅛ teaspoon pepper
2 tablespoons flour

Place chicken on rack in each 9x13-inch baking pan. Bake in preheated 450-degree oven for 20 minutes or until brown. Remove chicken; drain. Stir bouillon dissolved in ¾ cup boiling water into baking pan. Add carrots, onion, mushrooms, green beans, and seasonings. Add chicken. Spoon sauce over chicken. Bake, covered, at 350 degrees until chicken is tender. Arrange chicken and vegetables on serving plate. Blend pan drippings and mixture of flour and 2 tablespoons water in saucepan. Cook until thickened, stirring constantly. Spoon over chicken. Serve with rice. Yield: 4 servings.

Approx per serving: Cal 272, Prot 41.1 gr, Fat 4.5 gr, Chol 90.3 mg, Carbo 16.3 gr, Sod 1017.8 mg, Potas 1217.6 mg.

Maureen Dwyer, Omicron Tau
Kimberling City, Missouri

Chicken and Broccoli with Mushroom Sauce

3 tablespoons margarine
3 tablespoons flour
1 cup chicken broth
1 4-ounce can sliced mushrooms
10 ounces frozen broccoli, cooked

2 cups chopped cooked chicken
2 tablesppoons chopped parsley
2 tablespoons bread crumbs

Combine margarine and flour in saucepan. Cook over medium heat for 1 minute. Blend in broth. Cook until thick and smooth, stirring constantly. Add mushrooms with liquid. Season with salt and pepper to taste. Layer broccoli, chicken and sauce in shallow baking dish. Sprinkle with parsley and crumbs. Bake at 375 degrees for 15 to 25 minutes or until bubbly and brown on top. Yield: 4 servings.

Approx per serving: Cal 253, Prot 26.0 gr, Fat 11.5 gr, Chol 56:2 mg, Carbo 11.2 gr, Sod 425.0 mg, Potas 485.2 mg.

Lemon-Baked Chicken

1 2½ to 3-pound chicken, cut up
2 tablespoons oil
3 tablespoons fresh lemon juice

1 clove of garlic, crushed
½ teaspoon salt
⅛ teaspoon pepper

Arrange chicken in baking pan. Drizzle with mixture of oil, lemon juice, garlic, salt and pepper. Bake, covered, for 40 minutes or until tender, basting frequently. Bake, uncovered, for 10 minutes longer. Garnish with chopped parsley. Yield: 4 servings.

Approx per serving: Cal 270, Prot 35.9 gr, Fat 10.7 gr, Chol 89.6 mg, Carbo 1.1 gr, Sod 339.3 mg, Potas 486.1 mg.

Patsy Quint, Laureate Omicron
Wichita, Kansas

Chicken in Wine

2 pounds chicken
  pieces
Seasoned flour
6 tablespoons oil
2 cups sliced fresh
  mushrooms
1 tablespoon butter
1 cup mushroom
  soup

½ cup chicken broth
½ cup orange juice
½ cup dry white wine
1 tablespoon
  brown sugar
½ teaspoon salt
4 carrots, cut into
  julienne strips

Coat chicken with seasoned flour. Brown in oil in skillet. Drain on paper towel. Sauté mushrooms in butter. Combine soup, broth, orange juice, wine, brown sugar, salt and carrots in large casserole; mix well. Arrange chicken in casserole. Spoon mushrooms over chicken. Bake at 350 degrees for 1 hour. Serve with rice and green salad. Yield: 4 servings.

Ann Connolly, Xi Omicron
Quispamsis, New Brunswick, Canada

Chinese Chicken and Vegetables

6 cups chopped
  cooked chicken
2 cups chicken
  bouillon
¼ cup cornstarch
10 ounces frozen
  snow peas

1 10-ounce
  package frozen
  oriental stir-fry
  vegetables with
  seasonings

Combine chicken, bouillon and cornstarch dissolved in ¼ cup cold water in Crock•Pot; mix well. Cook on High for 2 to 3 hours or until thickened. Add snow peas and oriental vegetables. Cook on High for 1 hour or until vegetables are tender-crisp. Serve over rice. Yield: 6 servings.

Approx per serving: Cal 253, Prot 44.5 gr, Fat 4.8 gr, Chol 111.6 mg, Carbo 4.7 gr, Sod 409.6 mg, Potas 576.7 mg.

Jan Britson, Kappa Beta
Ames, Iowa

Macil's Chicken Enchiladas

¼ cup chopped
  onion
¼ cup chopped
  celery
1 tablespoon
  margarine
2 cans cream of
  chicken soup
1 large can
  evaporated milk

1 3-ounce can
  chopped green
  chilies
2 cups grated
  Cheddar cheese
2½ cups chopped
  cooked chicken
12 corn tortillas

Sauté onion and celery in margarine in skillet until tender. Add soup, milk and chilies; mix well. Spoon cheese and chicken onto tortillas. Roll to enclose filling. Arrange in 9x12-inch baking dish. Pour sauce over top. Sprinkle with additional cheese if desired. Bake at 350 degrees for 30 minutes or until bubbly. Serve with rice. Yield: 6 servings.

Approx per serving: Cal 660, Prot 41.2 gr, Fat 28.8 gr, Chol 113.1 mg, Carbo 60.3 gr, Sod 1218.7 mg, Potas 594.2 mg.

Macil Larson, Preceptor Alpha Psi
Kingman, Arizona

Stove-Top Chicken Casserole

1 package chicken-
  flavored stuffing
  mix
1 cup chopped
  cooked chicken
1 can cream of
  chicken soup
⅓ cup milk
½ cup sliced
  mushrooms

½ cup chopped
  green pepper
¼ cup chopped
  ripe olives
2 tablespoons
  chopped pimento
½ cup chopped
  almonds
2 tablespoons
  chopped parsley

Prepare stuffing mix using package directions. Pat over bottom and up sides of greased 8-inch square baking dish. Place chicken in prepared dish. Pour mixture of soup, milk, mushrooms, green pepper, olives and pimento over chicken. Sprinkle with almonds and parsley. Bake, covered, at 350 degrees for 35 minutes. Yield: 8 servings.

Approx per serving: Cal 227, Prot 12.1 gr, Fat 8.8 gr, Chol 19.3 mg, Carbo 26.0 gr, Sod 735.8 mg, Potas 269.2 mg.

Dorothy McDougall, Laureate Beta
Roseville, Minnesota

Hot Chicken Salad

2 cups chopped
  cooked chicken
1 cup thinly sliced
  celery
½ cup chopped
  blanched
  almonds
½ teaspoon salt
1 cup mayonnaise

2 tablespoons
  grated onion
2 tablespoons
  lemon juice
½ cup grated
  sharp Cheddar
  cheese
1 cup crushed
  potato chips

Combine chicken, celery, almonds, salt, mayonnaise and onion lemon juice in bowl; mix well. Spoon into greased casserole. Sprinkle with cheese and potato chips. Bake at 450 degrees for 10 to 15 minutes or until bubbly. Yield: 4 servings.

Approx per serving: Cal 832, Prot 30.9 gr, Fat 70.8 gr, Chol 108.5 mg, Carbo 21.0 gr, Sod 880.1 mg, Potas 875.5 mg.

Jane Walton
Pomeroy, Ohio

Bettye's Hot Chicken Salad

2 cups chopped
   cooked chicken
1 cup thinly sliced
   celery
½ cup chopped
   walnuts
1 cup reduced-calorie
   mayonnaise

1 onion, grated
2 tablespoons
   lemon juice
½ cup shredded
   Cheddar cheese
1 cup crushed unsalted
   potato chips

Combine chicken, celery, walnuts, mayonnaise, onion and lemon juice in bowl; mix well. Spoon into 2-quart casserole. Sprinkle with cheese and potato chips. Bake at 400 degrees for 20 minutes or until bubbly and cheese melts. Yield: 6 servings.

Approx per serving: Cal 442, Prot 20.7 gr, Fat 32.9 gr, Chol 59.5 mg, Carbo 20.0 gr, Sod 243.3 mg, Potas 628.0 mg.

Bettye J. Weekley, Preceptor Iota Kappa
Dickinson, Texas

Turkey Soufflé

6 slices bread,
   cubed
2 cups chopped
   cooked turkey
½ cup chopped
   onion
½ cup chopped
   green pepper
½ cup chopped
   celery

½ cup mayonnaise
½ teaspoon salt
Dash of pepper
2 eggs, beaten
1½ cups milk
1 can cream of
   mushroom soup
½ cup shredded
   sharp Cheddar
   cheese

Place half the bread in greased 9x13-inch baking dish. Combine turkey, vegetables, mayonnaise and seasonings; mix well. Spoon into prepared dish. Top with remaining bread. Beat eggs and milk in bowl until smooth. Pour over layers. Chill, covered, for 1 hour to overnight. Spread soup over top. Bake at 325 degrees for 50 minutes. Sprinkle with cheese. Bake for 10 minutes longer. Yield: 12 servings.

Approx per serving: Cal 234, Prot 12.7 gr, Fat 14.9 gr, Chol 80.8 mg, Carbo 12.2 gr, Sod 510.4 mg, Potas 224.1 mg.

Kathleen Radcliffe, Preceptor Kappa
Lancaster, Pennsylvania

Party Spaghetti

2 medium green
   peppers,
   chopped
2 stalks celery,
   chopped
2 medium onions,
   chopped
2 cloves of garlic,
   minced
¼ cup margarine
¼ teaspoon
   Worcestershire
   sauce
3 cups chopped
   cooked turkey
1 can mushroom
   soup

1 can tomato soup
1 4-ounce jar
   chopped
   pimento,
   drained
8 ounces process
   American
   cheese, chopped
8 ounces spaghetti,
   cooked
1 4-ounce can
   sliced
   mushrooms,
   drained
8 ounces Cheddar
   cheese, grated

Sauté green peppers, celery, onions and garlic in margarine in skillet. Add Worcestershire sauce, turkey, soups, pimento, American cheese, spaghetti and mushrooms; mix well. Season to taste. Pour into greased 2-quart casserole. Sprinkle Cheddar cheese over top. Bake at 350 degrees for 30 minutes. Yield: 8 servings.

Approx per serving: Cal 558, Prot 35.5 gr, Fat 29.2 gr, Chol 98.2 mg, Carbo 38.3 gr, Sod 1413.8 mg, Potas 641.9 mg.

Octavia Famuliner, Laureate Nu
Carrollton, Missouri

Microwave Turkey Chow Mein

2 4-ounce turkey
   thighs, cubed
2 tablespoons
   cornstarch
2 teaspoons instant
   chicken bouillon
2 tablespoons soy
   sauce
8 ounces fresh
   mushrooms,
   sliced

1 cup thinly sliced
   celery
1 medium onion,
   chopped
1 16-ounce can
   chow mein
   vegetables,
   drained
½ cup chow mein
   noodles

Place turkey in 2-quart glass baking dish. Microwave, covered, on High for 3 minutes. Turn turkey over. Microwave, covered, for 2 to 3 minutes or until turkey is no longer pink; drain. Add cornstarch dissolved in ¼ cup water and next 6 ingredients; mix well. Microwave, covered, on High for 10 to 12 minutes or until thickened, stirring occasionally. Top with chow mein noodles. Yield: 6 servings.

Approx per serving: Cal 100, Prot 10.0 gr, Fat 2.6 gr, Chol 22.2 mg, Carbo 9.4 gr, Sod 860.3 mg, Potas 369.7 mg. Nutritional information does not include chow mein vegetables.

Juanita McGann, Preceptor Alpha Beta
Colorado Springs, Colorado

Dilled Cucumber Sauce for Turkey

1 cucumber, peeled,
   seeded, thinly
   sliced
1 cup yogurt

1 teaspoon chopped
   chives
1 teaspoon dillweed

Combine all ingredients with salt to taste in bowl; mix well. Use as sandwich spread for turkey sandwiches or spread on thin slices of turkey and roll up. Yield: 32 tablespoons.

Approx per tablespoon: Cal 5, Prot 0.3 gr, Fat 0.1 gr, Chol 0.6 mg, Carbo 0.7 gr, Sod 4.2 mg, Potas 25.1 mg.

Sherry Murray, Xi Gamma Sigma
Marion, Iowa

Turkey and Cabbage Rolls

1 medium head
  cabbage
1 pound ground
  fresh turkey
1¼ cups cooked
  rice
½ cup chopped
  onion

½ cup applesauce
2 eggs, beaten
2 tablespoons
  chopped dates
1 tablespoon curry
  powder
1 cup chicken
  stock

Cook cabbage in water to cover in large saucepan. Cook until 12 outer leaves become tender enough to separate and be removed; drain. Combine next 7 ingredients in bowl; mix well. Spoon onto cabbage leaves; roll up from stem end to enclose filling. Place seam side down in 9x13-inch baking pan. Pour chicken stock over rolls. Bake, covered, for 1¼ hours, basting occasionally.
Yield: 6 servings.

Approx per serving: Cal 171, Prot 9.1 gr, Fat 5.4 gr, Chol 106.2 mg, Carbo 21.7 gr, Sod 360.7 mg, Potas 187.3 mg.

Dorothy Auer, Preceptor Upsilon
Scottsdale, Arizona

Linda's Turkey-Cabbage Skillet

8 ounces ground
  fresh turkey
3 cups shredded
  cabbage
½ cup chopped
  onion
3 ounces chopped
  green pepper

1 stalk celery,
  chopped
¼ cup rice
½ cup tomato
  sauce
½ teaspoon salt
½ teaspoon pepper

Brown ground turkey in nonstick skillet, stirring until crumbly. Add vegetables. Cook until onions are transparent, stirring constantly. Add rice, tomato sauce and seasonings. Simmer, covered, for 20 minutes or until rice is tender. Spoon into serving dish.
Yield: 4 servings.

Approx per serving: Cal 123, Prot 6.9 gr, Fat 2.8 gr, Chol 16.1 mg, Carbo 18.5 gr, Sod 475.1 mg, Potas 441.0 mg.

Linda F. Trahan, Kappa
New Iberia, Louisiana

Barbara's Turkey Loaf

1 pound ground
  fresh turkey
1 cup herb-
  seasoned stuffing
  mix
½ cup chopped
  parsley
2 stalks celery,
  grated
1 carrot, grated

1 small onion,
  grated
2 cloves of garlic,
  minced
½ teaspoon salt
¼ teaspoon pepper
¼ teaspoon poultry
  seasoning
1 egg, beaten

Line loaf pan with foil, allowing foil to extend over edge. Combine all ingredients in order listed in bowl; mix well. Press into prepared pan. Bake at 350 degrees for 45 minutes or until firm. Lift from pan with foil; remove foil. Place on serving plate; slice.
Yield: 4 servings.
Note: May serve cold as first-course paté or party snack.

Approx per serving: Cal 190, Prot 13.2 gr, Fat 7.3 gr, Chol 96.1 mg, Carbo 18.3 gr, Sod 581.1 mg, Potas 372.8 mg.

Barbara Israels, Preceptor Tau
Holland, Michigan

Turkey Loaf

1 pound ground
  fresh turkey
½ cup dry bread
  crumbs
1 teaspoon poultry
  seasoning
¼ cup minced
  onion

2 eggs, beaten
½ teaspoon celery
  seed
½ teaspoon salt
½ teaspoon pepper
1 can cream of
  chicken soup

Combine first 8 ingredients in bowl; mix well. Press into greased loaf pan. Bake at 350 degrees for 1 hour. Spread soup over top. Bake for 10 to 15 minutes longer. Remove to serving plate; slice.
Yield: 4 servings.

Approx per serving: Cal 233, Prot 15.0 gr, Fat 12.1 gr, Chol 165.1 mg, Carbo 15.3 gr, Sod 1019.8 mg, Potas 218.3 mg.

Dawn Clemons, Delta Omega
Carthage, Tennessee

Low-Calorie Pizza

1 pound ground
  fresh turkey
4 ounces reduced-
  calorie bread,
  crumbled
2 teaspoons onion
  powder
½ teaspoon garlic
  powder
½ teaspoon
  oregano
1 teaspoon salt
½ teaspoon pepper

1 8-ounce can
  tomato sauce
2 tablespoons
  onion flakes
2 green peppers,
  sliced
1 cup sliced
  mushrooms
Italian seasoning
  to taste
4 ounces
  mozzarella
  cheese, grated

Combine first 7 ingredients in bowl; mix well. Press into bottom of 9x13-inch baking dish. Bake at 350 degrees for 10 minutes or until firm. Layer tomato sauce, onion flakes, green peppers, mushrooms, Italian seasoning and cheese over turkey. Bake at 375 degrees for 15 minutes. Cut into squares. Yield: 4 servings.

Approx per serving: Cal 212, Prot 16.6 gr, Fat 12.2 gr, Chol 57.1 mg, Carbo 9.9 gr, Sod 1016.4 mg, Potas 585.8 mg.
Nutritional information does not include reduced-calorie bread.

Susan J. Wallace, Preceptor Laureate Beta Lambda
Springfield, Illinois

Spinach-Filled Turkey Roll

1½ pounds ground
 fresh turkey
½ cup finely
 chopped onion
¼ cup tomato
 sauce
2 slices bread,
 crumbled
1 teaspoon dry
 mustard
½ teaspoon
 oregano

2 eggs, beaten
¼ teaspoon garlic
 powder
1 10-ounce
 package frozen
 spinach, thawed
½ cup shredded
 mozzarella
 cheese
¾ cup tomato
 sauce

Combine first 8 ingredients in bowl; mix well. Pat into 8x12-inch rectangle on foil. Spread spinach over turkey mixture. Sprinkle with cheese. Roll from narrow side as for jelly roll. Place seam side down in ungreased baking pan. Bake at 350 degrees for 1 hour. Let stand for 10 minutes. Heat ¾ cup tomato sauce in saucepan. Place turkey roll on serving platter. Serve with warm tomato sauce.
Yield: 6 servings.

Approx per serving: Cal 194, Prot 15.6 gr, Fat 9.8 gr,
Chol 125.0 mg, Carbo 11.4 gr, Sod 381.1 mg, Potas 483.7 mg.

Edna Arp, Preceptor Psi
Custer, South Dakota
Joan Stockman, Preceptor Pi
Gering, Nebraska

Low-Fat Turkey Chili

1 pound fresh
 ground turkey
1 medium onion,
 chopped

1 package chili
 seasoning
1 20-ounce can
 tomatoes

Brown ground turkey with onion in heavy nonstick skillet, stirring until turkey is crumbly. Add chili seasoning and tomatoes; mix well. Simmer until of desired consistency. Ladle into serving bowls.
Yield: 4 servings.

Approx per serving: Cal 122, Prot 10.2 gr, Fat 5.3 gr,
Chol 32.2 mg, Carbo 8.9 gr, Sod 214.4 mg, Potas 1411.0 mg.

Margaret Bell, Xi Psi
Oklahoma City, Oklahoma

Turkey Lasagna

1 pound ground
 fresh turkey
1 large onion,
 chopped
1 16-ounce can
 tomatoes
1 6-ounce can
 tomato paste
1 tablespoon sugar
2 tablespoons
 parsley flakes
1 teaspoon basil

2⅔ cups cottage
 cheese
4 ounces Parmesan
 cheese
1 tablespoon
 parsley
1 teaspoon oregano
8 ounces uncooked
 lasagna noodles
8 ounces
 mozzarella
 cheese, grated

Brown ground turkey with onion in nonstick skillet, stirring until crumbly. Add tomatoes, tomato paste, sugar, parsley flakes, basil and 1 cup water; mix well. Combine cottage cheese, Parmesan cheese, parsley and oregano in bowl; mix well. Layer turkey mixture, uncooked noodles and cheese mixture ½ at a time in greased 9x13-inch baking dish. Top with mozzarella cheese. Bake, covered, at 350 degrees for 1 hour. Bake, uncovered, for 15 minutes longer.
Yield: 8 servings.

Approx per serving: Cal 422, Prot 31.8 gr, Fat 17.2 gr,
Chol 70.7 mg, Carbo 34.6 gr, Sod 510.4 mg, Potas 567.4 mg.

Charlotte Jones, Preceptor Kappa
Huron, South Dakota

Turkey Cheeseburger Pie

1 package
 refrigerator.
 crescent dinner
 rolls
1 pound ground
 fresh turkey
Onion flakes to
 taste

1 8-ounce can
 tomato sauce
Italian seasoning
 to taste
4 ounces
 mozzarella
 cheese, shredded

Separate roll dough. Arrange triangles in pie plate; press to seal edges. Brown ground turkey with onion flakes in heavy nonstick skillet, stirring until crumbly. Stir in tomato sauce and Italian seasoning. Spoon into prepared plate. Top with cheese. Bake at 375 degrees for 12 minutes or until crust is golden brown. Cut into wedges. Yield: 4 servings.

Approx per serving: Cal 191, Prot 15.3 gr, Fat 12.0 gr,
Chol 57.1 mg, Carbo 5.6 gr, Sod 471.1 mg, Potas 353.6 mg,
Nutritional information does not include refrigerator crescent rolls.

Carol Cronister, Preceptor Upsilon
Cantrall, Illinois

Macaroni Skillet Supper

1 pound ground
 fresh turkey
½ onion, chopped
½ cup chopped
 celery
½ cup chopped
 green pepper
1 16-ounce can
 tomatoes

3 ounces tiny shell
 macaroni
½ teaspoon salt
¼ teaspoon pepper
4 ounces Cheddar
 cheese, grated

Brown ground turkey with onion in nonstick skillet, stirring until crumbly. Add next 6 ingredients; mix well. Simmer, covered, for 25 minutes. Stir in cheese. Spoon into serving bowl.
Yield: 4 servings.

Approx per serving: Cal 312, Prot 19.9 gr, Fat 14.7 gr,
Chol 60.2 mg, Carbo 25.0 gr, Sod 663.2 mg, Potas 537.3 mg.

Linda Patten, Xi Rho Zeta
Deer Park, Texas

Crispy Fish Sticks

1 pound cod fillets
½ cup milk
1 teaspoon
  Worcestershire
  sauce
1 teaspoon soy
  sauce

12 soda crackers,
  finely crushed
1 cup cornflakes,
  crushed
Pinch of pepper
2 teaspoons corn oil

Cut fish into 8 pieces. Combine milk, Worcestershire sauce and soy sauce in shallow dish; mix well. Combine cracker crumbs, cornflake crumbs and pepper in shallow dish. Add oil; mix well. Dip each fillet into milk mixture then into crumbs. Repeat process. Place 1 inch apart on greased baking sheet. Bake at 450 degrees for 6 minutes. Turn fillets over. Bake for 5 to 6 minutes longer or until brown. Yield: 4 servings. Each serving has about 245 calories.

Kate Rolfvondenbaumen, Alpha Pi
Lloydminster, Alberta, Canada

Fish Cakes

5 tablespoons
  butter, melted
5 tablespoons flour
½ teaspoon salt
1½ cups milk
1½ tablespoons
  minced onion
1½ tablespoons
  minced parsley

1 teaspoon lemon
  juice
3 cups flaked
  cooked fish
1 egg, beaten
1 cup (or more) fine
  dry bread crumbs
2 tablespoons butter

Blend 5 tablespoons butter, flour and salt in saucepan. Stir in milk gradually. Cook until thickened, stirring constantly. Stir in onion, parsley, lemon juice and fish. Chill for several minutes. Shape into 12 cakes. Beat egg with 2 tablespoons water in bowl. Coat fish cakes with bread crumbs. Dip into egg mixture then into bread crumbs. Chill for 1 hour. Brown in 2 tablespoons butter in skillet; drain. Arrange on serving plate. Yield: 6 servings.

Approx per serving: Cal 301, Prot 24.9 gr, Fat 17.2 gr, Chol 92.2 mg, Carbo 10.8 gr, Sod 406.6 mg, Potas 125.1 mg.

Crunchy Baked Fish

2 pounds flounder
  fillets
½ cup low-fat
  yogurt
¼ cup whole
  wheat flour
¼ cup Grape Nuts

½ teaspoon garlic
  powder
½ teaspoon onion
  powder
1 tablespoon
  chopped parsley

Dip fillets into yogurt; coat with mixture of remaining ingredients. Arrange in shallow foil-lined baking dish. Bake at 400 degrees for 20 to 25 minutes or until fish flakes easily. Brown under broiler for 2 to 3 minutes if desired for crispy crust. Yield: 4 servings.

Approx per serving: Cal 264, Prot 73.0 gr, Fat 2.4 gr, Chol 114.8 mg, Carbo 30.0 gr, Sod 396.6 mg, Potas 1459.4 mg.

Diana Allen, Preceptor Alpha Zeta
Grand Prairie, Texas

Flounder Valenciennes

¼ cup chopped
  onion
2 cups sliced fresh
  mushrooms
2 tablespoons
  margarine
2 pounds flounder
  fillets

2 tablespoons
  lemon juice
1 tablespoon
  chopped parsley
1 teaspoon oregano
⅛ teaspoon pepper

Sauté onion and mushrooms in margarine in skillet until tender. Arrange fillets over sautéed vegetables; sprinkle with remaining ingredients. Simmer, covered, for 20 minutes or until fish flakes easily. Arrange fillets on serving plate. Spoon sauce over top. Yield: 6 servings.

Approx per serving: Cal 178, Prot 46.1 gr, Fat 5.1 gr, Chol 75.0 mg, Carbo 2.1 gr, Sod 169.9 mg, Potas 1007.5 mg.

Irene Paterline, Pi Phi
Mascoutah, Illinois

Flounder Florentine

1 pound flounder
  fillets
2 10-ounce
  packages frozen
  spinach, thawed,
  drained
2 tablespoons
  margarine,
  melted

3 tablespoons flour
1½ cups low-fat
  milk
⅛ teaspoon nutmeg
1 cup grated
  Cheddar cheese
½ cup fine bread
  crumbs

Arrange fillets on bed of spinach in 9x13-inch baking pan. Blend margarine and flour in saucepan. Stir in milk gradually. Cook until thickened, stirring constantly. Add nutmeg, cheese and salt and pepper to taste. Cook until cheese melts, stirring constantly. Spoon over fillets. Top with bread crumbs. Bake at 350 degrees for 30 minutes or until fish flakes easily. Yield: 4 servings.

Approx per serving: Cal 377, Prot 49.8 gr, Fat 17.7 gr, Chol 88.1 mg, Carbo 18.5 gr, Sod 519.6 mg, Potas 1348.9 mg.

Barbara Fitsell, Laureate Alpha Alpha
Kingston, Ontario, Canada

Poor Man's Lobster

1 tablespoon
  vinegar
½ teaspoon salt

1 teaspoon seafood
  seasoning
1 pound flounder fillets

Combine vinegar, salt and seafood seasoning with 2 cups water in saucepan. Bring to a boil. Add flounder. Simmer for 15 minutes or until fish flakes easily. Place on rack in broiler pan. Broil until brown. Serve with drawn butter. Yield: 4 servings.

Approx per serving: Cal 140, Prot 27.3 gr, Fat 2.5 gr, Chol 64.3 mg, Carbo 0.4 gr, Sod 333.4 mg, Potas 266.4 mg.

Favorite Flounder

1 8-ounce package
   stuffing mix
2 tablespoons flour
1 cup low-fat milk
½ cup grated
   Cheddar cheese
1 tablespoon
   minced onion

½ teaspoon
   seasoned salt
1 10-ounce
   package frozen
   chopped broccoli,
   thawed
1¼ pounds
   flounder fillets

Prepare stuffing mix using package directions. Blend flour and 1 cup water in saucepan. Cook over low heat until thickened, stirring constantly. Add milk, cheese, onion and seasoned salt. Cook until well-blended, stirring constantly. Layer ½ cup sauce, stuffing, broccoli, flounder and remaining sauce in greased 7x11-inch baking dish. Bake at 350 degrees for 30 minutes or until fish flakes easily. Yield: 6 servings.

Approx per serving: Cal 303, Prot 38.8 gr, Fat 5.9 gr, Chol 29.7 mg, Carbo 68.3 gr, Sod 1027.0 mg, Potas 810.0 mg.

Ann Oster, Gamma Iota
Berlin, Maryland

Creole Flounder

1 cup sliced green
   onions with tops
1 large green
   pepper, sliced
   into thin strips
1½ tablespoons
   margarine
1 16-ounce can
   tomatoes

1 8-ounce can
   tomato sauce
1 bay leaf
½ teaspoon thyme
6 4-ounce
   flounder fillets
¼ teaspoon salt
⅛ teaspoon pepper

Sauté green onions and green pepper in margarine in skillet until tender. Drain and chop tomatoes, reserving liquid. Stir tomatoes, reserved liquid, tomato sauce, bay leaf and thyme into skillet. Simmer for 20 minutes. Discard bay leaf. Arrange fillets in 9x13-inch baking dish; sprinkle with salt and pepper. Spoon sauce over fillets. Bake, covered, at 350 degrees for 20 minutes. Serve over rice. Yield: 6 servings.

Approx per serving: Cal 167, Prot 35.9 gr, Fat 4.1 gr, Chol 56.3 mg, Carbo 9.0 gr, Sod 533.9 mg, Potas 1079.9 mg.

Ellen R. Wilkinson, Preceptor Upsilon
Chesapeake, Virginia

Crab-Stuffed Flounder Rolls

1 4-ounce can
   mushroom pieces,
   drained
3 tablespoons
   chopped onion
1 7-ounce can
   crabmeat, drained
¼ cup dry bread
   crumbs
1 tablespoon
   parsley flakes

2 pounds flounder
   fillets
3 tablespoons flour
1½ cups low-fat
   milk
¼ cup dry white
   wine
½ cup shredded
   Swiss cheese
Paprika to taste

Combine first 5 ingredients and salt and pepper to taste in bowl; mix well. Cut fillets into 8 pieces. Spread each with mushroom mixture; roll to enclose filling. Place seam side down in shallow baking dish. Combine flour, milk and wine in saucepan. Cook over medium heat until thickened, stirring constantly. Add cheese. Cook until cheese melts, stirring constantly. Spoon over rolls. Sprinkle with paprika. Bake at 400 degrees for 30 minutes or until fish flakes easily. Yield: 8 servings.

Approx per serving: Cal 174, Prot 38.4 gr, Fat 3.6 gr, Chol 62.4 mg, Carbo 7.6 gr, Sod 185.7 mg, Potas 759.7 mg.

Jean Engel, Mu Epsilon
Freeport, Illinois

Lemon Haddock Bake

2 16-ounce
   packages frozen
   haddock fillets,
   thawed
½ teaspoon salt
1 cup sliced fresh
   mushrooms

¼ cup chopped
   onion
¼ cup chopped
   green pepper
8 thin lemon slices
¼ cup dry Sauterne
Paprika to taste

Arrange fillets in greased baking dish; sprinkle with salt. Layer mushrooms, onion, green pepper and lemon slices over fillets. Drizzle wine over top. Sprinkle with paprika. Bake, covered, at 350 degrees for 30 minutes or until fish flakes easily. Yield: 8 servings.

Approx per serving: Cal 110, Prot 18.3 gr, Fat 0.2 gr, Chol 57.9 mg, Carbo 1.8 gr, Sod 206.0 mg, Potas 382.3 mg.

Lila Warrell, Preceptor Upsilon
Muncie, Indiana

Tomato-Baked Fish

2 pounds haddock
   fillets
¼ cup chopped
   onion
¼ cup chopped
   celery
1 medium green
   pepper, chopped
1 teaspoon oil
2 cups canned
   tomatoes

2 teaspoons salt
¼ teaspoon pepper
¼ teaspoon garlic
   powder
1 teaspoon chili
   powder
1 tablespoon
   Worcestershire
   sauce
1 bay leaf

Arrange fillets in baking dish; sprinkle with salt and pepper to taste. Chill for several minutes. Sauté onion, celery and green pepper in oil in skillet until light brown. Add tomatoes and seasonings. Cook over low heat for 20 minutes, stirring frequently. Discard bay leaf. Pour into blender container. Process until smooth. Pour over fillets. Bake at 350 degrees for 50 minutes or until fish flakes easily, basting frequently. Yield: 6 servings.

Approx per serving: Cal 181, Prot 25.1 gr, Fat 2.6 gr, Chol 77.2 mg, Carbo 6.1 gr, Sod 948.0 mg, Potas 699.2 mg.

Ann Titus, Xi Gamma Zeta
Dallas, Texas

Haddock Creole

1 pound haddock
  fillets
¼ cup chopped
  onion
2 tablespoons
  chopped green
  pepper

1 tablespoon
  margarine
1 cup chopped
  stewed tomatoes
¼ teaspoon
  oregano

Arrange fillets in baking dish. Sauté onion and green pepper in margarine in skillet. Add tomatoes, oregano and salt and pepper to taste. Simmer for several minutes. Spoon over fillets. Bake at 350 degrees for 40 minutes or until fish flakes easily. Yield: 4 servings.

Approx per serving: Cal 141, Prot 18.6 gr, Fat 3.1 gr, Chol 58.0 mg, Carbo 3.3 gr, Sod 184.5 mg, Potas 464.9 mg.

Michelle L. Schmidt, Xi Alpha Xi
Kaukauna, Wisconsin

Baked Halibut

1 onion, thinly
  sliced
2 pounds halibut
  fillets
1½ cups sliced
  fresh mushrooms
⅓ cup chopped
  tomato
¼ cup chopped
  green pepper

¼ cup chopped
  parsley
½ cup dry white
  wine
2 tablespoons
  lemon juice
¼ teaspoon
  dillweed
⅛ teaspoon pepper

Layer onion, fillets, mushrooms, tomato, green pepper and parsley in baking dish. Drizzle mixture of wine, lemon juice and seasonings over layers. Bake at 350 degrees for 30 minutes or until fish flakes easily. Yield: 6 servings.

Approx per serving: Cal 179, Prot 31.9 gr, Fat 1.9 gr, Chol 73.0 mg, Carbo 5.2 gr, Sod 90.8 mg, Potas 825.8 mg.

Dorothy Kelly, Preceptor Zeta Chi
Concord, California

Hawaiian Halibut Steaks

1 pound halibut
  fillets
1 tablespoon soy
  sauce
1 tablespoon lemon
  juice
3 green onions,
  sliced
½ cup chopped
  green pepper
1 tomato, chopped

1 16-ounce can
  unsweetened
  pineapple chunks
2 teaspoons
  cornstarch
2 teaspoons
  Worcestershire
  sauce
Garlic powder to
  taste
Ginger to taste

Arrange fillets in lightly oiled baking dish. Brush with mixture of soy sauce and lemon juice. Sprinkle with green onions, green pepper and tomato. Bake, covered, at 450 degrees for 10 minutes or until fish flakes easily. Drain pineapple, reserving juice. Blend cornstarch and reserved juice in saucepan. Cook until thickened, stirring constantly. Add pineapple and seasonings. Pour over fillets. Bake for 5 minutes longer. Garnish with additional chopped green onion. Serve over fluffy rice. Yield: 4 servings.

Approx per serving: Cal 237, Prot 24.4 gr, Fat 1.7 gr, Chol 54.8 mg, Carbo 32.9 gr, Sod 421.2 mg, Potas 784.1 mg.

Rolla Chambers, Preceptor Eta
Lethbridge, Alberta, Canada

Poached Halibut

½ medium onion,
  sliced
1 tablespoon lemon
  juice
Chopped parsley
  to taste

1 bay leaf
1 teaspoon salt
3 to 6 peppercorns
1 pound halibut
  fillets

Combine first 6 ingredients in saucepan. Add 2 to 3 cups water. Simmer for 5 minutes. Arrange fillets in saucepan. Simmer for 5 minutes or until fish flakes easily. Do not overcook. Remove fish to serving plate. Garnish with lemon wedges, tomato slices and fresh parsley. Yield: 4 servings.

Approx per serving: Cal 115, Prot 23.0 gr, Fat 1.4 gr, Chol 54.8 mg, Carbo 2.2 gr, Sod 596.9 mg, Potas 517.8 mg.

Mary Jane Bergmann, Laureate Delta
Kalispell, Montana

Halibut Cakes

2 pounds halibut
1 medium onion
¼ green pepper
3 tablespoon flour
2 eggs
1 cup milk

1 teaspoon nutmeg
1½ teaspoons salt
⅛ teaspoon pepper
½ cup margarine
1½ tablespoons
  flour

Put halibut, onion and green pepper through food grinder. Mix with 3 tablespoons flour in bowl. Add eggs 1 at a time, mixing well after each addition. Add milk and seasonings; mix well. Shape into small patties. Brown in about ¼ cup margarine in skillet. Remove fish cakes. Blend 3 tablespoons margarine and flour into pan drippings. Stir in 2 cups water gradually. Cook until thickened, stirring constantly. Return fish cakes to skillet. Simmer, covered, for 1 hour. Place fish cakes on serving plate. Spoon sauce over cakes. Yield: 6 servings.

Approx per serving: Cal 333, Prot 34.7 gr, Fat 16.3 gr, Chol 163.0 mg, Carbo 9.4 gr, Sod 780.6 mg, Potas 772.3 mg.

Carol A. Bruce, Xi Delta
Juneau, Alaska

Microwave Orange Roughy

2 pounds orange roughy fillets	6 green onions, chopped
1 cup milk	¼ cup lemon juice
3 small tomatoes, chopped	

Soak fillets in milk for 30 minutes. Drain and rinse. Arrange in glass baking dish sprayed with nonstick cooking spray. Layer tomatoes and green onions over fillets; sprinkle with lemon juice. Microwave on High for 9 to 12 minutes or until fish flakes easily. Remove to serving platter. Garnish with sprinkle of paprika. Yield: 6 servings.

Eugenia W. Bell, PL563
Louisville, Kentucky

Salmon Casserole

1 15-ounce can pink salmon	¼ teaspoon salt
1 cup cracker crumbs	Pepper to taste
2 tablespoons minced onion	¼ cup no-cholesterol egg substitute
1 tablespoon lemon juice	⅔ cup low-fat milk
	1½ cups frozen chopped broccoli

Drain and flake salmon. Combine with next 7 ingredients in bowl; mix well. Stir in broccoli. Press into lightly greased casserole. Bake at 350 degrees for 45 minutes. Yield: 6 servings.

Approx per serving: Cal 188, Prot 19.4 gr, Fat 6.3 gr, Chol 26.8 mg, Carbo 13.9 gr, Sod 526.7 mg, Potas 501.3 mg. Nutritional information does not include egg substitute.

Susan Crewe, Laureate Alpha Theta
Springfield, Ohio

Cucumber and Salmon Casserole

3 cups soft bread crumbs	1 egg yolk, beaten
¼ cup margarine	Juice of ½ lemon
¼ cup flour	1 15-ounce can pink salmon, drained, flaked
2 tablespoons margarine, melted	½ cucumber, chopped
1¼ cups low-fat milk	¼ cup chopped parsley

Sauté bread crumbs in ¼ cup margarine in skillet until golden brown. Mix with salt and pepper to taste. Blend flour and melted margarine in saucepan. Stir in milk gradually. Cook until thickened, stirring constantly. Stir a small amount of hot mixture into beaten egg yolk; stir egg yolk into hot mixture. Add lemon juice and salmon; mix well. Cook over low heat for 2 minutes, stirring constantly; do not boil. Stir in cucumber. Alternate layers of salmon mixture and crumbs in 2-quart casserole. Sprinkle with parsley. Bake at 375 degrees for 15 minutes. Yield: 6 servings.

Approx per serving: Cal 275, Prot 20.5 gr, Fat 11.1 gr, Chol 70.5 mg, Carbo 22.2 gr, Sod 509.8 mg, Potas 448.5 mg.

Judy Jamieson, Zeta
Grand Falls, Newfoundland, Canada

Salmon Loaf

½ cup milk	2 teaspoons lemon juice
1 slice bread, crumbled	2 eggs, separated
1 cup flaked pink salmon	¼ teaspoon salt
	⅛ teaspoon paprika

Heat milk and bread crumbs in double boiler over very low heat. Add salmon and lemon juice; mix well. Add well-beaten egg yolks; mix well. Cook until thickened, stirring constantly. Add salt and paprika. Fold in stiffly beaten egg whites. Pour into greased casserole; place in larger pan of hot water. Bake at 300 degrees for 1 hour or until set. Serve with peas. Yield: 4 servings.

Approx per serving: Cal 158, Prot 16.2 gr, Fat 7.4 gr, Chol 150.1 mg, Carbo 5.5 gr, Sod 427.9 mg, Potas 285.9 mg.

Ginny Cooper, Xi Omicron
Harlingen, Texas

Barbara's Salmon Loaf

½ cup low-fat milk	⅛ teaspoon paprika
1½ slices bread, crumbled	⅛ teaspoon pepper
1 cup flaked pink salmon	2 teaspoons lemon juice
¼ teaspoon salt	2 egg whites, stiffly beaten

Mix milk and bread crumbs in double boiler. Heat until warm. Add salmon, seasonings and lemon juice; mix well. Fold gently into egg whites. Pour into casserole; place in larger pan of hot water. Bake at 300 degrees for 1 hour. Yield: 4 servings.

Approx per serving: Cal 129, Prot 15.0 gr, Fat 3.9 gr, Chol 20.8 mg, Carbo 7.6 gr, Sod 439.4 mg, Potas 291.0 mg.

Barbara Eberle, Mu Tau
Lombard, Illinois

Salmon-Potato Cakes

½ cup chopped onion	¼ teaspoon salt
½ cup chopped green pepper	¼ teaspoon pepper
2 tablespoons butter	2 cups mashed potatoes
2 eggs, beaten	1 16-ounce can pink salmon, drained, flaked
½ cup flour	

Sauté onion and green pepper in butter in skillet. Cool. Combine with remaining ingredients in bowl; mix well. Drop by heaping spoonfuls onto hot greased griddle. Brown on both sides. Place on serving plate. Yield: 4 servings.

Approx per serving: Cal 415, Prot 30.2 gr, Fat 19.9 gr, Chol 196.3 mg, Carbo 27.8 gr, Sod 1012.0 mg, Potas 781.7 mg.

Sabina Beckett
Milwaukie, Oregon

Hot Salmon Salad Loaf

1   16-ounce can
    salmon
2 eggs, beaten
1 cup fine bread
    crumbs
1 tablespoon
    minced onion
½ cup milk
¼ cup chopped
    pimento-stuffed
    olives
½ teaspoon dry
    mustard
1 teaspoon lemon juice

Drain salmon, reserving liquid. Flake salmon in bowl. Add remaining ingredients and enough reserved liquid to make of desired consistency; mix well. Spoon into buttered loaf pan. Bake at 350 degrees for 40 minutes. Let stand for 10 minutes. Invert on serving plate. Yield: 6 servings.

Approx per serving: Cal 221, Prot 20.6 gr, Fat 8.7 gr, Chol 114.4 mg, Carbo 13.7 gr, Sod 600.5 mg, Potas 356.5 mg.

Salmon Steaks for Two

2 salmon steaks
3 tablespoons
    reduced-calorie
    mayonnaise
1 tablespoon sliced
    green onion
¼ teaspoon dry
    mustard
1 egg white, stiffly
    beaten

Place salmon steaks on broiler pan sprayed with nonstick cooking spray. Broil for 5 to 6 minutes on each side. Fold mayonnaise, green onions and mustard into stiffly beaten egg white. Spoon over salmon. Broil until light brown. Yield: 2 servings.

Joan Stockman, Preceptor Pi
Gering, Nebraska

Baked Red Snapper

12 ounces red
    snapper fillets
2 teaspoons
    mayonnaise
1 teaspoon Dijon
    mustard
1 teaspoon lemon
    juice
1 teaspoon chopped
    chives
1 teaspoon chopped
    parsley
2 teaspoons
    Parmesan cheese

Arrange fillets in shallow flameproof baking dish sprayed with nonstick cooking spray. Combine mayonnaise, mustard, lemon juice, chives and parsley in small bowl; mix well. Spread over fillets. Sprinkle with cheese. Bake at 400 degrees for 20 minutes. Broil for 1 minute. Yield: 2 servings.

Approx per serving: Cal 216, Prot 39.0 gr, Fat 2.5 gr, Chol 105.5 mg, Carbo 0.5 gr, Sod 196.7 mg, Potas 1105.9 mg.

Barbara Jennison, Preceptor Iota Omicron
San Angelo, Texas

Trout Cyremort

8 trout fillets
Red pepper to taste
Onion powder to
    taste
Garlic powder to
    taste
⅛ teaspoon celery
    salt
Paprika to taste
¼ cup margarine,
    melted
1   10-ounce bottle
    of Worcestershire
    sauce
¼ cup lemon juice

Arrange fillets on foil baking tray. Sprinkle with seasonings. Pour mixture of margarine, Worcestershire sauce and lemon juice over fillets. Place on grill over hot coals. Cook for 15 minutes or until fish flakes easily. Punch holes in foil to allow juices to drain. Close grill cover and vents. Smoke for 5 minutes. Remove to serving plate. Garnish with lemon wedges and parsley sprigs. Yield: 8 servings.

Debbie Mattson, Eta Chi
Ft. Pierce, Florida

Microwave Favorite Trout

1½ pounds frozen
    trout
1 envelope Butter
    Buds, prepared
3 tablespoons
    Dijon mustard
Fresh lemon juice
1 tablespoon
    dillweed
Chopped fresh
    parsley

Thaw trout, covered, in microwave, turning frequently. Rinse and pat dry. Place in baking dish. Microwave for 3 minutes; turn trout. Microwave for 2 minutes. Trout will not be completely cooked. Remove skin and bones. Place on serving platter. Drizzle with Butter Buds. Top with mustard, lemon juice and dillweed. Microwave, covered, for 1 to 2 minutes. Let stand for several minutes. Sprinkle with parsley. Yield: 8 servings.

Carol McLennan, Preceptor Alpha Tau
Lawton, Oklahoma

Tuna-Broccoli Bake

2 tablespoons
    margarine,
    melted
3 tablespoons flour
1 cup low-fat milk
4 eggs, separated
1   7-ounce can
    water-pack tuna,
    drained
¼ cup shredded
    Cheddar cheese
1   10-ounce
    package frozen
    chopped broccoli,
    thawed
3 green onions,
    chopped
1 tablespoon
    mustard
¼ teaspoon hot
    pepper sauce

Blend margarine and flour in saucepan. Stir in milk gradually. Cook until thickened, stirring constantly. Cool slightly. Add egg yolks, tuna, cheese, broccoli, green onions, mustard, hot sauce and salt to taste; mix well. Fold into stiffly beaten egg whites. Spoon into 6-cup soufflé dish. Bake at 350 degrees for 45 minutes or until brown and firm. Yield: 4 servings.

Approx per serving: Cal 294, Prot 26.3 gr, Fat 15.3 gr, Chol 291.2 mg, Carbo 13.0 gr, Sod 291.1 mg, Potas 503.1 mg.

Connie Barnes, Eta Delta
Topeka, Kansas

Main Dishes   117

Tuna-Broccoli Casserole

2   10-ounce
   packages frozen
   broccoli,cooked
1 can cream of
   mushroom soup
½ cup milk
2   7-ounce cans
   water-pack tuna,
   drained

1 cup grated
   Cheddar cheese
½ cup bread
   crumbs
2 tablespoons
   melted
   margarine

Drain broccoli; place in shallow 2-quart casserole. Blend soup and milk in bowl. Layer tuna, soup mixture and cheese over broccoli. Sprinkle mixture of crumbs and margarine over top. Bake at 350 degrees for 20 minutes. Serve with fresh fruit salad. Yield: 5 servings.

Approx per serving: Cal 378, Prot 33.2 gr, Fat 18.9 gr, Chol 77.4 mg, Carbo 19.9 gr, Sod 823.4 mg, Potas 598.2 mg.

Helen Heath, Preceptor Upsilon
Muncie, Indiana

Baked Tuna Ring

1 egg, beaten
2   7-ounce cans
   water-pack tuna,
   drained
1   10-ounce
   package frozen
   mixed vegetables
½ cup grated
   Cheddar cheese

½ cup chopped onion
¼ cup chopped
   parsley
¼ teaspoon celery
   seed
4 cups buttermilk
   baking mix
1⅓ cups low-fat
   milk

Reserve 2 tablespoons beaten egg. Combine remaining egg with tuna, vegetables, cheese, onion, parsley, celery seed and salt and pepper to taste in bowl; mix well. Combine baking mix and milk in bowl; mix well. Roll on floured surface into 13x18-inch rectangle. Spread with tuna mixture. Roll as for jelly roll from wide side. Shape into ring on greased baking sheet. Cut almost through ring at 1-inch intervals. Brush with reserved egg. Bake at 350 degrees for 35 minutes or until golden. Remove to serving plate. Yield: 6 servings.

Approx per serving: Cal 528, Prot 30.4 gr, Fat 15.3 gr, Chol 92.2 mg, Carbo 65.7 gr, Sod 1198.2 mg, Potas 475.0 mg.

Melody Bellini, Chi
Tacoma, Washington

Tuna Barbecue

2   6-ounce cans
   water-pack tuna,
   drained
1 cup finely
   chopped celery

½ cup chopped
   onion
1 cup (about)
   Sugar-Free
   Barbecue Sauce

Combine tuna, celery, onion and enough Barbecue Sauce to make of desired consistency in saucepan. Simmer for 35 to 45 minutes. Serve in whole wheat pita pockets if desired. Yield: 4 servings.

Sugar-Free Barbecue Sauce

1   46-ounce can
   tomato juice
6 chicken
   bouillon cubes
1⅛ cups lemon
   juice
¾ cup
   Worcestershire
   sauce
5 cloves of garlic,
   chopped

2 tablespoons dry
   mustard
2 tablespoons dried
   onion flakes
2 teaspoons paprika
1 teaspoon pepper
Cayenne pepper
   to taste
Artificial sweetener
   to equal ½ cup
   sugar

Combine all ingredients in saucepan; mix well. Simmer, loosely covered, for 2 hours. Cool. Store in airtight container in refrigerator. Yield: 8 cups.

Approx per serving: Cal 195, Prot 29.2 gr, Fat 1.1 gr, Chol 60.3 mg, Carbo 18 gr, Sod 1368.3 mg, Potas 1030.1 mg.

Mary Meddles, Preceptor Delta Tau
Richwood, Ohio

Easy Tuna Casserole

1   6-ounce can
   water-pack tuna,
   drained
2 cups noodles,
   cooked
1 can cream of
   mushroom soup
1 can chicken and
   rice soup

⅛ teaspoon garlic
   salt
⅛ teaspoon onion
   salt
1 cup grated
   Cheddar cheese

Combine all ingredients in casserole; mix well. Bake at 350 degrees for 20 minutes. Yield: 4 servings.

Approx per serving: Cal 383, Prot 26.6 gr, Fat 17.4 gr, Chol 96.6 mg, Carbo 29.0 gr, Sod 1507.6 mg, Potas 308.9 mg.

Judi Stribe, Lambda Eta
Manning, Iowa

Microwave Tuna Lasagna

1   12-ounce carton
     cottage cheese
1 egg
1 ounce Parmesan
     cheese
1   7-ounce can
     tuna, drained

1 can mushrooms
1 can mushroom soup
1 pound lasagna
     noodles, cooked
8 ounces mozzarella
     cheese, shredded

Combine cottage cheese, egg and Parmesan cheese in bowl; mix well. Mix tuna, mushrooms and soup in bowl. Arrange double layers of noodles in 9x13-inch glass baking dish in the following order: noodles, half the cottage cheese mixture, noodles, tuna mixture, noodles, remaining cottage cheese mixture and noodles. Top with mozzarella cheese. Microwave, covered on Medium-High for 8 minutes. Let stand for several minutes. Yield: 8 servings.

Sherry Pendlebury, Xi Alpha
Ottawa, Ontario, Canada

Tuna-Macaroni Casserole

1 cup elbow
     macaroni,
     cooked
1 can cream of
     mushroom soup
¼ cup milk
¼ cup sour cream
¼ cup minced
     onion
1   8-ounce can
     green peas,
     drained

½   4-ounce can
     mushrooms,
     drained
1   7-ounce can
     water-pack tuna,
     drained, flaked
1   2-ounce jar
     chopped pimento,
     drained
½ cup chopped
     Cheddar cheese

Combine macaroni, soup, milk, sour cream, vegetables, tuna, pimento and cheese in bowl; mix well. Pour into 1½-quart casserole. Bake at 350 degrees for 30 minutes. Yield: 4 servings.

Approx per serving: Cal 495, Prot 28.3 gr, Fat 15.4 gr, Chol 57.4 mg, Carbo 59.8 gr, Sod 0.0 mg, Potas 831.3 mg.

Sylvia McCowan, Preceptor Tau
Anderson, Indiana

Tuna-Rice Casserole

1   6-ounce can
     tuna, drained
1 can cream of
     celery soup
¾ cup minute rice
¼ cup milk
2 eggs, separated

1 tablespoon chopped
     pimento
2 teaspoons minced
     onion
½ cup milk
1 tablespoon
     chopped parsley

Combine tuna, half the soup, rice, ¼ cup milk, lightly beaten egg yolks, pimento and onion in bowl. Fold in stiffly beaten egg whites gently. Pour into greased 6x10-inch baking dish. Bake at 350 degrees for 20 minutes or until set. Heat remaining soup, ½ cup milk and parsley in saucepan, stirring constantly. Spoon over casserole. Yield: 6 servings.

Approx per serving: Cal 218, Prot 12.3 gr, Fat 11.4 gr, Chol 108.4 mg, Carbo 15.6 gr, Sod 677.7 mg, Potas 217.6 mg.

Tuna Stir-Fry

¼ cup chopped
     onion
½ clove of garlic,
     minced
1 tablespoon
     margarine
2 cups shredded
     Chinese cabbage

1 tomato, peeled,
     chopped
1   6-ounce can
     water-pack tuna,
     drained
2 cups cooked
     noodles
½ teaspoon salt

Stir-fry onion and garlic in butter in skillet. Add cabbage. Stir-fry for 5 minutes. Add remaining ingredients. Cook for 5 to 10 minutes, stirring frequently. Spoon into serving bowl. Yield: 4 servings.

Approx per serving: Cal 200, Prot 17.2 gr, Fat 4.6 gr, Chol 53.8 mg, Carbo 22.3 gr, Sod 332.6 mg, Potas 352.9 mg.

Carole Pipetti, Xi Xi
Altoona, Pennsylvania

Baked Fish Louise

8   4-ounce white fish
     fillets
Onion powder to
     taste
Garlic powder to
     taste
¼ cup finely
     chopped celery

¼ cup finely
     chopped green
     onions with tops
¼ cup reduced-
     calorie Italian
     dressing
¼ cup lemon juice

Sprinkle fillets with salt, pepper, onion and garlic powder to taste. Arrange in single layer in shallow baking dish. Sprinkle with mixture of remaining ingredients. Bake, covered with foil, at 350 degrees for 20 minutes or until fish flakes easily. Yield: 8 servings.

Approx per serving: Cal 183, Prot 21.5 gr, Fat 13.9 gr, Chol 62.3 mg, Carbo 1.2 gr, Sod 121.9 mg, Potas 370.5 mg.

Mary Ann O'Sullivan, Xi Beta Alpha
Gretna, Louisiana

Foiled Fish

4 4-ounce white
  fish fillets,
  ½-inch thick
½ cup buttermilk
  salad dressing
2 cups broccoli
  flowerets

1 green pepper,
  cut into strips
1 small onion,
  thinly sliced

Place 1 fillet on each of four 12-inch foil squares. Top with 2 tablespoons salad dressing and ¼ of the mixture of vegetables. Seal foil. Place on baking sheet. Bake at 450 degrees for 20 minutes. Let stand for 1 to 2 minutes. Yield: 4 servings.

Approx per serving: Cal 334, Prot 27.1 gr, Fat 20.7 gr, Chol 72.2 mg, Carbo 11.6 gr, Sod 189.9 mg, Potas 911.6 mg.

Pat Koeppen, Preceptor Alpha Tau
Bloomington, Indiana

Portuguese Stew

2 28-ounce cans
  tomatoes
2 green peppers,
  chopped
3 carrots, sliced
2 beef bouillon
  cubes
1 tablespoon basil

1 teaspoon cayenne
  pepper
1 teaspoon Tabasco
  sauce
1 tablespoon sugar
1½ pounds white
  fish, cut into
  pieces

Combine all ingredients except fish in large saucepan. Add 1 cup water and salt and pepper to taste. Simmer for 1 hour or until vegetables are tender. Add fish. Simmer for 30 minutes or until fish flakes easily. Ladle into serving bowls. Yield: 10 servings.

Approx per serving: Cal 160, Prot 15.2 gr, Fat 6.0 gr, Chol 38.0 mg, Carbo 11.6 gr, Sod 450.1 mg, Potas 686.8 mg.

Paula Middleton, Xi Mu Eta
Houston, Texas

Minced Clams and Tomatoes

1 7-ounce can
  minced clams
2 cups bread crumbs
¼ cup chopped
  parsley

1 20-ounce can
  tomatoes,
  chopped
¼ cup oil

Drain clams, reserving juice. Alternate layers of clams and bread crumbs in greased 1½-quart baking dish. Sprinkle with parsley and salt and pepper to taste. Spread tomatoes over top. Mix reserved clam juice with oil in small bowl. Pour over layers. Bake at 250 degrees for 20 minutes. Yield: 4 servings.

Approx per serving: Cal 376, Prot 12.2 gr, Fat 16.6 gr, Chol 20.1 mg, Carbo 44.7 gr, Sod 867.5 mg, Potas 487.9 mg.

Sabina I. Beckett, XP2140
Milwaukie, Oregon

Crab Meat Casserole

2 eggs
1 cup milk
1 tablespoon
  Worcestershire
  sauce

½ cup melted
  butter
1 cup fine cracker
  crumbs
1 pound crab meat

Combine first 4 ingredients in bowl. Beat until smooth. Add cracker crumbs and salt and pepper to taste; mix well. Stir in crab meat. Pour into greased baking dish. Bake at 350 degrees for 40 minutes or until set. Yield: 4 servings.

Approx per serving: Cal 466, Prot 26.8 gr, Fat 32.3 gr, Chol 319.3 mg, Carbo 16.6 gr, Sod 784.3 mg, Potas 361.8 mg.

Mary Ellen McCarter, Alpha Sigma
Kindersley, Saskatchewan, Canada

Crab Imperial

1 tablespoon
  melted margarine
1 tablespoon flour
½ cup milk
1 teaspoon minced
  onion
1½ teaspoons
  Worcestershire
  sauce

2 slices bread, cubed
½ cup mayonnaise
1 tablespoon lemon
  juice
½ teaspoon salt
Dash of pepper
2 tablespoons margarine
1 pound crab meat
Paprika to taste

Blend 1 tablespoon margarine and flour in saucepan. Stir in milk gradually. Cook over medium heat until thickened, stirring constantly. Add onion, Worcestershire sauce and bread; mix well. Cool. Blend in mayonnaise, lemon juice, salt and pepper. Brown 2 tablespoons margarine in saucepan. Add crab meat; toss lightly. Stir into sauce. Spoon into greased 1-quart casserole. Sprinkle with paprika. Bake at 350 degrees for 15 minutes or until light brown. Yield: 6 servings.

Approx per serving: Cal 300, Prot 15.1 gr, Fat 23.1 gr, Chol 91.8 mg, Carbo 8.0 gr, Sod 588.3 mg, Potas 198.9 mg.

Crab Meat Strata

8 slices bread,
  crusts trimmed
2 7-ounce cans
  crab meat,
  drained
½ cup mayonnaise
1 cup chopped
  celery
1 onion, chopped

1 green pepper,
  chopped
½ teaspoon salt
4 eggs, slightly beaten
3 cups milk
1 can cream of
  mushroom soup
½ cup shredded
  Cheddar cheese

Cut bread into cubes. Place half the cubes in buttered 9x13-inch baking dish. Combine crab meat, mayonnaise, celery, onion, green pepper and salt in bowl; mix well. Spoon over bread crumbs. Top with remaining bread cubes. Beat eggs and milk in bowl. Pour over layers. Chill, covered, for several hours to overnight. Bake, uncovered, at 325 degrees for 15 minutes. Spread soup over top. Bake for 45 minutes. Top with cheese. Bake for 15 minutes longer. Yield: 8 servings.

Approx per serving: Cal 403, Prot 19.8 gr, Fat 24.6 gr, Chol 205.3 mg, Carbo 25.5 gr, Sod 1254.2 mg, Potas 380.3 mg.

Crab-Zucchini Bake

4 medium zucchini,
   sliced
1 onion, chopped
2 cloves of garlic,
   chopped
½ cup butter
3 tomatoes, cut
   into quarters
1 teaspoon basil
½ teaspoon
   paprika
1 teaspoon salt

½ teaspoon pepper
½ cup seasoned
   bread crumbs
1 cup Swiss cheese
   strips
2 7-ounce cans
   crab meat,
   drained
⅓ cup Swiss
   cheese strips
¼ cup seasoned
   bread crumbs

Cook zucchini, onion and garlic in butter in covered saucepan for 12 minutes. Add tomatoes, seasonings, ½ cup bread crumbs, 1 cup cheese and crab meat; mix well. Pour into greased 2-quart baking dish. Bake at 375 degrees for 30 minutes. Sprinkle ⅓ cup cheese and ¼ cup bread crumbs over top. Bake for 15 minutes longer. Yield: 4 servings.

Approx per serving: Cal 590, Prot 33.4 gr, Fat 37.2 gr, Chol 200.6 mg, Carbo 33.4 gr, Sod 2129.3 mg, Potas 998.0 mg.

Linda Schwartzberg, Xi Iota Kappa
St. Peters, Missouri

Hot Pineapple-Crab Salad

¾ cup pineapple
   chunks
¾ cup sliced celery
1 teaspoon minced
   onion
1½ teaspoons
   lemon juice

⅓ cup mayonnaise
3 tablespoons
   chopped
   almonds
1 tablespoon
   chopped pimento
1 cup crab meat

Combine first 7 ingredients in bowl. Fold in crab meat. Spoon into casserole. Bake at 350 degrees for 30 minutes or until heated through. Yield: 4 servings.

Approx per serving: Cal 249, Prot 7.8 gr, Fat 15.4 gr, Chol 47.4 mg, Carbo 26.7 gr, Sod 478.9 mg, Potas 226.0 mg.

Tommye Barker, Rho Omega
Houston, Texas

Chinese Lobster

1 ounce dried
   mushrooms
6 ounces lobster,
   thinly sliced
1½ cups thinly
   sliced onions
1 8-ounce can
   bean sprouts

1 3-ounce can
   bamboo shoots,
   thinly sliced
2 tablespoons oil
1 teaspoon
   cornstarch
1 teaspoon sweet
   and sour sauce

Soak mushrooms in hot water in bowl for 15 minutes; drain and slice thinly. Stir-fry mushrooms, lobster, onions, bean sprouts and bamboo shoots in oil for several minutes. Season with salt and pepper to taste. Blend cornstarch with 3 tablespoons water and sweet and sour sauce. Pour over lobster mixture. Cook for 1 minute, stirring constantly. Serve over hot deep-fried noodles with additional sweet and sour sauce. Yield: 2 servings.

Mildred Kaufman, Laureate Alpha Epsilon
Kitchener, Ontario, Canada

Cioppino

2½ pounds lobster
   meat
24 mussels
½ cup dry white
   wine
1 large onion,
   thinly sliced
2 cloves of garlic,
   bruised
6 tablespoons olive
   oil
1 green pepper,
   thinly sliced
½ pound green
   onions, cut into
   2-inch pieces
2 bay leaves

1 sprig of thyme
Oregano to taste
8 ounces
   mushrooms,
   thinly sliced
Freshly ground
   pepper to taste
1 cup tomato puree
½ pound sole fillets,
   cut into 1x2-inch
   pieces
1 cup dry white
   wine
¼ pound crab meat
½ cup Parmesan
   cheese

Combine lobster, mussels, ½ cup wine and ½ cup water in large saucepan. Cook, covered, over high heat for 5 minutes. Remove lobster and mussels; cut lobster into pieces. Cook liquid until reduced to ½. Saute onion and garlic in olive oil in skillet. Add green pepper, green onions, bay leaves, thyme and oregano. Cook over medium-high heat, stirring constantly. Discard garlic. Add mushrooms, pepper and salt to taste, tomato puree, fish and 1 cup wine. Poach, covered, for 2 minutes. Add reduced liquid, lobster and crab meat. Bring to a boil; remove herbs. Ladle into copper serving dish. Arrange mussels on top. Garnish with lobster claws and pieces of lobster meat. Sprinkle with Parmesan cheese. Serve with hot Italian bread. Yield: 10 servings.

Patricia Thorpe, Xi Iota Mu
Crescent City, California

Scallops with Vegetables

½ pound scallops,
   sliced
2 tablespoons
   oyster sauce
1 teaspoon soy
   sauce
2 teaspoons
   cornstarch

¼ teaspoon sugar
1½ cups snow
   peas
2 green onions,
   chopped
2 tablespoons
   margarine

Combine scallops with next 4 ingredients in bowl. Sauté snow peas and onions in margarine in skillet for 3 minutes or until tender-crisp. Add scallops mixture. Cook over high heat for 3 minutes or just until scallops are tender and sauce is slightly thickened, stirring constantly. Serve with rice. Yield: 4 servings.

Marilyn West, Xi Beta
Las Vegas, Nevada

Shrimp and Asparagus Casserole

8 ounces
   mushrooms,
   sliced
¼ cup margarine
2 tablespoons flour
1 cup low-fat milk
2 tablespoons
   Sherry
½ cup grated
   Swiss cheese

⅛ teaspoon nutmeg
12 asparagus
   spears, cooked
1 pound cooked
   shrimp
½ cup dry bread
   crumbs
½ cup grated
   Swiss cheese

Sauté mushrooms in margarine in skillet. Sprinkle with flour; mix well. Stir in milk and Sherry gradually. Cook until thickened, stirring constantly. Add ½ cup cheese and nutmeg. Layer asparagus and shrimp in 8x12-inch baking dish. Spoon sauce over layers. Sprinkle with mixture of crumbs and ½ cup cheese. Bake at 350 degrees for 20 minutes or until golden. Yield: 6 servings.

Approx per serving: Cal 308, Prot 27.9 gr, Fat 14.8 gr, Chol 134.3 mg, Carbo 14.1 gr, Sod 421.4 mg, Potas 407.7 mg.

Kelly Smith, Laureate Gamma
Eagle River, Alaska

Shrimp and Artichoke Casserole

4½ tablespoons
   butter, melted
4½ tablespoons
   flour
1 cup whipping
   cream
½ cup half and half
¼ cup dry Sherry
1 tablespoon
   Worcestershire
   sauce
8 ounces mushrooms,
   sliced

2 tablespoons butter
¼ teaspoon flour
1 14-ounce can
   artichoke hearts,
   drained
1½ pounds cooked
   shrimp
¼ cup Parmesan
   cheese
Paprika to taste

Blend 4½ tablespoons butter and flour in saucepan. Stir in whipping cream and half and half gradually. Cook until thickened, stirring constantly. Add Sherry and Worcestershire sauce. Sauté mushrooms in 2 tablespoons butter in skillet. Sprinkle with ¼ teaspoon flour; mix well. Slice artichokes into halves. Layer artichokes, shrimp, mushrooms and sauce in baking dish. Top with cheese and paprika. Bake at 375 degrees for 20 minutes. Yield: 6 servings.

Approx per serving: Cal 473, Prot 32.5 gr, Fat 32.5 gr, Chol 274.6 mg, Carbo 10.4 gr, Sod 399.5 mg, Potas 404.7 mg. Nutritional information does not include artichoke hearts.

Margie Gugino Hendricks, Xi Beta Tau
Little Rock, Arkansas

Baked Shrimp-Cheese Puff

4 slices bread
4 teaspoons
   margarine,
   softened
8 ounces shrimp,
   cut up

8 ounces Cheddar
   cheese, grated
3 eggs, beaten
2 cups low-fat milk
¼ teaspoon dry
   mustard

Spread bread with margarine; cut into cubes. Alternate layers of bread cubes, shrimp and ¾ of the cheese in casserole. Beat eggs with milk, dry mustard and salt and pepper to taste. Pour over layers. Top with remaining cheese. Bake at 350 degrees for 40 minutes or until puffed and golden. Yield: 4 servings.

Approx per serving: Cal 514, Prot 39.3 gr, Fat 29.2 gr, Chol 336.5 mg, Carbo 22.1 gr, Sod 772.5 mg, Potas 385.3 mg.

Marjorie E. Towslee, Preceptor Rho
Cartersville, Georgia

Shrimp Casserole

1 green pepper,
   chopped
1½ cups chopped
   onion
2 stalks celery,
   chopped
2 tablespoons
   margarine
3 cups shrimp

1 can Ro-Tel
   tomatoes
1 can cream of
   mushroom soup
2 cups cooked rice
¼ cup chopped
   parsley
½ cup bread
   crumbs

Sauté green pepper, onion and celery in margarine in saucepan. Add shrimp, tomatoes and salt and pepper to taste; mix well. Cook for 5 minutes. Stir in soup. Cook for 5 minutes longer. Add rice and parsley; mix well. Spoon into greased 9x13-inch casserole. Top with bread crumbs. Bake at 450 degrees for 30 minutes. Yield: 6 servings.

Approx per serving: Cal 284, Prot 19.8 gr, Fat 8.9 gr, Chol 100.1 mg, Carbo 30.9 gr, Sod 888.3 mg, Potas 413.6 mg.

Marlene Roy, Kappa
New Iberia, Louisiana

Shrimp Creole

1 onion, finely
   chopped
1 green pepper,
   finely chopped
¼ cup butter
2 tablespoons flour

⅛ teaspoon pepper
2 8-ounce cans
   tomato sauce
1 tablespoon vinegar
1½ pounds shrimp

Sauté onion and green pepper in butter in large skillet. Stir in flour and pepper. Add tomato sauce and vinegar; mix well. Simmer, covered, for 10 minutes. Add shrimp and salt to taste. Simmer, covered, for 5 minutes. Serve over fluffy rice. Yield: 6 servings.

Approx per serving: Cal 372, Prot 25.1 gr, Fat 20.2 gr, Chol 193.8 mg, Carbo 22.4 gr, Sod 745.5 mg, Potas 635.1 mg.

Delicious Shrimp Casserole

3 slices bread
½ cup low-fat milk
2 tablespoons
   margarine,
   melted
2 tablespoons flour
1 cup low-fat milk
1 cup chopped
   onion
1 cup chopped
   celery
1 cup chopped
   green pepper
4 cloves of garlic,
   minced
¼ cup margarine

¼ cup white wine
1 cup chopped
   mushrooms
3 cups cooked rice
3 cups shrimp
2 tablespoons
   chopped parsley
½ cup chopped
   green onion tops
⅛ teaspoon curry
   powder
¾ cup bread
   crumbs
2 tablespoons
   margarine

Soak bread in ½ cup milk for several minutes. Blend 2 tablespoons melted margarine and flour in saucepan. Stir in 1 cup milk gradually. Cook until thickened, stirring constantly. Sauté onion, celery, green pepper and garlic in ¼ cup margarine in skillet. Add bread mixture, white sauce, wine, mushrooms, rice, shrimp, parsley, green onion tops and curry powder; mix well. Add ¼ cup water if necessary. Cook for 8 minutes, stirring constantly. Pour into 2-quart casserole. Top with crumbs; dot with 2 tablespoons margarine. Bake at 350 degrees for 30 minutes. Yield: 6 servings.

Approx per serving: Cal 451, Prot 23.3 gr, Fat 17.7 gr, Chol 99.1 mg, Carbo 48.0 gr, Sod 433.2 mg, Potas 493.5 mg.

Tommie Billingsley, Xi Beta Eta
Horseshoe Bend, Arkansas

Lemon Broiled Shrimp Kabobs

2 pounds peeled
   shrimp
1 cup soy sauce
¼ cup lemon juice
1 medium onion,
   minced

8 cherry tomatoes
1 green pepper,
   cut into large
   pieces

Marinate shrimp in mixture of soy sauce, lemon juice and onion for 2 hours or longer. Drain. Thread shrimp, tomatoes and green pepper onto skewers. Broil for 10 minutes, turning frequently. Yield: 4 servings.

Approx per serving: Cal 285, Prot 56.0 gr, Fat 2.7 gr, Chol 340.2 mg, Carbo 6.3 gr, Sod 324.2 mg, Potas 506.4 mg.

Maureen Dwyer, Omicron Tau
Kimberling City, Missouri

Shrimp Fried Rice

2 eggs, beaten
1 tablespoon oil
1 cup fresh bean
   sprouts
½ cup canned
   sliced
   mushrooms,
   drained
2 tablespoons oil

3 cups cooked rice
2 tablespoons oil
2 tablespoons soy
   sauce
2 green onions,
   chopped
1 cup cooked
   shrimp

Scramble eggs in 1 tablespoon hot oil in wok until soft; remove eggs. Stir-fry bean sprouts and mushrooms with salt to taste in 2 tablespoons hot oil for 1 minute; remove vegetables. Stir-fry rice in 2 tablespoons hot oil until heated through. Stir in soy sauce. Add remaining ingredients, eggs and vegetables. Heat to serving temperature, stirring constantly. Spoon into serving bowl. Yield: 6 servings.

Approx per serving: Cal 280, Prot 10.7 gr, Fat 13.8 gr, Chol 116.3 mg, Carbo 27.9 gr, Sod 876.0 mg, Potas 197.1 mg.

Carol Terpstra, Alpha
Billings, Montana

Egg Rolls

½ pound lean
   ground pork
1 tablespoon oil
½ teaspoon sugar
1 tablespoon soy
   sauce
½ pound shrimp
½ cup chopped
   mushrooms
1 cup finely
   chopped celery
2 tablespoons oil

¼ cup chopped
   onion
2 teaspoons salt
½ pound fresh
   bean sprouts
1 tablespoon
   cornstarch
2 tablespoons
   chicken stock
Egg roll wrappers
Oil for deep frying

Preheat 12-inch wok over high heat for 30 seconds. Stir-fry pork in 1 tablespoon oil for 2 minutes. Stir in sugar, soy sauce, shrimp and mushrooms. Cook just until shrimp are pink; do not overcook. Remove to bowl. Stir-fry celery in 2 tablespoons oil in wok over medium heat for 5 minutes. Add onion. Stir-fry until clear. Stir in salt and bean sprouts. Add pork mixture. Cook until liquid comes to a boil. Pour cornstarch dissolved in chicken stock into center; mix well. Cook for 1 to 2 minutes, stirring constantly. Cool. Place ¼ cup mixture in center of each wrapper; fold envelope-style to enclose filling, sealing moistened edges. Deep-fry at 350 to 375 degrees; drain. Arrange on serving platter. Serve with Sweet and Sour Sauce. Yield: 24 servings.

Sweet and Sour Sauce

4 teaspoons
   cornstarch
¾ cup pineapple
   juice
½ cup packed
   brown sugar

⅓ cup rice vinegar
3 tablespoons
   catsup
1 tablespoon soy
   sauce

Blend cornstarch and pineapple juice in saucepan. Add remaining ingredients. Cook until clear and thickened, stirring constantly. Do not overcook. Yield: 16 tablespoons.

Approx per tablespoon: Cal 39, Prot 0.2 gr, Fat 0.0 gr, Chol 0.0 mg, Carbo 9.9 gr, Sod 113.9 mg, Potas 60.4 mg.

Ann Stone, Xi Xi
Eielson AFB, Alaska

Shrimp Divan

1 medium onion,
  finely chopped
½ cup chopped
  green pepper
1 apple, chopped
1 tablespoon curry
  powder
3 tablespoons
  margarine
3 tablespoons flour
2 cups low-fat milk
¼ cup lemon juice

1 can Cheddar
  cheese soup
3 cups cooked egg
  noodles
1 16-ounce
  package frozen
  broccoli, thawed
3 chicken breasts,
  cooked, sliced
1 pound small
  shrimp, cooked
Paprika to taste

Sauté onion, green pepper, apple, curry powder and salt to taste in margarine in saucepan. Stir in flour. Combine milk, lemon juice and soup in bowl. Stir into vegetable mixture. Cook until heated through, stirring frequently. Layer noodles, broccoli, chicken, shrimp and soup mixture in 9x13-inch baking dish. Sprinkle with paprika. Bake at 350 degrees for 1 hour. Yield: 8 servings.

Approx per serving: Cal 306, Prot 32.6 gr, Fat 7.6 gr, Chol 118.6 mg, Carbo 26.9 gr, Sod 201.0 mg, Potas 583.9 mg.

Elizabeth Jackson, Xi Alpha
Mililani, Hawaii

Fruited Shrimp Kabobs

1 cup orange juice
½ cup vinegar
½ cup oil
½ cup soy sauce
1 pound fresh
  shrimp

2 lemons, cut into
  wedges
4 bananas, cut into
  thick slices

Combine first 4 ingredients in bowl. Add shrimp, lemons and bananas. Marinate in refrigerator for 1 hour or longer. Drain, reserving marinade. Thread onto skewers. Broil 3 inches from heat source for 6 minutes, turning frequently and basting with reserved marinade. Serve with heated marinade as sauce. Yield: 4 servings.

Approx per serving: Cal 457, Prot 31.7 gr, Fat 29.4 gr, Chol 170.1 mg, Carbo 48.1 gr, Sod 2798.9 mg, Potas 1036.1 mg.

Linda Thorstenson, Alpha Theta Zeta
Houston, Texas

Shrimp St. Jacques

3 green onions,
  chopped
½ cup sliced fresh
  mushrooms
½ clove of garlic,
  chopped
2 tablespoons
  margarine

2 tablespoons flour
¾ cup low-fat milk
2 tablespoons
  white wine
¼ cup grated
  Swiss cheese
1½ cups cooked
  shrimp

Sauté green onions, mushrooms and garlic in margarine in skillet; remove vegetables. Blend flour into pan juices. Stir in milk and wine gradually. Cook until thickened, stirring constantly. Add cheese, Cook until melted, stirring constantly. Stir in sautéed vegetables and shrimp. Pour into buttered casserole. Bake at 350 degrees for 15 minutes or until bubbly. Yield: 4 servings.

Approx per serving: Cal 177, Prot 15.9 gr, Fat 8.9 gr, Chol 80.9 mg, Carbo 7.4 gr, Sod 212.7 mg, Potas 210.0 mg.

Maxine Prentice, Xi Iota
Peterborough, Ontario, Canada

Savory Shrimp

2 cups sliced
  mushrooms
½ cup chopped
  green onions
7 tablespoons
  margarine
¼ cup flour
1 can chicken
  bouillon
1 teaspoon nutmeg

¼ cup pale dry
  Sherry
1 tablespoon lemon
  juice
1 19-ounce can
  pineapple
  chunks, drained
2 pounds shrimp,
  cooked, peeled

Sauté mushrooms and green onions in margarine in skillet; remove vegetables. Blend flour into pan juices. Stir in bouillon gradually. Cook until thickened, stirring constantly. Stir in nutmeg, Sherry, lemon juice and salt and pepper to taste. Stir in sautéed vegetables, pineapple and shrimp. Heat to serving temperature. Serve on fluffy rice. Garnish with additional chopped green onions.
Yield: 8 servings.

Approx per serving: Cal 536, Prot 47.0 gr, Fat 18.6 gr, Chol 272.8 mg, Carbo 42.5 gr, Sod 652.8 mg, Potas 691.1 mg.

Vera Wilson, Preceptor Alpha Phi
Ottawa, Ontario, Canada

Skewered Seafood

1 pound shrimp,
  cooked
1 pound scallops
3 green peppers,
  cut in 1-inch
  pieces
1 20-ounce can
  pineapple
  chunks, drained

⅔ pound fresh
  mushroom caps
¼ cup melted
  margarine
¼ cup lemon juice
¼ cup soy sauce
1 tablespoon
  chopped parsley

Combine shrimp, scallops, green peppers, pineapple chunks and mushroom caps in shallow dish. Mix remaining ingredients in small bowl. Pour over seafood. Marinate, covered, in refrigerator for 2 hours. Drain, reserving marinade. Alternate marinated ingredients on 6 skewers. Place on grill 4 inches from medium-hot coals. Grill for 7 minutes on each side, brushing occasionally with marinade. Yield: 6 servings.

Approx per serving: Cal 361, Prot 39.2 gr, Fat 10.1 gr, Chol 153.5 mg, Carbo 31.5 gr, Sod 1297.4 mg, Potas 988.2 mg.

Kathy Webb, Tau Epsilon
Wauconda, Illinois

Broccoli Frittata

1 bunch broccoli
1 cup sliced onion
2 cloves of garlic,
  minced
1 tablespoon oil
6 eggs, lightly
  beaten

1 teaspoon salt
Pinch of nutmeg
Pinch of freshly
  ground pepper
½ cup grated
  mozzarella cheese

Trim tough ends from broccoli; peel stems. Cut into ¾-inch pieces. Steam broccoli in boiling water in saucepan until tender-crisp. Drain. Sauté onion and garlic in oil in oven-proof skillet. Add broccoli. Stir-fry for 1 minute. Combine eggs, salt, nutmeg and pepper; mix well. Pour over broccoli. Sprinkle with cheese. Cook over medium heat for 5 to 10 minutes or until set but moist. Broil for 2 to 3 minutes or until brown. Cut into wedges. Yield: 4 servings.

Helen Stokaluk, Laureate Eta
Thunder Bay, Ontario, Canada

Broccoli Puff with Cheese Sauce

1 10-ounce
  package frozen
  chopped broccoli,
  cooked
6 eggs, separated
¼ teaspoon salt
¼ teaspoon pepper
½ teaspoon cream
  of tartar
3 tablespoons flour

2 tablespoons
  margarine
2 cups low-fat milk
1 8-ounce package
  sliced American
  cheese, chopped
1 tablespoon
  Worcestershire sauce
1 teaspoon dry mustard

Combine broccoli, egg yolks, salt and pepper in blender container. Process until smooth. Beat egg whites and cream of tartar until stiff but not dry. Fold in broccoli mixture gently. Spoon into ungreased 1-quart baking dish. Bake at 350 degrees for 20 minutes or until puffed and set. Blend flour and melted margarine in saucepan. Cook over medium heat until bubbly, stirring constantly. Stir in milk gradually. Cook over medium heat until thickened, stirring constantly. Add remaining ingredients; stir until well blended. Spoon hot broccoli puff onto serving plates. Top with cheese sauce. Yield: 6 servings.

Approx per serving: Cal 317, Prot 19.1 gr, Fat 19.8 gr, Chol 283.3 mg, Carbo 16.0 gr, Sod 890.4 mg, Potas 429.7 mg.

Linda Jordan, Iota Kappa
Avon, New York

Cheese Blintz

1 egg, beaten
¼ cup ricotta cheese
Cinnamon to taste

Artificial sweetener
  to taste

Pour egg into 6-inch nonstick skillet. Cook until lightly browned on bottom and almost set on top. Remove from heat. Sprinkle mixture of remaining ingredients over half the egg; fold over to enclose filling. Place on serving plate. Yield: 1 serving.

Approx per serving: Cal 82, Prot 6.5 gr, Fat 5.8 gr, Chol 252.8 mg, Carbo 0.5 gr, Sod 61.2 mg, Potas 64.7 mg.

Deborah Woodard, Xi Eta Theta
Sepulveda, California

Cheese Custard

4 eggs, separated
1½ cups low-fat
  milk
⅛ teaspooon nutmeg

1½ cups grated
  Swiss cheese
Salt substitute to
  taste

Beat egg yolks with remaining ingredients in bowl. Fold in stiffly beaten egg whites gently. Pour into shallow 9-inch baking dish. Bake at 350 degrees for 30 minutes or until set. Serve immediately. Yield: 4 servings.

Approx per serving: Cal 278, Prot 21.2 gr, Fat 18.7 gr, Chol 299.0 mg, Carbo 5.6 gr, Sod 408.9 mg, Potas 251.7 mg.

Jackie Vogler, Xi Sigma Pi
Hilltop Lakes, Texas

Vegetable Custard

1 cup bread crumbs
1 cup sliced fresh
  mushrooms
1 cup sliced
  zucchini
1 cup fresh green
  beans
1 cup sliced carrots
½ cup chopped
  green pepper

1 cup chopped
  onion
2 tablespoons butter
4 eggs, well beaten
2 cups milk
1 tomato, sliced
¼ cup Parmesan
  cheese
2 tablespoons
  melted butter

Sprinkle bread crumbs in greased springform pan. Sauté next 6 vegetables in 2 tablespoons butter in skillet until tender-crisp. Spoon into prepared pan. Combine eggs and milk with salt, pepper and nutmeg to taste in bowl; mix well. Pour over vegetables. Top with sliced tomatoes, Parmesan cheese and 2 tablespoons melted butter. Bake at 375 degrees for 35 minutes or until set. Place on serving plate; remove side of pan. Cut into wedges. Yield: 8 servings.

Approx per serving: Cal 151, Prot 7.3 gr, Fat 8.3 gr, Chol 144.0 mg, Carbo 12.4 gr, Sod 144.3 mg, Potas 331.1 mg.

Joanie Hagel, Preceptor Phi
Fairfax, Virginia

Eggnog Oven Omelet

10 eggs
½ cup sugar
½ cup yogurt
½ cup sugar-free
    carbonated cream
    soda
1 tablespoon grated
    orange rind

1 tablespoon vanilla
    extract
½ teaspoon nutmeg
¼ teaspoon salt
1 tablespoon
    confectioners' sugar
1½ cups blueberries

Beat eggs and sugar in mixer bowl at high speed until thick and lemon-colored. Combine yogurt, cream soda, orange rind, vanilla, nutmeg and salt in bowl; beat until smooth. Add egg mixture; mix well. Pour into rectangular baking dish. Bake for 45 minutes or until set. Sprinkle with confectioners' sugar. Cut into squares. Top with blueberries. Yield: 12 servings.

Approx per serving: Cal 121, Prot 5.8 gr, Fat 5.2 gr, Chol 211.5 mg, Carbo 12.7 gr, Sod 100.5 mg, Potas 83.4 mg.

Brenda Latimer, Delta Epsilon
Bowling Green, Kentucky

Vegetable Swiss Omelets

1 small onion,
    chopped
1 zucchini, sliced
1 cup fresh sliced
    mushrooms
½ cup chopped
    green pepper
1 tomato, peeled,
    chopped

½ teaspoon dried
    oregano leaves
½ teaspoon salt
¼ teaspoon pepper
8 eggs
½ cup low-fat milk
½ cup shredded Swiss
    cheese

Sauté onion, zucchini, mushrooms and green pepper in nonstick skillet for 3 minutes or until tender. Add tomato, oregano and salt. Cook until heated through. Set aside. Beat eggs and milk in bowl until smooth. Heat nonstick skillet over medium heat until hot enough to sizzle a drop of water. Pour ½ cup egg mixture into skillet. Cook until set. Sprinkle ¼ of the sautéed vegetables and ¼ ot the cheese over half the omelet; fold over to enclose filling. Place on serving plate. Repeat with remaining ingredients. Yield: 4 servings.

Approx per serving: Cal 264, Prot 20.0 gr, Fat 16.1 gr, Chol 521.0 mg, Carbo 9.9 gr, Sod 513.5 mg, Potas 543.8 mg.

Louise Witte, Alpha Epsilon
Yoakum, Texas

Broccoli Quiche

2 cups chopped
    fresh broccoli
⅓ cup chopped
    onion
½ cup chopped
    green pepper
6 slices Lite Line
    cheese

1 cup low-fat milk
½ cup buttermilk
    baking mix
3 eggs
¼ teaspoon salt
¼ teaspoon pepper

Combine broccoli, onion and green pepper with a small amount of water in saucepan. Cook, covered, for 10 minutes; drain. Place in lightly greased 9-inch pie plate. Top with cheese. Combine remaining ingredients in blender container. Process until smooth. Pour over vegetables. Bake at 375 degrees for 25 minutes or until set. Let stand for 5 minutes. Cut into wedges. Yield: 6 servings.

Approx per serving: Cal 192, Prot 13.4 gr, Fat 9.1 gr, Chol 130.3 mg, Carbo 14.8 gr, Sod 692.7 mg, Potas 359.0 mg.

Linda F. Trahan, Kappa
New Iberia, Louisiana

Broccoli-Rice Quiche

1½ cups cooked rice
3 ounces Cheddar
    cheese, grated
1 egg
¾ teaspoon salt
¼ cup low-fat milk

1   10-ounce
    package chopped
    broccoli, cooked
¾ cup sliced
    mushrooms
2 eggs

Combine rice, half the cheese, 1 egg and salt in bowl; mix well. Press over bottom and side of 9-inch pie plate. Mix milk, broccoli, mushrooms and 2 eggs in bowl. Pour into prepared pie plate. Bake at 350 degrees for 20 minutes. Sprinkle with remaining cheese. Bake for 10 minutes longer. Yield: 3 servings.

Approx per serving: Cal 347, Prot 19.8 gr, Fat 15.6 gr, Chol 281.7 mg, Carbo 32.5 gr, Sod 1204.8 mg, Potas 449.0 mg.

Jan Britson, Kappa Beta
Ames, Iowa

Confetti Cheese Quiche

⅔ cup flour
¼ teaspoon salt
3 tablespoons
    shortening
⅓ cup low-fat
    cottage cheese,
    sieved
½ cup shredded
    low calorie
    cheese
1   8-ounce can
    mixed vegetables,
    drained

¼ cup finely
    chopped green
    onion
3 eggs, slightly
    beaten
1 cup evaporated
    skim milk
½ teaspoon salt
⅛ teaspoon pepper
½ cup shredded
    low-calorie cheese

Mix flour and ¼ teaspoon salt in bowl. Cut in shortening until crumbly. Stir in cottage cheese with fork. Roll into circle on lightly floured surface. Fit into 9-inch pie plate; trim and flute edge. Sprinkle with ½ cup shredded cheese. Add mixture of mixed vegetables and green onion. Combine eggs, milk, ½ teaspoon salt, pepper in bowl; mix well. Pour over vegetables. Sprinkle with ½ cup shredded cheese. Bake at 325 degrees for 45 minutes or until set. Let stand for 10 minutes. Cut into wedges. Yield: 8 servings.

Approx per serving: Cal 176, Prot 8.0 gr, Fat 9.8 gr, Chol 95.9 mg, Carbo 14.3 gr, Sod 451.5 mg, Potas 149.7 mg.

Dorothy Gessinger, Xi Alpha Psi
Federal Way, Washington

No-Crust Quiche

¼ cup chopped
   jalapeño peppers
¾ cup grated
   Cheddar cheese

6 eggs
Lemon pepper to taste

Sprinkle jalapeño peppers in greased 8-inch pie plate. Top with Cheddar cheese. Combine eggs with salt and lemon pepper to taste in bowl. Beat with fork until smooth. Pour over cheese and peppers. Bake at 350 degrees for 25 minutes or until set. Cut into wedges. Yield: 6 servings.

Approx per serving: Cal 139, Prot 10.1 gr, Fat 10.3 gr, Chol 266.8 mg, Carbo 1.0 gr, Sod 160.6 mg, Potas 84.7 mg.

Ann Ball, Xi Lambda Iota
Houston, Texas

Vegetable Quiche for One

1 egg
½ cup evaporated
   milk
2 to 3 tablespoons
   chopped
   mushrooms
2 to 3 tablespoons
   chopped spinach

2 to 3 tablespoons
   chopped broccoli
⅓ ounce Cheddar
   cheese, grated
⅓ ounce Swiss cheese,
   grated
4 teaspoons
   Parmesan cheese

Combine egg and evaporated milk with salt and pepper to taste in bowl. Beat until smooth. Stir in remaining ingredients. Pour into individual quiche pan. Bake at 350 degrees for 30 minutes. Yield: 1 serving.

Approx per serving: Cal 372, Prot 23.6 gr, Fat 23.1 gr, Chol 342.7 mg, Carbo 13.3 gr, Sod 389.0 mg, Potas 633.0 mg.

Teresa Wash, Mu Zeta
Big Spring, Texas

Rice Soufflé

3 eggs, separated
1 cup cold cooked
   rice
½ cup milk

2 tablespoons butter
1 cup grated
   Cheddar cheese
⅛ teaspoon salt

Combine beaten egg yolks, rice, milk, butter and cheese in bowl; mix well. Fold in stiffly beaten egg whites and salt gently. Spoon into greased rectangular baking dish. Bake at 300 degrees for 30 minutes or until set and brown on top. Yield: 4 servings.
Note: May add chicken or tuna if desired.

Approx per serving: Cal 300, Prot 14.1 gr, Fat 20.3 gr, Chol 239.6 mg, Carbo 14.9 gr, Sod 589.9 mg, Potas 131.6 mg.

Shirley L. Knight, Laureate Pi
Central Point, Oregon

Egg-Stuffed Zucchini

4 medium zucchini
1 large tomato,
   chopped
2 tablespoons
   butter
3 eggs, beaten

¼ teaspoon salt
⅛ teaspoon pepper
½ cup shredded sharp
   American cheese

Cut zucchini in half lengthwise. Scoop out pulp leaving ¼-inch thick shells. Chop enough pulp to measure 1 cup. Place zucchini shells cut side down in ½ cup water in skillet. Simmer, covered, for 5 minutes or just until tender; drain. Turn cut side up in skillet. Sprinkle with salt to taste. Sauté zucchini pulp and tomato in butter in medium skillet for 3 minutes. Add eggs, salt and pepper. Cook over low heat just until set. Spoon into zucchini shells. Top with cheese. Heat, covered, until cheese melts. Yield: 4 servings.

Approx per serving: Cal 175, Prot 9.1 gr, Fat 11.2 gr, Chol 209.9 mg, Carbo 11.4 gr, Sod 309.3 mg, Potas 658.4 mg.

Virginia L. Beach, Laureate Lambda
Aurora, Colorado

Microwave Eggplant Parmesan

1 eggplant, peeled,
   sliced
1 tablespoon salt
1 cup flour
2 eggs, beaten
3 tablespoons oil

8 ounces grated
   mozzarella cheese
2½ cups spaghetti
   sauce
½ cup Parmesan
   cheese

Combine eggplant with water to cover and 1 tablespoon salt in bowl. Let stand for 30 minutes; drain. Rinse eggplant well; pat dry. Coat with flour; dip into beaten eggs. Brown in oil in skillet. Drain on paper towel. Alternate layers of eggplant, mozzarella cheese and spaghetti sauce in 2-quart baking dish until all ingredients are used. Top with Parmesan cheese. Microwave, covered, for 10 minutes or until almost tender. Microwave, uncovered, for 5 minutes. Let stand for several minutes. Yield: 4 servings.

Approx per serving: Cal 500, Prot 25.0 gr, Fat 31.2 gr, Chol 190.4 mg, Carbo 29.9 gr, Sod 609.4 mg, Potas 276.2 mg.
Nutritional information does not include any salt.

Mary Hildebrand, Omicron Tau
Elgin, Illinois

Eggplant alla Parmigiana

2 eggplant, peeled,
  sliced
1 28-ounce can
  tomatoes
2 tablespoons butter
2 tablespoons basil
4 ounces mozzarella
  cheese, grated

4 ounces Swiss cheese,
  grated
¼ cup oil
½ cup Parmesan
  cheese

Sprinkle eggplant with salt. Let stand for 30 minutes. Process tomatoes in blender container until smooth. Combine with butter, basil and salt and pepper to taste in saucepan. Simmer for 20 minutes or until thickened to desired consistency. Mix mozzarella and Swiss cheeses in bowl. Rinse eggplant; pat dry. Heat oil to 300 degrees in skillet. Fry eggplant slices several at a time for 3 minutes or until golden brown. Drain on paper towel. Spread 6 tablespoons tomato sauce in 9x13-inch baking dish. Alternate layers of eggplant slices and cheese mixture in prepared dish until all ingredients are used. Top with Parmesan cheese. Bake at 375 degrees for 25 minutes. Yield: 6 servings.

Approx per serving: Cal 335, Prot 15.5 gr, Fat 25.9 gr, Chol 56.8 mg, Carbo 12.3 gr, Sod 818.9 mg, Potas 536.7 mg.

Kitty Whitehead, Eta
Calgary, Alberta, Canada

Enchilada Bake

¾ cup chopped
  onion
¾ cup chopped
  green pepper
1 teaspoon minced
  garlic
2 teaspoons oil
1 19-ounce can
  red kidney beans
1 16-ounce can
  stewed tomatoes

1 tablespoon chili
  powder
1 teaspoon cumin
6 corn tortillas
¾ cup ricotta cheese
½ cup shredded
  mozzarella cheese
¼ cup sliced ripe olives

Sauté onion, green pepper and garlic in oil in saucepan. Add beans, tomatoes, chili powder and cumin; mix well. Simmer, partially covered, for 30 minutes. Place 2 tortillas in lightly greased 1½-quart baking dish. Layer scant ¾ cup tomato sauce over tortillas. Spoon 2 tablespoons ricotta over sauce. Sprinkle with 2 tablespoons mozzarella cheese. Repeat layers twice. Top with remaining ricotta, mozzarella and olives. Bake at 350 degrees for 20 minutes or until bubbly. Yield: 4 servings.

Approx per serving: Cal 481, Prot 22.2 gr, Fat 15.1 gr, Chol 12.5 mg, Carbo 68.1 gr, Sod 352.0 mg, Potas 762.4 mg.

Nancy Scott, Alpha
Beatrice, Nebraska

Hoppin' Juan

1½ cups brown rice,
  cooked
½ cup dried black-
  eyed peas, cooked
3 cloves of garlic,
  minced
1 large onion,
  chopped
1 8-ounce can
  green chilies,
  chopped

3 cups shredded
  Monterey Jack
  cheese
½ pound ricotta cheese
2 tablespoons low-fat
  milk
1 cup shredded
  Monterey Jack
  cheese

Combine rice, peas, garlic, onion, chilies and salt to taste in bowl; mix well. Mix 3 cups Monterey Jack cheese, ricotta cheese and milk in bowl. Alternate layers of rice mixture and cheese mixture in large casserole until all ingredients are used, ending with rice mixture. Bake at 350 degrees for 25 minutes. Sprinkle with 1 cup Monterey Jack cheese. Bake for 5 minutes longer. Yield: 12 servings.

Approx per serving: Cal 281, Prot 13.5 gr, Fat 12.8 gr, Chol 37.4 mg, Carbo 27.9 gr, Sod 499.3 mg, Potas 207.4 mg.

Janet McCamant, Theta Zeta
Hotchkiss, Colorado

Spinach Lasagna

1 4-ounce can
  mushrooms
1½ cups ricotta
  cheese
1 cup grated
  mozzarella cheese
1 10-ounce
  package frozen
  spinach, thawed,
  drained

1 egg
1 teaspoon salt
½ teaspoon pepper
¾ teaspoon oregano
8 ounces lasagna
  noodles
1 32-ounce jar
  spaghetti sauce
1 cup grated
  mozzarella cheese

Drain mushrooms, reserving liquid. Add enough water to measure 1 cup. Combine ricotta cheese, 1 cup mozzarella cheese, spinach, mushrooms, egg and seasonings in bowl; mix well. Layer uncooked noodles, spinach mixture and spaghetti sauce ½ at a time in 9x13-inch baking dish. Top with 1 cup mozzarella cheese. Pour reserved mushroom liquid carefully around edge of dish. Bake at 350 degrees for 1¼ hours. Cut into squares. Yield: 12 servings.

Approx per serving: Cal 143, Prot 7.8 gr, Fat 5.4 gr, Chol 37.7 mg, Carbo 15.8 gr, Sod 274.1 mg, Potas 140.5 mg.

Linda Owens, Xi Epsilon Kappa
Legonier, Indiana

Vegetable Lasagna

½ cup chopped
  onion
¼ cup chopped
  celery
1 clove of garlic,
  crushed
3 tablespoons oil
8 ounces
  mushrooms,
  sliced
1 5-ounce can
  tomato paste
1 16-ounce can
  tomato sauce
1 teaspoon sugar

1 teaspoon salt
½ teaspoon oregano
¼ teaspoon pepper
¼ teaspoon thyme
¼ teaspoon basil
12 ounces lasagna
  noodles, cooked
8 ounces ricotta cheese
2 cups chopped
  cooked spinach
1 8-ounce
  package mozzarella
  cheese slices
¼ cup Parmesan
  cheese

Sauté onion, celery and garlic in oil in saucepan. Add mushrooms. Cook for 3 minutes longer. Add tomato paste, tomato sauce, sugar and seasonings; mix well. Simmer for 10 minutes. Spread thin layer of sauce in 9x13-inch dish. Layer noodles, remaining sauce, ricotta cheese, spinach and mozzarella ½ at a time in prepared dish. Top with Parmesan cheese. Bake at 350 degrees for 30 minutes or until bubbly. Let stand for 10 minutes. Cut into squares. Yield: 6 servings.

Approx per serving: Cal 503, Prot 22.4 gr, Fat 20.5 gr, Chol 91.3 mg, Carbo 59.6 gr, Sod 1040.5 mg, Potas 1056.5 mg.

Emily Bisdorf, Preceptor Beta Pi
Delta, British Columbia, Canada

Vegetarian Lasagna

2 carrots, sliced
¾ cup chopped
  onion
3 tablespoons oil
1 jar meatless
  spaghetti sauce
1 teaspoon oregano
½ teaspoon basil
2 cups sliced fresh
  mushrooms
2 medium zucchini,
  sliced

1 16-ounce
  package lasagna
  noodles, cooked
1 10-ounce
  package spinach,
  thawed, drained
1 can pitted ripe olives
1 16-ounce carton
  cottage cheese
4 cups shredded
  mozzarella cheese

Sauté carrots and onion with garlic salt to taste in oil in saucepan. Stir in spaghetti sauce, oregano and basil. Simmer, covered, until carrots are tender. Add mushrooms and zucchini; mix well. Spoon into 9x13-inch baking dish. Add layers of noodles, spinach, olives, cottage cheese and mozzarella cheese. Bake at 375 degrees for 35 minutes. Let stand for 10 minutes. Cut into squares.
Yield: 12 servings.

Approx per serving: Cal 389, Prot 20.5 gr, Fat 18.9 gr, Chol 76.5 mg, Carbo 34.8 gr, Sod 371.6 mg, Potas 395.0 mg.

Brenda Johnson, Alpha
Springfield, Missouri

Zucchini Lasagna

8 ounces mushrooms,
  sliced
4 medium zucchini,
  chopped
1 small onion,
  chopped
1 clove of garlic,
  chopped
1 tablespoon oil
1 32-ounce jar
  salt-free spaghetti
  sauce

1 small package
  artichoke lasagna
  noodles, cooked
8 ounces mozzarella
  cheese, shredded
1 pint dry curd
  cottage cheese
½ cup Parmesan
  cheese

Sauté mushrooms, zucchini, onion and garlic in oil in saucepan. Add spaghetti sauce. Simmer for 20 minutes. Alternate layers of noodles, spaghetti sauce mixture and cheeses in 9x13-inch baking dish until all ingredients are used. Bake at 350 degrees for 45 minutes. Cut into squares. Yield: 10 servings.

Approx per serving: Cal 159, Prot 13.9 gr, Fat 8.7 gr, Chol 27.6 mg, Carbo 7.0 gr, Sod 225.9 mg, Potas 363.8 mg.
Nutritional information does not include spaghetti sauce.

Patricia A. Bowman, Preceptor Delta Pi
San Clemente, California

Italian Shell Pasta

¼ cup margarine,
  melted
¼ cup flour
2½ cups milk
½ teaspoon salt
2 tablespoons
  tomato paste
1 10-ounce
  package frozen
  chopped spinach,
  thawed, drained

1 cup ricotta cheese
¾ cup Italian-style
  bread crumbs
½ teaspoon garlic
  powder
1 8-ounce package
  jumbo pasta shells,
  cooked
¼ cup Parmesan
  cheese

Blend margarine and flour in saucepan. Cook over low heat until smooth and bubbly, stirring constantly. Stir in milk gradually. Cook for 5 minutes or until thickened, stirring constantly. Whisk in salt and tomato paste. Combine spinach, ricotta cheese, bread crumbs and garlic powder in bowl; mix well. Stuff heaping teaspoonful into each pasta shell. Layer ⅓ of the tomato sauce and half the stuffed shells in 8x12-inch baking dish. Repeat layers. Top with remaining sauce and Parmesan cheese. Bake, covered, at 350 degrees for 30 minutes. Yield: 6 servings.

Photograph for this recipe on page 36.

Pasta with Tomatoes and Cheese

1 16-ounce can tomatoes, drained, chopped	12 ounces pasta cooked
1 large clove of garlic, cut into quarters	2 ounces mozzarella cheese, cubed
7 fresh basil leaves, chopped	15 ripe olives, cut into halves
½ cup olive oil	1 tablespoon capers
	2 teaspoons oregano

Combine tomatoes, garlic and basil with salt and pepper to taste in saucepan. Simmer for 15 minutes. Remove garlic and discard. Mix olive oil and pasta in serving bowl. Add tomato sauce, cheese, olives and capers; mix well. Season with salt and pepper to taste. Sprinkle oregano over top. Yield: 4 servings.

Approx per serving: Cal 651, Prot 15.0 gr, Fat 34.9 gr, Chol 12.5 mg, Carbo 69.9 gr, Sod 318.6 mg, Potas 432.2 mg.

Vicky Jager, Zeta Eta
Eureka, California

Tofu Spaghetti Sauce

½ pound tofu	½ cup Cheddar cheese
2 tablespoons olive oil	1 teaspoon sugar
½ onion, chopped	½ teaspoon oregano
12 ounces tomato paste	½ teaspoon basil
1 beef bouillon cube	¼ teaspoon garlic powder
¼ cup vermouth	1 bay leaf

Sauté tofu in 1 tablespoon olive oil in saucepan. Remove with slotted spoon. Add 1 tablespoon olive oil and onion. Sauté until transparent. Add remaining ingredients and salt and pepper to taste; mix well. Simmer for 20 minutes or to desired consistency. Stir in tofu. Simmer for 5 minutes longer. Serve over whole wheat spaghetti. Yield: 4 servings.

Approx per serving: Cal 258, Prot 11.4 gr, Fat 14.1 gr, Chol 14.7 mg, Carbo 21.0 gr, Sod 377.9 mg, Potas 835.6 mg.

Sherry Raitiere, Alpha Upsilon
Danville, Kentucky

Crustless Vegetable Pie

1 medium eggplant, peeled, chopped	3 eggs
2 medium zucchini, chopped	½ tablespoon basil
1 onion, chopped	½ teaspoon oregano
¼ cup oil	⅛ teaspoon salt
4 medium tomatoes, peeled, chopped	⅛ teaspoon pepper
1 tablespoon minced parsley	¾ cup Parmesan cheese
	¼ pound mozzarella cheese, sliced

Sauté eggplant, zucchini and onion in oil in saucepan. Add tomatoes. Simmer, covered, for 20 to 25 minutes. Cool. Combine parsley, eggs, seasonings and ¼ cup Parmesan cheese in bowl; beat until smooth. Add vegetables; mix well. Layer vegetable mixture and remaining Parmesan cheese ½ at a time in greased 10-inch pie plate. Top with mozzarella cheese. Bake at 350 degrees for 40 minutes or until set. Cut into wedges. Yield: 5 servings.

Approx per serving: Cal 354, Prot 18.8 gr, Fat 25.0 gr, Chol 188.6 mg, Carbo 16.0 gr, Sod 512.6 mg, Potas 705.4 mg.

Mary Gamble, Xi Beta Alpha
Huntsville, Alabama

Spinach-Bulgur Casserole

1 cup bulgur	3 eggs, beaten
1 10-ounce package frozen chopped spinach, cooked	1 small tomato, chopped
	½ cup yogurt
1 17-ounce can chicken bouillon	1½ cups grated Cheddar cheese

Combine bulgur and 2 cups water in saucepan. Cook for 15 minutes. Add next 5 ingredients; mix well. Pour into greased 9x13-inch baking dish. Top with cheese. Bake at 350 degrees for 25 minutes. Yield: 6 servings.

Approx per serving: Cal 288, Prot 15.4 gr, Fat 13.3 gr, Chol 157.0 mg, Carbo 27.8 gr, Sod 586.7 mg, Potas 377.7 mg.

Audrey Spaulding, Zeta Epsilon
Carbondale, Colorado

Curried Cheese and Olive Sandwich

1 cup chopped ripe olives	½ cup reduced-calorie mayonnaise
1 cup thinly sliced green onions	½ teaspoon curry powder
1½ cups shredded American cheese	8 English muffins, split

Combine first 5 ingredients in bowl; mix well. Spread on muffin halves. Place on broiler pan. Broil until bubbly. Serve as open-face sandwiches. Yield: 16 servings.

Approx per serving: Cal 141, Prot 4.3 gr, Fat 7.3 gr, Chol 10.2 mg, Carbo 15.1 gr, Sod 361.2 mg, Potas 115.9 mg.

Joan Miller, Xi Delta Pi
Mason City, Iowa

Fruited Cheese Pockets

½ cup cottage
cheese
½ cup shredded
Monterey Jack
cheese
1   8-ounce can fruit
cocktail, drained

2 tablespoons sliced
almonds
1 to 2 tablespoons
milk
2 whole wheat pita
bread rounds
2 lettuce leaves

Combine cheeses, fruit cocktail and almonds in bowl; mix well. Moisten with milk as desired. Spoon into pita rounds. Add lettuce leaf to each pocket sandwich. Yields: 2 servings.

Approx per serving: Cal 327, Prot 17.9 gr, Fat 16.1 gr, Chol 41.7 mg, Carbo 29.9 gr, Sod 353.0 mg, Potas 394.5 mg. Nutritional information does not include pita bread rounds.

Eileen Veldman, Lambda Chi
Dayton, Ohio

Good Witch

12 flour tortillas
1 cup chopped
broccoli
1 cup shredded
carrots
1 cup chopped
onion

1 cup shredded cabbage
1 cup alfalfa sprouts
1 cup sliced avocado
2 tablespoons chopped
dill pickle
¼ cup salad dressing

Wrap tortillas in damp cloth. Warm in oven for 15 minutes. Combine broccoli, carrots, onion and cabbage in glass bowl. Microwave until tender-crisp. Add alfalfa sprouts, avocado and dill pickle; mix gently. Spread tortillas with salad dressing. Spoon vegetable filling into tortillas. Roll tightly to enclose filling. Wrap in plastic wrap. Eat like sandwich. Yield: 24 servings.
Note: May add barbecue sauce to filling if desired.

Approx per serving: Cal 78, Prot 2.0 gr, Fat 3.0 gr, Chol 1.2 mg, Carbo 11.4 gr, Sod 28.0 mg, Potas 112.1 mg. Nutritional information does not include alfalfa sprouts.

Carol McLennan, Preceptor Alpha Tau
Lawton, Oklahoma

Mediterranean Salad Sandwich Filling

2 cloves of garlic,
chopped
2 teaspoons olive oil
1 tablespoon corn oil
1½ tablespoons
lemon juice
3 cups chopped
parsley

2 cups chopped
watercress
1 cup finely sliced
celery
1 cup chopped tomato
1 small onion, chopped
2 cups alfalfa sprouts
1 cup bulgur, cooked

Sauté garlic in olive oil in skillet. Cool. Stir in corn oil and lemon juice. Combine remaining ingredients in salad bowl. Add oil mixture, tossing to mix well. Serve in pita bread rounds or lettuce cups. Yield: 20 servings.

Approx per serving: Cal 50, Prot 1.3 gr, Fat 1.3 gr, Chol 0.0 mg, Carbo 8.8 gr, Sod 12.6 mg, Potas 133.7 mg.

Diane Bevis Jacobs, Xi Delta Mu
Cocoa, Florida

Taco Casserole

1½ cups whole
wheat baking mix
1 package taco
seasoning mix
¾ cup milk
1   15-ounce can
chili beans
¾ cup shredded
Cheddar cheese

1½ cups shredded
lettuce
1 cup chopped tomato
¼ cup shredded
Cheddar cheese
1 avocado, sliced
1 cup sour cream

Combine baking mix and taco seasoning in bowl. Add milk; mix well. Spread in ungreased 8x8-inch baking dish. Layer chili beans and ¾ cup cheese over dough. Bake at 400 degrees for 25 minutes or until light brown and bubbly. Top with lettuce, tomato, ¼ cup cheese and avocado. Spoon sour cream over top.
Yield: 6 servings.

Approx per serving: Cal 321, Prot 13.0 gr, Fat 21.7 gr, Chol 39.8 mg, Carbo 21.0 gr, Sod 173.2 mg, Potas 630.4 mg.

Peggy Simpson, Gamma Pi
Snohomish, Washington

Vegetable Cheese Skillet

2 teaspoons
margarine
¼ cup chopped
green pepper
¼ cup chopped
celery
½ cup chopped
onion
1 clove of garlic,
minced

½ cup chopped
mushrooms
⅛ teaspoon salt
⅛ teaspoon pepper
1 cup cooked noodles
½ cup buttermilk
2 teaspoons chopped
parsley
1 cup shredded
Cheddar cheese

Melt margarine in 9-inch ovenproof skillet. Add green pepper, celery, onion and garlic. Sauté for 5 minutes or until vegetables are tender. Add mushrooms, salt and pepper. Sauté for 2 minutes. Stir in noodles, buttermilk and parsley; mix well. Sprinkle with cheese. Broil until cheese melts. Yield: 2 servings.

Approx per serving: Cal 412, Prot 21.2 gr, Fat 23.5 gr, Chol 82.0 mg, Carbo 29.5 gr, Sod 691.3 mg, Potas 415.1 mg.

Betty Benson, Xi Epsilon Eta
Union, Michigan

Vegetarian Chop Suey

1 large onion,
  chopped
1 cup sliced celery
8 ounces
  mushrooms,
  sliced
2 tablespoons oil

6 cups bean sprouts
1 green pepper,
  chopped
¼ cup chicken broth
1 tablespoon honey
2 tablespoons soy sauce

Stir-fry onion, celery and mushrooms in oil in wok until tender-crisp. Add bean sprouts and green pepper. Stir-fry until tender-crisp. Add remaining ingredients. Cook just until heated through. Serve with brown rice. Yield: 6 servings.

Approx per serving: Cal 120, Prot 6.3 gr, Fat 5.1 gr, Chol 0.1 mg, Carbo 16.1 gr, Sod 816.7 mg, Potas 544.2 mg.

Janice Erickson, Chi Iota
Vista, California

Vegetarian Loaf

1½ cups cottage
  cheese
1 cup cornflake
  crumbs
½ cup chopped
  celery
¼ cup chopped
  onion
4 eggs, beaten

1 teaspoon poultry
  seasoning
½ cup chopped
  walnuts
⅛ teaspoon
  monosodium
  glutamate
2 tablespoons oil

Combine all ingredients in bowl; mix well. Shape into 1½-inch thick loaf. Place in shallow baking pan. Bake at 350 degrees for 50 minutes. Yield: 4 servings.

Approx per serving: Cal 416, Prot 23.3 gr, Fat 25.0 gr, Chol 270.3 mg, Carbo 25.1 gr, Sod 531.2 mg, Potas 303.6 mg.

Raymona Wohlheter, Epsilon
Richmond, Indiana

Athenian Baked Macaroni

1 medium green
  pepper, chopped
1 medium onion,
  chopped
3 tablespoons butter
2 cups macaroni,
  cooked
1   4-ounce can
  sliced mushrooms,
  drained
1   20-ounce can
  green peas,
  drained

3 slices Swiss cheese
4 eggs, beaten
½ cup half and half
½ teaspoon cinnamon
¼ teaspoon allspice
¼ teaspoon pepper
1 cup grated Cheddar
  cheese
1 medium tomato,
  sliced
6 ripe olives,
  sliced

Sauté green pepper and onion in butter in skillet. Add macaroni, mushrooms and peas; mix gently. Spoon half the macaroni mixture, Swiss cheese and remaining macaroni mixture in 2½-quart baking dish. Combine next 5 ingredients with ¾ cup Cheddar cheese in bowl; mix well. Pour over macaroni. Top with remaining Cheddar cheese. Bake at 325 degrees for 35 minutes or until bubbly. Arrange tomato and olives over top. Garnish with parsley sprigs. Yield: 8 servings.

Approx per serving: Cal 368, Prot 17.3 gr, Fat 17.8 gr, Chol 170.8 mg, Carbo 35.3 gr, Sod 420.5 mg, Potas 356.2 mg.

Macaroni and Cheese Soufflé

2 tablespoons
  melted butter
3 tablespoons flour
½ teaspoon salt
½ teaspoon paprika
Dash of cayenne
  pepper

1¼ cups milk
1½ cups shredded
  sharp Cheddar
  cheese
3 eggs, separated
1½ cups macaroni,
  cooked

Blend first 5 ingredients in saucepan. Stir in milk gradually. Cook over medium heat until thickened, stirring constantly. Remove from heat. Stir in cheese until melted. Add beaten egg yolk and macaroni; mix well. Fold in stiffly beaten egg whites gently. Pour into greased 2-quart casserole. Bake at 350 degrees for 35 minutes or until set. Yield: 6 servings.

Approx per serving: Cal 339, Prot 16.1 gr, Fat 18.0 gr, Chol 173.3 mg, Carbo 27.7 gr, Sod 478.8 mg, Potas 189.5 mg.

Chili Relleno Strata

6 slices bread,
  trimmed
2 tablespoons
  margarine,
  softened
1   4-ounce can
  chopped chilies
2 cups shredded
  Cheddar cheese
2 cups shredded
  Monterey Jack
  cheese

6 eggs, beaten
2 cups milk
¼ teaspoon dry
  mustard
¼ teaspoon garlic
  powder
2 teaspoons paprika
2 teaspoons salt
2 teaspoons oregano
½ teaspoon pepper

Spread 1 side of bread with margarine. Place buttered side down in 7x11-inch baking dish. Layer chilies and mixture of cheeses over bread. Combine eggs with remaining ingredients in bowl; mix well. Pour over layers. Chill, covered, for 4 hours to overnight. Bake, uncovered, at 325 degrees for 55 minutes or until set and light brown. Cut into squares. Yield: 12 servings.

Approx per serving: Cal 353, Prot 19.6 gr, Fat 23.1 gr, Chol 186.9 mg, Carbo 16.4 gr, Sod 826.6 mg, Potas 321.3 mg.

Breads

Oat-Wheat Bread

2½ cups whole
    wheat flour
1½ teaspoons salt
2 packages dry
    yeast
⅔ cup nonfat dry
    milk powder
1 cup shredded
    carrots

¼ cup oil
¼ cup honey
1 egg
1 cup oats
1 cup whole
    wheat flour
2½ cups all-
    purpose flour
1 cup raisins

Mix first 5 ingredients in large mixer bowl. Combine oil, honey and 2½ cups water in saucepan. Heat until warm. Add to flour mixture; mix well. Add egg. Beat for 4 minutes. Stir in remaining ingredients. Knead on floured surface until smooth and elastic. Place in greased bowl, turning to grease surface. Let rise, covered, in warm place for 1 hour or until doubled in bulk. Place in 2 greased loaf pans. Let rise for 30 minutes or until doubled in bulk. Bake at 350 degrees for 40 minutes or until bread tests done. Cool on wire rack.
Yield: 32 servings.

Approx per serving: Cal 140, Prot 4.3 gr, Fat 2.5 gr, Chol 8.2 mg, Carbo 26.4 gr, Sod 118.2 mg, Potas 186.2 mg.

Becky Wohlford, Beta Gamma
Lynchburg, Virginia

Corn and Rice Bread

1 cup yellow
    cornmeal
½ cup flour
4 teaspoons baking
    powder
¾ teaspoon soda
1 teaspoon salt

2 tablespoons
    sugar
2 eggs
1 cup buttermilk
2 tablespoons corn
    oil
½ cup cooked rice

Sift dry ingredients into bowl. Beat eggs with buttermilk and oil in small bowl. Add to dry ingredients; mix well. Stir in rice. Pour into greased 8x8-inch baking pan. Bake at 425 degrees for 40 minutes or until golden. Serve hot. Yield: 8 servings.

Approx per serving: Cal 180, Prot 5.2 gr, Fat 5.2 gr, Chol 63.8 mg, Carbo 27.7 gr, Sod 611.1 mg, Potas 93.1 mg.

Fran Naylor
Clendenin, West Virginia

Cornmeal Dumplings

1 cup yellow
    cornmeal
⅓ cup self-rising
    flour
1 teaspoon baking
    powder
¾ teaspoon salt

1 teaspoon sugar
1 egg, beaten
½ cup half and
    half
1½ tablespoons
    melted
    shortening

Sift dry ingredients into bowl. Beat egg with half and half. Add to dry ingredients; mix well. Add shortening; mix well. Drop by teaspoonfuls into simmering soup or stew. Simmer, covered, for 15 minutes. Yield: 24 dumplings.

Approx per dumpling: Cal 46, Prot 1.0 gr, Fat 1.8 gr, Chol 12.7 mg, Carbo 6.2 gr, Sod 103.8 mg, Potas 17.8 mg. Nutritional information does not include soup or stew.

Jill Kepler Campbell, Gamma Pi
Cleveland, Mississippi

Cornmeal-Sesame Seed Pancakes

1 cup cornmeal
¼ teaspoon salt
1 egg, beaten
1 cup low-fat milk
3 tablespoons oil

½ cup whole
    wheat flour
1 teaspoon baking
    powder
¾ cup sesame seed

Pour 1 cup boiling water over mixture of cornmeal and salt in bowl. Let stand for several minutes. Add mixture of egg, milk and oil; mix well. Add mixture of flour and baking powder; mix well. Pour onto hot lightly greased griddle. Bake until bubbly and dry around edges. Sprinkle generously with sesame seed; turn pancakes over. Bake until golden. Yield: 12 pancakes.

Approx per pancake: Cal 159, Prot 4.5 gr, Fat 9.3 gr, Chol 21.9 mg, Carbo 15.3 gr, Sod 92.9 mg, Potas 137.8 mg.

Mary Thompson, Xi Nu
Weiser, Idaho

Vegetable Spoon Bread

2 eggs, beaten
1 10-ounce
    package frozen
    chopped
    spinach, thawed
1 9-ounce can
    cream-style corn
1 cup sour cream

½ cup melted
    margarine
1 cup chopped ham
1 8½-ounce
    package corn
    muffin mix
½ cup shredded
    processed cheese

Combine first 6 ingredients in bowl; mix well. Stir in corn muffin mix. Pour into greased 9-inch baking pan. Bake at 350 degrees for 35 minutes. Sprinkle with cheese. Bake for 2 minutes longer or until cheese melts. Yield: 8 servings.
Note: May substitute broccoli or cauliflower for spinach.

Approx per serving: Cal 417, Prot 11.3 gr, Fat 28.3 gr, Chol 96.5 mg, Carbo 31.0 gr, Sod 706.8 mg, Potas 297.4 mg.

Barbara Palmer, Alpha Rho Alpha
Joshua, Texas

New England Apple Bread

½ cup shortening
1 cup sugar
2 eggs
2 cups flour
1 teaspoon baking
    powder
½ teaspoon salt
½ teaspoon soda

1½ tablespoons
    sour milk
1 teaspoon vanilla
    extract
1 cup grated apple
¼ cup chopped
    walnuts

Cream shortening and sugar in bowl until light and fluffy. Blend in eggs. Add dry ingredients alternately with sour milk and vanilla, mixing well after each addition. Stir in apple and walnuts. Spoon into greased loaf pan. Bake at 350 degrees for 1 hour. Cool on wire rack. Yield: 16 servings.

Approx per serving: Cal 195, Prot 2.8 gr, Fat 9.2 gr, Chol 31.8 mg, Carbo 25.9 gr, Sod 121.8 mg, Potas 42.8 mg.

Esther Levesque, Alpha Alpha
Hudson, New Hampshire

Banana-Nut Bread

¼ cup butter,
   softened
¾ cup sugar
2 eggs, well beaten
2 cups flour

1 teaspoon soda
½ teaspoon salt
3 bananas, mashed
¾ cup chopped
   pecans

Cream butter and sugar in mixer bowl until light and fluffy. Blend in eggs. Add sifted dry ingredients alternately with bananas, mixing well after each addition. Stir in pecans. Spoon into greased loaf pan. Bake at 400 degrees for 1 hour. Cool on wire rack.
Yield: 16 servings.

Approx per serving: Cal 186, Prot 3.2 gr, Fat 7.7 gr,
Chol 40.5 mg, Carbo 27.1 gr, Sod 161.2 mg, Potas 139.9 mg.

Maxine B. Mayer, Preceptor Omicron
Littleton, Colorado

Banana-Nut High-Fiber Bread

1 cup shortening
1½ cups sugar
4 eggs, beaten
2 cups mashed
   bananas
1 teaspoon vanilla
   extract
2 cups flour
2 teaspoons soda

4 teaspoons baking
   powder
½ teaspoon salt
1 cup All-Bran
   cereal
1 cup quick-
   cooking oats
1½ cups chopped
   pecans

Cream shortening and sugar in mixer bowl until light and fluffy. Blend in eggs, bananas and vanilla. Add sifted dry ingredients gradually, mixing well after each addition. Stir in cereal, oats and pecans. Pour into 3 greased 4x8-inch loaf pans. Bake at 350 degrees for 35 minutes or until loaves test done. Cool on wire racks. Yield: 36 servings.

Approx per serving: Cal 180, Prot 2.6 gr, Fat 14.0 gr,
Chol 28.1 mg, Carbo 20.4 gr, Sod 129.1 mg, Potas 108.1 mg.

Grace C. Friese, Laureate Alpha
Council Bluffs, Iowa

Natural Sugarless Banana Bread

2 cups oat flour
1 cup instant
   nonfat dry milk
   powder
¾ teaspoon soda
1¼ teaspoons
   cream of tartar
¼ teaspoon salt
½ cup chopped
   peanuts

⅔ cup sunflower
   seed
2 eggs
1 cup mashed
   banana
1 tablespoon
   vanilla extract
⅓ cup melted
   margarine

Mix first 7 ingredients in bowl. Combine eggs, banana and vanilla in mixer bowl; beat until smooth. Add margarine; mix well. Pour over dry ingredients; mix well. Pour into greased loaf pan. Bake at 350 degrees for 45 minutes or until bread tests done. Cool on wire rack. Yield: 16 servings.

Approx per serving: Cal 190, Prot 7.3 gr, Fat 10.8 gr,
Chol 32.5 mg, Carbo 17.7 gr, Sod 185.3 mg, Potas 281.8 mg.

Bonnie Ditmyer, Alpha Alpha Zeta
Palmdale, California

Beer Bread

3 cups self-rising
   flour
3 tablespoons
   sugar

1 egg
1 12-ounce can
   beer

Combine all ingredients in bowl; mix well. Pour into greased and floured loaf pan. Let stand for 10 minutes. Bake at 350 degrees for 1 hour. Cool on wire rack. Yield: 16 servings.

Approx per serving: Cal 106, Prot 2.7 gr, Fat 0.6 gr,
Chol 15.8 mg, Carbo 20.6 gr, Sod 258.3 mg, Potas 30.8 mg.

Patti Dutton, Zeta Eta
Eureka, California

Cottage Cheese-Fruit Bread

6 tablespoons
   margarine,
   softened
½ cup packed
   brown sugar
2 eggs
1 tablespoon grated
   orange rind
1 tablespoon grated
   lemon rind
1½ cups cream-
   style cottage
   cheese

2 cups flour
2 teaspoons baking
   powder
¾ teaspoon soda
¼ teaspoon salt
¼ cup raisins
¼ cup dried
   apples, chopped
¼ cup dried
   apricots,
   chopped
½ cup chopped
   pecans

Cream margarine and brown sugar in mixer bowl until light and fluffy. Add eggs 1 at a time, mixing well after each addition. Mix in grated rinds and cottage cheese. Add mixture of dry ingredients gradually. Stir in fruit and pecans. Pour into greased loaf pan. Bake at 350 degrees for 45 minutes or until bread tests done. Cool on wire rack. Yield: 16 servings.

Approx per serving: Cal 199, Prot 6.1 gr, Fat 8.8 gr,
Chol 36.0 mg, Carbo 24.6 gr, Sod 229.3 mg, Potas 139.9 mg.

Donna Lou Keller, Preceptor Pi
Scottsbluff, Nebraska

Cranberry-Nut Bread

1 egg
¾ cup sugar
1 cup sour cream
2¼ cups flour
1 teaspoon baking
  powder
1 teaspoon soda
1 teaspoon salt

3 tablespoons
  grated orange
  rind
½ cup chopped
  walnuts
1 cup coarsely
  chopped
  cranberries

Beat egg and sugar in bowl until thick and lemon-colored. Stir in sour cream. Sift flour, baking powder, soda and salt together. Add to egg mixture, stirring just until moistened. Stir in remaining ingredients. Pour into greased loaf pan. Bake at 350 degrees for 55 minutes or until bread tests done. Remove to wire rack to cool. Yield: 12 servings.

Approx per serving: Cal 220, Prot 4.4 gr, Fat 8.0 gr, Chol 29.5 mg, Carbo 33.4 gr, Sod 289.6 mg, Potas 89.2 mg.

Margaret Mahoney, Laureate Phi
LaMarque, Texas

Health Bread

1 cup raisins
1 cup whole wheat
  flour
1 cup oats
1 cup All-Bran cereal

½ cup packed
  brown sugar
1 tablespoon soda
1 teaspoon salt
1 cup buttermilk

Combine raisins and 1 cup water in saucepan. Cook for 5 minutes. Combine next 6 ingredients in large bowl. Add raisin mixture and buttermilk; mix well. Pour into greased loaf pan. Bake at 350 degrees for 1 hour. Cool on wire rack. Yield: 16 servings.

Approx per serving: Cal 113, Prot 3.0 gr, Fat 0.6 gr, Chol 0.3 mg, Carbo 26.9 gr, Sod 334.9 mg, Potas 181.8 mg.

Kate Williams, X5616
Oscoda, Michigan

Jean's Health Bread

2 cups sugar
1 cup honey
1½ cups oil
4 eggs, beaten
6 cups All-Bran
  cereal

2 tablespoons soda
3 cups flour
1 tablespoon salt
4 cups buttermilk
1 cup raisins

Combine sugar, honey and oil in bowl; beat until smooth. Blend in eggs. Add cereal and dry ingredients alternately with buttermilk, mixing well after each addition. Stir in raisins. Pour into 3 greased 4x8-inch loaf pans. Bake at 350 degrees for 1 hour or until bread tests done. Cool on wire rack. Yield: 36 servings.

Approx per serving: Cal 246, Prot 4.2 gr, Fat 10.0 gr, Chol 28.3 mg, Carbo 92.4 gr, Sod 416.0 mg, Potas 148.7 mg.

Jean L. Kuhn, Xi Iota
Wyoming, Michigan

Irish Brown Bread

1½ cups stone-
  ground whole
  wheat flour
1 cup self-rising
  flour

½ cup wheat germ
¼ teaspoon salt
1 teaspoon soda
2 cups buttermilk

Mix first 4 ingredients in bowl. Make a well in center. Stir in mixture of soda and buttermilk. Place in greased 8-inch round baking pan. Cut shallow cross in top. Bake at 400 degrees for 1 hour. Cool in pan for 5 minutes. Brush with melted butter if desired. Remove to wire rack to cool completely. Yield: 8 servings.

Approx per serving: Cal 175, Prot 8.5 gr, Fat 1.4 gr, Chol 1.2 mg, Carbo 33.7 gr, Sod 418.3 mg, Potas 239.9 mg.

Maureen Fitzgerald, Xi Gamma Lambda
Falls Church, Virginia

Pineapple Yogurt-Walnut Loaf

2½ cups whole
  wheat flour
½ cup 40% bran
  flakes
2 tablespoons
  wheat germ
1 teaspoon soda
1 teaspoon baking
  powder
2 8-ounce cartons
  low-fat
  pineapple yogurt
¼ cup milk

1 egg
2 tablespoons oil
2 tablespoons
  light molasses
2 tablespoons
  honey
1 teaspoon lemon
  juice
1 cup raisins
½ cup chopped
  walnuts
½ cup chopped
  dates

Mix first 5 dry ingredients in bowl. Combine yogurt, milk, egg, oil, molasses, honey and lemon juice in bowl; mix well. Add to dry ingredients; mix just until moistened. Stir in raisins, walnuts and dates. Pour into 2 greased 4x8-inch loaf pans. Bake at 325 degrees for 50 minutes or until bread tests done. Cool in pans for 10 minutes. Remove to wire rack to cool completely. Yield: 24 servings.

Approx per serving: Cal 179, Prot 2.9 gr, Fat 3.4 gr, Chol 10.9 mg, Carbo 36.9 gr, Sod 62.3 mg, Potas 393.6 mg. Nutritional information does not include pineapple yogurt.

Sandra Miller, Preceptor Beta Lambda
Lakewood, Colorado

Pumpkin Bread

¼ cup sugar
1½ cups flour
¼ teaspoon baking powder
1 teaspoon soda
1 teaspoon cinnamon
½ teaspoon ginger

¾ teaspoon salt
2 cups canned pumpkin
½ cup oil
2 eggs
½ cup raisins
1 cup chopped pecans

Mix first 7 dry ingredients in bowl. Add ¼ cup water, pumpkin, oil and eggs; mix well. Stir in raisins and pecans. Pour into greased loaf pan. Bake at 350 degrees for 45 minutes or until bread tests done. Cool on wire rack. Yield: 16 servings.

Approx per serving: Cal 199, Prot 3.1 gr, Fat 13.0 gr, Chol 31.6 mg, Carbo 19.1 gr, Sod 237.8 mg, Potas 171.9 mg.

Aileen M. Bennett, Phi
Gulfport, Mississippi

Sprout Flat Bread

2 cups rye meal
¾ cup nonfat dry milk powder
½ cup sunflower seed

½ cup sesame seed
½ cup wheat sprouts
3 tablespoons oil
1 egg, beaten

Mix first 4 dry ingredients with desired amount of salt in bowl. Stir in wheat sprouts, oil and 1 cup water. Mix to form smooth dough. Stir in egg gently. Spread ¼ to ½ inch thick on oiled and floured baking sheet. Bake at 450 degrees for 10 minutes or until firm. Brown top under broiler. Cut and serve while hot.
Yield: 20 servings.

Approx per serving: Cal 123, Prot 2.8 gr, Fat 6.1 gr, Chol 13.2 mg, Carbo 15.3 gr, Sod 20.1 mg, Potas 118.3 mg. Nutritional information does not include wheat sprouts.

Barbara Ostrom, Theta Iota
Arcadia, California

Three-Grain Peanut Bread

1 cup flour
½ cup quick-cooking oats
½ cup yellow cornmeal
½ cup nonfat dry milk powder
½ cup sugar

1 tablespoon baking powder
½ teaspoon salt
⅔ cup peanut butter
1 egg
1½ cups low-fat milk

Mix first 7 dry ingredients in bowl. Cut in peanut butter until crumbly. Beat egg and milk in small bowl. Pour into crumb mixture; mix well. Pour into greased loaf pan. Bake at 325 degrees for 1 hour and 10 minutes or until bread tests done. Cool in pan for 10 minutes. Remove to wire rack to cool completely. Yield: 16 servings.

Approx per serving: Cal 164, Prot 6.1 gr, Fat 6.4 gr, Chol 17.2 mg, Carbo 21.7 gr, Sod 219.7 mg, Potas 165.9 mg.

Lois Ferguson, Xi Epsilon Epsilon
Stockton, California

Whole Wheat Soda Bread

1 cup all-purpose flour
2 tablespoons brown sugar
1 teaspoon soda
¼ teaspoon salt
2 tablespoons margarine

2 cups whole wheat flour
⅓ cup oats
1½ cups buttermilk
2 tablespoons melted margarine

Combine first 4 dry ingredients in bowl. Cut in 2 tablespoons margarine until crumbly. Mix in whole wheat flour and oats. Add buttermilk and melted margarine; mix well. Knead 10 times on floured surface. Shape into ball. Place in greased 9-inch pie pan. Cut cross on top. Bake at 375 degrees for 40 minutes or until bread tests done. Cool slightly before serving. Yield: 10 servings.

Approx per serving: Cal 199, Prot 6.2 gr, Fat 5.4 gr, Chol 0.7 mg, Carbo 32.6 gr, Sod 241.0 mg, Potas 171.0 mg.

Mary Charles, Preceptor Theta Xi
Pleasanton, California

Zucchini Bread

3 eggs, beaten
2 cups sugar
2 teaspoons vanilla extract
1 cup oil
3 cups grated unpeeled zucchini
3 cups flour

½ teaspoon baking powder
1 teaspoon soda
1½ teaspoons cinnamon
1 teaspoon salt
1 cup chopped pecans

Beat eggs, sugar, vanilla and oil in mixer bowl until thick and lemon-colored. Mix in zucchini. Add sifted dry ingredients gradually, mixing well after each addition. Stir in pecans. Pour into 2 greased loaf pans. Bake at 350 degrees for 50 minutes or until bread tests done. Cool on wire rack. Yield: 32 servings.

Approx per serving: Cal 166, Prot 3.1 gr, Fat 10.2 gr, Chol 23.7 mg, Carbo 15.9 gr, Sod 103.7 mg, Potas 71.6 mg.

Karen Zahn, Alpha Phi
Moorcroft, Wyoming

Zucchini-Pineapple Bread

3 eggs
2 cups sugar
2 teaspoons vanilla
  extract
1 cup oil
2 cups grated
  zucchini
3 cups flour
1 teaspoon soda

1 teaspoon baking
  powder
1 teaspoon salt
1 cup crushed
  pineapple,
  drained
½ cup raisins
1 cup chopped
  pecans

Beat eggs, sugar, vanilla and oil in mixer bowl until thick and lemon-colored. Mix in zucchini. Add sifted dry ingredients gradually, mixing well after each addition. Stir in pineapple, raisins and pecans. Pour into 2 greased loaf pans. Bake at 325 degrees for 1 hour. Cool on wire rack. Yield: 32 servings.

Approx per serving: Cal 142, Prot 2.4 gr, Fat 3.7 gr, Chol 23.7 mg, Carbo 25.6 gr, Sod 109.4 mg, Potas 81.3 mg.

Kathy Welch, Alpha Omega Lambda
Corrigan, Texas

Sugarless Banana Muffins

1 cup mashed
  banana
½ cup oil
1 egg, beaten
1 teaspoon vanilla
  extract
½ teaspoon salt

1 cup whole wheat
  flour
½ cup wheat germ
1 tablespoon
  baking powder
1 teaspoon soda

Combine first 4 ingredients in bowl; mix well. Add salt, whole wheat flour and mixture of remaining ingredients; mix well. Spoon into greased muffin cups. Bake at 350 degrees for 15 minutes or until muffins test done. Yield: 12 muffins.

Approx per muffin: Cal 145, Prot 3.2 gr, Fat 10.2 gr, Chol 21.1 mg, Carbo 11.6 gr, Sod 245.0 mg, Potas 118.1 mg.

Mary O. Pankey, Laureate Eta
Carbondale, Illinois

Blueberry Muffins

½ cup butter,
  softened
1 cup sugar
2 eggs
1 teaspoon vanilla
  extract

2 cups flour
1½ teaspoons
  baking powder
¼ teaspoon salt
½ cup milk
1 cup blueberries

Combine butter, sugar, eggs and vanilla in mixer bowl. Beat at high speed for 4 minutes. Add sifted dry ingredients alternately with milk, mixing well at low speed after each addition. Fold in blueberries. Fill paper-lined muffin cups ⅔ full. Bake at 375 degrees for 20 minutes or until muffins test done. Cool on wire rack. Yield: 18 muffins.

Approx per muffin: Cal 157, Prot 2.5 gr, Fat 6.2 gr, Chol 44.8 mg, Carbo 23.3 gr, Sod 129.9 mg, Potas 38.8 mg.

Renee Mathews, Zeta Eta
Eureka, California

Microwave Apple-Bran Muffins

4 large apples,
  quartered
3 eggs
½ cup protein powder
2 teaspoons cinnamon
½ teaspoon allspice
¼ teaspoon cloves
1 teaspoon vanilla
  extract

1 teaspoon banana
  extract
2 teaspoons sugar
  substitute
1 teaspoon liquid
  butter
3 cups unprocessed
  bran
1 teaspoon soda

Combine unpeeled apples, eggs and ⅓ cup water in blender container. Process until finely chopped. Pour into bowl. Process 1 cup water in blender until container sides are clean. Add to apples. Add protein powder, spices, flavorings, sugar substitute, butter, bran and soda; mix well. Spoon into microwave-safe muffin cups sprayed with nonstick cooking spray. Microwave on Medium-High for 8 minutes or until muffins test done, turning muffin pan several times. Yield: 6 muffins.

Approx per muffin: Cal 123, Prot 3.5 gr, Fat 3.7 gr, Chol 126.4 mg, Carbo 20.7 gr, Sod 168.8 mg, Potas 187.5 mg. Nutritional information does not include unprocessed bran.

Eldena Stevens, Laureate Rho
Hutchinson, Kansas

Buttermilk Bran Muffins

1½ cups whole
  bran cereal
1½ cups
  buttermilk
2 tablespoons
  reduced-calorie
  margarine,
  melted

1 egg, beaten
1¼ cups flour
2 tablespoons
  sugar
2 teaspoons baking
  powder
½ teaspoon soda
¼ teaspoon salt

Combine bran cereal and buttermilk in bowl. Let stand for 5 minutes. Add margarine and egg; mix well. Mix remaining ingredients in bowl; make well in center. Pour in bran mixture, stirring just until moistened. Fill greased muffin cups ⅔ full. Bake at 400 degrees for 20 minutes or until golden brown. Yield: 12 muffins.

Approx per muffin: Cal 108, Prot 4.0 gr, Fat 2.1 gr, Chol 21.7 mg, Carbo 21.0 gr, Sod 242.8 mg. Potas 105.8 mg.

Bessie Wade, Preceptor Pi
Loyall, Kentucky

Carrot-Bran Muffins

2 tablespoons
  vinegar
¼ cup blackstrap
  molasses
⅓ cup honey
¼ cup oil
2 eggs
1½ cups whole
  wheat flour
1½ cups
  unprocessed
  miller's bran

1½ cups low-fat
  milk
1½ teaspoons soda
1 teaspoon
  cinnamon
½ teaspoon
  nutmeg
1 cup grated
  carrots
½ cup raisins
½ cup chopped
  walnuts

Combine vinegar, molasses, honey, oil and eggs in mixer bowl; beat until smooth. Add mixture of dry ingredients; mix just until moistened. Stir in carrots, raisins and walnuts. Fill greased muffin cups ⅔ full. Bake at 375 degrees for 20 minutes.
Yield: 24 muffins.

Approx per muffin: Cal 108, Prot 2.5 gr, Fat 4.7 gr, Chol 21.7 mg, Carbo 15.4 gr, Sod 68.0 mg, Potas 141.8 mg. Nutritional information does not include miller's bran.

Mary Louise Simpson, Preceptor Delta
Alexandria, Virginia

Mock Date-Bran Muffins

3 eggs
4 packages vanilla
  Alba 77
1 teaspoon baking
  powder

1 teaspoon soda
1 tablespoon maple
  flavoring
1 cup Bran Buds
1 apple, grated

Combine first 5 ingredients in food processor or blender container. Process until smooth. Combine with Bran Buds and apple in bowl; mix well. Pour into greased muffin cups. Bake at 350 degrees for 15 minutes or until brown. Yield: 13 muffins.

Approx per muffin: Cal 55, Prot 3.8 gr, Fat 2.1 gr, Chol 61.8 mg, Carbo 7.1 gr, Sod 131.0 mg, Potas 60.5 mg.

Susan J. Wallace, Preceptor Beta Lambda
Springfield, Illinois

Gayle's Refrigerator Bran Muffins

2 cups All-Bran
  cereal
1 cup vegetable oil
2½ cups sugar
4 eggs, beaten
4 cups buttermilk
2½ cups whole
  wheat flour
2½ cups oat flour

5 teaspoons soda
1 teaspoon salt
3 cups All-Bran
  cereal
1 cup chopped
  pecans
1 cup chopped
  dates

Mix 2 cups cereal and 2 cups boiling water in bowl. Let stand for several minutes. Combine oil, sugar, eggs and buttermilk in bowl. Beat until smooth. Add sifted flours, soda and salt; mix well. Stir in soaked and dry cereal, pecans and dates. Spoon into greased muffin cups. Bake at 400 degrees for 20 minutes. Store unused batter, covered, in refrigerator for up to 2 months.
Yield: 72 muffins.

Approx per muffin: Cal 120, Prot 2.6 gr, Fat 5.0 gr, Chol 14.3 mg, Carbo 19.0 gr, Sod 133.5 mg, Potas 100.5 mg.

Gayle Hudson, Preceptor Zeta Xi
Austin, Texas

LeAnne's Bran Muffins

2 cups All-Bran
  cereal
1 cup Bran Buds
  cereal
2 cups buttermilk
2½ teaspoons soda
1 cup honey

2 eggs, beaten
½ cup oil
2 cups unprocessed
  miller's bran
1 cup flour
1 cup raisins

Mix cereals with 1 cup boiling water in bowl. Let stand for several minutes. Combine buttermilk, soda, honey, eggs and oil in mixer bowl. Beat until smooth. Add cereal mixture; mix well. Beat in miller's bran and flour. Stir in raisins. Pour into greased muffin cups. Bake at 375 degrees for 20 minutes or until muffins test done.
Yield: 48 muffins.

Approx per muffin: Cal 78, Prot 1.5 gr, Fat 2.6 gr, Chol 10.7 mg, Carbo 14.3 gr, Sod 82.8 mg, Potas 68.3 mg. Nutritional information does not include miller's bran.

LeAnne Emerson, Beta Nu
Columbus, Nebraska

Minute Bran Muffins

2 cups 100% bran
  cereal
1 cup plus 3
  tablespoons
  shortening
2½ cups sugar
4 eggs

1 quart buttermilk
6 cups flour
4 cups Bran Buds
  cereal
5 teaspoons soda
2 teaspoons salt

Pour 2 cups boiling water over 100% bran cereal in bowl. Let stand for several minutes. Cream shortening and sugar in mixer bowl until light and fluffy. Blend in eggs. Add buttermilk, soaked cereal and remaining ingredients; mix well. Fill greased muffin cups ⅔ full. Bake at 400 degrees for 16 minutes or until brown. Store unused batter, covered, in refrigerator for up to 6 weeks.
Yield: 72 muffins.

Approx per muffin: Cal 117, Prot 2.4 gr, Fat 4.2 gr, Chol 14.3 mg, Carbo 18.8 gr, Sod 158.0 mg, Potas 52.5 mg.

Mary Louise Eayrs, Laureate Delta
Kalispell, Montana

Refrigerator Honey-Bran Muffins

1 cup All-Bran
  cereal
1 cup raisins
½ cup oil
½ cup sugar
¼ cup honey
2 cups buttermilk
2 eggs, beaten
1½ teaspoons
  vanilla extract

2 tablespoons
  molasses
2 teaspoons grated
  orange rind
2½ cups whole
  wheat flour
1 tablespoon soda
1 teaspoon salt
2 cups All-Bran
  cereal

Combine 1 cup All-Bran, raisins and 1 cup boiling water in bowl. Let stand for several minutes. Stir in oil, sugar, honey and buttermilk. Add eggs, vanilla, molasses and orange rind; mix well. Stir in mixture of remaining ingredients. Chill, covered, for 24 hours to 2 weeks. Fill greased muffin cups ⅔ full. Bake at 350 degrees for 25 minutes or until brown. Yield: 30 muffins.

Approx per muffin: Cal 133, Prot 3.3 gr, Fat 4.4 gr, Chol 17.2 mg, Carbo 24.1 gr, Sod 217.2 mg, Potas 150.4 mg.

Lori Nolan, Delta Upsilon
Angel Fire, New Mexico

Refrigerator Bran Muffins

1 cup 100% bran
  cereal
½ cup shortening
½ cup sugar
2 eggs, beaten
2 cups buttermilk
2½ cups flour

2½ teaspoons soda
1½ teaspoons salt
2 cups 100% bran
  cereal
½ cup chopped
  pecans
1 cup raisins

Combine 1 cup bran cereal and 1 cup boiling water in bowl. Let stand for 10 minutes. Cream shortening and sugar in mixer bowl until light and fluffy. Blend in eggs. Add buttermilk and soaked cereal; mix well. Add sifted flour, soda and salt and 2 cups bran cereal, mixing well after each addition. Stir in pecans and raisins. Spoon into greased muffin cups. Bake at 400 degrees for 20 minutes. Store unused batter, covered, in refrigerator for up to 3 weeks. Let stand for 2 to 3 hours at room temperature before baking. Yield: 36 muffins.

Approx per muffin: Cal 117, Prot 2.7 gr, Fat 4.8 gr, Chol 14.3 mg, Carbo 18.4 gr, Sod 198.8 mg, Potas 101.2 mg.

Dorothy Gessinger, Xi Alpha Psi
Federal Way, Washington

Regina's Bran Muffins

4 cups All-Bran
  cereal
1 cup shortening
2½ cups sugar
4 eggs, beaten

5 cups flour, sifted
5 teaspoons soda
1 teaspoon salt
4 cups buttermilk
2 cups bran cereal

Combine All-Bran cereal and 2 cups boiling water in bowl. Let stand for 10 minutes. Cream shortening and sugar in mixer bowl until light and fluffy. Blend in eggs. Add sifted mixture of flour, soda and salt alternately with buttermilk, mixing well after each addition. Stir in soaked and dry cereals. Spoon into greased muffin cups. Bake at 400 degrees for 20 minutes or until brown. Store unused batter in airtight container in refrigerator for up to 1 month. Yield: 40 muffins.

Approx per muffin: Cal 198, Prot 4.4 gr, Fat 6.6 gr, Chol 25.8 mg, Carbo 34.5 gr, Sod 249.4 mg, Potas 109.2 mg.

Regina Wiitala, XP2257
Connell, Wisconsin

Ruby's Bran Muffins

½ cup flour
1 teaspoon soda
2 cups bran flakes
1 cup buttermilk
1 cup reduced-
  calorie
  margarine

1 egg, beaten
Liquid artificial
  sweetener to
  equal ¼ cup
  sugar
6 tablespoons
  raisins

Sift flour and soda into bowl. Mix in bran flakes. Combine buttermilk, margarine, egg and artificial sweetener in mixer bowl; beat until smooth. Add to dry ingredients, mixing just until moistened. Stir in raisins. Spoon into greased muffin cups. Bake at 400 degrees for 18 minutes or until brown. Yield: 12 muffins.

Approx per muffin: Cal 123, Prot 3.3 gr, Fat 5.1 gr, Chol 21.5 mg, Carbo 18.4 gr, Sod 236.0 mg, Potas 133.1 mg.

Ruby Smedley, 12060
DeQueen, Arkansas

Six-Week Muffins

5 teaspoons soda
1 cup shortening
1½ cups honey
4 eggs, beaten
5 cups flour
1 teaspoon salt
4 cups 100% bran
  cereal

2 cups 40% bran
  flakes
1 quart buttermilk
2 cups chopped
  dates
1 cup chopped
  pecans
1 cup raisins

Dissolve soda in 2 cups boiling water. Cool. Cream shortening in mixer bowl until light and fluffy. Blend in honey and eggs. Add next 4 ingredients alternately with buttermilk and soda mixture, mixing well after each addition. Stir in dates, pecans and raisins. Spoon into greased muffin cups. Bake at 400 degrees for 20 minutes. Store unused batter in airtight container in refrigerator for up to 6 weeks. Yield: 84 muffins.

Approx per muffin: Cal 114, Prot 2.3 gr, Fat 4.1 gr, Chol 12.3 mg, Carbo 19.3 gr, Sod 115.7 mg, Potas 98.8 mg.

Myrna DuBois, Preceptor Kappa Phi
Hemet, California

Super Muffins

1½ cups reduced-
sugar 100% bran
cereal
1 cup low-fat milk
1 egg, beaten
⅓ cup molasses
⅓ cup
unsweetened
applesauce
½ cup all-purpose
flour

½ cup whole
wheat flour
2 tablespoons
toasted wheat
germ
2 teaspoons baking
powder
½ teaspoon soda
½ cup raisins
½ cup chopped
pecans

Mix bran cereal and milk in bowl. Let stand for 3 minutes. Add egg, molasses and applesauce. Combine flours, wheat germ, baking powder and soda in bowl. Make well in center. Pour in bran cereal mixture; mix just until moistened. Stir in raisins and pecans. Fill greased muffin cups ⅔ full. Bake at 400 degrees for 25 minutes or until brown. Store unused batter in airtight container in refrigerator for several weeks. Yield: 12 muffins.

Approx per muffin: Cal 129, Prot 3.3 gr, Fat 4.5 gr,
Chol 21.9 mg, Carbo 20.4 gr, Sod 155.4 mg, Potas 225.7 mg.
Nutritional information does not include reduced-sugar bran cereal.

Stacy Zuger, Theta Delta
Endicott, Washington

Three-Month Muffins

4 shredded wheat
biscuits, crushed
1½ cups raisins
¾ cup shortening
2½ cups sugar
4 eggs

5 cups flour
4 cups buttermilk
2 teaspoons salt
5 teaspoons soda
4 cups All-Bran
cereal

Combine crushed wheat biscuits, raisins and 2 cups boiling water in bowl. Cool. Cream shortening and sugar in mixer bowl until light and fluffy. Add wheat mixture; mix well. Add remaining ingredients in order listed, mixing well after each addition. Spoon into greased muffin cups. Bake at 400 degrees for 20 minutes or until brown. Store unused batter in airtight container in refrigerator; do not stir before using. Yield: 60 muffins.

Approx per muffin: Cal 134, Prot 2.9 gr, Fat 3.4 gr,
Chol 17.2 mg, Carbo 25.2 gr, Sod 190.6 mg, Potas 94.4 mg.

Gladys M. Cook, Laureate Alpha Omega
San Diego, California

Orange Juicy Muffins

2 cups buttermilk
baking mix
1 teaspoon grated
orange rind
⅔ cup orange juice

2 tablespoons sugar
1 egg
¼ teaspoon cinnamon
⅛ teaspoon nutmeg
2 tablespoons sugar

Grease bottoms of muffin cups. Combine first 5 ingredients in mixer bowl; beat for 30 seconds. Fill prepared muffin cups ⅔ full. Sprinkle with mixture of remaining ingredients. Bake at 400 degrees for 15 minutes. Serve with whipped honey butter. Yield: 12 muffins.

Approx per muffin: Cal 114, Prot 2.2 gr, Fat 3.0 gr,
Chol 21.1 mg, Carbo 19.4 gr, Sod 265.3 mg, Potas 49.5 mg.

Gaye Tate, Zeta Gamma
Jasper, Alabama

Saucy Pear Muffins

1½ cups pear
purée
1 egg
2 tablespoons corn
oil
2 cups unbleached
flour

2 teaspoons baking
powder
1 teaspoon soda
½ teaspoon
nutmeg
1 cup chopped
dates

Combine pear purée, egg and oil in mixer bowl. Beat until smooth. Add dry ingredients gradually, mixing well after each addition. Stir in dates. Spoon into greased muffin cups. Sprinkle with additional nutmeg. Bake at 350 degrees for 15 minutes. Cool on wire rack. Yield: 12 muffins.

Approx per muffin: Cal 169, Prot 3.3 gr, Fat 3.2 gr,
Chol 21.1 mg, Carbo 33.2 gr, Sod 129.7 mg, Potas 175.7 mg.

Beverly Tudor, Laureate Beta Psi
Port Neches, Texas

Whole Wheat-Applesauce Muffins

½ cup oil
¾ cup brownulated
brown sugar
1½ cups unsweetened
chunky applesauce

1½ teaspoons soda
1½ cups whole
wheat flour
1 teaspoon
cinnamon

Mix oil and brown sugar in bowl with spoon until smooth. Blend in applesauce and soda. Add flour and cinnamon; mix well. Fill paper-lined muffin cups ¾ full. Bake at 375 degrees for 20 minutes or until brown. Yield: 12 muffins.

Approx per muffin: Cal 194, Prot 2.1 gr, Fat 9.4 gr,
Chol 0.0 mg, Carbo 27.2 gr, Sod 107.8 mg, Potas 126.6 mg.

Mildred L. Neel, Preceptor Gamma Sigma
Sarasota, Florida

Diet Pancakes

3 eggs, separated
3 tablespoons sour
  cream

3 tablespoons
  buttermilk
  pancake mix

Combine egg yolks, sour cream and pancake mix in bowl; mix well. Beat egg whites until stiff peaks form. Fold gently into batter. Pour ¼ cup at a time onto hot griddle. Bake until lightly browned on both sides. Serve with reduced-calorie syrup. Store unused batter in airtight container in refrigerator for several days. Yield: 10 pancakes.

Approx per pancake: Cal 44, Prot 2.3 gr, Fat 2.9 gr, Chol 77.8 mg, Carbo 1.9 gr, Sod 50.3 mg, Potas 27.5 mg.

Lottie Inman, Laureate Gamma Theta
La Habra, California

Melt-In-Your-Mouth Pancakes

2 eggs
2 cups buttermilk
3 tablespoons oil
1 teaspoon salt

1 teaspoon soda
1 tablespoon sugar
1 cup flour

Combine all ingredients in bowl; mix well. Pour ¼ cup at a time onto hot griddle. Bake until light brown on both sides. Yield: 12 pancakes.

Approx per pancake: Cal 100, Prot 3.6 gr, Fat 4.5 gr, Chol 43.0 mg, Carbo 11.1 gr, Sod 309.6 mg, Potas 77.9 mg.

Lori Brodhag, Zeta Eta
McKinleyville, California

Whole Grain Oatmeal Pancakes

1 egg, beaten
1¼ cups milk
1 tablespoon oil
1 tablespoon honey

1½ cups Whole
  Grain Pancake
  Mix

Combine egg, milk, oil and honey in bowl; mix well. Add Pancake Mix; mix just until moistened. Pour ¼ cup at a time onto hot griddle. Bake until brown on both sides. Serve with honey or syrup. Yield: 4 servings.

Whole Grain Pancake Mix

8 cups whole
  wheat flour
2 cups instant
  nonfat dry milk
  powder

1 tablespoon salt
2 teaspoons sugar
3 cups quick-
  cooking oats

Combine all ingredients in bowl; mix well. Store in airtight container.

Nancy G. Smith, Xi Phi
Plano, Texas

Whole Wheat Pancakes

1 cup whole red
  wheat kernels
1½ cups milk
½ teaspoon salt

1 tablespoon
  baking powder
½ cup oil
2 eggs

Combine wheat kernels and 1 cup milk in blender container. Process at high speed for 3 minutes. Add ½ cup milk. Process for 2 minutes longer. Add remaining ingredients. Process until smooth. Pour ¼ cup at a time onto hot griddle. Bake until lightly browned on both sides. Yield: 10 pancakes.

Approx per pancake: Cal 198, Prot 4.5 gr, Fat 13.6 gr, Chol 55.7 mg, Carbo 15.0 gr, Sod 236.4 mg, Potas 105.9 mg.

Jennifer L. Anderson, Theta Delta
Endicott, Washington

Pineapple Spice Scones

3 cups unbleached
  flour
⅓ cup sugar
2½ teaspoons
  baking powder
½ teaspoon salt
¾ cup reduced-
  calorie
  margarine

1 8-ounce can
  crushed
  pineapple
3 tablespoons
  chopped
  almonds
1 tablespoon sugar
½ teaspoon
  cinnamon

Mix first 4 ingredients in bowl. Cut in margarine until crumbly. Stir in undrained pineapple just until moistened. Knead 10 to 12 times on lightly floured surface. Roll ¼ inch thick. Cut with 2½-inch biscuit cutter. Place on ungreased baking sheet. Brush with milk. Combine remaining ingredients in bowl. Sprinkle 1 tablespoon on each scone. Bake at 425 degrees for 15 minutes. Yield: 24 scones.

Approx per scone: Cal 118, Prot 1.8 gr, Fat 4.7 gr, Chol 0.0 mg, Carbo 17.5 gr, Sod 134.1 mg, Potas 32.7 mg.

Joanie Hazel, Preceptor Phi
Fairfax, Virginia

Scones

2 cups flour
¼ cup sugar
1 tablespoon
  baking powder
1 teaspoon salt
⅓ cup shortening
2 eggs
½ cup milk
¼ cup raisins

Sift dry ingredients into bowl. Cut in shortening until crumbly. Blend in 1 egg and 1 egg yolk. Add milk and raisins, mix just until moistened. Knead several times on lightly floured surface. Roll into ½-inch thick square. Cut diagonally into triangles. Brush with egg white. Sprinkle with additional sugar. Place on greased baking sheet. Bake at 425 degrees for 12 minutes or until light brown. Yield: 18 scones.

Approx per scone: Cal 118, Prot 2.5 gr, Fat 5.1 gr, Chol 29.0 mg, Carbo 15.4 gr, Sod 184.2 mg, Potas 46.4 mg.

Joyce Barbach, Xi Alpha Tau
Tonawanda, New York

Brunch Peach Puff with Brandy Sauce

½ cup butter
½ cup peach
  Brandy
Egg substitute
  to equal 6 eggs
3½ cups low-fat
  milk
1 cup flour
1   10-ounce
  package frozen
  peaches, thawed
½ cup peach
  Brandy
2 teaspoons
  cornstarch
2 teaspoons lemon
  juice
1 tablespoon brown
  sugar

Melt butter in 12-inch iron skillet in oven. Combine next 4 ingredients in mixer bowl. Beat until smooth. Pour into hot skillet. Bake at 450 degrees for 25 minutes or until puffed and brown. Drain peaches, reserving syrup. Blend reserved syrup, ½ cup peach Brandy, cornstarch, lemon juice and brown sugar in saucepan. Cook until thickened, stirring constantly. Stir in peaches. Serve over hot puff. Yield: 6 servings.

Approx per serving: Cal 378, Prot 7.2 gr, Fat 17.1 gr, Chol 53.0 mg, Carbo 39.6 gr, Sod 261.6 mg, Potas 344.3 mg, Nutritional information does not include egg substitute.

Rose Mareczko, XP862
El Paso, Texas

Riz Biscuits

1 cake yeast
1 cup warm
  buttermilk
½ teaspoon soda
2½ cups flour
2 tablespoons
  sugar
½ cup shortening
2 tablespoons
  butter

Dissolve crumbled yeast in warm buttermilk in bowl. Add remaining ingredients; mix well. Roll thin on floured surface. Brush with melted butter; fold in half. Brush with melted butter. Roll thin. Cut with small biscuit cutter. Place in baking pan. Let rise for 1 hour. Bake at 425 degrees until golden brown. Yield: 36 biscuits.

Margaret Mahoney, Laureate Phi
La Marque, Texas

Dilly Bread

1 package dry
  yeast
1 cup small-curd
  cottage cheese
2 tablespoons
  sugar
¼ teaspoon soda
1 tablespoon
  minced onion
1 tablespoon
  margarine,
  softened
1 teaspoon salt
2 teaspoons
  dillseed
1 egg
2¼ to 2½ cups
  flour

Dissolve yeast in ¼ cup warm water. Combine next 8 ingredients in bowl; mix well. Stir in yeast. Add flour gradually, kneading after each addition. Knead on floured surface until smooth and elastic. Place in greased bowl, turning to grease surface. Let rise, covered, in warm place for 50 minutes or until doubled in bulk. Place in greased loaf pan. Let rise for 30 minutes or until doubled in bulk. Bake at 350 degrees for 40 minutes or until bread tests done. Yield: 16 servings.
Note: For whole wheat dilly bread, substitute 1 cup whole wheat flour for 1 cup all-purpose flour.

Approx per serving: Cal 106, Prot 4.7 gr, Fat 1.9 gr, Chol 18.7 mg, Carbo 17.1 gr, Sod 196.6 mg, Potas 45.6 mg.

Marilyn Cleveland, Laureate Rho
Hutchinson, Kansas

Sally's Dilly Bread

1 package dry
  yeast
1 cup cottage
  cheese
2 tablespoons
  sugar
1 tablespoon
  butter, melted
1 egg, at room
  temperature
1 tablespoon onion
  flakes
1 tablespoon
  dillseed
1 teaspoon salt
¼ teaspoon soda
1½ cups all-
  purpose flour
1½ cups whole
  wheat flour

Dissolve yeast in ¼ cup warm water. Heat cottage cheese to lukewarm in saucepan. Combine with yeast and remaining ingredients in bowl; mix well. Knead on floured surface until smooth and elastic. Place in greased bowl, turning to grease surface. Let rise, covered, in warm place for 50 minutes or until doubled in bulk. Place in greased loaf pan. Let rise for 45 minutes or until doubled in bulk. Bake at 350 degrees for 40 minutes. Brush with melted butter. Yield: 16 servings.

Approx per serving: Cal 115, Prot 5.4 gr, Fat 2.1 gr, Chol 20.9 mg, Carbo 19.1 gr, Sod 194.6 mg, Potas 79.8 mg.

Sally Schreck, Theta Theta
Goshen, Indiana

Easy Seven-Grain Bread

1 cup seven-grain
  cereal
2 packages dry
  yeast
6 tablespoons
  safflower oil
½ cup honey

2 teaspoons salt
2 eggs, beaten
2½ cups whole
  wheat flour
3 cups unbleached
  flour

Pour ½ cup boiling water over cereal in bowl. Let stand until lukewarm. Dissolve yeast in ½ cup warm water. Add to cereal mixture; mix well. Add oil, honey, salt, eggs and whole wheat flour. Beat for 2 minutes. Stir in unbleached flour. Knead on floured surface until smooth and elastic. Place in 2 greased loaf pans. Let rise, covered, in warm place until doubled in bulk. Bake at 350 degrees for 50 minutes. Yield: 32 servings.

Approx per serving: Cal 119, Prot 3.1 gr, Fat 3.2 gr,
Chol 15.8 mg, Carbo 20.1 gr, Sod 138.1 mg, Potas 61.3 mg.
Nutritional information does not include seven-grain cereal.

Jennifer Cohn, Xi Psi Omega
Longview, Texas

Herb Cheese Bread

1 package hot roll
  mix
1 tablespoon
  oregano
1 tablespoon basil
8 ounces mozzarella
  cheese, shredded

8 ounces Cheddar
  cheese, shredded
1 egg, beaten
⅓ cup Parmesan
  cheese
1 tablespoon
  paprika

Prepare roll mix according to package instructions, adding oregano and basil. Knead on floured surface until smooth and elastic. Place in greased bowl, turning to grease surface. Let rise, covered, in warm place for 30 minutes or until doubled in bulk. Knead on floured surface. Roll into 12-inch square. Sprinkle with mozzarella and Cheddar cheeses. Roll tightly as for jelly roll. Place seam side down on greased baking sheet. Cut slashes every 2 inches. Let rise for 30 minutes. Brush with egg. Sprinkle Parmesan cheese and paprika over top. Bake at 350 degrees for 30 minutes or until golden brown. Yield: 16 servings.

Approx per serving: Cal 200, Prot 10.4 gr, Fat 10.3 gr,
Chol 45.8 mg, Carbo 16.2 gr, Sod 267.8 mg, Potas 64.7 mg.

Maxine F. Schoenrock, Xi Lambda Omega
Freeport, Florida

Logger's Bread

4 packages dry
  yeast
3 cups oats
⅓ cup oil
½ cup molasses
2 tablespoons salt
4 eggs

6 cups stone-
  ground whole
  wheat flour
1 cup cracked
  wheat flour
5 cups unbleached
  flour

Dissolve yeast in 1 cup warm water. Mix oats with 3 cups boiling water in bowl. Let stand for 5 minutes. Add oil, molasses, salt, eggs and yeast; mix well. Mix flours in bowl. Add to batter gradually, mixing well after each addition. Knead in remaining flour on floured surface until smooth and elastic. Place in greased bowl, turning to grease surface. Let rise, covered, in warm place until doubled in bulk. Punch dough down. Let rise, covered, until doubled in bulk. Place in 4 greased loaf pans. Let rise, covered, until doubled in bulk. Bake at 325 degrees for 45 minutes or until bread tests done. Cool on wire rack. Yield: 64 servings.
Note: For soft crust, brush hot bread with shortening and cover with towel for several minutes.

Approx per serving: Cal 117, Prot 3.9 gr, Fat 2.1 gr,
Chol 15.8 mg, Carbo 21.2 gr, Sod 204.9 mg, Potas 107.3 mg.

Diane Rodd, Xi Alpha Omicron
Necedah, Wisconsin

Whole Wheat Bread

2 cups whole
  wheat flour
2 packages dry
  yeast
¼ cup low-fat milk

3 tablespoons
  blackstrap molasses
3 to 4 cups whole
  wheat flour

Mix 2 cups flour and yeast in bowl. Combine milk, molasses and 2 cups water in saucepan. Heat to 110 degrees. Pour over yeast mixture. Beat at low speed until moistened. Beat at medium speed for 3 minutes. Add 2 to 3 cups flour, mixing by hand until dough pulls from side of bowl. Knead in ½ to 1 cup additional flour on floured surface. Dough will be slightly sticky. Place in greased bowl, turning to grease surface. Let rise, covered, for 1 to 1½ hours or until doubled in bulk. Divide into 2 portions. Let rest, covered, for 15 minutes. Place in greased loaf pans. Let rise, covered, for 1 hour or until doubled in bulk. Bake at 375 degrees for 35 minutes or until bread tests done. Remove to wire rack to cool. Store in refrigerator. Yield: 32 servings.

Lori L. Jordan, Alpha
Beatrice, Nebraska

Vegetables

Microwave Zesty Vegetable Medley

Flowerets of 1
  medium head
  cauliflower
1 bunch broccoli,
  cut into 1-inch
  pieces
1 pound carrots,
  cut into ½-inch
  pieces
¼ cup chopped
  onion

¼ cup horseradish,
  drained
1 cup reduced-
  calorie
  mayonnaise
14 saltine crackers,
  crumbled
2 tablespoons
  margarine,
  melted
⅛ teaspoon paprika

Combine first 3 vegetables and ¼ cup water in glass casserole. Microwave, covered on High for 16 minutes, stirring once; drain. Add mixture of onion, horseradish, mayonnaise and salt and pepper to taste; toss lightly. Sprinkle mixture of cracker crumbs, margarine and paprika over top. Microwave for 1 to 2 minutes.
Yield: 5 servings.

Approx per serving: Cal 335, Prot 9.8 gr, Fat 22.3 gr,
Chol 16.0 mg, Carbo 32.6 gr, Sod 250.7 mg, Potas 1187.3 mg.

Alice Cooper, Preceptor Theta
Beatrice, Nebraska

Asparagus alla Fontina

2½ pounds
   asparagus
¼ cup margarine
⅛ teaspoon salt
Pepper to taste
Nutmeg to taste
⅓ cup grated
   Gruyère cheese

¾ cup finely
   chopped
   prosciutto
2 tablespoons
   chopped parsley
3 eggs, beaten
¼ cup Parmesan
   cheese

Cut asparagus into 1-inch pieces. Combine asparagus with water to cover in saucepan. Cook for 7 minutes or just until tender-crisp, drain. Add margarine, salt, pepper and nutmeg. Cook for several minutes, stirring to coat well. Spoon into buttered 9-inch pie plate. Sprinkle with Gruyère cheese, prosciutto and parsley. Pour beaten eggs over top. Sprinkle with Parmesan cheese. Bake at 350 degrees for 35 minutes or until set. Cut into wedges.
Yield: 8 servings.

Approx per serving: Cal 171, Prot 10.3 gr, Fat 12.8 gr, Chol 130.1 mg, Carbo 5.4 gr, Sod 267.5 mg, Potas 316.2 mg.

Kristina Scott, Gamma Gamma
Virginia Beach, Virginia

Asparagus the Easy Way

1 pound fresh
   asparagus,
   trimmed

1 tablespoon
   margarine

Place asparagus in 6x10-inch baking dish. Sprinkle with 2 tablespoons water. Dot with margarine. Cover tightly with foil. Bake at 350 degrees for 25 minutes or until tender.
Yield: 2 servings.

Approx per serving; Cal 110, Prot 5.7 gr, Fat 6.2 gr, Chol 0.0 mg, Carbo 11.4 gr, Sod 74.6 mg, Potas 632.1 mg.

Olava C. Lee, Preceptor Alpha Delta
Albuquerque, New Mexico

Asparagus-Noodle Casserole

1 14-ounce can
   asparagus
1 5-ounce package
   noodles, cooked
2 hard-boiled eggs,
   chopped

1 can cream of
   mushroom soup
1 cup grated
   Cheddar cheese

Drain asparagus, reserving liquid. Layer noodles, asparagus and eggs in baking dish. Combine reserved asparagus liquid and soup in bowl; mix until smooth. Pour over layers. Sprinkle with seasonings to taste. Top with cheese. Bake at 350 degrees until bubbly.
Yield: 8 servings.

Approx per serving: Cal 197, Prot 9.3 gr, Fat 10.0 gr, Chol 96.8 mg, Carbo 18.0 gr, Sod 529.2 mg, Potas 165.4 mg.

Nell Absher, Xi Beta Phi
Lilburn, Georgia

String Beans

1 pound fresh
   green beans
6 chicken bouillon
   cubes
¼ cup chopped
   onion

2 cups tomato
   juice
1 teaspoon salt
¼ to ½ teaspoon
   pepper

Combine beans, bouillon cubes, onion and 6 cups water in saucepan. Bring to a boil; reduce heat. Simmer for 20 minutes. Add remaining ingredients. Simmer for 10 minutes longer. Pour into serving bowl.
Yield: 4 servings.

Approx per serving: Cal 71, Prot 4.6 gr, Fat 0.5 gr, Chol 4.6 mg, Carbo 14.5 gr, Sod 2224.9 mg, Potas 574.1 mg.

Jickie Simpson, Preceptor Alpha Psi
Golden, Colorado

Green Bean Puff

1 16-ounce can
   green beans
1 tablespoon
   chopped onion
2 tablespoons
   margarine
2 tablespoons flour
⅛ teaspoon
   marjoram

¼ teaspoon salt
⅛ teaspoon pepper
¾ cup low-fat milk
2 eggs, separated
¼ teaspoon salt
½ cup shredded
   sharp Cheddar
   cheese

Drain green beans, reserving ¼ cup liquid. Place beans in 8-inch round baking dish. Sauté onion in margarine in saucepan. Stir in flour, marjoram, ¼ teaspoon salt and pepper. Stir in milk and reserved liquid gradually. Cook over medium heat until thickened, stirring constantly. Pour over beans. Beat egg whites and ¼ teaspoon salt in bowl until stiff peaks form. Fold in cheese and well beaten egg yolks gently. Spread over bean mixture. Bake at 375 degrees for 15 minutes or until light brown and heated through.
Yield: 4 servings.

Approx per serving: Cal 199, Prot 9.7 gr, Fat 13.9 gr, Chol 142.2 mg, Carbo 9.5 gr, Sod 648.5 mg, Potas 188.8 mg.

Vivian Martin, Delta Omega
Beaverton, Oregon

Green Beans in Tomato Cups

6 medium tomatoes
1 9-ounce
   package frozen
   French-style
   green beans,
   cooked
1 4-ounce can
   sliced mushrooms,
   drained

6 tablespoons
   reduced-calorie
   Italian salad
   dressing
¼ cup sliced green
   onions
¼ teaspoon salt
⅛ teaspoon pepper

Cut thin slice from each tomato. Scoop out pulp, reserving shells. Sprinkle shells with salt and pepper to taste. Invert on paper towel-lined plate to drain. Chill in refrigerator. Combine remaining ingredients in bowl; mix well. Chill for 2 hours to overnight. Spoon into tomato cups. Serve on lettuce-lined plate.
Yield: 6 servings.

Approx per serving: Cal 44, Prot 2.0 gr, Fat 1.0 gr,
Chol 0.0 mg, Carbo 8.0 gr, Sod 210.8 mg, Potas 338.5 mg.

Patricia Hancock, Iota Beta
Kalona, Iowa

Mary Ann's Beets in Orange Sauce

1 16-ounce can
   sliced beets
Ginger to taste
Cinnamon to taste

1 tablespoon frozen
   orange juice
   concentrate

Combine undrained beets with seasonings and orange juice concentrate in saucepan. Cook until heated through. Spoon into serving dish. Yield: 4 servings.

Approx per serving: Cal 39, Prot 1.0 gr, Fat 0.1 gr,
Chol 0.0 mg, Carbo 9.2 gr, Sod 200.7 mg, Potas 171.9 mg.

Mary Ann Madar, Laureate Alpha Delta
Elizabeth Township, Pennsylvania

Beets with Orange Sauce

1 tablespoon
   margarine,
   melted
¼ cup packed
   brown sugar
2 tablespoons flour
¾ cup orange juice

¼ cup slivered
   orange rind
2½ cups chopped
   cooked beets
⅛ teaspoon paprika
⅛ teaspoon salt
Juice of 1 lime

Blend margarine, brown sugar and flour in saucepan. Add orange juice and rind gradually. Cook until thickened, stirring constantly. Simmer for 5 minutes, stirring constantly. Add beets, paprika and salt. Simmer for 30 minutes. Stir in lime juice. Spoon into serving bowl. Yield: 6 servings.

Approx per serving: Cal 103, Prot 1.4 gr, Fat 2.1 gr,
Chol 0.0 mg, Carbo 20.8 gr, Sod 268.7 mg, Potas 260.4 mg.

Shirley Chontos, Xi Iota Xi
Vallejo, California

Beets with Pineapple

2 tablespoons
   brown sugar
1 tablespoon
   cornstarch
¼ teaspoon salt
1 9-ounce can
   pineapple tidbits

1 tablespoon
   margarine
1 tablespoon lemon
   juice
1 16-ounce can
   sliced beets,
   drained

Mix first 3 ingredients in saucepan. Stir in pineapple with juice. Cook until thickened, stirring constantly. Add remaining ingredients; mix well. Cook for 5 minutes or until heated through. Spoon into serving bowl. Yield: 4 servings.

Approx per serving: Cal 138, Prot 1.1 gr, Fat 3.0 gr,
Chol 0.0 mg, Carbo 28.5 gr, Sod 371.6 mg, Potas 233.0 mg.

Christa Belknap, Alpha Delta
Knoxville, Iowa

Broccoli with Parmesan

1 onion, minced
¼ cup margarine
¼ cup flour
2 cups low-fat milk
1 egg yolk, beaten
1 cup Parmesan
   cheese
½ teaspoon salt

⅛ teaspoon pepper
2½ pounds
   broccoli, cooked
½ cup bread
   crumbs
2 tablespoons
   margarine

Sauté onion in ¼ cup margarine in skillet. Stir in flour. Stir in milk gradually. Cook until thickened, stirring constantly. Add a small amount of hot mixture to egg yolk; stir egg yolk into hot mixture. Stir in cheese, salt and pepper. Pour half the sauce into 2-quart baking dish. Arrange broccoli on top. Cover with remaining sauce. Sprinkle with bread crumbs. Dot with 2 tablespoons margarine. Bake at 400 degrees for 20 minutes. Yield: 8 servings.

Approx per serving: Cal 343, Prot 13.7 gr, Fat 25.8 gr,
Chol 71.0 mg, Carbo 17.9 Sod 420.1 mg, Potas 691.7 mg.

Claire Hebert, Preceptor Delta
Sulphur, Louisiana

Broccoli Neapolitan

½ cup chopped
   onion
½ teaspoon garlic
   salt
2 teaspoons oil
2 teaspoons flour
1 pound fresh
   broccoli,
   chopped

1 large carrot,
   chopped
2 medium tomatoes,
   chopped
½ teaspoon basil
½ teaspoon
   oregano
3 slices low-fat
   cheese

Sauté onion with garlic salt in oil in saucepan. Stir in flour. Add ½ cup water gradually. Cook for 2 minutes or until thickened, stirring constantly. Add vegetables and seasonings. Simmer, covered, for 20 minutes or until vegetables are tender. Arrange cheese slices on top. Heat until cheese melts. Yield: 6 servings.

Approx per serving: Cal 97, Prot 6.8 gr, Fat 4.1 gr, Chol 1.1 mg, Carbo 10.5 gr, Sod 404.7 mg, Potas 487.5 mg.

Debbie Hinze, Beta Nu
Columbus, Nebraska

Broccoli with Lemon Cream

2 pounds fresh
   broccoli,
   trimmed
2 3-ounce
   packages cream
   cheese, softened
6 tablespoons milk
1 teaspoon grated
   lemon rind

1 tablespoon lemon
   juice
½ teaspoon ginger
½ teaspoon
   cardamom
½ cup slivered
   almonds
1 tablespoon butter

Combine broccoli with water to cover in saucepan. Cook for 7 minutes or until tender-crisp; drain. Arrange spears in 9x13-inch baking dish. Combine next 6 ingredients in mixer bowl; beat until smooth. Spoon over broccoli. Bake, covered, at 350 degrees for 15 minutes or until bubbly. Sauté almonds in butter in small saucepan until golden brown. Sprinkle over broccoli. Yield: 6 servings.

Approx per serving: Cal 240, Prot 10.1 gr, Fat 18.8 gr, Chol 39.5 mg, Carbo 12.4 gr, Sod 125.1 mg, Potas 699.5 mg.

Barb Sanders, Xi Alpha Omega
Oelwein, Iowa

Broccoli Casserole

½ cup chopped
   onion
½ cup chopped
   celery
½ cup chopped
   green pepper
2 tablespoons butter
1 can cream of
   mushroom soup

1 8-ounce jar
   Cheez Whiz
1 cup rice, cooked
1 10-ounce
   package frozen
   chopped broccoli,
   cooked
½ cup evaporated
   milk

Sauté onion, celery and green pepper in butter in skillet. Mix soup and Cheez Whiz in saucepan. Cook until heated through, stirring constantly. Add sautéed vegetables, remaining ingredients and salt and pepper to taste; mix well. Spoon into greased baking dish. Bake at 300 degrees for 30 minutes. Yield: 4 servings.

Approx per serving: Cal 563, Prot 20.9 gr, Fat 28.3 gr, Chol 74.3 mg, Carbo 57.6 gr, Sod 1642.3 mg, Potas 626.1 mg.

Sarah Gray, Preceptor Iota Omicron
San Angelo, Texas

Chinese-Style Cabbage

3 cups shredded
   cabbage
1 medium green
   pepper, cut into
   strips
1 cup diagonally
   sliced celery

⅔ cup chopped
   onion
¼ teaspoon salt
⅛ teaspoon pepper
1 tablespoon soy
   sauce

Combine vegetables and 1 tablespoon water in saucepan. Steam, covered, for 5 minutes or until vegetables are tender-crisp, stirring occasionally. Add salt, pepper and soy sauce; mix well. Spoon into serving dish. Yield: 4 servings.

Approx per serving: Cal 40, Prot 2.1 gr, Fat 0.3 gr, Chol 0.0 mg, Carbo 9.4 gr, Sod 519.1 mg, Potas 365.4 mg.

Carol Robinson, Xi Alpha Phi
Boulder, Colorado

Pat's Cabbage Patch

2 heads cabbage,
   shredded
½ pound bacon,
   chopped
3 onions, finely
   chopped

1 20-ounce can
   sauerkraut,
   drained
⅓ cup packed
   brown sugar

Combine cabbage with a small amount of water in saucepan. Cook for 15 minutes; drain. Sauté bacon with onions in saucepan until bacon is crisp. Add sauerkraut, brown sugar, cabbage and salt and pepper to taste. Simmer until heated through. Spoon into serving dish. Yield: 8 servings.

Approx per serving: Cal 314, Prot 7.0 gr, Fat 20.3 gr, Chol 19.8 mg, Carbo 29.7 gr, Sod 795.5 mg, Potas 795.2 mg.

Patricia Cruger, Laureate Gamma Tau
North Hollywood, California

Stir-Fried Cabbage

3 tablespoons oil
8 cups shredded
   cabbage
½ cup raisins
1 teaspoon caraway
   seed

½ teaspoon salt
Dash of allspice
1 cup sour cream
2 tablespoons milk

Heat oil over medium heat in large skillet or wok. Add cabbage, raisins and seasonings. Stir-fry for 15 minutes or until cabbage is tender-crisp. Stir in mixture of sour cream and milk. Cook until heated through. Spoon into serving dish. Yield: 8 servings.

Approx per serving: Cal 157, Prot 2.5 gr, Fat 11.5 gr, Chol 13.2 mg, Carbo 13.3 gr, Sod 170.9 mg, Potas 326.0 mg.

Eugenia W. Bell, PL563
Louisville, Kentucky

Christmas Cabbage

1 medium head
  red cabbage,
  sliced
2 tablespoons red
  wine vinegar
1 teaspoon sugar
½ teaspoon salt
3 tablespoons oil
10 ounces frozen
  peas

1 medium head
  green cabbage,
  sliced
1 medium onion,
  chopped
½ teaspoon
  caraway seed
½ teaspoon salt
3 tablespoons oil

Combine red cabbage, vinegar, sugar, ½ teaspoon salt and 3 tablespoons oil in saucepan. Cook for 25 minutes or until cabbage is tender, stirring occasionally. Stir in peas. Cook until heated through. Combine green cabbage with remaining ingredients in saucepan. Cook for 20 minutes or until cabbage and onion are tender, stirring occasionally. Arrange as desired on serving platter. Yield: 10 servings.

Approx per serving: Cal 262, Prot 12.0 gr, Fat 9.3 gr, Chol 0.0 mg, Carbo 41.5 gr, Sod 387.2 mg, Potas 1492.7 mg.

Mary Muller, Beta Beta
Eureka Springs, Arkansas

Red Cabbage Casserole

2 strips bacon
1 onion, finely
  chopped
2 tart apples,
  peeled, sliced
1 cup dry white
  wine

2 pounds red
  cabbage,
  shredded
1 tablespoon brown
  sugar
1 tablespoon
  vinegar

Fry bacon in saucepan until crisp. Remove bacon, drain and crumble. Add onion and apples. Sauté until tender-crisp. Add wine. Bring to a boil. Stir in remaining ingredients, crumbled bacon and salt and pepper to taste. Spoon into 1½-quart baking dish. Bake, covered, at 350 degrees for 1½ hours or until cabbage is tender. Yield: 6 servings.

Approx per serving: Cal 640, Prot 8.5 gr, Fat 53.0 gr, Chol 52.9 mg, Carbo 24.0 gr, Sod 539.6 mg, Potas 463.2 mg.

Patricia Webb, Xi Beta Chi
Metropolis, Illinois

German Sour Red Cabbage

6 cups shredded
  red cabbage
2 tablespoons
  margarine,
  melted
½ cup vinegar

1 medium onion,
  sliced into rings
1 teaspoon liquid
  artificial
  sweetener

Rinse cabbage in colander; do not drain completely dry. Combine with margarine in saucepan. Cook, covered, over low heat for 3 minutes or until wilted. Add vinegar, onion and ¼ cup water. Cook, covered, over low heat for 10 minutes or until cabbage is tender. Stir in sweetener and seasonings to taste. Spoon into serving dish. Yield: 6 servings.

Approx per serving: Cal 67, Prot 1.7 gr, Fat 4.0 gr, Chol 0.0 mg, Carbo 7.9 gr, Sod 67.2 mg, Potas 242.1 mg.

Emily Bisdorf, Preceptor Beta Pi
Delta, British Columbia, Canada

Red Cabbage with Caraway Seed

1 1-pound head
  red cabbage,
  shredded
¼ cup red wine
  vinegar

1 tablespoon
  currant jelly
1 teaspoon caraway
  seed

Combine all ingredients and 1 cup water in saucepan. Steam, covered, for 20 minutes or until cabbage is tender. Spoon into serving dish. Yield: 4 servings.

Approx per serving: Cal 50, Prot 2.3 gr, Fat 0.2 gr, Chol 0.0 mg, Carbo 11.9 gr, Sod 30.4 mg, Potas 322.3 mg.

Shirley E. Baker, Preceptor Delta Kappa
Springfield, Ohio

Microwave Red Cabbage

5 cups shredded
  red cabbage
1 cup chopped
  peeled apple
½ cup raisins
½ cup chopped
  onion

1 tablespoon sugar
2 tablespoons butter
2 tablespoons cider
  vinegar
¼ teaspoon cinnamon
1 teaspoon salt
¼ teaspoon pepper

Combine all ingredients and ¼ cup water in glass baking dish. Microwave, covered, on High for 12 minutes or until cabbage is tender-crisp, stirring once. Let stand for several minutes. Yield: 6 servings.

Approx per serving: Cal 113, Prot 1.8 gr, Fat 4.1 gr, Chol 11.8 mg, Carbo 19.9 gr, Sod 422.1 mg, Potas 299.9 mg.

Margaret Mahoney, Laureate Phi
LaMarque, Texas

Carrot Casserole

4 cups shredded
  carrots
¼ cup chopped
  onion
¼ cup chopped
  green pepper

1 cup Cheddar
  cheese soup
¼ cup bread
  crumbs
1 tablespoon butter,
  melted

Combine carrots, onion and green pepper in bowl; mix well. Spoon into oiled 1-quart baking dish. Spread soup over vegetables. Toss bread crumbs with butter in bowl. Sprinkle over top. Bake at 350 degrees for 30 minutes. Yield: 6 servings.

Approx per serving: Cal 58, Prot 1.2 gr, Fat 2.2 gr, Chol 6.0 mg, Carbo 9.2 gr, Sod 71.3 mg, Potas 277.5 mg.

Helen Lacina, Preceptor Beta Omicron
Grinnell, Iowa

Eileen's Carrot Casserole

2 pounds carrots
2 tablespoons sugar
2 teaspoons salt
¼ to ½ teaspoon pepper

½ cup chopped parsley
3 tablespoons margarine

Shred carrots in food processor. Combine carrots with next 4 ingredients in bowl. Spoon into 2-quart baking dish. Dot with margarine. Bake, covered, at 350 degrees for 1 hour.
Yield: 6 servings.

Approx per serving: Cal 134, Prot 1.9 gr, Fat 6.1 gr,
Chol 0.0 mg, Carbo 19.4 gr, Sod 854.0 mg, Potas 553.8 mg.

Eileen Veldman, Lambda Chi
Dayton, Ohio

Cheesy Scalloped Carrots

1 small onion, minced
2 teaspoons chopped green pepper
2 tablespoons margarine
¼ cup flour
¼ teaspoon salt
¼ teaspoon dry mustard

2 cups low-fat milk
⅛ teaspoon pepper
¼ teaspoon celery salt
12 medium carrots, sliced, cooked
1 8-ounce package sliced American cheese
3 cups soft bread crumbs

Sauté onion and green pepper in margarine in saucepan. Stir in flour, salt, dry mustard and milk. Cook until thickened, stirring constantly. Add pepper and celery salt. Alternate layers of carrots and cheese in 2-quart casserole ending with carrots. Add sauce. Sprinkle with bread crumbs. Bake at 350 degrees for 25 minutes or until brown and bubbly. Yield: 8 servings.

Approx per serving: Cal 277, Prot 12.2 gr, Fat 13.0 gr,
Chol 28.6 mg, Carbo 28.6 gr, Sod 680.7 mg, Potas 531.7 mg.

Gloria Dyck, Phi
Swift Current, Saskatchewan, Canada

Glazed Carrots

2 large carrots, cut into julienne strips
1 navel orange, sectioned
Pinch of cinnamon

1 teaspoon butter flavoring
1 teaspoon liquid artificial sweetener

Combine carrots with a small amount of water in saucepan. Cook for 10 minutes or until tender; drain. Add remaining ingredients; mix gently. Cook until heated through. Spoon into serving dish.
Yield: 2 servings.

Approx per serving: Cal 66, Prot 1.7 gr, Fat 0.2 gr,
Chol 0.0 mg, Carbo 15.9 gr, Sod 34.6 mg, Potas 381.7 mg.

Lynn S. Collins, Xi Gamma
Winston-Salem, North Carolina

Jane's Glazed Carrots

1 pound carrots, sliced
⅓ cup packed brown sugar

1 teaspoon lemon juice
2 tablespoons butter

Combine carrots with water to cover and salt to taste in saucepan. Cook until tender; drain. Mix in brown sugar, lemon juice, butter and 1 teaspoon water in saucepan. Heat until sugar dissolves, stirring constantly. Add carrots. Simmer for 5 minutes or until carrots are glazed, stirring occasionally. Spoon into serving dish.
Yield: 4 servings.

Approx per serving: Cal 167, Prot 1.3 gr, Fat 6.0 gr,
Chol 17.7 mg, Carbo 28.6 gr, Sod 128.8 mg, Potas 452.5 mg.

Jane Walton, XP1188
Pomeroy, Ohio

Spanish Carrots

1 cup chopped onion
½ cup chopped green pepper
3 tablespoons butter
1½ cups sliced carrots

1 8-ounce can tomato sauce
¼ teaspoon oregano
½ teaspoon salt
Pepper to taste

Sauté onion and green pepper in butter in skillet. Add remaining ingredients and ¼ cup water; mix well. Spoon into greased 1½-quart casserole. Bake, covered, at 400 degrees for 1 hour.
Yield: 4 servings.

Approx per serving: Cal 135, Prot 2.3 gr, Fat 8.9 gr,
Chol 26.6 mg, Carbo 13.5 gr, Sod 725.7 mg, Potas 481.3 mg.

Patricia Cruger, Laureate Gamma Tau
North Hollywood, California

Cauliflower Casserole

1 head cauliflower,
  chopped, cooked
1 tablespoon
  chopped onion
¼ cup margarine
¼ cup flour
1½ cups low-fat
  milk

3 eggs, separated
1 cup grated
  Cheddar cheese
⅛ teaspoon salt
⅛ teaspoon white
  pepper
⅛ teaspoon paprika

Place cauliflower in buttered 2-quart baking dish. Sauté onion in margarine in saucepan. Stir in flour. Stir in milk gradually. Cook over low heat until thickened, stirring constantly. Stir a small amount of hot mixture into beaten egg yolks; stir egg yolks into hot mixture. Stir in cheese, salt and pepper. Fold in stiffly beaten egg whites gently. Spoon over cauliflower. Sprinkle with paprika. Place baking dish in pan of water. Bake at 325 degrees for 1¼ hours. Yield: 6 servings.

Approx per serving: Cal 254, Prot 13.4 gr, Fat 16.7 gr, Chol 105.4 mg, Carbo 15.1 gr, Sod 339.5 mg, Potas 564.8 mg.

Marion Grandin, Preceptor Beta
Montreal, Quebec, Canada

Microwave Cauliflower with a Flair

1 medium head
  cauliflower,
  trimmed
1 10-ounce
  package frozen
  peas
1 teaspoon mustard

½ cup reduced-
  calorie
  mayonnaise
½ teaspoon onion
  flakes
½ cup shredded
  Cheddar cheese

Place cauliflower in glass baking dish. Add 2 tablespoons water if desired. Microwave, tightly covered with plastic wrap, on High for 8 to 10 minutes or until tender-crisp. Let stand for several minutes. Microwave peas in unwrapped package on High for 5 minutes. Let stand for several minutes. Place cauliflower in serving dish. Spread with mixture of mustard, mayonnaise and onion flakes. Sprinkle with cheese. Microwave on High for 1 minute or until cheese melts. Spoon peas around cauliflower. Yield: 3 servings.

Approx per serving: Cal 342, Prot 17.5 gr, Fat 20.3 gr, Chol 31.9 mg, Carbo 30.1 gr, Sod 325.0 mg, Potas 995.4 mg.

Susan J. Wallace, Preceptor Beta Lambda
Springfield, Illinois

Cauliflower-Tomato Scallop

½ cup chopped
  celery
¼ cup chopped
  onion
¼ cup chopped
  green pepper
5 tablespoons
  margarine
¼ cup flour
¾ teaspoon salt
¼ teaspoon pepper

2 cups low-fat milk
1½ cups shredded
  sharp Cheddar
  cheese
Flowerets of 1 large
  head cauliflower,
  cooked
3 large tomatoes,
  sliced
½ cup soft bread
  crumbs

Sauté celery, onion and green pepper in margarine in saucepan. Add flour, salt and pepper. Stir in milk gradually. Cook until thickened, stirring constantly. Add cheese; stir until cheese melts. Layer half the cauliflower, ⅓ of the cheese sauce, tomato slices, ⅓ of the cheese sauce, remaining cauliflower and remaining cheese sauce in baking dish. Top with bread crumbs. Bake at 400 degrees for 25 minutes or until brown and bubbly. Yield: 6 servings.

Approx per serving: Cal 341, Prot 17.5 gr, Fat 20.4 gr, Chol 31.4 mg, Carbo 26.3 gr, Sod 689.6 mg, Potas 1005.4 mg,

Pam Berry, Lambda Psi
Marine City, Michigan

Low-Calorie Creole Celery

1 tablespoon
  margarine
¼ cup chopped
  onion
1½ cups chopped
  tomatoes

2 cups sliced celery
¼ teaspoon salt
⅛ teaspoon pepper
2 tablespoons
  chopped parsley

Melt margarine in saucepan. Add onion, tomatoes, celery, salt and pepper. Simmer, covered, for 5 minutes or until celery is tender. Stir in parsley. Spoon into serving dish. Yield: 4 servings.

Approx per serving: Cal 51, Prot 1.3 gr, Fat 3.0 gr, Chol 0.0 mg, Carbo 5.6 gr, Sod 247.1 mg, Potas 347.2 mg.

Martha Thompson, Rho
Ely, Nevada

Corn in Foil

½ cup margarine,
  softened
1 teaspoon
  horseradish
1 tablespoon
  mustard

1 teaspoon salt
Freshly ground
  pepper to taste
4 ears sweet corn

Cream margarine with horseradish, mustard, salt and pepper in mixer bowl until light and fluffy. Spread on corn. Wrap each ear loosely in foil. Bake at 450 degrees for 20 minutes or until tender. Serve with additional butter sprinkled with parsley. Yield: 4 servings.

Approx per serving: Cal 279, Prot 3.0 gr, Fat 24.0 gr, Chol 0.0 mg, Carbo 16.8 gr, Sod 862.2 mg, Potas 178.7 mg.

Joyce Barbach, Xi Alpha Tau
Tonawanda, New York

Corn on the Cob

10 ears unhusked
corn

Remove outer husks from corn. Pull back inner husks; remove silks. Pull up inner husks to enclose ear. Soak in cold water for 30 minutes. Wrap each ear in foil. Bake at 400 degrees for 40 minutes or until tender. Yield: 10 servings.

Approx per serving: Cal 118, Prot 4.4 gr, Fat 1.3 gr, Chol 0.0 mg, Carbo 27.2 gr, Sod 1.3 mg, Potas 290.9 mg.

Patricia Thorpe, Xi Iota Mu
Crescent City, California

Squaw Corn

4 slices bacon
1 medium onion,
  chopped
½ medium green
  pepper, chopped
2 cups whole
  kernel corn

2 eggs, beaten
½ teaspoon salt
⅛ teaspoon
  Worcestershire
  sauce

Fry bacon in skillet until crisp. Remove bacon, drain and crumble. Sauté onion in bacon drippings in skillet. Add green pepper and corn. Cook over low heat for 5 minutes. Add eggs and salt. Cook until eggs are set, stirring constantly. Stir in Worcestershire sauce and bacon. Spoon into serving dish. Yield: 4 servings.

Approx per serving: Cal 313, Prot 8.4 gr, Fat 23.2 gr, Chol 146.2 mg, Carbo 20.1 gr, Sod 690.5 mg, Potas 220.3 mg.

Rena Longlois, Preceptor Iota Omicron
San Angelo, Texas

Easy Eggplant Casserole

1 medium eggplant,
  peeled, cubed
½ cup low-fat milk
2 tablespoons
  melted
  margarine
1 small onion,
  chopped

1 egg, beaten
1 cup seasoned dry
  bread crumbs
1 tablespoon
  melted
  margarine
½ cup soft bread
  crumbs

Cook eggplant in water to cover in saucepan for 8 minutes; drain. Add next 5 ingredients; mix well. Spoon into greased 2-quart baking dish. Sprinkle with mixture of margarine and soft crumbs. Bake at 350 degrees for 30 minutes. Yield: 4 servings.

Approx per serving: Cal 221, Prot 6.9 gr, Fat 11.5 gr, Chol 65.3 mg, Carbo 23.8 gr, Sod 643.6 mg, Potas 287.1 mg.

Ellen Gates, Preceptor Laureate Eta
Carbondale, Illinois

Eggplant Casserole

4 small eggplant,
  peeled, sliced
2 eggs, beaten
2 large onions,
  finely chopped

1 pound sharp cheese,
  grated
12 crackers,
  crumbled
2 tablespoons butter

Cook eggplant in salted water in saucepan for 10 minutes or until tender. Drain and mash eggplant. Add eggs; mix well. Add onions, cheese and salt and pepper to taste; mix well. Spoon into greased 9x13-inch baking dish. Sprinkle crackers over top; dot with butter. Bake at 350 degrees for 35 to 45 minutes or until brown. Yield: 4 servings.

Joanne Anderson, Alpha Pi
Lloydminster, Saskatchewan, Canada

Eggplant Parmigiana

1 small onion,
  chopped
1 tablespoon olive
  oil
2 8-ounce cans
  tomato sauce
1 teaspoon sugar
1 bay leaf
⅛ teaspoon garlic
  powder
1 teaspoon oregano
½ teaspoon salt

Pepper to taste
1 medium eggplant,
  cut into ⅛-inch
  slices
2 eggs, beaten
1 cup bread crumbs
1 cup Parmesan
  cheese
2 tablespoons oil
8 ounces mozzarella
  cheese, thinly
  sliced

Sauté onion in 1 tablespoon olive oil in saucepan. Add next 7 ingredients and 2 cups water; mix well. Simmer for 30 minutes, stirring occasionally. Dip eggplant into beaten eggs; coat with mixture of bread crumbs and Parmesan cheese. Brown on both sides in oil in skillet; drain on paper towels. Layer eggplant, mozzarella cheese and tomato sauce ½ at a time in 2-quart baking dish. Bake, covered, at 350 degrees for 30 minutes. Yield: 4 servings.

Approx per serving: Cal 536, Prot 30.4 gr, Fat 35.5 gr, Chol 204.9 mg, Carbo 25.9 gr, Sod 1478.0 mg, Potas 779.9 mg.

Brenda Owens, Upsilon Zeta
Edwardsville, Illinois

Eggplant with Tomatoes

½ cup canned
  tomatoes
4 thin slices
  eggplant

4 teaspoons butter
1 teaspoon chopped
  green onion

Heat tomatoes in small saucepan. Brown eggplant on both sides in butter in skillet; drain. Place on serving plate. Top with warm tomatoes and sprinkle of green onion. Yield: 1 serving.

Approx per serving: Cal 234, Prot 5.3 gr, Fat 16.0 gr, Chol 46.1 mg, Carbo 21.8 gr, Sod 342.9 mg, Potas 870.3 mg.

Josephine Monty, Xi Omicron
Greenville, Mississippi

Layered Eggplant Parmesan

1 large eggplant,
  peeled, sliced
3 eggs, beaten
1 cup bread crumbs
½ cup oil
2 teaspoons
  oregano

½ cup grated
  Parmesan cheese
8 ounces shredded
  mozzarella cheese
3 8-ounce cans
  tomato sauce

Dip eggplant into beaten eggs; coat with bread crumbs. Brown on both sides in oil in skillet; drain. Alternate layers of eggplant sprinkled with oregano, Parmesan cheese, mozzarella cheese and tomato sauce in 2-quart baking dish ending with mozzarella cheese. Bake at 350 degrees for 30 minutes or until bubbly.
Yield: 6 servings.

Approx per serving: Cal 440, Prot 18.2 gr, Fat 33.5 gr,
Chol 169.3 mg, Carbo 18.7 gr, Sod 962.6 mg, Potas 648.0 mg.

Gail Cummins, Xi Alpha Eta
Cleveland, Mississippi

Eggplant Dressing

1 large eggplant,
  peeled, chopped
½ cup chopped
  onion
½ cup chopped
  celery
2 cups corn bread
  crumbs

1 cup bread crumbs
1 can cream of
  chicken soup
2 tablespoons
  margarine
2 eggs, beaten
1 cup grated Swiss
  cheese

Cook eggplant in water to cover in saucepan until tender; drain. Cook onion and celery in a small amount of water in saucepan until tender; drain. Combine vegetables, crumbs, next 3 ingredients and salt and pepper to taste in 2-quart baking dish; mix well. Top with cheese. Bake at 375 degrees for 20 minutes or until bubbly.
Yield: 6 servings.

Approx per serving: Cal 768, Prot 22.5 gr, Fat 31.7 gr,
Chol 204.1 mg, Carbo 99.0 gr, Sod 1779.4 mg, Potas 524.7 mg.

Marlene Baucum, Xi Xi
Phoenix, Arizona

Curried Onions and Cucumber

3 large onions, cut
  into eighths
1 large cucumber,
  peeled, chopped
¼ cup nonfat dry
  milk powder

3 tablespoons flour
½ to 1 teaspoon
  curry powder
1 tablespoon
  margarine

Bring 1 cup water to a boil in saucepan. Add onions and cucumber. Simmer, covered, for 5 minutes. Mix milk powder, flour and curry powder in small bowl. Blend in ½ cup water. Stir into vegetable mixture gradually. Cook until thickened, stirring constantly. Add margarine and salt and pepper to taste. Yield: 6 servings.

Approx per serving: Cal 77, Prot 2.9 gr, Fat 2.1 gr,
Chol 0.6 mg, Carbo 12.6 gr, Sod 48.3 mg, Potas 225.3 mg.

Cindy Neal, Delta Rho
Danville, Indiana

Onions en Casserole

4 large onions,
  sliced
3 tablespoons
  margarine
¾ cup shredded
  Cheddar cheese
⅔ cup bread
  crumbs

2 tablespoons
  margarine,
  melted
½ cup low-fat milk
⅛ teaspoon paprika

Sauté onions in margarine in skillet until tender. Alternate layers of onions, cheese and crumbs mixed with melted margarine in greased 8-inch square baking dish. Pour milk over layers. Sprinkle with salt and pepper to taste and paprika. Bake at 350 degrees for 30 minutes. Yield: 6 servings.

Approx per serving: Cal 209, Prot 6.5 gr, Fat 14.7 gr,
Chol 15.0 mg, Carbo 14.2 gr, Sod 267.1 mg, Potas 230.2 mg.

Betty Lou Wright, Preceptor Zeta
Buhl, Idaho

Grilled Onions

4 Vidalia onions,
  cored
4 teaspoons
  margarine

4 beef bouillon
  cubes

Place each onion on square of heavy-duty foil. Place 1 teaspoon margarine, 1 bouillon cube and salt and pepper to taste in center of each onion; seal foil. Place on grill preheated on Low. Cook for 45 minutes or until tender. Yield: 4 servings.

Approx per serving: Cal 103, Prot 3.4 gr, Fat 4.1 gr,
Chol 3.0 mg, Carbo 15.0 gr, Sod 1023.6 mg, Potas 272.0 mg.

Nell Absher, Xi Beta Phi
Lilburn, Georgia

Onion-Mushroom Casserole

1 small loaf
  French bread,
  sliced
3 tablespoons
  margarine,
  softened
4 onions, thinly
  sliced
8 ounces
  mushrooms,
  sliced

3 stalks celery,
  chopped
2 tablespoons
  margarine
½ pound Swiss
  cheese, shredded
1 can cream of
  mushroom soup
½ cup low-fat milk
2 teaspoons soy
  sauce

Spread bread slices with softened margarine; place on baking sheet. Bake at 350 degrees for 8 minutes or until toasted. Sauté onions, mushrooms and celery in 2 tablespoons margarine in skillet. Layer sautéed vegetables, cheese and toasted bread in 9x13-inch baking dish. Blend remaining ingredients in bowl; pour over layers. Bake at 350 degrees for 30 minutes. Yield: 6 servings.

Approx per serving: Cal 452, Prot 18.3 gr, Fat 25.7 gr, Chol 43.7 mg, Carbo 38.5 gr, Sod 1192.3 mg, Potas 545.8 mg.

Deanna Rowe, Xi Epsilon Sigma
Lawrenceburg, Indiana

Chinese Green Peas

2   10-ounce
  packages frozen
  green peas
3 small onions,
  chopped
1½ cups chopped
  celery
1 can sliced water
  chestnuts,
  drained

¼ cup oil
4 teaspoons
  cornstarch
1 cup beef broth
1 teaspoon soy
  sauce
⅛ teaspoon salt

Sauté peas, onions, celery and water chestnuts in oil in skillet for 2 minutes. Cook over low heat for 10 minutes, stirring occasionally. Dissolve cornstarch in broth. Stir into vegetable mixture. Cook until thickened, stirring constantly. Add soy sauce and salt. Cook for 1 minute longer. Yield: 10 servings.

Approx per serving: Cal 130, Prot 4.6 gr, Fat 5.7 gr, Chol 2.4 mg, Carbo 16.1 gr, Sod 245.1 mg, Potas 233.2 mg.

Kathryn R. Young, Preceptor Iota
Shreveport, Louisiana

Creole Black-Eyed Peas

1⅓ cups sliced
  onion
¼ cup margarine
2   16-ounce cans
  black-eyed peas,
  drained

1   20-ounce can
  tomatoes
1½ cups bread
  crumbs
½ teaspoon salt
½ teaspoon pepper

Sauté onion in margarine in skillet. Add remaining ingredients; mix well. Pour into 2-quart casserole. Bake at 350 degrees for 20 minutes or until bubbly. Yield: 8 servings.

Approx per serving: Cal 200, Prot 8.5 gr, Fat 6.7 gr, Chol 0.3 mg, Carbo 28.1 gr, Sod 362.1 mg, Potas 500.0 mg.

Marguerite Truelove, Preceptor Alpha Delta
Columbia, Tennessee

Cheddar-Potato Puff

6 medium potatoes,
  peeled, chopped
2½ tablespoons
  margarine
⅓ cup milk

½ teaspoon salt
¼ teaspoon nutmeg
1 egg, beaten
1 cup grated
  Cheddar cheese

Cook potatoes in water in saucepan until tender. Drain and mash with margarine, milk, salt and nutmeg. Fold in egg and cheese. Spoon into greased 8-inch square baking dish. Bake at 350 degrees for 30 minutes or until puffed and golden brown. Yield: 6 servings.

Approx per serving: Cal 282, Prot 10.2 gr, Fat 12.5 gr, Chol 62.7 mg, Carbo 33.2 gr, Sod 390.4 mg, Potas 810.1 mg.

Marjorie Svacina, Xi Beta Beta
Council Bluffs, Iowa

Chicken-Flavored Colcannon

1 pound potatoes,
  peeled, cooked
½ cup low-fat milk
1 tablespoon
  margarine
2 cups shredded
  cabbage

¾ cup chopped
  leeks
2 cups chicken
  broth

Mash potatoes with milk, margarine and salt and pepper to taste in bowl. Cook cabbage and leeks in broth in saucepan until tender; drain. Add to potato mixture; mix well. Spoon into casserole. Bake at 350 degrees for 20 minutes. Yield: 4 servings.

Approx per serving: Cal 134, Prot 4.3 gr, Fat 3.5 gr, Chol 2.7 mg, Carbo 22.5 gr, Sod 540.6 mg, Potas 510.1 mg.

Nancy Kimmel, Xi Epsilon Psi
Terre Haute, Indiana

Grilled Potatoes

4 large baking
  potatoes
1 tablespoon
  reduced-calorie
  margarine
1 tablespoon
  Parmesan cheese

1 teaspoon chopped
  chives
½ teaspoon pepper
⅛ teaspoon garlic
  powder
1 medium onion,
  thinly sliced

Cut potatoes into halves crosswise. Cut ¾ inch slices to but not through bottom. Mix margarine, cheese, chives, pepper and garlic powder in small bowl. Place a small amount of mixture and 1 onion slice in each slit. Wrap potatoes in foil. Bake at 400 degrees for 45 minutes or until tender. Yield: 4 servings.

Approx per serving: Cal 162, Prot 5.1 gr, Fat 0.7 gr, Chol 1.7 mg, Carbo 34.9 gr, Sod 21.9 mg, Potas 815.8 mg.

Marlene Mallon, Mu Theta
Salina, Kansas

Low-Calorie Potato Scallop

4 cups sliced
  peeled potatoes
2 tomatoes, sliced
¼ cup sliced green
  onions

2 tablespoons
  Parmesan cheese
½ teaspoon salt
¼ teaspoon pepper
2 bouillon cubes

Layer potatoes, tomatoes, green onions and mixture of cheese, salt and pepper ½ at a time in 1½-quart casserole. Dissolve bouillon in ½ cup boiling water. Pour over layers. Bake, covered, at 325 degrees for 1 hour. Bake, uncovered, for 15 minutes longer. Yield: 6 servings.

Approx per serving: Cal 97, Prot 3.6 gr, Fat 0.7 gr, Chol 2.9 mg, Carbo 19.7 gr, Sod 516.6 mg, Potas 522.8 mg.

Jean Lynch, Beta Delta
Woodbury, New Jersey

Potato-Cheddar Broil

8 ounces potatoes,
  sliced ¼ inch
  thick

4 ounces Cheddar
  cheese strips
2 tomatoes, sliced

Sprinkle potato slices on both sides with salt and pepper to taste. Arrange on foil-lined baking sheet sprayed with nonstick cooking spray. Broil for 2 to 3 minutes or until brown; turn slices over. Broil until brown. Top with cheese. Broil until cheese melts. Arrange potato and tomato slices on serving plate. Yield: 2 servings.

Approx per serving: Cal 317, Prot 17.4 gr, Fat 18.5 gr, Chol 56.1 mg, Carbo 21.2 gr, Sod 364.0 mg, Potas 792.7 mg.

Terry Brooks, Preceptor Iota Omicron
San Angelo, Texas

Microwave Scalloped Potatoes

4 medium potatoes,
  thinly sliced
1 tablespoon flour
¼ cup chopped
  onion

½ teaspoon salt
1½ cups low-fat
  milk
2 tablespoons
  margarine

Layer potatoes in 3-quart glass casserole. Sprinkle with flour, onion and salt. Add milk; dot with margarine. Microwave, tightly covered, on High for 20 minutes, stirring twice. Let stand for 5 minutes. Yield: 4 servings.

Approx per serving: Cal 243, Prot 7.4 gr, Fat 7.0 gr, Chol 3.7 mg, Carbo 38.8 gr, Sod 389.0 mg, Potas 926.0 mg.

Helen Schoenrock, Epsilon
Fairbury, Nebraska

Potato-Cheese Casserole

1 32-ounce
  package frozen
  hashed brown
  potatoes
2½ cups shredded
  Colby cheese
1 8-ounce carton
  sour cream

1 can cream of
  chicken soup
¼ cup chopped
  onion
1 cup melted
  margarine
1 cup cornflakes,
  crushed

Combine potatoes, cheese, sour cream, soup, onion and ½ cup margarine in bowl; mix well. Spoon into 9x13-inch baking dish. Mix remaining ½ cup margarine and cornflakes in small bowl. Spread over potato mixture. Bake at 350 degrees for 1 hour. Yield: 8 servings.

Approx per serving: Cal 533, Prot 12.5 gr, Fat 42.2 gr, Chol 50.6 mg, Carbo 27.4 gr, Sod 885.1 mg, Potas 306.3 mg.

Robin Kryder, Delta Zeta Delta
Ridgecrest, California

Diet Baked Potatoes

6 baking potatoes
6 ¼-inch thick
  onion slices
6 slices green
  pepper

Garlic salt to taste
Pepper to taste
6 tablespoons
  chicken broth

Cut each potato in half lengthwise. Sandwich onion and green pepper slice between halves. Sprinkle with garlic salt and pepper to taste. Place on foil. Drizzle 1 tablespoon broth over each. Seal foil tightly. Bake at 425 degrees for 1 hour or until tender. This method results in a flavorful potato without using butter or sour cream. Yield: 6 servings.

Approx per serving: Cal 166, Prot 5.9 gr, Fat 0.4 gr, Chol 4.6 mg, Carbo 36.0 gr, Sod 1451.7 mg, Potas 866.9 mg.

Margie Gugino Hendricks, Xi Beta Tau
Little Rock, Arkansas

Vegetable Casserole

1 10-ounce
  package frozen
  French-style
  green beans
1 10-ounce
  package frozen
  green peas
1 10-ounce
  package frozen
  fordhook lima
  beans
1 can sliced water
  chestnuts,
  drained

1 medium onion,
  grated
1⅓ cups
  mayonnaise
1 teaspoon mustard
1 teaspoon
  Worcestershire
  sauce
¼ teaspoon Tabasco
  sauce
Juice of ½ lemon
⅛ teaspoon garlic
  powder
2 hard-boiled eggs

Cook green beans, peas and lima beans according to package directions just until tender-crisp; drain. Combine cooked vegetables in bowl. Add water chestnuts, onion and mixture of mayonnaise and next 5 ingredients; mix well. Pour into 2-quart casserole. Bake at 350 degrees for 25 minutes. Bake for 5 minutes longer. Grate eggs over top. Yield: 8 servings.

Approx per serving: Cal 384, Prot 7.1 gr, Fat 31.5 gr, Chol 89.3 mg, Carbo 20.3 gr, Sod 332.4 mg, Potas 300.8 mg.

Oneta Gentry, Xi Alpha Mu
Birmingham, Alabama

Onion-Potato Bake

½ cup low-fat milk
2 tablespoons
  chopped pimento
2 tablespoons
  chopped parsley
2 medium potatoes,
  peeled, thinly
  sliced

3 medium onions,
  thinly sliced
½ cup shredded
  Swiss cheese

Combine milk, pimento and parsley in bowl. Layer potatoes, onions, salt and pepper to taste and milk mixture ½ at a time in greased 6x10-inch baking dish. Bake, covered, at 350 degrees for 60 minutes or until potatoes are tender. Top with cheese. Bake until cheese melts. Yield: 6 servings.

Approx per serving: Cal 120, Prot 5.7 gr, Fat 3.0 gr, Chol 10.3 mg, Carbo 18.4 gr, Sod 87.9 mg, Potas 426.3 mg.

Darlene Norris, Xi Gamma Eta
Russell, Iowa

Oven-Fried Potatoes

4 medium potatoes,
  sliced

2 tablespoons oil
Thyme to taste

Coat potatoes with oil; place in shallow baking pan. Sprinkle on all sides with thyme, pepper and seasoned salt to taste. Bake at 350 degrees for 45 minutes or until brown and tender. Yield: 4 servings.

Approx per serving: Cal 203, Prot 3.9 gr, Fat 7.0 gr, Chol 0.0 mg, Carbo 32.1 gr, Sod 5.6 mg, Potas 763.1 mg.

Joyce Bielfeldt, Preceptor Zeta Iota
Abilene, Texas

Scalloped Potatoes

2 cups thinly
  sliced potatoes
½ cup sliced
  mushrooms
½ cup sliced onion

4 beef bouillon
  cubes
½ teaspoon thyme
Dash of pepper

Layer potatoes, mushrooms and onion in 9-inch square baking dish sprayed with nonstick cooking spray. Dissolve bouillon in 1½ cups boiling water. Add seasonings. Pour over vegetables. Bake, covered, at 350 degrees for 30 minutes. Bake, uncovered, 15 minutes longer. Yield: 4 servings.

Approx per serving: Cal 72, Prot 2.9 gr, Fat 0.2 gr, Chol 3.0 mg, Carbo 15.3 gr, Sod 965.7 mg, Potas 378.8 mg.

Carol Cronister, Preceptor Upsilon
Cantrell, Illinois

Specialty Mashed Potatoes

6 medium potatoes,
  cooked, mashed
2 10-ounce
  package frozen
  chopped spinach,
  cooked
10 tablespoons
  margarine,
  melted

1 cup sour cream
¼ teaspoon pepper
6 green onions,
  chopped
⅛ teaspoon
  dillweed
1 cup grated
  Cheddar cheese

Combine mashed potatoes, well-drained spinach, next 5 ingredients and half the cheese in bowl; mix well. Spoon into baking dish. Top with remaining cheese. Bake at 350 degrees for 20 minutes. Yield: 8 servings.

Approx per serving: Cal 351, Prot 8.5 gr, Fat 25.2 gr, Chol 26.6 mg, Carbo 24.6 gr, Sod 312.9 mg, Potas 610.6 mg.

Mildred L. Neel, Preceptor Gamma Sigma
Sarasota, Florida

Potato-Tomato Scallop

4 cups sliced
  peeled potatoes
2 tomatoes, sliced
¼ cup sliced
  green onion

2 tablespoons
  Parmesan cheese
1 teaspoon salt
¼ teaspoon pepper
2 bouillon cubes

Alternate layers of potatoes, tomatoes, green onions, cheese and seasonings in 1½-quart baking dish until all ingredients are used. Dissolve bouillon cubes in ½ cup boiling water. Pour over layers. Bake, covered, at 325 degrees for 1 hour. Bake, uncovered, for 15 minutes longer. Yield: 6 servings.

Approx per serving: Cal 97, Prot 3.7 gr, Fat 0.8 gr, Chol 3.3 mg, Carbo 19.5 gr, Sod 697.1 mg, Potas 521.1 mg.

Jeanne Banes, Laureate Beta
Waukegan, Illinois

Cheesy Spinach Bake

2 10-ounce
  packages frozen
  chopped spinach,
  thawed
8 eggs, well beaten
1 8-ounce
  package cream
  cheese, cubed

1 stick margarine,
  sliced
1 pound brick
  cheese, shredded
½ cup milk
½ cup flour
⅛ teaspoon salt
⅛ teaspoon pepper

Grease and flour bottom of 9x13-inch baking dish. Drain spinach; press dry. Combine with remaining ingredients in bowl; mix well. Pour into prepared baking dish. Bake at 350 degrees for 45 minutes or until knife inserted in center comes out clean. Yield: 8 servings.

Approx per serving: Cal 570, Prot 26.5 gr, Fat 47.0 gr, Chol 342.3 mg, Carbo 11.7 gr, Sod 750.6 mg, Potas 416.0 mg.

Linda Jachino, Xi Kappa Iota
McHenry, Illinois

Spinach Casserole

1 16-ounce carton
  cottage cheese
1 10-ounce
  package frozen
  spinach, thawed,
  drained
2 cups grated
  Cheddar cheese
3 eggs

2 tablespoons flour
¼ cup melted
  margarine
¾ teaspoon dried
  onion flakes
⅛ teaspoon garlic
  salt
Pepper to taste

Combine all ingredients in bowl; mix well. Spoon into greased baking dish. Bake at 350 degrees for 1 hour. Yield: 8 servings. Note: May substitute zucchini for spinach.

Approx per serving: Cal 278, Prot 19.3 gr, Fat 19.7 gr, Chol 134.4 mg, Carbo 6.2 gr, Sod 484.6 mg, Potas 229.6 mg.

Lori Brodhag, Zeta Eta
McKinleyville, California

Squash Creole

4 cups chopped
  squash
1 teaspoon instant
  chicken bouillon
2 medium green
  peppers, chopped
2 stalks celery,
  chopped
1½ cups tomato
  juice

1 teaspoon onion
  flakes
1 clove of garlic,
  crushed
½ teaspoon salt
Freshly ground
  pepper to taste

Combine squash, 1 cup water and bouillon in saucepan. Cook, uncovered, over medium heat until squash is tender and nearly dry. Add remaining ingredients. Cook, covered, until green peppers and celery are tender. Cook, uncovered, until liquid is reduced to desired consistency. Spoon into serving dish. Yield: 4 servings.

Approx per serving: Cal 55, Prot 3.0 gr, Fat 0.3 gr, Chol 0.4 mg, Carbo 12.2 gr, Sod 600.2 mg, Potas 620.7 mg.

Roberta LeClair, Preceptor Iota Omicron
San Angelo, Texas

Mexican Squash Casserole

5 medium squash,
  sliced
1 medium onion,
  chopped
1 8-ounce jar
  jalapeño Cheez
  Whiz
1 can cream of
  mushroom soup

1 4-ounce can
  chopped green
  chilies
2 cups crushed
  tortilla chips
1 cup shredded
  Cheddar cheese

Cook squash and onion in ½ cup water in saucepan until tender; drain. Mix with Cheez Whiz, soup and green chilies in bowl. Alternate layers of tortilla chips and squash mixture in casserole. Top with cheese. Bake at 350 degrees for 20 minutes. Yield: 4 servings.

Approx per serving: Cal 501, Prot 24.7 gr, Fat 31.2 gr, Chol 76.8 mg, Carbo 35.2 gr, Sod 1704.4 mg, Potas 933.0 mg.

Denise Hefley, Alpha Psi Epsilon
McAllen, Texas

Rice and Acorn Squash

1 acorn squash
1 cup cooked
  brown rice
1 cup shredded
  carrot
1 to 2 tablespoons
  honey
¼ teaspoon
  cinnamon

¼ cup raisins
¼ cup apple juice
1 apple, cut into
  8 wedges
2 tablespoons
  margarine
2 tablespoons
  toasted walnuts

Cut two 12x18-inch pieces heavy foil. Cut squash into 4 slices; cut slices into halves. Combine rice, carrot, honey, cinnamon and raisins in bowl; mix well. Mound half the mixture onto each piece foil. Arrange squash around rice mixture, pressing halves close together. Sprinkle with apple juice, top with apple wedges and dot with butter. Seal foil tightly; place on baking sheet. Bake at 450 degrees for 45 minutes. Open foil. Sprinkle with walnuts. Yield: 2 servings.

Approx per serving: Cal 581, Prot 8.5 gr, Fat 17.8 gr, Chol 0.0 mg, Carbo 106.8 gr, Sod 453.3 mg, Potas 1432.7 mg.

Dr. Denise Rollette, Alpha Iota
Hammond, Louisiana

Orange Yamboree Bake

6 tablespoons
  margarine,
  melted
⅔ cup packed
  brown sugar
⅔ cup sugar
2 tablespoons
  cornstarch
½ teaspoon salt

4 teaspoons grated
  orange rind
2 cups orange juice
8 yams, cooked,
  peeled, sliced
5 navel oranges,
  peeled, sliced
½ cup chopped
  peanuts

Blend first 6 ingredients in saucepan. Stir in orange juice gradually. Cook over low heat until thickened, stirring constantly. Layer yams, oranges and peanuts in 1½-quart casserole. Pour sauce over layers. Bake at 350 degrees for 1 hour. Yield: 8 servings.

Approx per serving: Cal 504, Prot 6.4 gr, Fat 13.9 gr, Chol 0.0 mg, Carbo 92.7 gr, Sod 296.7 mg, Potas 764.5 mg.

Elizabeth Cocks, Alpha Iota
Walden, New York

Baked Tomatoes

1 medium onion,
  chopped
1 clove of garlic,
  minced
¼ cup butter
2 10-ounce
  packages frozen
  spinach, thawed

1 cup dry bread
  crumbs
2 eggs, beaten
2 teaspoons salt
4 tomatoes, cut
  into halves

Sauté onion and garlic in butter in skillet until tender. Add spinach. Cook for 8 minutes, stirring occasionally. Remove from heat. Add crumbs, eggs and salt; mix well. Arrange tomatoes cut side up in 9x13-inch baking dish. Top each with ½ cup spinach mixture. Chill, covered, for 45 minutes. Bake at 350 degrees for 35 minutes or until bubbly. Yield: 4 servings.

Approx per serving: Cal 315, Prot 12.7 gr, Fat 16.2 gr, Chol 163.2 mg, Carbo 32.8 gr, Sod 1508.5 mg, Potas 930.2 mg.

Linda Schwartzberg, Xi Iota Kappa
St. Peters, Missouri

Zucchini Italian Squash

1 small zucchini,
  sliced ½ inch
  thick
1 small onion,
  sliced

1 teaspoon butter
¼ cup milk
1 tablespoon
  grated American
  cheese

Alternate layers of zucchini and onion in small baking dish; spread with butter. Sprinkle with salt and pepper to taste. Add milk. Bake at 350 degrees for 15 minutes. Top with cheese. Bake for 15 minutes longer. Yield: 1 serving.

Approx per serving: Cal 173, Prot 8.0 gr, Fat 8.0 gr, Chol 25.4 mg, Carbo 20.3 gr, Sod 201.0 mg, Potas 763.8 mg.

Josephine Monty, Xi Omicron
Greenville, Mississippi

Zucchini Pancakes

3 cups coarsely
　grated zucchini
1 egg, beaten
Pinch of nutmeg

½ cup flour
1 teaspoon baking
　powder

Combine zucchini, egg, nutmeg and salt and pepper to taste in bowl; mix well. Sift in flour and baking powder; mix well. Pour ¼ cup batter at a time onto lightly oiled griddle over medium-high heat. Cook until golden on both sides, turning once. Place on serving plate. Garnish with sprinkle of Parmesan cheese. Yield: 4 servings.

Approx per serving: Cal 100, Prot 4.8 gr, Fat 1.7 gr, Chol 63.2 mg, Carbo 16.9 gr, Sod 99.1 mg, Potas 294.7 mg.

Nivia Wilson, Preceptor Epsilon
Galveston, Texas

Zucchini Patties

2 cups shredded
　zucchini
1 onion, grated
1 egg, beaten
2 tablespoons
　wheat germ

½ teaspoon
　tarragon
2 to 3 tablespoons
　flour
3 tablespoons oil

Drain zucchini in colander. Combine with onion, egg, wheat germ, tarragon and pepper to taste in bowl. Add enough flour to bind mixture; mix well. Drop by tablespoonfuls into hot oil in skillet over medium heat. Cook until brown and crisp, turning once. Drain on paper towels. Sprinkle with salt to taste. Yield: 4 servings.

Approx per serving: Cal 177, Prot 4.9 gr, Fat 12.2 gr, Chol 63.2 mg, Carbo 13.3 gr, Sod 20.7 mg, Potas 313.9 mg.

Sue Patterson Taylor, Kappa Rho
Springfield, Illinois

Stuffed Zucchini

4 medium zucchini
¾ cup chopped
　tomato
⅓ cup chopped
　green pepper

¼ cup chopped
　onion
¼ teaspoon salt
⅓ cup grated
　Cheddar cheese

Simmer whole zucchini in boiling water to cover in covered saucepan for 8 minutes. Drain and cool. Cut zucchini in half lengthwise. Scoop out and chop pulp, reserving shells. Combine chopped pulp, tomato, green pepper, onion and salt in bowl; mix well. Spoon into reserved shells. Place in 8x12-inch baking dish. Bake at 400 degrees for 15 minutes. Sprinkle with cheese. Bake for 5 minutes longer. Yield: 8 servings.

Approx per serving: Cal 47, Prot 3.0 gr, Fat 1.7 gr, Chol 4.6 mg, Carbo 6.1 gr, Sod 102.2 mg, Potas 316.1 mg.

Rebecca Payne Howell, Alpha Psi Epsilon
Pharr, Texas

Microwave Vegetable Della Robbia

2 pounds broccoli,
　trimmed
Flowerets of 1 small
　head cauliflower
1 carrot, thinly
　sliced
1 zucchini, sliced
　¼ inch thick

4 ounces
　mushrooms,
　sliced
1 small red pepper,
　cut into wide
　strips
¼ cup melted
　margarine

Arrange broccoli around outer edge of microproof platter with stalks toward center. Mound cauliflowerets in center. Arrange carrot, zucchini and mushrooms around cauliflower. Shape red pepper strips as for poinsettia over cauliflower. Drizzle margarine over vegetables. Microwave, covered with plastic wrap, on High for 10 to 12 minutes or until vegetables are tender, turning platter every 4 minutes. Let stand for 5 minutes. Garnish with Parmesan cheese. Yield: 8 servings.

Approx per serving: Cal 134, Prot 8.1 gr, Fat 6.4 gr, Chol 2.7 mg, Carbo 15.9 gr, Sod 95.2 mg, Potas 946.9 mg.

Barb Seifert, Omicron Tau
Elgin, Illinois

Microwave Vegetables Extraordinaire

Flowerets of 1 small
　bunch broccoli
Flowerets of 1 small
　head cauliflower
3 carrots, sliced
2 zucchini, sliced
¼ cup margarine,
　melted
¼ teaspoon thyme

½ teaspoon garlic
　salt
1 tomato, cut into
　wedges
⅓ pound fresh
　mushroom
　halves
½ cup Parmesan
　cheese

Arrange broccoli, cauliflower, carrots and zucchini in desired pattern on microproof platter. Microwave, tightly covered, with plastic wrap for 6 minutes, turning 2 or 3 times. Drizzle mixture of margarine and seasonings over vegetables. Arrange tomato and mushrooms on platter. Sprinkle with cheese. Microwave, covered, for 1 to 2 minutes or until cheese melts. Yield: 6 servings.

Approx per serving: Cal 211, Prot 12.5 gr, Fat 11.0 gr, Chol 9.4 mg, Carbo 20.9 gr, Sod 395.7 mg, Potas 1179.8 mg.

Patty Kopp, Xi Kappa
Pasco, Washington

Simple Veggie Bake

1   17-ounce can
     cream-style corn
1 can cream of
     celery soup
2 cups shredded
     Swiss cheese
1   20-ounce
     package frozen
     cauliflower, cooked
1   10-ounce
     package frozen
     broccoli cuts,
     cooked

1   17-ounce can
     whole kernel
     corn, drained
1   4-ounce can
     sliced mushrooms,
     drained
1 cup shredded
     American cheese
1½ cups soft bread
     crumbs
2 tablespoons
     melted butter

Combine cream-style corn, soup and Swiss cheese in bowl; mix well. Fold in remaining well-drained vegetables. Pour into 9x13-inch baking dish. Layer American cheese and mixture of bread crumbs and butter over top. Bake at 375 degrees for 30 minutes. Let stand for 10 minutes before serving. Yield: 10 servings.

Approx per serving: Cal 282, Prot 13.8 gr, Fat 13.7 gr, Chol 40.0 mg, Carbo 29.7 gr, Sod 896.0 mg, Potas 378.6 mg.

Rosanna Marlatt, Zeta Nu
Boardman, Oregon

Ratatouille

6 cups cubed
     eggplant
3 cups sliced
     zucchini
¾ cup chopped
     green pepper
1 cup chopped
     celery
¾ cup chopped
     onion
1 clove of garlic,
     chopped

⅓ cup oil
3 tomatoes, chopped
1   4-ounce can
     mushrooms, drained
½ cup sliced green
     olives
1½ teaspoons salt
1 teaspoon oregano
½ teaspoon thyme
¼ teaspoon pepper

Sauté eggplant, zucchini, green pepper, celery, onion and garlic in oil in 4-quart saucepan for 7 to 10 minutes or until vegetables are tender-crisp, stirring occasionally. Add tomatoes, mushrooms, olives and seasonings. Simmer, covered, until heated through. Yield: 8 servings.

Approx per serving: Cal 134, Prot 2.7 gr, Fat 9.9 gr, Carbo 10.9 gr, Sod 703.9 mg, Potas 473.0 mg.

Three-Vegetable Casserole

1   10-ounce
     package frozen
     chopped broccoli
1   10-ounce
     package frozen
     French-style green
     beans
1   10-ounce
     package frozen
     cauliflower

2 cans cream of
     mushroom soup
1 cup shredded
     Cheddar cheese
½ cup croutons

Cook vegetables in a small amount of water in saucepan until tender-crisp. Drain well. Add soup and ¾ cup cheese; mix well. Spoon into greased 9x13-inch baking dish. Bake at 350 degrees for 30 minutes. Sprinkle with remaining ¼ cup cheese and croutons. Bake for 30 minutes longer. Yield: 10 servings.

Approx per serving: Cal 146, Prot 6.4 gr, Fat 8.7 gr, Chol 16.1 mg, Carbo 12.2 gr, Sod 608.0 mg, Potas 240.0 mg.

Audrey Guith, Laureate Beta
St. Paul, Minnesota

Ratatouille Stir-Fry

1 tablespoon oil
1 clove of garlic,
     minced
2½ cups thinly
     sliced zucchini
1 small onion,
     thinly sliced
1 cup green pepper
     strips

1 cup chopped
     tomato
1 tablespoon
     chopped parsley
1 tablespoon vinegar
¼ teaspoon crushed
     dried basil
¼ teaspoon crushed
     dried oregano

Heat oil in heavy skillet. Add garlic. Stir-fry for 15 seconds. Add zucchini and onion. Stir-fry for 2 minutes. Add green pepper. Stir-fry for 2 minutes. Add tomato and mixture of remaining ingredients. Simmer, covered, for 1 minute. Season with salt to taste. Spoon into serving dish. Yield: 8 servings.

Approx per serving: Cal 41, Prot 1.6 gr, Fat 1.8 gr, Chol 0.0 mg, Carbo 5.8 gr, Sod 5.0 mg, Potas 265.4 mg.

Cora L. Campbell, Preceptor Pi
Loyall, Kentucky

Beta Rice

1 large onion, diced
1 large green pepper, diced
½ cup diced celery
6 tablespoons margarine, melted
1 cup minute rice
1 can beef consomme
1 12-ounce can mushrooms
1 chicken bouillon cube
½ teaspoon salt
½ teaspoon pepper
½ teaspoon Italian seasoning
1 tablespoon parsley flakes

Combine onion, green pepper, celery and melted margarine in 8x8-inch baking dish. Bake at 350 degrees for 15 minutes. Add remaining ingredients; mix well. Bake at 350 degrees for 1 hour, stirring occasionally. Yield: 6 servings.

Approx per serving: Cal 202, Prot 4.8 gr, Fat 11.7 gr, Chol 9.9 mg, Carbo 19.5 gr, Sod 820.5 mg, Potas 189.4 mg.

Betty Lou Buttars, Xi Delta Gamma
Burns, Oregon

Cumin Rice

½ medium onion, finely chopped
¼ teaspoon cumin
1 tablespoon margarine
½ cup rice
1 teaspoon tarragon vinegar

Sauté onion with cumin in margarine in saucepan until tender. Add rice. Sauté for several minutes. Add vinegar and 1½ cups boiling water. Simmer, covered, for 20 minutes or until rice is tender. Spoon into serving dish. Yield: 2 servings.

Approx per serving: Cal 235, Prot 3.7 gr, Fat 6.0 gr, Chol 0.0 mg, Carbo 41.0 gr, Sod 52.6 mg, Potas 111.7 mg.

Shirley E. Baker, Preceptor Delta Kappa
Springfield, Ohio

Golden Rice Bake

2 cups cooked rice
3 cups shredded carrots
½ cup milk
2 tablespoons minced onion
2 eggs, beaten
1½ teaspoons salt
¼ teaspoon pepper
2 cups grated American cheese

Combine first 7 ingredients and 1½ cups cheese in bowl; mix well. Pour into greased 1½-quart baking dish. Top with remaining ½ cup cheese. Bake at 350 degrees for 1 hour. Yield: 6 servings.

Approx per serving: Cal 262, Prot 12.4 gr, Fat 11.9 gr, Chol 114.3 mg, Carbo 26.2 gr, Sod 1448.7 mg, Potas 352.6 mg.

Carey Anderson, Zeta Nu
Boardman, Oregon

Green Rice

1 stick margarine
1 cup rice, cooked
2 cups shredded Cheddar cheese
2 tablespoons parsley flakes
1 teaspoon onion powder
1 cup milk
3 eggs, separated
1 can cream of mushroom soup

Melt margarine in 9x13-inch baking dish. Combine margarine with rice and next 4 ingredients in bowl; mix well. Stir in egg yolks and salt and pepper to taste. Beat egg whites until stiff peaks form. Fold gently into rice mixture. Pour into prepared baking dish. Bake at 350 degrees for 30 minutes. Warm soup in saucepan until heated through. Serve soup over rice. Yield: 6 servings.

Approx per serving: Cal 522, Prot 17.3 gr, Fat 35.9 gr, Chol 173.4 mg, Carbo 32.2 gr, Sod 898.4 mg, Potas 212.2 mg.

Virginia Webb, Alpha Pi
Tacoma, Washington

Philippine-Style Rice

3 cups rice
Soy sauce to taste (optional)
Butter, sugar and milk to taste (optional)

Combine rice and 4½ to 5½ cups water in saucepan; cover. Bring to a boil over high heat. Stir until well mixed; reduce heat. Simmer, covered, for 15 to 25 minutes or until rice is tender and fluffy. Serve hot rice as side dish sprinkled with soy sauce to taste or serve as hot cereal with butter, sugar and milk. Yield: 6 servings.

Approx per serving: Cal 336, Prot 6.2 gr, Fat 0.4 gr, Chol 0.0 mg, Carbo 74.4 gr, Sod 4.6 mg, Potas 85.1 mg. Nutritional information is for rice only.

Norie Mitchell, Xi Iota Mu
Crescent City, California

Wild Rice Dish

4 ounces fresh mushrooms, sliced
2 beef bouillon cubes
2 medium onions, chopped
2 tablespoons chopped parsley
½ cup wild rice
1 cup long grain rice
2 tablespoons butter

Combine mushrooms, bouillon cubes, onions, parsley and 2 cups water in saucepan. Bring to a boil; stir in rices and butter. Simmer, covered, for 20 minutes or until tender. Spoon into serving dish. Yield: 4 servings.

Approx per serving: Cal 325, Prot 8.1 gr, Fat 6.3 gr, Chol 17.0 mg, Carbo 59.3 gr, Sod 518.0 mg, Potas 318.7 mg.

Barbara Madison, Xi Alpha Alpha
Kent, Washington

Vegetables 161

Quick and Easy Raw Applesauce

4 apples, peeled
2 tablespoons
lemon juice
½ cup honey
Cinnamon to taste

Combine all ingredients in blender container. Process until smooth. Pour into serving dish. Yield: 2 servings.

Approx per serving: Cal 505, Prot 1.2 gr, Fat 2.6 gr, Chol 0.0 mg, Carbo 131.7 gr, Sod 8.6 mg, Potas 529.8 mg.

Donna M. Roth, Preceptor Beta Epsilon
Marion, Iowa

Casserole Sauce Mix

2 cups nonfat dry
milk powder
¼ cup instant
chicken bouillon
2 tablespoons onion
flakes
¾ cup cornstarch
1 teaspoon dried
thyme
1 teaspoon dried
basil

Combine all ingredients in bowl; mix well. Store in airtight container. Combine ⅓ cup mix with 1 tablespoon margarine and 1¼ cups water in saucepan. Cook until thickened, stirring constantly. Use as substitute for 1 can soup in casserole recipes. Mix will make enough sauce for 9 recipes at a cost of about $.15 per recipe. Yield: 9 recipes.

Approx per recipe: Cal 96, Prot 5.9 gr, Fat 0.2 gr, Chol 5.4 mg, Carbo 17.3 gr, Sod 195.4 mg, Potas 263.3 mg.

Mildred Ormiston, Preceptor Alpha Upsilon
Kismet, Kansas

Low-Sodium Chutney

6 cups grated
unpeeled
zucchini
2 green peppers,
coarsely ground
2 cups grated
unpeeled tart
apples
1 onion, finely
ground
1 cup honey
¾ pound raisins,
ground
1 tablespoon celery
seed
Juice and grated
rind of 1 lemon
1⅓ cups vinegar
⅓ cup frozen
orange juice
concentrate

Combine all ingredients in stockpot; mix well. Simmer until of desired consistency. Ladle into hot sterilized jars, leaving ½-inch headspace; seal with 2-piece lids. Process in boiling water bath for 10 minutes. Let stand for 1 to 2 weeks before serving to allow flavors to mellow. Yield: 80 tablespoons.

Approx per tablespoon: Cal 34, Prot 0.4 gr, Fat 0.1 gr, Chol 0.0 mg, Carbo 9.0 gr, Sod 2.1 mg, Potas 88.2 mg.

Sue Patterson Taylor, Kappa Rho
Springfield, Illinois

Cranberry-Mushroom Stuffing

1½ cups Ocean
Spray fresh
cranberries
1 teaspoon barley
malt
2 tablespoons honey
1 large onion,
diced
1 tablespoon butter
1 teaspoon sage
1 stalk celery, diced
2 pounds small
mushrooms, cut into
quarters
6 cups whole wheat
croutons
½ cup coarsely
chopped pecans
1 egg, beaten
½ cup skim milk

Combine cranberries with barley malt, honey and 2 cups water in bowl. Let stand for 2 hours. Saute onion in butter in saucepan. Add sage, celery and mushrooms; mix well. Cool. Combine mushroom mixture with croutons and pecans; toss to mix. Drain cranberries. Add to dressing; mix well. Add mixture of egg and milk; toss for 30 seconds. Stuff turkey. Bake turkey according to package directions. Each serving has approximately 100 calories. Yield: 16 servings.

Photograph for this recipe on page 103.

Sugarless Apple Jelly

2½ tablespoons
unflavored
gelatin
1 quart unsweetened
apple juice
Artificial sweetener
to equal 1 cup
sugar

Soften gelatin in apple juice in saucepan. Bring to a boil, stirring until gelatin is dissolved. Cook for 1 minute, stirring constantly; remove from heat. Stir in artificial sweetener and several drops of green food coloring if desired. Pour into hot sterilized jelly jars leaving ¼-inch headspace. Seal with 2-piece lids. Process in boiling water bath for 10 minutes. Yield: 64 tablespoons.

Approx per tablespoon: Cal 8, Prot 0.2 gr, Fat 0.0 gr, Chol 0.0 mg, Carbo 1.8 gr, Sod 0.4 mg, Potas 15.7 mg.

Lorraine Kirkpatrick, Xi Eta Kappa
Barstow Heights, California

Desserts

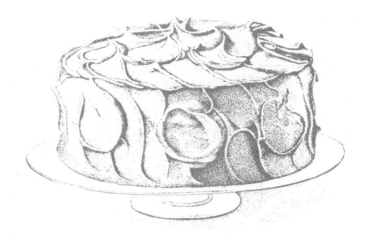

Carrot-Pineapple Cake

2 cups flour
2 teaspoons baking
  powder
1½ teaspoons soda
1 teaspoon salt
2 teaspoons
  cinnamon
1½ cups oil
2 cups sugar

4 eggs
2 teaspoons vanilla
  extract
2 cups grated carrots
1 8-ounce can
   crushed pineapple
½ cup chopped
  walnuts
½ cup raisins

Cream Cheese Frosting

½ cup butter,
  softened
1 16-ounce
   package
   confectioners'
   sugar

1 3-ounce package
   cream cheese,
   softened
1 teaspoon vanilla
  extract

Sift first 5 ingredients into mixer bowl. Add oil, sugar and eggs in order listed, beating well after each addition. Add remaining ingredients; mix well. Pour into 2 greased and floured 9-inch cake pans. Bake at 350 degrees for 35 minutes or until cake tests done. Cool in pans for 10 minutes. Remove to wire rack to cool completely. Spread Cream Cheese Frosting. between layers and over top and side of cake. Yield: 20 servings.

Combine all ingredients in mixer bowl. Beat until smooth and creamy.

Approx per serving: Cal 328, Prot 3.3 gr, Fat 19.6 gr, Chol 50.6 mg, Carbo 36.4 gr, Sod 220.0 mg, Potas 116.8 mg.

Connie Lohmann, Iota Phi
Tracy, California

Apple Cake

2 cups chopped
  apples
1 cup sugar
⅓ cup oil
1 egg, beaten
1 teaspoon vanilla
  extract

1½ cups flour
1 teaspoon baking
  powder
1 teaspoon soda
½ teaspoon salt
½ cup raisins

Mix apples and sugar in bowl. Let stand for 10 minutes. Add oil, egg and vanilla; mix well. Add mixture of dry ingredients; mix well. Stir in raisins. Pour into greased 8-inch square cake pan. Bake at 350 degrees for 35 minutes or until cake tests done. Yield: 8 servings.

Approx per serving: Cal 316, Prot 3.6 gr, Fat 10.2 gr, Chol 31.6 mg, Carbo 54.4 gr, Sod 288.1 mg, Potas 135.2 mg.

Julie Ann M. Prahler, Preceptor Omega
Pontiac, Michigan

Lush Apple Dump Cake

2 cups flour
2 cups sugar
2 eggs
1 teaspoon soda
1 teaspoon
  cinnamon

1 teaspoon vanilla
  extract
½ cup oil
1 cup chopped pecans
1 can apple pie filling

Combine all ingredients in bowl. Beat until well mixed. Pour into greased and floured 9x13-inch cake pan. Bake at 350 degrees for 1 hour or until cake tests done. Cool on wire rack. Cut into squares. Serve with scoop of vanilla ice milk. Yield: 12 servings.

Approx per serving: Cal 340, Prot 4.2 gr, Fat 8.7 gr, Chol 42.1 mg, Carbo 62.9 gr, Sod 79.4 mg, Potas 90.9 mg.

Barbara Jensen, Laureate Phi
Texas City, Texas

Blueberry Cake

1 cup butter,
  softened
1 cup sugar
1 cup sour cream
2 eggs
1 teaspoon almond
  extract
3 cups flour
1 teaspoon soda

1 teaspoon baking powder
1 can blueberry
  pie filling
¾ cup packed
  brown sugar
½ cup chopped pecans
1 tablespoon melted
  butter

Cream softened butter and sugar in bowl until light and fluffy. Add sour cream, eggs and flavoring; mix well. Fold in mixture of flour, soda and baking powder. Layer half the batter, pie filling and remaining batter in greased and floured 8x12-inch baking dish. Mix brown sugar, pecans and melted butter in small bowl. Sprinkle over batter. Bake at 350 degrees for 45 minutes or until cake tests done. Cool on wire rack. Yield: 12 servings.

Approx per serving: Cal 456, Prot 5.6 gr, Fat 17.4 gr, Chol 77.2 mg, Carbo 70.4 gr, Sod 226.2 mg, Potas 148.3 mg.

Amy Beer, Laureate Pi
Mansfield, Ohio

Carrot Cake

2 cups sugar
1 cup oil
4 eggs
2 cups flour

2 teaspoons soda
1 teaspoon salt
2 teaspoons cinnamon
2½ cups grated carrots

Blend sugar and oil in mixer bowl. Add eggs 1 at a time, beating well after each addition. Add mixture of flour, soda, salt and cinnamon; mix well. Stir in carrots. Pour into 2 greased and floured 9-inch cake pans. Bake at 350 degrees for 30 minutes or until layers test done. Cool on wire rack. Spread Cream Cheese-Coconut Frosting between layers and over top and side of cake. Yield: 24 servings.

Cream Cheese-Coconut Frosting

½ cup margarine,
  softened
3 ounces cream cheese,
  softened
2 teaspoons vanilla
  extract

2 cups confectioners'
  sugar
1 cup flaked coconut
½ cup chopped pecans

Beat margarine and cream cheese in mixer bowl until light. Add vanilla and confectioners' sugar gradually, beating until of spreading consistency. Fold in coconut and pecans.

Approx per serving: Cal 312, Prot 2.9 gr, Fat 18.1 gr, Chol 37.0 mg, Carbo 37.4 gr, Sod 236.0 mg, Potas 90.3 mg.

Georgia Brazil, Xi Beta Kappa
Santa Rosa, New Mexico

Carrot Spice Cake

4 eggs
1 cup honey
1 cup oil
2 cups flour
2 teaspoons baking
  powder
½ teaspoon soda
2 teaspoons
  cinnamon
½ teaspoon nutmeg
¼ teaspoon allspice
3 cups grated carrots
½ cup grated apple
¾ cup chopped
  walnuts
¾ cup raisins
½ cup unsweetened
  coconut

Beat eggs in mixer bowl until thick. Add honey in a fine stream, beating constantly. Add oil; mix well. Mix in sifted dry ingredients. Stir in carrots, apple, walnuts, raisins and coconut. Pour into greased and floured 9x13-inch cake pan. Bake at 325 degrees for 45 minutes or until cake tests done. Cool on wire rack. Sprinkle with confectioners' sugar or frost with cream cheese frosting if desired. This cake freezes well. Yield: 15 servings.

Approx per serving: Cal 363, Prot 4.9 gr, Fat 21.0 gr, Chol 67.4 mg, Carbo 41.6 gr, Sod 107.3 mg, Potas 215.4 mg.

Emily Bisdorf, Preceptor Beta Pi
Delta, British Columbia, Canada

Chocolate-Strawberry Cake

2 cups chopped
  apples
2 cups frozen
  unsweetened
  strawberries,
  thawed
7 eggs
1 tablespoon vanilla
  extract
1 tablespoon
  chocolate extract
1 tablespoon
  strawberry
  extract
1 tablespoon
  Sweet 'N' Low
1 cup chocolate protein
  powder
¼ cup nonfat dry milk
  powder
2 teaspoons soda
1 cup unprocessed bran

Combine apples, strawberries, eggs and flavorings in food processor or blender container. Process until smooth. Pour into mixer bowl. Add dry ingredients; beat until well mixed. Pour into bundt pan sprayed with nonstick cooking spray. Bake at 350 degrees for 30 minutes. Cool. Invert onto serving plate. Yield: 8 servings.

Janine C. Shaw, Xi Eta
Lexington, Kentucky

Cinnamon-Cream Torte

¾ cup margarine,
  softened
½ cup sugar
1 egg
1 tablespoon
  cinnamon
1½ cups flour
2 cups whipping cream

Combine margarine, sugar, egg, cinnamon and 1 cup flour in mixer bowl. Beat at low speed until blended. Beat at medium speed for 3 minutes or until light and fluffy. Stir in ½ cup flour. Moisten cookie sheets; press nine 8-inch waxed paper circles onto moistened surface to secure. Spread each circle with ¼ cup dough. Bake at 375 degrees for 6 to 8 minutes or until light brown around edge. Remove cookies on waxed paper to wire rack to cool completely. Allow cookie sheets to cool completely between batches. Stack cooled cookies on waxed paper circles on flat plate. Cover with plastic wrap. Store in cool dry place for up to 3 days. Peel waxed paper carefully from cookies. Layer cookies and about ½ cup stiffly whipped cream alternately on serving plate, ending with whipped cream. Garnish with light sifting of cocoa. Score into 16 wedges with dull edge of knife. Refrigerate for 4 hours or longer until cookies soften for easier cutting. Yield: 16 servings.

Approx per serving: Cal 256, Prot 2.4 gr, Fat 20.5 gr, Chol 55.4 mg, Carbo 16.1 gr, Sod 118.8 mg, Potas 44.3 mg.

Deborah Peek, Psi
Little Rock, Arkansas

Crumb Cake

1 cup sugar
2 cups flour
¾ cup margarine,
  softened
1 egg
1 cup buttermilk
2 teaspoons
  baking powder
1 teaspoon cloves
1 teaspoon cinnamon

Mix sugar and flour in bowl. Cut in margarine until crumbly. Reserve 1 cup mixture. Add egg, buttermilk, baking powder and spices to remaining mixture; mix well. Pour into greased and floured 9x13-inch cake pan. Sprinkle reserved crumb mixture over top. Bake at 375 degrees for 45 minutes or until cake tests done. Cool on wire rack. Yield: 16 servings.

Approx per serving: Cal 173, Prot 2.7 gr, Fat 9.1 gr, Chol 16.1 mg, Carbo 25.4 gr, Sod 170.2 mg, Potas 43.6 mg.

Carolyn Russell, Eta Tau Alpha
Calgary, Alberta, Canada

Spiced Chocolate Zucchini Cake

¾ cup butter,
  softened
2 cups sugar
2 teaspoons
  cinnamon
¾ teaspoon nutmeg
3 eggs
2 cups grated
  zucchini

2 teaspoons vanilla
  extract
2½ cups flour
½ cup cocoa
2½ teaspoons baking
  powder
1½ teaspoons soda
1 teaspoon salt
½ cup milk

Cream butter, sugar, cinnamon and nutmeg in mixer bowl until light and fluffy. Add eggs; mix well. Fold in zucchini and vanilla. Add mixture of dry ingredients alternately with milk, mixing well after each addition. Pour into 2 greased and floured 9-inch cake pans. Bake at 350 degrees for 30 minutes or until cake tests done. Cool in pans for 5 minutes. Remove to wire rack to cool completely. Spread Cinnamon-Cream Cheese Frosting between layers and over top of cake. Yield: 16 servings.

Cinnamon-Cream Cheese Frosting

⅓ cup butter,
  softened
1 3-ounce package
  cream cheese,
  softened
¾ teaspoon
  cinnamon

4 cups confectioners'
  sugar
1 teaspoon vanilla
  extract
1½ to 2 tablespoons
  milk

Cream butter, cream cheese and cinnamon in mixer bowl until light and fluffy. Add remaining ingredients. Beat until creamy.

Photograph for this recipe on page 1.

Diabetic Date Cake

1 cup chopped dates
2 teaspoons soda
1 teaspoon vanilla
  extract

2 cups flour
1 cup mayonnaise
1 teaspoon salt
½ cup chopped pecans

Sprinkle dates with soda in bowl. Add 1 cup boiling water. Let stand, covered, until cool. Add remaining ingredients; mix well. Pour into greased and floured 9-inch square baking pan. Bake at 350 degrees for 45 minutes or until cake tests done. Yield: 8 servings.

Approx per serving: Cal 426, Prot 4.8 gr, Fat 28.0 gr, Chol 19.6 mg, Carbo 41.7 gr, Sod 639.7 mg, Potas 227.9 mg.

Carol Allison, Zeta Nu
Boardman, Oregon

Hawaiian Delight Upside-Down Cake

2 tablespoons
  margarine
1 cup grated coconut
1 14-ounce can
  crushed pineapple

1 2-layer package
  yellow cake
  mix

Melt margarine in 9x13-inch baking pan. Sprinkle coconut and drained pineapple into prepared pan. Prepare cake mix according to package directions. Pour over pineapple. Bake at 350 degrees for 35 minutes or until cake tests done. Cool in pan for 2 minutes. Invert onto serving tray. Cut into squares. Serve with whipped cream. Yield: 12 servings.

Approx per serving: Cal 390, Prot 4.1 gr, Fat 14.5 gr, Chol 44.3 mg, Carbo 64.0 gr, Sod 248.1 mg, Potas 164.3 mg.

Sharon Evansen, Preceptor Gamma Epsilon
Aberdeen, Washington

Guess-What Snack Cake

2 cups drained
  cooked pinto
  beans
¼ cup bean liquid
½ cup margarine,
  softened
⅔ cup sugar
1 egg
2 teaspoons vanilla
  extract
1 cup whole wheat
  flour

½ cup instant nonfat
  dry milk powder
1½ teaspoons baking
  powder
1 teaspoon cinnamon
1 teaspoon allspice
1 cup raisins
½ cup chopped
  walnuts

Mash beans with bean liquid in bowl until smooth; set aside. Cream margarine and sugar in bowl until light and fluffy. Add egg, vanilla and beans; mix well. Add mixture of dry ingredients; mix well. Fold in raisins and walnuts. Pour into 9-inch square baking pan sprayed with nonstick cooking spray. Bake at 350 degrees for 1 hour or until cake tests done. Cool on wire rack. Garnish with sprinkle of confectioners' sugar. Yield: 20 servings.

Approx per serving: Cal 149, Prot 3.1 gr, Fat 7.0 gr, Chol 13.0 mg, Carbo 20.1 gr, Sod 95.4 mg, Potas 159.1 mg.

Tonya Holmes, Xi Beta Lambda
Midvale, Idaho

Microwave Raspberry Jam Cake

½ cup sugar
¼ cup margarine,
  softened
2 eggs
1 cup flour
½ teaspoon soda
1 teaspoon
  cinnamon
¼ teaspoon cloves
½ teaspoon nutmeg

⅓ cup buttermilk
¼ cup chopped pecans
½ cup raspberry jam
3 tablespoons
  margarine
¾ cup packed brown
  sugar
3 cups sifted
  confectioners' sugar

Cream sugar and softened margarine in bowl until light and fluffy. Add eggs; beat until smooth. Add mixture of flour, soda and spices alternately with buttermilk, mixing just until blended after each addition. Fold in pecans and jam, leaving swirls of jam. Pour into ungreased glass 8x12-inch cake pan. Microwave on Medium for 9 minutes, turning ¼ turn every 3 minutes. Microwave on High for 3 minutes. Cool on wire rack. Microwave 3 tablespoons margarine in 1½-quart glass bowl on High for 30 seconds or until melted. Add brown sugar. Microwave on High for 2 minutes, stirring twice. Let stand for 5 minutes. Add confectioners' sugar; beat until smooth. Spread over cooled cake. Yield: 8 servings.

Approx per serving: Cal 503, Prot 4.1 gr, Fat 14.3 gr, Chol 63.4 mg, Carbo 92.5 gr, Sod 211.1 mg, Potas 155.0 mg.

Dorothy Gessinger, Xi Alpha Psi
Federal Way, Washington

Omelette Cake Supreme

4 cups sliced
  strawberries
¼ cup sugar
4 eggs, separated

6 tablespoons sugar
⅓ cup flour
1 pint whipping cream,
  whipped

Sprinkle strawberries with ¼ cup sugar in bowl. Let stand for several minutes. Beat egg whites until stiff peaks form. Add 3 tablespoons sugar, 1 tablespoon at a time, beating constantly. Beat egg yolks with remaining 3 tablespoons sugar until thick and lemon-colored. Fold in egg whites gently. Fold in flour gradually. Pour ½ of the mixture into lightly greased electric skillet, spreading evenly. Bake at 250 degrees for 15 minutes or until cake tests done. Cool on towel. Repeat process. Spread half the whipped cream and half the strawberries over each cake; fold cakes in half to enclose filling. Chill, wrapped in plastic wrap. Place on serving plate. Garnish with additional whipped cream and strawberries. Yield: 8 servings.

Approx per serving: Cal 356, Prot 5.6 gr, Fat 25.7 gr, Chol 205.5 mg, Carbo 27.7 gr, Sod 50.6 mg, Potas 212.9 mg.

Terri Bourland, Preceptor Eta Omega
Oakland, California

Pea Picking Cake

1 16-ounce can
   crushed
   pineapple
1 2-layer package
   golden butter
   cake mix
½ cup oil
4 eggs

1 11-ounce can
   mandarin oranges,
   drained
1 8-ounce carton
   whipped topping
1 small package
   vanilla instant
   pudding mix

Drain crushed pineapple. Reserve ⅓ cup. Combine remaining pineapple with cake mix, oil, eggs and orange sections in bowl; mix well. Pour into greased and floured 9x13-inch cake pan. Bake at 350 degrees for 35 minutes or until cake tests done. Cool completely in pan. Combine whipped topping, pudding mix and reserved pineapple in bowl; mix well. Spread over cake. Store in refrigerator for up to 1 week. Yield: 16 servings.

Approx per serving: Cal 320, Prot 3.8 gr, Fat 14.2 gr, Chol 63.2 mg, Carbo 44.9 gr, Sod 354.7 mg, Potas 76.4 mg.

Karen Zahn, Alpha Phi
Moorcroft, Wyoming

Orange-Date Cake

½ cup butter,
  softened
1 cup packed
  brown sugar
2 eggs, separated
1½ cups flour
⅛ teaspoon salt
1 teaspoon baking
  powder

¾ cup sour milk
1 teaspoon soda
8 ounces dates,
  chopped
1 orange, thinly sliced
1½ cups packed
  brown sugar
2 tablespoons butter

Cream ½ cup butter, 1 cup brown sugar and egg yolks in bowl until light and fluffy. Add mixture of flour, salt and baking powder alternately with mixture of sour milk and soda, mixing well after each addition. Add dates and orange; mix well. Fold in stiffly beaten egg whites gently. Pour into greased and floured 10-inch square cake pan. Bake at 375 degrees for 50 to 60 minutes or until cake tests done. Cool. Bring 1½ cups brown sugar dissolved in ⅓ cup water in saucepan to a boil. Cook to soft-ball stage. Remove from heat. Add 2 tablespoons butter; mix well. Spread warm frosting over cake. Yield: 8 servings.

Approx per serving: Cal 586, Prot 5.9 gr, Fat 16.3 gr, Chol 99.2 mg, Carbo 86.8 gr, Sod 418.9 mg, Potas 533.1 mg.

Jean Turnbull, Laureate Mu
North Vancouver, British Columbia, Canada

Pineapple-Carrot Cupcakes

1 cup chopped
  dates
1 cup raisins,
  chopped
½ cup corn oil
  margarine
2 cups whole wheat
  flour
1 teaspoon soda
1 teaspoon vanilla
  extract

1 egg
½ cup brown sugar
  substitute
1 cup grated carrots
1 cup unsweetened
  crushed
  pineapple
½ cup freshly grated
  coconut
1 cup chopped pecans

Combine dates, raisins and 1 cup water in saucepan. Bring to a boil. Boil for 3 minutes. Add margarine. Cool. Combine date mixture with flour, soda, vanilla, egg and brown sugar substitute in bowl; mix well. Add remaining ingredients; mix well. Spoon into 24 greased and floured muffin cups. Bake at 375 degrees for 25 minutes or until cupcakes test done. Cool for 10 minutes before serving. Garnish with additional cream cheese and pineapple.
Yield: 24 cupcakes.
Note: May substitute unsweetened applesauce for pineapple.

Approx per cupcake: Cal 160, Prot 2.5 gr, Fat 8.4 gr, Chol 10.5 mg, Carbo 21.1 gr, Sod 91.4 mg, Potas 196.0 mg.

Mary Meddles, Preceptor Delta Tau
Richwood, Ohio

Pound Cake

¼ cup margarine,
  softened
½ cup sugar
2 teaspoons vanilla
  extract

2 eggs
¾ cup flour
1½ teaspoons baking
  powder

Cream margarine and sugar in bowl until light and fluffy. Add vanilla and eggs; beat well. Fold in sifted flour and baking powder. Pour into 4x8-inch loaf pan sprayed with nonstick cooking spray. Bake at 350 degrees for 20 to 30 minutes or until cake tests done. Cool on wire rack. Remove to serving plate. Serve with fruit.
Yield: 8 servings.

Approx per serving: Cal 163, Prot 2.9 gr, Fat 7.3 gr, Chol 63.2 mg, Carbo 21.7 gr, Sod 147.3 mg, Potas 30.2 mg.

Linda Patten, Xi Rho Zeta
Deer Park, Texas

Pumpkin Pudding Cake

1 29-ounce can
  pumpkin
1 large can
  evaporated milk
1 cup sugar
3 eggs

1 teaspoon nutmeg
1 teaspoon cinnamon
1 2-layer package
  yellow cake mix
1 cup melted margarine
½ cup chopped pecans

Combine pumpkin, evaporated milk, sugar, eggs and spices in bowl; beat well. Pour into greased 9x13-inch cake pan. Sprinkle dry cake mix over top. Drizzle margarine over cake mix. Top with pecans. Bake at 350 degrees for 60 to 70 minutes. Yield: 12 servings.

Approx per serving: Cal 503, Prot 7.3 gr, Fat 26.2 gr, Chol 74.1 mg, Carbo 60.8 gr, Sod 792.2 mg, Potas 303.9 mg.

Ruth King, Preceptor Beta Gamma
Leon, Kansas

Rhubarb Upside-Down Cake

4 cups chopped
  rhubarb
1 3-ounce package
  strawberry gelatin

1 cup sugar
1 2-layer package
  yellow cake mix

Layer rhubarb and mixture of gelatin and sugar in greased 9x13-inch cake pan. Prepare cake mix using package directions. Pour into prepared pan. Bake at 350 degrees for 40 minutes or until cake tests done. Invert onto serving plate. Cool. Serve with whipped topping.
Yield: 12 servings.

Approx per serving: Cal 277, Prot 2.9 gr, Fat 3.1 gr, Chol 0.0 mg, Carbo 59.3 gr, Sod 427.4 mg, Potas 117.4 mg.

Jeanette Smith, Alpha Xi
Glen Carbon, Illinois

Strawberry Angel Cake

1 small package
  sugar-free gelatin
1 10-ounce
  package frozen
  unsweetened
  strawberries

2 cups whipped
  topping
1 angel food cake,
  torn into 2-inch
  pieces.

Dissolve gelatin in 1¼ cups boiling water. Add strawberries; mix well. Chill until partially set. Beat until fluffy. Fold in half the whipped topping. Layer cake and gelatin mixture alternately in tube pan, packing each cake layer lightly. Chill for 12 hours or longer. Unmold on serving plate. Frost with remaining whipped topping.
Yield: 12 servings.

Approx per serving: Cal 180, Prot 3.6 gr, Fat 2.9 gr, Chol 0.0 mg, Carbo 35.2 gr, Sod 96.8 mg, Potas 59.2 mg.

Jacqueline E. Neil, Xi Gamma Alpha
Dubuque, Iowa

Sugar-Free Cake

2 cups raisins
1 cup unsweetened
 applesauce
2 eggs
8 packets
 Sweet 'N' Low

¾ cup oil
2 cups flour
1 teaspoon soda
½ teaspoon salt
1 teaspoon cinnamon

Cook raisins in 2 cups water in saucepan until raisins plump and water is almost completely absorbed. Remove from heat. Cool slightly. Add applesauce and eggs; mix well. Add Sweet 'N' Low and oil; mix well. Add mixture of dry ingredients; mix well. Pour into greased and floured 9x13-inch cake pan. Bake at 350 degrees for 45 minutes or until cake tests done. Serve with whipped topping. Yield: 12 servings.

Approx per serving: Cal 288, Prot 3.9 gr, Fat 14.9 gr,
Chol 42.1 mg, Carbo 36.8 gr, Sod 174.8 mg, Potas 230.8 mg.

Lorraine Kirkpatrick, Xi Eta Kappa
Barstow Heights, California

Fresh Tomato Cake

7 medium tomatoes
½ cup butter,
 softened
1 cup packed
 brown sugar
1 teaspoon allspice
¾ teaspoon grated
 orange rind
½ teaspoon ginger
2 eggs

½ cup raisins
½ cup chopped dates
3 cups flour
2 teaspoons baking
 powder
1 teaspoon soda
½ teaspoon salt
¼ cup confectioners'
 sugar

Parboil tomatoes for 1 minute. Rinse with cold water; remove skins. Seed and chop tomatoes; drain well. Cream butter, brown sugar, allspice, orange rind and ginger in mixer bowl until light and fluffy. Add eggs; beat well. Fold in tomatoes, raisins and dates. Add mixture of flour, baking powder, soda and salt; mix well. Pour into greased 5x9-inch loaf pan. Bake at 350 degrees for 1 hour or until cake tests done. Cool in pan for 5 minutes. Remove to wire rack to cool completely. Sprinkle with confectioners' sugar. Yield: 12 servings.

Photograph for this recipe on page 1.

Upside-Down Cake

¼ cup corn syrup
1 tablespoon lemon
 juice
1 tablespoon melted
 butter
¼ cup packed
 brown sugar
Sliced fresh fruit
2½ teaspoons
 baking powder

1½ cups sifted flour
¼ teaspoon salt
5 tablespoons butter,
 softened
¾ cup sugar
1 egg, well beaten
½ cup milk
½ teaspoon vanilla
 extract

Combine corn syrup, lemon juice, melted butter and brown sugar in bowl; mix well. Spread in buttered 8-inch square baking pan. Arrange fruit in prepared pan. Sift baking powder, flour and salt together three times. Cream softened butter and sugar in bowl until light and fluffy. Add egg, a small amount at a time, beating well after each addition. Add sifted dry ingredients alternately with milk and vanilla, beating well after each addition. Drop by spoonfuls over fruit; spread evenly. Bake at 350 degrees for 50 minutes. Cool for 5 minutes. Invert onto serving plate. Yield: 6 servings.

Theresa E. MacDonald, Xi Laureate Alpha
Nepean, Ontario, Canada

Charlene's Swiss Chocolate Roll

1 medium banana,
 chopped
2 eggs
2 teaspoons vanilla
 extract
2 slices bread,
 crumbled
⅔ cup instant
 nonfat dry milk
 powder
4 teaspoons cocoa

1 teaspoon soda
1 teaspoon cream of
 tartar
2 teaspoons artificial
 sweetener
⅔ cup ricotta cheese
1 teaspoon vanilla
 extract
4 teaspoons Equal
 artificial sweetener

Line 9x13-inch cake pan with waxed paper; spray with nonstick cooking spray. Combine banana, eggs and 2 teaspoons vanilla in blender container. Process until smooth. Add next 6 ingredients. Process until well mixed. Pour into prepared pan. Bake at 325 degrees for 10 minutes or until cake tests done. Invert onto towel. Remove waxed paper. Roll from narrow end as for jelly roll. Combine ricotta cheese, 1 teaspoon vanilla and Equal in bowl. Mix with fork until fluffy. Unroll cake. Spread ricotta mixture over top. Roll to enclose filling. Cut cake roll in half. Place on serving plates. Yield: 2 servings.
Note: Do not use Equal in cake layer as baking heat decreases sweetness.

Approx per serving: Cal 411, Prot 27.2 gr, Fat 16.6 gr,
Chol 258.7 mg, Carbo 40.7 gr, Sod 913.1 mg, Potas 770.2 mg.
Nutritional information does not include cholesterol value for ricotta cheese.

Charlene Cassity, Xi Epsilon Eta
Union, Michigan

Double Chocolate Roll

4 eggs, separated
⅛ teaspoon salt
¾ cup sugar
½ cup cake flour,
  sifted
2 tablespoons cocoa
2 tablespoons
  confectioners' sugar

1 small package
  chocolate sugar-free
  pudding mix
2 cups low-fat milk
2 egg whites
1 teaspoon
  confectioners' sugar

Beat 4 egg whites with salt until stiff peaks form. Add ½ cup sugar gradually, beating until very stiff. Set aside. Beat egg yolks until light. Add ¼ cup sugar; beat until thick. Fold ¼ of the egg whites into egg yolks gently. Fold in remaining egg whites gently. Sift flour and cocoa together. Fold into egg mixture gradually. Spread in waxed paper-lined 10x15-inch cake pan. Bake at 325 degrees for 30 minutes. Invert onto towel sprinkled with 2 tablespoons confectioners' sugar. Peel off waxed paper. Roll cake and towel as for jelly roll. Cool. Prepare pudding mix with milk using package directions. Beat 2 egg whites until soft peaks form. Fold ¼ of the egg whites into pudding gently. Fold in remaining egg whites gently. Unroll cake; remove towel. Spread with pudding mixture; reroll. Place on serving plate. Sift 1 teaspoon confectioners' sugar over top. Chill for 24 hours before serving. Yield: 12 servings.

Approx per serving: Cal 125, Prot 4.6 gr, Fat 2.6 gr, Chol 85.9 mg, Carbo 21.5 gr, Sod 117.8 mg, Potas 110.6 mg.

Jackie Vogler, Xi Sigma Pi
Hilltop Lake, Texas

Easy Rocky Road Candy

1 can sweetened
  condensed milk
1 12-ounce
  package
  chocolate chips

2 cups salted peanuts
2½ cups miniature
  marshmallows

Combine condensed milk and chocolate chips in saucepan. Heat over medium heat until chocolate chips melt; mix well. Remove from heat. Stir in peanuts and half the marshmallows. Spread remaining marshmallows in buttered 9x9-inch dish. Pour chocolate mixture into prepared pan. Chill for 2 hours. Cut into squares. Yield: 36 pieces.

Approx per piece: Cal 152, Prot 3.8 gr, Fat 8.7 gr, Chol 5.4 mg, Carbo 17.1 gr, Sod 52.2 mg, Potas 134.7 mg.

Jerrie Cannon, Xi Eta Kappa
Barstow, California

Date Candy Roll

3 cups sugar
1 cup milk
1 8-ounce
  package dates,
  chopped

1½ cups chopped
  pecans
1 teaspoon vanilla
  extract

Combine sugar and milk in saucepan. Cook to 234 to 240 degrees on candy thermometer, soft-ball stage. Stir in dates. Cook to 250 to 268 degrees on candy thermometer, hard-ball stage; stir frequently. Add pecans, vanilla and salt to taste. Beat until mixture thickens and loses its luster. Pour onto damp cloth. Shape into roll. Let stand until firm. Cut into slices. Yield: 40 slices.

Approx per slice: Cal 108, Prot 0.7 gr, Fat 3.4 gr, Chol 0.9 mg, Carbo 2.0 gr, Sod 3.3 mg, Potas 73.4 mg.

Maxine B. Mayer, Preceptor Omicron
Littleton, Colorado

Grandkid's Fudge

2 cups sugar
⅔ cup evaporated
  milk

1 cup peanut butter
1 7-ounce jar
  marshmallow creme

Combine sugar and evaporated milk in saucepan. Cook to 234 to 240 degrees on candy thermometer, soft-ball stage. Remove from heat. Stir in peanut butter and marshmallow creme. Pour into buttered pan. Let stand until cool. Cut into squares. Yield: 36 pieces.

Approx per piece: Cal 109, Prot 2.2 gr, Fat 4.0 gr, Chol 1.5 mg, Carbo 17.3 gr, Sod 52.0 mg, Potas 60.9 mg.

Edith Scott, Xi Lambda Psi
Venice, Florida

Microwave Brittle

1½ cups sugar
¾ cup light corn
  syrup
1 teaspoon butter
¼ teaspoon salt

1 teaspoon vanilla
  extract
2 cups dry-roasted
  peanuts
1 teaspoon soda

Combine sugar and corn syrup in glass dish; mix well. Microwave on High for 7 minutes, stirring once. Add butter, salt, vanilla and peanuts; mix well. Microwave on High for 5½ minutes longer. Stir in soda. Pour into buttered 9x13-inch dish. Cool for 20 minutes. Break into pieces. Yield: 50 pieces.

Approx per piece: Cal 72, Prot 1.5 gr, Fat 2.9 gr, Chol 0.2 mg, Carbo 10.7 gr, Sod 55.4 mg, Potas 39.2 mg.

Bonni Arrigoni, Alpha Phi
Moorcroft, Wyoming

Buttermilk Chiffon Cheesecake

1½ cups Grape Nuts
¼ cup frozen apple
  juice concentrate,
  thawed
3½ cups dry curd
  cottage cheese
1 cup buttermilk
2 envelopes
  unflavored
  gelatin
1 8-ounce can
  unsweetened
  crushed pineapple
½ cup frozen apple
  juice concentrate,
  thawed

1 teaspoon vanilla
  extract
3 egg whites,
  stiffly beaten
2 10-ounce packages
  frozen unsweetened
  blueberries, thawed
½ cup frozen apple
  juice concentrate,
  thawed
1 tablespoon cornstarch
1 teaspoon vanilla
  extract

Mix Grape Nuts with ¼ cup apple juice concentrate in bowl. Press over bottom and sides of two 9-inch pie plates. Crumble cottage cheese into buttermilk in bowl. Fill blender container ¾ full. Process until smooth. Repeat until all cottage cheese mixture has been processed; set aside. Soften gelatin in crushed pineapple in bowl. Bring ½ cup apple juice concentrate and ½ cup water to a boil in saucepan. Pour over pineapple mixture; stir until gelatin dissolves. Cool. Stir in cottage cheese mixture and vanilla. Fold in stiffly beaten egg whites gently. Spoon into prepared pie plates. Chill for several hours. Combine blueberries, ½ cup apple juice concentrate and ½ cup water in saucepan. Bring to a boil. Stir in cornstarch blended with 1 tablespoon water. Cook until thickened, stirring constantly. Stir in 1 teaspoon vanilla. Cool. Spread over cheesecakes. Chill until set. Yield: 12 servings.

Approx per serving: Cal 191, Prot 11.7 gr, Fat 0.5 gr,
Chol 3.4 mg, Carbo 35.2 gr, Sod 265.7 mg, Potas 248.2 mg.

Connie Loetsch, Preceptor Zeta Alpha
Abilene, Texas

Swirled Chocolate Cheesecake

1¼ cups chocolate
  wafer crumbs
⅓ cup melted butter
1½ cups chocolate
  chips
½ cup sugar

16 ounces cream cheese,
  softened
¾ cup sugar
1 teaspoon vanilla
  extract
4 eggs

Combine cookie crumbs and melted butter in bowl; mix well. Press over bottom and halfway up side of springform pan. Bake at 350 degrees for 5 minutes. Cool. Melt chocolate chips with ½ cup sugar in double boiler; blend well. Beat cream cheese and ¾ cup sugar in mixer bowl until light and fluffy. Add vanilla and eggs; beat until smooth. Add half the cream cheese mixture to chocolate mixture; mix well. Reserve ½ cup. Pour remaining chocolate mixture into crust. Spread remaining cream cheese mixture over chocolate layer. Drizzle reserved chocolate mixture over top. Cut through all layers with knife to marbleize. Bake at 325 degrees for 50 minutes. Cool to room temperature. Chill in refrigerator. Place on serving plate; remove side of pan. Yield: 14 servings.

Approx per serving: Cal 375, Prot 5.5 gr, Fat 26.9 gr,
Chol 121.6 mg, Carbo 32.4 gr, Sod 152.2 mg, Potas 123.2 mg.
Nutritional information does not include chocolate wafer crumbs.

Nu Chapter
Thompson, Manitoba, Canada

Low-Calorie Citrus Cheesecake

⅔ cup cornflakes
¼ cup Grape Nuts
2 teaspoons melted
  butter
1 teaspoon brown
  sugar
1 teaspoon grated
  orange rind
1 teaspoon grated
  lemon rind
2 envelopes
  unflavored
  gelatin
¼ cup sugar
1½ cups low-fat
  milk

3 eggs, separated
3 cups ricotta cheese
1 tablespoon orange
  juice
1 tablespoon lemon
  juice
1 teaspoon grated
  lemon rind
1 teaspoon grated
  orange rind
1 teaspoon vanilla
  extract
½ cup sugar
2 kiwifruit, peeled,
  sliced

Process cornflakes and Grape Nuts in food processor until finely crushed. Combine with next 4 ingredients in bowl; mix well. Press over bottom of 8-inch springform pan. Bake at 350 degrees for 5 minutes. Cool. Mix gelatin and ¼ cup sugar in double boiler. Beat in milk and egg yolks. Let stand until gelatin softens. Cook over boiling water until gelatin dissolves and mixture coats spoon, stirring constantly. Chill until partially set. Process ricotta cheese in food processor until smooth. Combine with next 5 ingredients in bowl; mix well. Stir in partially congealed mixture. Beat egg whites until frothy. Add ½ cup sugar gradually, beating constantly until soft peaks form. Fold gently into cream cheese mixture. Spoon into prepared pan. Chill for 8 hours or longer. Place on serving plate; remove side of pan. Arrange kiwifruit on top.
Yield: 12 servings.

Approx per serving: Cal 188, Prot 10.0 gr, Fat 8.4 gr,
Chol 66.4 mg, Carbo 19.9 gr, Sod 124.8 mg, Potas 78.3 mg.
Nutritional information does not include kiwifruit or cholesterol value for ricotta cheese.

Debbie LoCicero, Gamma
Omaha, Nebraska

Crescent Cheesecake Squares

2   8-count
   packages
   refrigerator
   crescent rolls
2   8-ounce
   packages cream
   cheese, softened

1¼ cups sugar
1 egg, separated
1 teaspoon vanilla
   extract
½ teaspoon cinnamon
½ cup chopped pecans

Separate 1 can refrigerator rolls. Arrange in 9x13-inch baking pan; press edges to seal. Whip cream cheese and sugar in mixer bowl until light and fluffy. Beat in egg yolk and vanilla. Spread over crust. Arrange remaining roll dough over top to form crust; press edges to seal. Brush with stiffly beaten egg white. Sprinkle with cinnamon and pecans. Bake at 350 degrees for 45 minutes. Cut into squares. Yield: 12 squares.

Approx per square: Cal 262, Prot 4.0 gr, Fat 18.2 gr, Chol 63.0 mg. Carbo 22.3 gr, Sod 99.8 mg, Potas 63.6 mg. Nutritional information does not include crescent rolls.

Diane Rodd, Xi Alpha Omicron
Necedah, Wisconsin

Low-Calorie Peach Cheesecake

2 envelopes
   unflavored
   gelatin
¾ cup sugar
¼ teaspoon salt
2 eggs, separated
1 cup low-fat milk

1 teaspoon lemon juice
1   10-ounce package
   frozen peaches,
   thawed
¼ teaspoon almond
   extract
2 tablespoons sugar

Mix gelatin, ¾ cup sugar and salt in double boiler. Beat in egg yolks and milk. Let stand until gelatin is softened. Cook over boiling water until gelatin dissolves, stirring constantly. Remove from heat. Stir in lemon juice, peaches and flavoring. Chill until partially set. Beat until light and smooth. Beat egg whites until soft peaks form. Add 2 tablespoons sugar gradually, beating until stiff peaks form. Fold gently into partially congealed mixture. Spoon into mold. Chill until firm. Unmold on serving plate. Yield: 4 servings.

Approx per serving: Cal 308, Prot 8.5 gr, Fat 3.6 gr, Chol 128.8 mg, Carbo 56.6 gr, Sod 199.3 mg, Potas 219.2 mg.

Bessie Wade, Preceptor Pi
Loyall, Kentucky

Pineapple Cheatcake

1   20-ounce can
   pineapple tidbits
1 envelope unflavored
   gelatin
½ cup low-fat milk
8 ounces Neufchâtel
   cheese, softened

1 teaspoon vanilla
   extract
¼ teaspoon lemon juice
2 egg whites
12 packets Equal

Drain pineapple, reserving juice. Add enough water to measure 1 cup. Soften gelatin in cold milk in saucepan. Heat over low heat for 2 minutes, stirring constantly until gelatin dissolves. Remove from heat. Beat Neufchâtel cheese in mixer bowl until light and fluffy. Beat in gelatin mixture, reserved juice, vanilla and lemon juice. Chill for 30 minutes or until partially set. Beat egg whites until soft peaks form. Add Equal, beating constantly until stiff peaks form. Fold egg whites and pineapple gently into partially congealed mixture. Spoon into 9-inch pie plate or springform pan. Chill for 3 hours or until firm. Yield: 8 servings.

Approx per serving: Cal 153, Prot 5.4 gr, Fat 7.2 gr, Chol 0.6 mg, Carbo 17.3 gr, Sod 136.3 mg, Potas 112.2 mg.

Betty Kelly, XP1129
Fort Dodge, Iowa

Low-Fat Vanilla Cheesecake

2 cups ricotta cheese
1 cup plain low-fat
   yogurt
4 eggs

½ cup sugar
1½ teaspoons vanilla
   extract

Combine all ingredients in blender container. Process just until smooth. Pour into nonstick 9x9-inch baking pan. Place in larger pan of hot water. Bake at 325 degrees for 40 minutes or until set. Cool. Chill in refrigerator. Cut into squares. Yield: 12 servings.

Approx per serving: Cal 122, Prot 6.8 gr, Fat 6.2 gr, Chol 85.8 mg, Carbo 10.7 gr, Sod 63.3 mg, Potas 48.5 mg. Nutritional information does not include cholesterol value for ricotta cheese.

Karen Doran, Beta Eta
Longview, West Virginia

Honey-Carob Brownies

½ cup melted
  butter
½ cup carob
  powder
1 cup honey
2 eggs, beaten
1 cup whole wheat
  flour

1 teaspoon baking
  powder
¼ teaspoon salt
1 teaspoon vanilla
  extract
½ cup broken
  walnuts

Combine margarine, carob powder, honey and eggs in bowl; mix well. Sift in flour, baking powder and salt; mix well. Stir in vanilla and walnuts. Pour into greased 8-inch square baking dish. Bake at 350 degrees for 40 minutes. Cool. Cut into squares. Yield: 16 brownies.

Approx per brownie: Cal 182, Prot 2.7 gr, Fat 9.1 gr, Chol 49.4 mg, Carbo 26.9 gr, Sod 132.9 mg, Potas 65.3 mg.

Deborah Peek, Psi
Little Rock, Arkansas

Low-Calorie Brownies

2 cups graham
  cracker crumbs
3 ounces semisweet
  chocolate chips
1 cup low-fat milk

½ cup chopped
  walnuts
1½ teaspoons
  Sweet 'N' Low
¼ teaspoon salt

Combine all ingredients in bowl; mix well. Spoon into 8-inch square baking pan. Bake at 350 degrees for 30 minutes. Cut into 2-inch squares while warm. Yield: 16 brownies.

Approx per brownie: Cal 108, Prot 2.3 gr, Fat 5.7 gr, Chol 0.6 mg, Carbo 14.0 gr, Sod 129.1 mg, Potas 108.3 mg.

Deborah Peek, Psi
Little Rock, Arkansas

Chocolate-Caramel-Walnut Bars

1 package pudding-
  recipe German
  chocolate cake
  mix
½ cup margarine,
  softened
1 small can
  evaporated milk

1 14-ounce
  package caramels
1½ cups walnuts
1 6-ounce
  package
  semisweet
  chocolate chips

Combine cake mix, margarine and ⅓ cup evaporated milk in bowl; mix well. Press half the mixture into 9x13-inch baking dish. Bake at 350 degrees for 6 minutes. Melt caramels in ⅓ cup evaporated milk in saucepan, stirring frequently. Sprinkle half the walnuts and all the chocolate chips over baked layer. Spread with caramel mixture. Drop remaining dough by spoonfuls over caramel layer. Sprinkle with remaining walnuts. Bake at 350 degrees for 20 minutes. Cool slightly. Cut into bars. Yield: 60 bars.

Approx per bar: Cal 114, Prot 1.4 gr, Fat 6.0 gr, Chol 1.0 mg, Carbo 14.4 gr, Sod 117.9 mg, Potas 44.4 mg.

Carol Terpstra, Alpha
Billings, Montana

Fruit And Oat Bars

¾ cup melted
  margarine
⅓ cup packed
  brown sugar
2 cups oats
1 cup flour

⅓ cup chopped
  pecans
½ teaspoon salt
1 10-ounce jar
  fruit preserves

Combine margarine and brown sugar in bowl; mix well. Add oats, flour, pecans and salt; mix well. Reserve ¾ cup for topping. Pat remaining mixture into greased 7x11-inch glass baking dish. Bake at 350 degrees for 10 minutes. Spread preserves over baked layer to within ½ inch of edge. Sprinkle with reserved oats mixture. Bake for 10 minutes longer or until light brown. Cool. Cut into bars. Store in airtight container. Yield: 24 bars.

Approx per bar: Cal 138, Prot 1.3 gr, Fat 7.2 gr, Chol 0.0 mg, Carbo 17.7 gr, Sod 117.0 mg, Potas 48.9 mg.

Bettie A. Wilson, Preceptor Beta Mu
Hatfield, Pennsylvania

Goblin Bread Cookies

1 1-pound
  package light
  brown sugar
¾ cup melted
  margarine
3 eggs, beaten
2⅔ cups self-rising
  flour

1 6-ounce
  package
  chocolate chips
1 cup coconut
1 cup chopped
  pecans

Combine brown sugar and margarine in bowl; mix well. Blend in eggs. Add flour; mix well. Stir in remaining ingredients. Pour into greased 9x13-inch baking pan. Bake at 325 degrees for 45 minutes or until bread tests done. Cool in pan. Cut into squares. Yield: 15 squares.

Approx per square: Cal 449, Prot 4.8 gr, Fat 21.9 gr, Chol 50.6 mg, Carbo 61.7 gr, Sod 387.4 mg, Potas 263.9 mg.

Virginia S. Tyler, Delta Tau
Thomaston, Georgia

Oatmeal Carmelitas

1 cup flour
2 cups quick-cooking
  oats
¾ cup packed
  brown sugar
½ teaspoon soda
¼ teaspoon salt

¾ cup butter
1 6-ounce package
   chocolate chips
½ cup chopped pecans
¾ cup caramel ice
  cream topping
3 tablespoons flour

Combine flour, oats, brown sugar, soda, salt and butter in bowl; mix until crumbly. Press half the crumb mixture over bottom of 9x13-inch baking pan. Bake at 350 degrees for 10 minutes. Sprinkle with chocolate chips and pecans. Blend ice cream topping and flour in bowl. Spoon over chocolate chips and pecans. Sprinkle remaining crumb mixture over top. Bake at 350 degrees for 15 minutes or until brown. Chill for 1 hour or longer. Cut into squares.
Yield: 32 squares.

Approx per square: Cal 133, Prot 1.6 gr, Fat 7.9 gr, Chol 13.3 mg, Carbo 15.2 gr, Sod 96.7 mg, Potas 69.4 mg. Nutritional information does not include ice cream topping.

Patti Dutton, Zeta Eta
Eureka, California

Sugarless Bars

1 cup chopped
  dates
½ cup raisins
1 stick margarine
2 eggs
1 teaspoon soda

1 teaspoon vanilla
  extract
½ teaspoon
  cinnamon
½ teaspoon nutmeg
¼ teaspoon salt

Combine first 3 ingredients and 1 cup water in saucepan. Bring to a boil. Cook for 5 minutes. Cool. Stir in eggs, soda, vanilla, cinnamon, nutmeg and salt. Pour into greased 9-inch square baking pan. Bake for 25 minutes or until set. Cut into bars when cool. Yield: 16 bars.

Approx per bar: Cal 105, Prot 1.2 gr, Fat 6.5 gr, Chol 31.6 mg, Carbo 11.7 gr, Sod 163.7 mg, Potas 116.4 mg.

Joy Raye, Preceptor Delta Theta
Torrance, California

Twenty-Three Calorie Applesauce Cookies

8 ounces diet
  margarine
5 tablespoons
  packed brown
  sugar
1 teaspoon vanilla
  extract
1 egg
1⅔ cups flour

1 teaspoon soda
½ teaspoon salt
2 teaspoons apple
  pie spice
1 cup unsweetened
  applesauce
⅔ cup raisins
1 cup whole bran
  cereal

Cream first 4 ingredients in bowl until blended. Add sifted dry ingredients alternately with applesauce, mixing well after each addition. Stir in raisins and cereal. Drop by level measuring teaspoonfuls onto baking sheet sprayed with nonstick cooking spray. Bake at 375 degrees for 15 minutes or until golden brown. Cool on wire rack. Store in airtight container. Yield: 108 cookies.

Approx per cookie: Cal 23, Prot 0.4 gr, Fat 1.4 gr, Chol 2.6 mg, Carbo 3.9 gr, Sod 41.7 mg, Potas 18.0 mg.

Ann Titus, Xi Gamma Zeta
Dallas, Texas

Chocolate Chip Cookies

½ cup margarine,
  softened
¼ cup packed brown
  sugar
1 egg
1 teaspoon vanilla
  extract
1½ cups whole
  wheat flour

½ cup oats
¼ teaspoon salt
½ teaspoon soda
1 teaspoon baking
  powder
½ cup low-fat milk
1 cup chocolate
  chips

Cream margarine and brown sugar in bowl until light and fluffy. Add egg and vanilla; mix well. Add mixture of flour, oats, salt, soda and baking powder alternately with milk, beating well after each addition. Stir in chocolate chips. Drop by teaspoonfuls onto lightly greased cookie sheet. Bake at 350 degrees for 12 to 15 minutes or until light brown. Cool on wire rack.
Yield: 36 cookies.

Approx per cookie: Cal 77, Prot 1.3 gr, Fat 4.6 gr, Chol 7.2 mg, Carbo 8.7 gr, Sod 70.6 mg, Potas 51.0 mg.

Billy Jane Gabel, Xi Mu Eta
Houston, Texas

Colossal Cookies

½ cup margarine
1½ cups packed
  brown sugar
4 eggs
1 teaspoon vanilla
  extract
1 18-ounce jar
   chunky peanut
   butter

2½ teaspoons soda
18 ounces oats
6 ounces chocolate
  chips
1 cup raisins

Cream margarine and brown sugar in mixer bowl until light and fluffy. Blend in eggs and vanilla. Add peanut butter; mix well. Stir in remaining ingredients. Drop by scant ¼ cupfuls 4 inches apart onto ungreased cookie sheet. Flatten to 2½-inch diameter with fork. Bake at 350 degrees for 10 minutes or until brown. Cool for 1 minute. Remove to wire rack to cool completely. Store in airtight container. Yield: 54 cookies.

Approx per cookie: Cal 165, Prot 4.6 gr, Fat 9.3 gr, Chol 18.7 mg, Carbo 17.9 gr, Sod 130.6 mg, Potas 155.2 mg.

Erin Haugh, Alpha Eta
Green River, Wyoming

Chocolate-Freckled Cookies

½ cup shortening
½ cup packed
  brown sugar
¼ cup sugar
1 egg
2 tablespoons milk
1 teaspoon vanilla
  extract
¼ cup cocoa

1½ cups whole
  wheat flour
½ teaspoon soda
½ teaspoon
  cinnamon
¼ teaspoon salt
⅓ cup toasted
  wheat germ

Cream shortening and sugars in mixer bowl at medium speed until light and fluffy. Add egg, milk and vanilla; beat well. Add mixture of cocoa, flour, soda, cinnamon and salt gradually, beating at low speed until blended after each addition. Drop by rounded teaspoonfuls onto ungreased cookie sheet. Flatten with glass dipped in wheat germ. Bake at 350 degrees for 8 to 10 minutes or until edges are firm. Cool on wire rack. Yield: 36 cookies.

Approx per cookie: Cal 69, Prot 1.2 gr, Fat 3.6 gr,
Chol 7.1 mg, Carbo 8.7 gr, Sod 29.5 mg, Potas 49.6 mg.

Debbie DeButts, Kappa
South Sioux City, Nebraska

Cookies for Kids

¼ cup margarine,
  softened
1 cup peanut butter
1 2-layer package
  yellow cake mix

2 eggs
1 6-ounce
  package
  chocolate chips

Combine margarine, peanut butter, half the cake mix, eggs and ⅓ cup water in mixer bowl; beat until smooth. Stir in remaining cake mix and chocolate chips. Drop by rounded teaspoonfuls 2 inches apart onto ungreased cookie sheet. Bake at 375 degrees for 10 minutes or until brown. Remove to wire rack to cool.
Yield: 72 cookies.

Approx per cookie: Cal 71, Prot 1.5 gr, Fat 3.9 gr,
Chol 7.0 mg, Carbo 7.9 gr, Sod 98.4 mg, Potas 32.0 mg.

Pat Forney, Laureate Mu
Fort Collins, Colorado

Graham Cookies

⅔ cup shortening
1 cup packed
  brown sugar
1 tablespoon
  blackstrap
  molasses

½ teaspoon salt
1 teaspoon soda
2½ cups graham
  flour

Cream shortening and brown sugar in mixer bowl until light and fluffy. Add molasses and salt; mix well. Dissolve soda in ¼ cup hot water. Stir soda mixture and graham flour into molasses mixture. Roll on very lightly floured surface. Cut as desired. Place on ungreased cookie sheet. Bake at 350 degrees for 8 minutes or until brown. Cool on wire rack. Yield: 24 cookies.

Approx per cookie: Cal 133, Prot 1.7 gr, Fat 6.5 gr,
Chol 0.0 mg, Carbo 18.3 gr, Sod 81.8 mg, Potas 79.3 mg.

Heather Pilloud, Sigma
Brandon, Manitoba, Canada

Lighten Up Granola Goodies

3½ cups oats
1 cup chopped
  walnuts
1 cup raisins
⅔ cup melted
  butter
⅓ cup honey

1 egg, beaten
½ teaspoon vanilla
  extract
½ cup packed
  brown sugar
1 can cherry pie
  filling

Spread oats in 10x15-inch baking pan. Bake at 350 degrees for 15 minutes or until toasted. Mix with walnuts and raisins in bowl. Add remaining ingredients; mix well. Press into greased 10x15-inch baking pan. Bake at 350 degrees for 25 minutes or until brown. Cool on wire rack. Cut into squares. Yield: 24 squares.
Note: May use Lite Cherry Pie Filling.

Approx per square: Cal 203, Prot 2.9 gr, Fat 9.4 gr,
Chol 26.3 mg, Carbo 28.5 gr, Sod 68.4 mg, Potas 132.0 mg.

Olive Ambrose, Preceptor Beta Iota
Flint, Michigan

Health Cookies

1 cup shortening
1 cup packed brown
  sugar
2 eggs
2 cups whole
  wheat flour
1 teaspoon vanilla
  extract

1 tablespoon
  baking powder
1 teaspoon soda
1 cup peanut butter
1 cup bran flakes
1 cup oats
1 cup raisins

Cream shortening and brown sugar in mixer bowl until light and fluffy. Blend in eggs. Add remaining ingredients in order listed, mixing well after each addition. Drop by spoonfuls onto ungreased cookie sheet. Bake at 325 degrees for 12 minutes or until brown. Yield: 48 cookies.

Approx per cookie: Cal 132, Prot 1.4 gr, Fat 9.0 gr,
Chol 22.4 mg, Carbo 12.8 gr, Sod 96.9 mg, Potas 74.6 mg.

Donna Roth, Preceptor Beta Epsilon
Marion, Iowa

Desserts   175

Crisp Honey Cookies

½ cup margarine,
softened
½ cup honey
1¾ cups flour
1 teaspoon soda

½ teaspoon
cinnamon
¼ teaspoon cloves
⅓ cup wheat germ

Cream margarine and honey in mixer bowl until light and fluffy. Sift flour, soda and spices in bowl. Mix in wheat germ. Add to honey mixture; mix well. Chill for 1 hour. Roll ⅛ inch thick on lightly floured surface. Cut with floured cookie cutter. Place on greased cookie sheet. Bake at 350 degrees for 8 minutes or until light brown. Cool on wire rack. Frost if desired.
Yield: 36 cookies.

Approx per cookie: Cal 63, Prot 0.9 gr, Fat 2.7 gr, Chol 0.0 mg, Carbo 8.9 gr, Sod 54.3 mg, Potas 17.2 mg.

Elaine Shaughency, Preceptor Beta Zeta
Lexington, Ohio

Apple-Oatmeal Chewies

½ cup margarine,
softened
1 cup packed
brown sugar
¼ cup sugar
1 teaspoon vanilla
extract
2 eggs
1½ cups flour

¾ teaspoon soda
1 teaspoon cinnamon
2 cups quick-
cooking oats
1 cup chopped
pecans
1 large Golden
Delicious apple,
peeled, chopped

Combine first 5 ingredients in mixer bowl; mix well. Add flour, soda and cinnamon. Beat at low speed until blended. Fold in oats, pecans and apple. Spread in greased 9x13-inch baking dish. Bake at 350 degrees for 35 minutes or until toothpick inserted in center comes out clean. Cool in pan on wire rack. Cut into bars. Store in airtight container. Yield: 20 bars.

Approx per bar: Cal 212, Prot 3.4 gr, Fat 10.1 gr, Chol 25.3 mg, Carbo 28.1 gr, Sod 96.7 mg, Potas 130.0 mg.

Kathleen Radcliffe, Preceptor Kappa Xi
Lancaster, Pennsylvania

Cross-Country Cookies

¾ cup corn oil
1 cup packed brown
sugar
2 eggs
1 teaspoon vanilla
extract
1½ cups flour
1 cup oats

1½ teaspoons
baking powder
½ teaspoon salt
½ teaspoon
cinnamon
½ cup chopped
pecans

Combine first 4 ingredients in mixer bowl. Beat at medium speed until thick. Add flour, oats, baking powder, salt and cinnamon. Beat at low speed until smooth. Stir in pecans. Drop by level tablespoons 2 inches apart onto greased cookie sheet. Bake at 350 degrees for 12 minutes or until brown. Cool on wire rack.
Yield: 42 cookies.

Approx per cookie: Cal 91, Prot 1.2 gr, Fat 5.3 gr, Chol 12.0 mg, Carbo 10.0 gr, Sod 41.7 mg, Potas 40.7 mg.

Ginny Cooper, Xi Omicron
Harlingen, Texas

Good Cookies

1 cup margarine,
softened
1 cup packed brown
sugar
1 cup sugar
2 eggs
1 teaspoon vanilla
extract
1½ cups flour

1 teaspoon soda
1 teaspoon salt
1 cup All-Bran
2 cups oats
1   6-ounce package
chocolate chips
¼ to ½ cup wheat germ
1 cup raisins
1 cup chopped pecans

Cream margarine and sugars in mixer bowl until light and fluffy. Blend in eggs, vanilla and 1 tablespoon water. Add sifted flour, soda and salt; mix well. Stir in remaining ingredients. Drop by teaspoonfuls onto ungreased cookie sheet. Bake at 375 degrees for 8 minutes or until light brown. Yield: 48 cookies.

Approx per cookie: Cal 149, Prot 2.1 gr, Fat 7.5 gr, Chol 10.5 mg, Carbo 20.3 gr, Sod 120.9 mg, Potas 101.4 mg.

Renee Mathews, Zeta Eta
Eureka, California

Mrs. Field's Cookies

2 cups butter,
softened
2 cups sugar
2 cups packed
brown sugar
5 cups oats
4 cups flour
1 teaspoon salt

2 teaspoons baking
powder
2 teaspoons soda
24 ounces chocolate
chips
3 cups chopped
pecans

Cream butter and sugars in bowl until light and fluffy. Process mixture of oats and flour, a small amount at a time, in blender until pulverized. Combine with salt, baking powder and soda. Add to creamed mixture; mix well. Stir in chocolate chips and pecans. Shape into golf ball-sized cookies. Place 2 inches apart on ungreased cookie sheet. Bake at 375 degrees for 6 minutes. Cool on wire rack.
Yield: 112 cookies.

Approx per cookie: Cal 139, Prot 1.5 gr, Fat 8.0 gr, Chol 10.1 mg, Carbo 17.1 gr, Sod 80.8 mg, Potas 70.0 mg.

Doris Ann Love, Preceptor Gamma Phi
Rock Island, Illinois

No Cholesterol Oatmeal Cookies

1 cup shortening
1½ cups packed
   brown sugar
1½ cups oats
2 cups flour
½ teaspoon nutmeg

1 teaspoon
   cinnamon
1 teaspoon soda
1 cup raisins
½ cup chopped
   pecans

Cream shortening and brown sugar in mixer bowl until light and fluffy. Add next 4 ingredients and soda dissolved in 1 cup boiling water; mix well. Stir in raisins and pecans. Drop by spoonfuls onto greased cookie sheet. Bake at 350 degrees for 20 minutes or until brown. Cool on wire rack. Yield: 72 cookies.

Approx per cookie: Cal 75, Prot 0.7 gr, Fat 3.9 gr, Chol 0.0 mg, Carbo 9.9 gr, Sod 13.4 mg, Potas 45.2 mg.

Midge Dailey, Preceptor Alpha Kappa
Hillsboro, Oregon

Old-Fashioned Oatmeal Cookies

1 cup raisins
¾ cup shortening
1½ cups sugar
2 eggs
1 teaspoon vanilla
   extract
2½ cups whole
   wheat flour

2 cups oats
½ teaspoon baking
   powder
1 teaspoon soda
1 teaspoon
   cinnamon
½ teaspoon cloves
1 teaspoon salt

Combine raisins and 1 cup water in saucepan. Simmer, uncovered, until raisins are puffed. Drain, reserving liquid. Cream shortening and sugar in mixer bowl until light and fluffy. Blend in eggs and vanilla. Add dry ingredients alternately with reserved liquid, mixing well after each addition. Stir in raisins. Drop by rounded teaspoonfuls 2 inches apart onto ungreased cookie sheet. Bake at 400 degrees until light brown. Remove to wire rack to cool. Yield: 78 cookies.

Approx per cookie: Cal 44, Prot 1.0 gr, Fat 0.5 gr, Chol 6.5 mg, Carbo 9.4 gr, Sod 42.2 mg, Potas 37.4 mg.

Ethelyn Kidd, Alpha Laureate
Omaha, Nebraska

Magic Popcorn Macaroons

1 cup unsalted
   popped popcorn,
   chopped
1 cup finely
   chopped walnuts

3 egg whites
1 cup confectioners'
   sugar
¼ teaspoon vanilla
   extract

Mix chopped popcorn and walnuts in bowl. Beat egg whites until foamy. Add confectioners' sugar gradually, beating until stiff peaks form. Beat in vanilla. Fold in popcorn mixture gently. Drop by ½ teaspoonfuls onto lightly oiled cookie sheet. Bake at 300 degrees for 30 minutes or until very light brown. Cool on wire rack. Yield: 60 cookies.

Approx per cookie: Cal 22, Prot 0.5 gr, Fat 1.3 gr, Chol 0.0 mg, Carbo 2.3 gr, Sod 2.5 mg, Potas 11.4 mg.

Beverly Tudor, Preceptor Laureate
Port Neches, Texas

Praline Cookies

½ cup butter,
   softened
1½ cups packed
   light brown sugar
1 egg

1½ cups sifted flour
1 teaspoon vanilla
   extract
1 cup coarsely chopped
   pecans

Combine butter, brown sugar and egg in bowl; mix until creamy. Stir in flour, vanilla and pecans. Chill for several minutes until easy to handle. Shape into 1-inch balls. Place 3 inches apart on greased cookie sheet. Flatten to ⅛-inch with bottom of glass covered with dampened cheesecloth. Bake at 350 degrees for 12 minutes. Remove to wire rack to cool completely. Yield: 36 cookies.

Approx per cookie: Cal 99, Prot 1.0 gr, Fat 5.1 gr, Chol 14.9 mg, Carbo 13 gr, Sod 35.7 mg, Potas 58.4 mg.

Sugar-Free Cookies

1½ cups flour
1 teaspoon soda
½ teaspoon salt
1 tablespoon
   cinnamon
½ teaspoon nutmeg
½ teaspoon cloves
1 egg, beaten

½ cup margarine,
   softened
¼ teaspoon liquid
   saccharin
1 cup unsweetened
   applesauce
1 cup All-Bran
½ cup raisins

Sift first 6 ingredients together. Cream egg, margarine, and saccharin in bowl until light and fluffy. Add sifted dry ingredients alternately with applesauce, mixing well after each addition. Stir in All-Bran and raisins. Drop by level tablespoonfuls 1 inch apart onto greased cookie sheet. Bake at 350 degrees for 20 minutes. Remove to wire rack to cool. Yield: 48 cookies.

Approx per cookie: Cal 43, Prot 0.7 gr, Fat 2.1 gr, Chol 5.3 mg, Carbo 6.0 gr, Sod 60.7 mg, Potas 28.5 mg.

Mildred Ruppert, Laureate Pi
Independence, Missouri

Sugarless Cookies

¼ cup margarine
1 cup coarsely
  chopped dates
¼ teaspoon
  cinnamon
1 egg, beaten
1 teaspoon vanilla
  extract
1 cup flour

1 tablespoon
  artificial
  sweetener
½ teaspoon soda
½ teaspoon baking
  powder
⅛ teaspoon salt
1 cup chopped
  pecans

Combine margarine, dates, cinnamon and ¾ cup water in saucepan. Cook for 3 minutes, stirring occasionally. Cool. Add remaining ingredients; mix well. Spoon into greased baking pan. Bake at 350 degrees for 10 minutes. Cool on wire rack. Cut into squares. Yield: 16 cookies.

Approx per cookie: Cal 140, Prot 2.2 gr, Fat 8.6 gr, Chol 15.8 mg, Carbo 15.2 gr, Sod 91.7 mg, Potas 129.0 mg.

Mildred Ruppert, Laureate Pi
Independence, Missouri

Walnut Snacks

5 tablespoons instant
  nonfat dry milk
  powder
1 cup chopped
  walnuts
½ cup chopped dates

½ cup chopped raisins
½ teaspoon
  cinnamon
1 teaspoon nutmeg
2 egg whites

Combine first 6 ingredients in bowl; mix well. Beat egg whites until soft peaks form. Fold in dry ingredients gently. Drop by spoonfuls onto greased cookie sheet. Bake at 350 degrees for 12 minutes or until brown. Cool on cookie sheet for 5 minutes. Remove to wire rack to cool completely. Yield: 36 cookies.

Approx per cookie: Cal 37, Prot 1.0 gr, Fat 2.2 gr, Chol 0.1 mg, Carbo 4.2 gr, Sod 6.4 mg, Potas 59.0 mg.

Jane Anne Armstrong, Xi Gamma Omega
Guelph, Ontario, Canada

Sugarless Sweets

1 cup finely
  chopped dates
1 cup finely
  chopped pecans

1 cup finely
  chopped raisins
2 cups finely
  chopped coconut

Combine first 3 ingredients and salt to taste in bowl; mix well. Shape into small balls. Roll in coconut. Store in airtight container. Yield: 48 cookies.

Approx per cookie: Cal 47, Prot 0.5 gr, Fat 5.6 gr, Chol 0.0 mg, Carbo 3.0 gr, Sod 1.6 mg, Potas 70.4 mg.

Jean Rounds, Preceptor Laureate Zeta
Cheyenne, Wyoming

Wheat Germ Cookies

1 cup margarine
1 cup packed
  brown sugar
1 cup sugar
1 cup wheat germ
1 cup cottage
  cheese
2 eggs
1 cup molasses

3 cups flour
1 teaspoon soda
1 teaspoon
  cinnamon
¼ teaspoon nutmeg
1 cup mashed
  cooked pumpkin
1 cup raisins

Cream margarine and sugars in mixer bowl until light and fluffy. Add wheat germ, cottage cheese, eggs and molasses; mix well. Add sifted dry ingredients gradually, mixing well after each addition. Stir in pumpkin and raisins. Drop by teaspoonfuls onto ungreased cookie sheet. Bake at 375 degrees for 8 minutes or until brown. Remove to wire rack to cool. Yield: 96 cookies.
Note: May substitute drained crushed pineapple, applesauce or chopped peaches for pumpkin.

Approx per cookie: Cal 70, Prot 1.3 gr, Fat 2.3 gr, Chol 5.8 mg, Carbo 11.4 gr, Sod 40.8 mg, Potas 74.2 mg.

Linda Brower, Xi Delta Phi
Greensburg, Kansas

Whole Wheat Snack Cookies

½ cup butter-
  flavored
  shortening
½ cup packed
  brown sugar
1 teaspoon vanilla
  extract

⅓ cup honey
2 cups whole
  wheat flour
¼ cup wheat germ
1 teaspoon baking
  powder
½ cup milk

Cream shortening, brown sugar, vanilla and honey in mixer bowl until light and fluffy. Add dry ingredients alternately with milk, mixing well after each addition. Shape into 2 balls. Chill for several hours. Roll each ball ⅛ inch thick on lightly floured surface. Cut as desired. Place on ungreased cookie sheet. Prick lightly with fork. Bake at 350 degrees for 10 minutes. Remove to wire rack to cool. Spread with cream cheese or peanut butter if desired. Yield: 36 cookies.

Approx per cookie: Cal 71, Prot 1.2 gr, Fat 2.9 gr, Chol 8.4 mg, Carbo 10.8 gr, Sod 43.3 mg, Potas 48.8 mg.

Patricia Ostrom, Upsilon
Weiser, Idaho

Boiled Custard

1 quart milk
2 eggs
¼ cup sugar

1 tablespoon flour
6 marshmallows
⅛ teaspoon nutmeg

Heat milk almost to a simmer in double boiler. Combine eggs, sugar and flour in bowl; mix well. Add milk gradually, beating constantly. Pour into double boiler. Cook for 20 minutes or until thickened. Add marshmallows. Beat until marshmallows melt and blend well. Pour into serving glasses. Sprinkle with nutmeg. Chill until serving time. Yield: 16 servings.

Approx per serving: Cal 72, Prot 3.0 gr, Fat 2.9 gr, Chol 40.2 mg, Carbo 8.7 gr, Sod 39.2 mg, Potas 96.6 mg.

Martha Jo Thomas, Phi Lambda
Lexington, Kentucky

Island Float

3 egg yolks
¼ cup sugar
2 cups milk,
  scalded

1 teaspoon vanilla
  extract
2 egg whites
¼ cup sugar

Beat egg yolks with ¼ cup sugar and salt to taste in double boiler until thick and lemon-colored. Stir in milk gradually. Cook over hot water until mixture coats spoon, stirring frequently; remove from heat. Stir in vanilla. Cool. Spoon into dessert glasses. Chill in refrigerator. Beat egg whites until soft peaks form. Add ¼ cup sugar gradually, beating until stiff peaks form. Drop by spoonfuls on top of custard just before serving. Yield: 4 servings.

Approx per serving: Cal 226, Prot 8.1 gr, Fat 8.2 gr, Chol 205.8 mg, Carbo 30.5 gr, Sod 91.8 mg, Potas 211.5 mg.

Hazel Hill, Gamma Iota
Chillicothe, Missouri

Microwave Custard

3 eggs
¼ cup sugar
1 teaspoon vanilla
  extract

2 cups milk
½ teaspoon
  cinnamon
½ teaspoon nutmeg

Beat eggs lightly in bowl. Beat in sugar gradually. Stir in vanilla, milk, cinnamon and salt to taste. Pour into 4 individual glass serving dishes. Sprinkle with nutmeg. Place in shallow glass baking dish with 1 inch hot water. Microwave, covered, for 3 minutes or until bubbly. Turn baking dish around. Microwave for 3 minutes longer or until custard begins to set. Let stand for several minutes to set completely. Garnish with fruit. Yield: 4 servings.

Approx per serving: Cal 165, Prot 9.1 gr, Fat 8.6 gr, Chol 206.7 mg, Carbo 12.5 gr, Sod 107.0 mg, Potas 224.4 mg.

Arlene Ahlbrandt, Preceptor Alpha Kappa
Fort Collins, Colorado

Apricot Sherbet

1 16-ounce can
  unsweetened
  apricots, drained
⅓ cup apricot
  nectar
1 tablespoon sugar

2 teaspoons lemon
  juice
⅛ teaspoon ginger
2 egg whites
2 tablespoons sugar

Place apricots, apricot nectar, 1 tablespoon sugar, lemon juice and ginger in blender container. Process until smooth. Pour into small loaf pan. Freeze until partially frozen. Beat egg whites until foamy. Add 2 tablespoons sugar gradually, beating until stiff peaks form. Beat apricot mixture until smooth. Fold in egg whites gently. Spoon into loaf pan. Freeze, covered with foil, for 6 hours to overnight. Spoon into serving dishes. Yield: 6 servings.

Approx per serving: Cal 67, Prot 1.8 gr, Fat 0.1 gr, Chol 0.0 mg, Carbo 15.7 gr, Sod 16.9 mg, Potas 224.7 mg.

Gloria Smithers, Preceptor Laureate Kappa
Beatrice, Nebraska

Carob Tortoni

1 egg white
⅛ teaspoon salt
⅛ teaspoon cream
  of tartar
1 tablespoon sugar
2 tablespoons
  carob powder

6 maraschino
  cherries,
  chopped
1 tablespoon sliced
  almonds
1 cup whipped
  topping

Beat egg white with salt and cream of tartar until soft peaks form. Add sugar gradually, beating until stiff peaks form. Combine remaining ingredients in bowl; mix lightly. Fold in egg white gently. Spoon into 3 paper-lined muffin cups. Freeze until firm. Remove paper liners. Place in dessert glasses. Yield: 3 servings.

Approx per serving: Cal 132, Prot 2.2 gr, Fat 6.8 gr, Chol 0.0 mg, Carbo 18.7 gr, Sod 118.9 mg, Potas 41.5 mg.

Joan Stockman, Preceptor Pi
Gering, Nebraska

Cranberry Sherbet

1 tablespoon
  unflavored
  gelatin
4 cups cranberries

2 cups sugar
1 cup orange juice
⅛ teaspoon salt
2 egg whites

Soften gelatin in 1 cup water in saucepan. Add cranberries and sugar. Cook for 10 minutes, stirring frequently. Stir in orange juice and salt. Press through sieve into freezer tray. Freeze until partially frozen. Beat egg whites until stiff peaks form. Add partially frozen cranberry mixture. Beat for 1 minute. Pour into freezer tray. Freeze until firm. Spoon into orange shells. Yield: 4 servings.

Approx per serving: Cal 478, Prot 4.2 gr, Fat 0.9 gr, Chol 0.0 mg, Carbo 118.0 gr, Sod 96.1 mg, Potas 240.5 mg.

Dorothy Kramer, Laureate Theta
Omaha, Nebraska

Homemade Fruit Sherbet

1 egg, separated
½ cup instant
  nonfat dry milk
  powder
3 tablespoons
  lemon juice

⅓ cup sugar
1 10-ounce
   package frozen
   raspberries,
   thawed

Combine egg white, dry milk powder and ⅓ cup water in mixer bowl. Beat until stiff peaks form. Add lemon juice and sugar gradually, beating constantly. Add egg yolk. Beat just until mixed. Fold in raspberries. Spoon into freezer tray. Freeze for 1 hour or longer. Spoon into dessert glasses. Yield: 6 servings.

Approx per serving: Cal 125, Prot 3.5 gr, Fat 1.1 gr, Chol 43.4 mg, Carbo 26.2 gr, Sod 40.7 mg, Potas 166.9 mg.

Sharon Toutant, Beta Alpha Omicron
San Gabriel, California

Muskmelon Ice

½ cup sugar
2 very ripe
  cantaloupes

¼ cup lemon juice

Combine sugar and 1½ cups water in saucepan. Simmer for 5 minutes. Cool. Cut cantaloupes in half; discard seed. Scoop pulp and juice into mixer bowl. Add lemon juice and cooled syrup. Beat until smooth. Freeze until partially frozen. Beat until smooth. Spoon into freezer container. Freeze, covered, until firm. Let stand at room temperature for several minutes before spooning into dessert glasses. Yield: 6 servings.

Approx per serving: Cal 121, Prot 1.3 gr, Fat 0.2 gr, Chol 0.0 mg, Carbo 31.0 gr, Sod 22.0 mg, Potas 469.7 mg.

Kathy Welch, Alpha Omega Lambda
Corrigan, Texas

Strawberry Freeze

1 16-ounce
   package frozen
   whole
   strawberries
¼ cup sugar
1 tablespoon lemon
  juice

2 egg whites
1 cup whipped
  topping
½ 16-ounce
   package frozen
   whole
   strawberries

Combine first 4 ingredients in large mixer bowl. Beat at high speed for 12 minutes or until very stiff peaks form. Add whipped topping; mix well. Spoon into serving bowls. Freeze until firm. Crush remaining strawberries with fork in bowl. Serve over frozen mixture. Yield: 8 servings.

Approx per serving: Cal 132, Prot 1.3 gr, Fat 2.1 gr, Chol 0.0 mg, Carbo 29.3 gr, Sod 14.7 mg, Potas 104.2 mg.

Marlene Mallon, Mu Theta
Salina, Kansas

French Vanilla Ice Cream

2 eggs
1 cup sugar
½ small package
  vanilla instant
  pudding mix
2 cups 2% milk

2 cups half and
  half
1½ teaspoons
   vanilla extract
⅛ teaspoon salt

Beat eggs in mixer bowl until thick and lemon-colored. Add remaining ingredients; beat until smooth. Pour into ice cream freezer container. Freeze according to manufacturer's instructions. Spoon into dessert bowls. Yield: 8 servings.
Note: Make chocolate ice cream by substituting chocolate instant pudding mix for vanilla, 1 teaspoon chocolate extract for vanilla extract and adding ¼ teaspoon cinnamon. For fruit flavors, add chopped fresh fruit to ice cream toward end of freezing process.

Approx per serving: Cal 262, Prot 6.4 gr, Fat 9.8 gr, Chol 94.5 mg, Carbo 38.7 gr, Sod 146.3 mg, Potas 208.8 mg.

Paula Lipko, Beta Pi
Ellsworth AFB, South Dakota

Frozen Dessert Sandwiches

1 teaspoon
  unflavored
  gelatin
¼ cup frozen
  orange juice
  concentrate
5 packets Equal
½ teaspoon vanilla
  extract

⅛ teaspoon salt
½ cup instant
  nonfat dry milk
  powder
3¼ teaspoons
  lemon juice
112 graham
  crackers

Chill mixer bowl and beaters. Soften gelatin in orange juice concentrate in small bowl. Stir in Equal, vanilla and salt. Combine dry milk powder and ½ cup cold water in chilled bowl. Beat until soft peaks form. Add lemon juice. Beat until stiff peaks form. Fold in gelatin mixture. Spread between graham crackers. Freeze until firm. Yield: 56 servings.

Approx per serving: Cal 59, Prot 1.4 gr, Fat 1.3 gr, Chol 0.1 mg, Carbo 89.0 gr, Sod 106.5 mg, Potas 74.2 mg.

Gloria Smethers, Preceptor Laureate Kappa
Beatrice, Nebraska

Bailey's Irish Cream Mousse

1 6-ounce package
  semisweet chocolate
  chips
6 tablespoons butter
½ cup confectioners'
  sugar, sifted

3 eggs, separated
½ cup Bailey's
  Irish Cream
  liqueur
16 ounces whipping
  cream, whipped

Melt chocolate chips and butter in saucepan; mix well. Let stand for 5 minutes. Combine confectioners' sugar, egg yolks and liqueur in mixer bowl; beat until smooth. Blend in chocolate mixture. Fold in whipped cream gently. Beat egg whites until stiff peaks form. Fold gently into mousse. Spoon into dessert glasses. Garnish with shaved chocolate. Yield: 12 servings.

Approx per serving: Cal 302, Prot 3.1 gr, Fat 27.2 gr, Chol 133.7 mg, Carbo 14.4 gr, Sod 98.4 mg, Potas 99.3 mg. Nutritional information does not include liqueur.

Vicki Smith, Preceptor Beta Theta
Bellevue, Washington

Cranberry-Raspberry Mousse

¾ cup Ocean Spray
  cranberries
¾ cup frozen
  raspberries,
  drained
¼ teaspoon barley
  malt sweetener
2 tablespoons honey

2 dates, chopped
½ tablespoon
  arrowroot
1 tablespoon fresh
  orange juice
3 egg whites,
  stiffly beaten

Combine cranberries, raspberries, sweetener, honey and dates in saucepan. Bring to a boil over medium heat. Stir in mixture of arrowroot and orange juice. Cook until thickened, stirring constantly. Press hot mixture through fine sieve. Chill in refrigerator. Fold gently into egg whites. Spoon into serving glasses.
Yield: 6 servings.

Photograph for this recipe on page 103.

Pumpkin Mousse

1 envelope
  unflavored
  gelatin
⅓ cup evaporated
  skim milk
1 16-ounce can
  pumpkin
½ teaspoon
  cinnamon
¼ teaspoon nutmeg

¼ teaspoon salt
1 teaspoon vanilla
  extract
½ teaspoon butter
  extract
Artificial sweetener
  to equal ½ cup sugar
⅔ cup evaporated
  skim milk, chilled

Soften gelatin in ⅓ cup evaporated skim milk in saucepan. Combine with next 4 ingredients and ¼ cup water in saucepan. Cook until gelatin dissolves, stirring frequently. Stir in flavorings and artificial sweetener. Cool. Beat chilled evaporated milk in bowl until stiff peaks form. Fold gently into pumpkin mixture. Spoon into dessert glasses. Chill until serving time. Yield: 8 servings.

Leona Sayer, Laureate Lambda
Salmon, Idaho

Special Mousse

1 large package
  reduced-calorie
  pudding mix
1 envelope
  unflavored
  gelatin

1 tablespoon instant
  coffee powder
2½ cups milk
2 cups reduced-calorie
  whipped topping

Combine first 3 ingredients in saucepan. Stir in milk. Let stand for several minutes to soften gelatin. Bring to a boil, stirring until gelatin dissolves. Pour into bowl. Chill for 1 hour. Fold in whipped topping gently. Spoon into dessert glasses. Yield: 8 servings.

Approx per serving: Cal 53, Prot 46.0 gr, Fat 2.7 gr, Chol 10.3 mg, Carbo 3.9 gr, Sod 39.0 mg, Potas 120.9 mg.

Kathy Mills, Xi Gamma Eta
Russell, Iowa

Sugarless Apple Pie

6 to 8 Golden
  Delicious apples
1 12-ounce can
  frozen apple
  juice concentrate,
  thawed
2 tablespoons
  cornstarch

1 teaspoon
  cinnamon
½ teaspoon nutmeg
1 recipe 2-crust pie
  pastry
2 tablespoons butter

Peel and thinly slice apples. Blend apple juice concentrate, cornstarch and spices in saucepan. Cook until thickened, stirring constantly. Remove from heat. Add apples; mix well. Pour into pastry-lined 9-inch pie plate. Dot with butter. Top with remaining pastry; seal edge and cut vents. Bake at 350 degrees for 45 minutes or until crust is golden and apples are tender. Yield: 6 servings.

Approx per serving: Cal 629, Prot 4.5 gr, Fat 25.6 gr, Chol 11.8 mg, Carbo 100.1 gr, Sod 419.0 mg, Potas 601.3 mg.

Eleanor Smith, Lambda Xi
Sun City, California

Marie's Sugarless Apple Pie

6 cups thinly sliced
  apples
1 recipe 2-crust
  pie pastry
1 tablespoon
  cornstarch

½ teaspoon Sweeta
⅛ teaspoon salt
¼ teaspoon nutmeg
1 teaspoon
  cinnamon
2 tablespoons butter

Place apples in pastry-lined 9-inch pie plate. Combine cornstarch, Sweeta, salt, spices and 3 tablespoons water in bowl; mix well. Drizzle over apples. Dot with butter. Top with remaining pastry; seal edge and cut vents. Bake at 425 degrees for 15 minutes. Reduce temperature to 375 degrees. Bake for 25 minutes or until brown. Cool on wire rack. Yield: 8 servings.

Approx per serving: Cal 308, Prot 3.0 gr, Fat 18.5 gr, Chol 8.9 mg, Carbo 34.2 gr, Sod 345.6 mg, Potas 126.4 mg.

Marie Buccolo, Xi Tau Theta
Palestine, Texas

Coconut Pie

4 eggs
1¾ cups sugar
½ cup flour
¼ cup melted
  margarine

2 cups milk
1½ cups coconut
1 teaspoon vanilla
  extract

Beat eggs in bowl. Add remaining ingredients in order listed, mixing well after each addition. Pour into greased 10-inch pie plate. Bake at 350 degrees for 45 minutes or until set. Yield: 8 servings.

Approx per serving: Cal 396, Prot 6.7 gr, Fat 15.7 gr, Chol 134.9 mg, Carbo 58.6 gr, Sod 164.8 mg, Potas 180.9 mg.

Linda Higgins, Theta Chi
Fulton, Missouri

Cottage Cheese Pie

1 envelope
  unflavored
  gelatin
2 tablespoons
  lemon juice
2 egg yolks

¼ cup hot milk
⅓ cup sugar
2 cups low-fat
  cottage cheese
1 graham cracker
  pie shell

Soften gelatin in lemon juice. Combine with egg yolks in blender container. Process for several seconds. Add hot milk gradually, processing constantly. Add sugar. Process for 1 minute or until gelatin and sugar are dissolved. Add cottage cheese gradually, processing constantly until smooth. Pour into pie shell. Chill until set. Top with favorite reduced-calorie pie filling or glazed fresh fruit if desired. Yield: 6 servings.

Approx per serving: Cal 470, Prot 48.9 gr, Fat 13.7 gr, Chol 109.4 mg, Carbo 39.3 gr, Sod 1299.0 mg. Potas 113.2 mg.

Mareke Campbell, Theta Kappa
Belleville, Illinois

Kathy's Ice Cream Pie

3 tablespoons butter
2 tablespoons
  brown sugar
¼ cup light corn
  syrup
2½ cups Rice
  Krispies
¼ cup chocolate
  syrup

¼ cup peanut
  butter
3 tablespoons light
  corn syrup
1 quart vanilla
  ice cream,
  softened

Combine butter, brown sugar and ¼ cup corn syrup in saucepan. Cook over low heat for 7 minutes or to syrup consistency. Pour over rice cereal in bowl; mix lightly. Press over bottom and side of buttered 9-inch pie pan. Freeze for 1 hour. Combine chocolate syrup; peanut butter and corn syrup in bowl; mix well. Spoon into crust. Freeze until firm. Spoon ice cream over chocolate layer. Drizzle with additional chocolate sauce if desired. Freeze until firm. Yield: 6 servings.

Approx per serving: Cal 869, Prot 6.7 gr, Fat 28.8 gr, Chol 74.0 mg, Carbo 152.7 gr, Sod 300.8 mg, Potas 269.1 mg.

Melody Ott, Beta Eta
Longview, Washington

Ice Cream Pie

⅓ cup peanut
   butter
½ cup corn syrup
2 cups crisp rice
   cereal

1 quart mint-chocolate
   chip ice cream,
   softened
½ cup chocolate syrup

Combine peanut butter, corn syrup and rice cereal in bowl; mix well. Press over bottom and side of pie plate. Chill in refrigerator. Spoon ice cream into shell. Drizzle chocolate syrup over top. Freeze until firm. Yield: 7 servings.

Approx per serving: Cal 413, Prot 6.3 gr, Fat 20.2 gr, Chol 48.2 mg, Carbo 56.0 gr, Sod 209.4 mg, Potas 226.2 mg.

Renee Mathews, Zeta Eta
Eureka, California

Heaven-Light Lemon Pie

2 egg whites
½ teaspoon vinegar
½ teaspoon vanilla
   extract
⅛ teaspoon salt
3 tablespoons sugar
1 tablespoon finely
   shredded lemon
   rind

2 eggs
¼ cup lemon juice
¼ cup sugar
1 tablespoon butter
1 envelope whipped
   topping mix
½ cup low-fat milk
½ teaspoon vanilla
   extract

Spray 9-inch pie plate with nonstick cooking spray. Combine egg whites and next 3 ingredients in small mixer bowl. Beat until soft peaks form. Add 3 tablespoons sugar gradually, beating until stiff peaks form. Spread evenly over bottom and side of prepared pie plate to form crust. Bake at 325 degrees for 25 minutes or until light brown. Cool. Combine lemon rind, eggs, lemon juice, ¼ cup sugar and butter in saucepan. Cook over low heat until thickened, stirring constantly. Spread ¼ of the mixture over meringue. Prepare whipped topping mix according to package directions using low-fat milk and ½ teaspoon vanilla. Spread half the mixture in pie plate. Fold remaining lemon mixture into whipped topping. Spoon over top. Chill, covered, in refrigerator. Garnish with lemon twists. Yield: 8 servings.

Approx per serving: Cal 89, Prot 3.1 gr, Fat 3.1 gr, Chol 68.2 mg, Carbo 12.6 gr, Sod 87.4 mg, Potas 64.4 mg. Nutritional information does not include whipped topping mix.

Mary Louise Eayrs, Laureate Delta
Kalispell, Montana

Lemon-Kiwi Chiffon Pie

¾ cup flour
¼ teaspoon salt
8 teaspoons
   reduced-calorie
   margarine
¼ cup low-fat yogurt
1 2-serving envelope
   reduced-calorie
   lemon pudding mix

2 egg whites,
   at room
   temperature
1 tablespoon sugar
1 medium kiwifruit,
   peeled, thinly
   sliced

Mix flour and salt in bowl. Cut in margarine until crumbly. Stir in yogurt; shape into ball. Chill, wrapped in plastic wrap, for 1 hour to 3 days. Roll dough to 10-inch circle between waxed paper. Chill for several minutes. Fit into 8-inch pie plate. Trim and flute edge; prick with fork. Bake at 400 degrees for 15 minutes or until light brown. Cool on wire rack. Combine pudding mix and ¾ cup water in saucepan. Bring to a boil over medium heat, stirring constantly. Chill, covered, until slightly thickened, stirring occasionally. Beat egg whites until soft peaks form. Add sugar gradually, beating until stiff peaks form. Fold gently into pudding. Spoon into pie shell. Arrange kiwifruit slices over top. Chill, covered, until serving time. Yield: 8 servings.

Approx per serving: Cal 90, Prot 3.4 gr, Fat 3.3 gr, Chol 0.0 mg, Carbo 13.7 gr, Sod 159.1 mg, Potas 33.6 mg. Nutritional information does not include kiwifruit.

Frozen Peanut Butter Pie

3 ounces cream
   cheese, softened
1 cup sifted
   confectioners'
   sugar
7½ tablespoons
   peanut butter

½ cup milk
1 8-ounce carton
   whipped topping
1 graham cracker
   pie shell

Whip cream cheese in mixer bowl until light and fluffy. Blend in confectioners' sugar and peanut butter at medium speed. Beat in milk gradually. Fold in whipped topping. Pour into pie shell. Freeze, wrapped in plastic wrap, until firm. Let stand at room temperature for 30 minutes before serving. Garnish with finely chopped peanuts. Yield: 10 servings.

Approx per serving: Cal 303, Prot 5.0 gr, Fat 20.5 gr, Chol 23.6 mg, Carbo 27.4 gr, Sod 201.5 mg, Potas 131.7 mg.

Nancy Carol Mann, Epsilon Kappa
Beckley, West Virginia

Squash-Peanut Pie

¼ cup butter, softened	2 eggs, beaten
½ cup packed light brown sugar	1¾ cups milk
	¼ teaspoon salt
1½ teaspoons pumpkin pie spice	1½ teaspoons vanilla extract
¼ cup sour cream	1 unbaked 9-inch pie shell
1 cup mashed cooked winter squash	2 tablespoons butter
	2 tablespoons light brown sugar
	1 cup chopped peanuts

Cream ¼ cup butter, ½ cup brown sugar and pumpkin pie spice in mixer bowl until light and fluffy. Add sour cream, squash, eggs, milk, salt and vanilla in order listed, mixing well after each addition. Pour into pie shell. Bake at 400 degrees for 15 minutes. Melt 2 tablespoons butter in small saucepan. Blend in 2 tablespoons brown sugar. Heat until brown sugar dissolves, stirring constantly. Stir in peanuts until well coated. Spread over pie filling. Reduce temperature to 325 degrees. Bake for 40 minutes or until set. Cool. Garnish with whipped cream and sprinkle of nutmeg. Yield: 6 servings.

Photograph for this recipe on page 1.

Strawberry Pie

¾ cup flour	3 cups sliced strawberries
2 tablespoons confectioners' sugar	1 small package sugar-free strawberry Jell-O
3 tablespoons reduced-calorie margarine	1 tablespoon cornstarch

Combine flour, confectioners' sugar and margarine in bowl. Add several drops of water, mixing to form dough. Roll on lightly floured surface. Fit into 9-inch pie plate; flute edge and prick with fork. Bake at 350 degrees for 10 minutes. Cool. Place strawberries in pie shell. Combine Jell-O, cornstarch and 1 cup boiling water in saucepan. Cook until thickened, stirring constantly. Cool. Spoon over strawberries. Chill until serving time. Yield: 8 servings.

Approx per serving: Cal 104, Prot 5.1 gr, Fat 0.4 gr, Chol 0.0 mg, Carbo 16.3 gr, Sod 67.1 mg, Potas 102.8 mg.

Charlotte Jones, Preceptor Kappa
Huron, South Dakota

Dessert Tarts

24 vanilla wafers	2 eggs
2 8-ounce packages cream cheese, softened	½ teaspoon vanilla extract
¾ cup sugar	1 can cherry pie filling
¼ cup lemon juice	

Place 1 vanilla wafer in each paper-lined 2½-inch muffin cup. Combine cream cheese, sugar, lemon juice, eggs and vanilla in mixer bowl. Beat until light and fluffy. Spoon into muffin cups. Bake at 375 degrees for 15 minutes or until light brown. Cool. Top with pie filling. Chill until serving time. Yield: 24 tarts.

Jan Canby, Chi Omicron
Rancho Cordova, California

Dieter's Pie Crust

½ cup cottage cheese	⅓ cup sifted flour
2 tablespoons shortening	⅛ teaspoon salt

Drain cottage cheese; squeeze with towel until dry. Force through fine sieve. Cut shortening into mixture of flour and salt until crumbly. Add cottage cheese; mix with fork until mixture forms ball. Roll on very lightly floured pastry cloth. Fit into pie plate. Bake at 400 degrees for 20 minutes. Yield: 1 pie shell.

Approx per pie shell: Cal 516, Prot 20.6 gr, Fat 33.5 gr, Chol 23.3 mg, Carbo 32.4 gr, Sod 558.4 mg, Potas 140.2 mg.

Melody Dixon, Xi Delta Phi
Aurora, Indiana

Crescent Fruit Pizza

1 package refrigerator sugar cookie dough	2 bananas, sliced
½ cup sugar	1 11-ounce can mandarin oranges, drained
1 8-ounce package cream cheese, softened	1 16-ounce can chunky fruit, drained
½ cup sugar	2 tablespoons orange marmalade
1 teaspoon vanilla extract	

Slice cookie dough according to package directions. Arrange slices in greased pizza pan. Bake according to package directions. Cool. Cream sugar, cream cheese and vanilla in mixer bowl until light and fluffy. Spread evenly over cookie crust. Arrange banana slices around outer rim of pan. Arrange orange sections inside bananas. Place chunky fruit in center. blend marmalade with several drops of water to desired consistency. Drizzle over fruit. Chill for 3 to 4 hours. Garnish with strawberries. Yield: 10 servings.

Approx per serving: Cal 182, Prot 2.5 gr, Fat 8.8 gr, Chol 25.2 mg, Carbo 25.6 gr, Sod 58.6 mg, Potas 202.0 mg. Nutritional information does not include cookie dough.

Debbie Lungi, Zeta Eta
Eureka, California

Fruit Pizza

1 8-count
   package
   refrigerator
   crescent rolls
1 small package
   sugar-free
   pudding mix

1 small package
   sugar-free
   strawberry Jell-O
1 tablespoon
   cornstarch
8 fresh fruits in
   season

Separate refrigerator rolls. Place in pizza pan; press edges to seal. Bake at 350 degrees for 10 minutes or until light brown. Cool. Prepare pudding mix using package directions. Spread over crust. Chill in refrigerator. Combine Jell-O, cornstarch and 1 cup boiling water in saucepan; mix well. Cook until thickened, stirring constantly. Cool. Arrange fruit over pudding. Spoon glaze over fruit. Chill until set. Cut into wedges. Yield: 8 servings.

Charlotte Jones, Preceptor Kappa
Huron, South Dakota

Apple Pudding

2 cups crisp rice
   cereal, crushed
Artificial sweetener
   to equal ¼ cup
   sugar
1 tablespoon melted
   butter
¼ teaspoon
   cinnamon

1 large apple,
   thinly sliced
2 teaspoons brown
   sugar
½ teaspoon vanilla
   extract
½ cup low-fat milk
Nutmeg to taste

Mix cereal with artificial sweetener, melted butter and cinnamon in bowl; mix well. Layer cereal mixture, apples and brown sugar ⅓ at a time in small baking dish. Pour mixture of vanilla and milk gently over layers. Sprinkle with nutmeg. Bake at 350 degrees for 1 hour. Spoon warm pudding into serving dishes. Yield: 4 servings.

Approx per serving: Cal 136, Prot 2.0 gr, Fat 3.6 gr, Chol 10.1 mg, Carbo 24.4 gr, Sod 192.8 mg, Potas 128.4 mg.

Chris L. Mayer, Theta Delta
Endicott, Washington

Banana Bread Pudding

2 slices stale bread
1½ cups apricot
   nectar
2 eggs, separated
1 medium banana,
   sliced

2 tablespoons sugar
½ teaspoon vanilla
   extract
¼ teaspoon cream
   of tartar
2 tablespoons sugar

Cut bread into ½-inch cubes. Combine nectar, egg yolks, banana and 2 tablespoons sugar in bowl; mix well. Stir in bread cubes. Spoon into 1-quart baking dish. Bake at 350 degrees for 25 minutes. Beat egg whites with remaining ingredients in bowl until soft peaks form. Spread over pudding, sealing to edge of dish. Bake for 12 minutes longer or until light brown. Yield: 6 servings.

Approx per serving: Cal 134, Prot 3.3 gr, Fat 2.3 gr, Chol 84.6 mg, Carbo 25.9 gr, Sod 77.1 mg, Potas 189.6 mg.

Georgia Cuneo, Laureate Alpha
Winston-Salem, North Carolina

Pots de Crème

1 6-ounce
   package
   semisweet
   chocolate chips
1 egg

1 teaspoon vanilla
   extract
2 tablespoons sugar
¾ cup milk,
   scalded

Combine chocolate chips, egg, vanilla, sugar and salt to taste in blender container. Add hot milk gradually. Process at low speed for 1 minute. Chill for several hours. Fill demitasse cups ⅔ full. Garnish with whipped cream and grated unsweetened chocolate. Yield: 8 servings.

Approx per serving: Cal 150, Prot 2.5 gr, Fat 9.1 gr, Chol 34.8 mg, Carbo 16.4 gr, Sod 19.5 mg, Potas 110.2 mg.

Charlotte Harris, Xi Delta Nu
St. Petersburg, Florida

Cranberry Pudding

1 cup fresh
   cranberries
¼ cup chopped
   pecans
¼ cup sugar
1 egg, well beaten

½ cup sugar
½ cup flour, sifted
6 tablespoons
   melted
   margarine

Layer first 3 ingredients in greased 8-inch pie plate. Beat egg and ½ cup sugar in mixer bowl until thick and lemon-colored. Add flour and margarine; mix well. Pour into prepared pie plate. Bake at 325 degrees for 45 minutes. Cut into wedges. Serve hot with vanilla ice cream. Yield: 5 servings.

Approx per serving: Cal 362, Prot 3.5 gr, Fat 20.5 gr, Chol 50.6 mg, Carbo 43.0 gr, Sod 181.4 mg, Potas 92.7 mg.

Mabel Revelle, Xi Beta Eta
Fredericktown, Missouri

Creamy Rice Pudding

2 cups cooked rice
3 cups low-fat milk, scalded
1 teaspoon vanilla extract

2 tablespoons sugar
1 egg, beaten
¼ cup raisins
¼ teaspoon cinnamon

Combine all ingredients in bowl; mix well. Pour into buttered baking dish. Place in larger pan of hot water. Bake at 350 degrees for 1½ hours or until knife inserted in center comes out clean. Yield: 4 servings.

Approx per serving: Cal 259, Prot 9.9 gr, Fat 3.6 gr, Chol 70.5 mg, Carbo 46.9 gr, Sod 492.7 mg, Potas 399.7 mg.

Ann Titus, Xi Gamma Zeta
Dallas, Texas

Mary's Creamy Rice Pudding

½ cup rice
5 cups milk
½ cup raisins
¼ teaspoon salt

¼ cup sugar
½ teaspoon cinnamon

Combine rice with milk, raisins and salt in buttered 2-quart baking dish. Stir in mixture of sugar and cinnamon. Bake at 300 degrees for 2 hours or until rice is tender and liquid is absorbed. Serve warm or cold with milk or cream. Yield: 6 servings.

Approx per serving: Cal 255, Prot 8.5 gr, Fat 7.2 gr, Chol 28.5 mg, Carbo 40.0 gr, Sod 194.6 mg, Potas 399.4 mg.

Mary Wood, Preceptor Gamma Kappa
St. Louis, Missouri

Rice Pudding

½ cup cooked rice
¼ cup sugar
2 eggs

1½ cups warm milk
¼ teaspoon salt
½ cup raisins

Combine rice, sugar and eggs in bowl; mix well. Stir in remaining ingredients. Pour into 2-quart baking dish. Place in larger pan half filled with hot water. Bake at 350 degrees for 40 minutes or until knife inserted in center comes out clean. Yield: 6 servings.

Approx per serving: Cal 153, Prot 4.9 gr, Fat 4.1 gr, Chol 92.8 mg, Carbo 24.9 gr, Sod 207.0 mg, Potas 206.6 mg.

Margaret M. Berry, Preceptor Alpha Kappa
Trenton, Ontario, Canada

Tasty Baked Apples

6 red apples, cored
1 bottle of diet red soda
¼ cup reduced-calorie margarine

2 tablespoons cinnamon

Place apples in 8x8-inch baking dish. Pour soda over apples. Top each apple with margarine and cinnamon. Bake at 350 degrees for 30 minutes or until tender. Yield: 6 servings.
Note: Serve with pork roast and baked potatoes for an easy oven meal.

Approx per serving: Cal 169, Prot 0.4 gr, Fat 6.6 gr, Chol 0.0 mg, Carbo 30.7 gr, Sod 75.4 mg, Potas 232.8 mg.

Yvonne Sorge, Xi Kappa Theta
Lebanon, Ohio

Frothy Apple Snow with Custard Sauce

1 tablespoon unflavored gelatin
3 tablespoons sugar
1 large apple, grated
⅛ teaspoon nutmeg
⅛ teaspoon cinnamon

3 tablespoons lemon juice
3 egg whites
3 tablespoons sugar
3 egg yolks
3 tablespoons sugar
2 cups milk
1 teaspoon vanilla extract

Soften gelatin in 2 tablespoons cold water in bowl. Add 1 cup boiling water; mix until gelatin dissolves. Add 3 tablespoons sugar. Cool. Stir in apple, spices and lemon juice. Chill until partially set. Beat egg whites with 3 tablespoons sugar until stiff peaks form. Beat gelatin mixture until frothy. Fold in egg whites gently. Pour into 8x12-inch dish. Chill until set. Beat egg yolks and 3 tablespoons sugar in bowl until thick. Bring milk just to the simmering point in double boiler. Stir a small amount of hot milk into egg yolks; stir egg yolks into hot milk. Cook over hot water until mixture thickens and coats spoon. Stir in vanilla. Chill until serving time. Cut pudding into squares. Place on serving plates. Spoon custard sauce over top. Yield: 8 servings.

Approx per serving: Cal 143, Prot 5.3 gr, Fat 4.3 gr, Chol 102.9 mg, Carbo 21.6 gr, Sod 53.1 mg, Potas 149.0 mg.

Bev Wallstrum, Preceptor Zeta Lambda
Santa Rosa, California

Baked Fruit

1 16-ounce can
  peaches
1 16-ounce can pears
1 16-ounce can
  pineapple chunks
1 16-ounce can
  fruit cocktail

½ cup melted butter
½ cup packed
  brown sugar
3 tablespoons cornstarch
½ cup maraschino
  cherries

Drain peaches, pears, pineapple and fruit cocktail, reserving 1½ cups juice. Combine butter, brown sugar and cornstarch in saucepan; mix well. Add juice. Cook until thickened, stirring constantly. Arrange fruit in large glass baking dish. Pour juice mixture over fruit. Bake at 350 degrees for 45 minutes. Decorate with cherries and pecans. Yield: 10 servings.

Approx per serving: Cal 388, Prot 1.9 gr, Fat 17.9 gr, Chol 28.4 mg, Carbo 60.0 gr, Sod 119.9 mg, Potas 347.6 mg.

Connie McCasland, Beta Delta
Calmar, Iowa

Blueberry Squares

1 cup margarine,
  softened
2 cups sugar
1 teaspoon vanilla
  extract
4 eggs

2 cups flour
½ teaspoon baking
  powder
1 can blueberry pie
  filling

Cream margarine, sugar and vanilla in mixer bowl until light and fluffy. Add eggs, flour and baking powder; mix well. Pour half the batter into greased and floured 9x13-inch baking pan. Spread with pie filling. Spoon remaining batter evenly over top. Bake at 350 degrees for 55 minutes. Cut into squares. Yield: 16 servings.

Approx per serving: Cal 322, Prot 3.4 gr, Fat 13.1 gr, Chol 63.2 mg, Carbo 48.3 gr, Sod 166.3 mg. Potas 35.2 mg.

Esther Levesque, Alpha Alpha
Hudson, New Hampshire

Banana Split Cake

2 cups graham
  cracker crumbs
½ cup melted
  butter
2 eggs
2 cups
  confectioners'
  sugar
1 cup margarine,
  softened
4 bananas, sliced

¼ cup sugar
1 tablespoon lemon
  juice
1 20-ounce can
  crushed
  pineapple,
  drained
1 8-ounce carton
  whipped topping
½ cup chopped
  pecans

Mix crumbs and butter in bowl. Press over bottom of 9x13-inch dish. Beat eggs in mixer bowl for 15 minutes. Add confectioners' sugar and margarine; beat until light and fluffy. Spread over crumb layer. Sprinkle bananas with mixture of sugar and lemon juice. Layer bananas and pineapple over confectioners' sugar mixture. Spread whipped topping over layers. Sprinkle with pecans. Chill for 4 hours. Cut into squares. Yield: 24 servings.

Approx per serving: Cal 393, Prot 2.0 gr, Fat 17.0 gr, Chol 32.9 mg, Carbo 61.7 gr, Sod 207.1 mg, Potas 159.8 mg.

Bonnie Arrigoni, Alpha Phi
Moorcroft, Wyoming

Cannoli Cream

1 pound part-skim
  ricotta cheese
¼ cup orange
  marmalade
½ teaspoon rum
  extract

¼ cup low-fat milk
⅓ cup golden
  raisins
¼ cup slivered
  almonds, toasted

Combine ricotta cheese, marmalade, rum flavoring and milk in blender container. Process until smooth. Stir in raisins. Chill for 1 hour or longer. Stir in almonds. Spoon into dessert glasses. Garnish with shaved chocolate. Yield: 8 servings.

Approx per serving: Cal 148, Prot 7.1 gr, Fat 8.1 gr, Chol 0.3 mg, Carbo 14.7 gr, Sod 57.0 mg, Potas 88.6 mg. Nutritional analysis does not include cholesterol value of ricotta cheese.

Margaret Smith, Beta Omicron
Alamogordo, New Mexico

Cantaloupe Medley

1 small package
  strawberry
  gelatin

2 cantaloupes
1 banana, sliced

Prepare gelatin according to package directions. Cut cantaloupes in half crosswise; discard seed. Pour gelatin into cantaloupe cavities. Chill until set. Top with banana slices just before serving. Garnish with whipped cream and strawberries. Yield: 4 servings.

Approx per serving: Cal 171, Prot 4.2 gr, Fat 0.3 gr, Chol 0.0 mg, Carbo 44.4 gr, Sod 100.8 mg, Potas 714.7 mg.

Rhonda England, Alpha Sigma
Kindersley, Saskatchewan, Canada

Cherry Delights

4 egg whites
1 cup sugar
½ teaspoon baking
 powder
1 cup chopped
 pecans
40 Ritz crackers,
 crushed
2 teaspoons sugar

1 cup confectioners'
 sugar
1 8-ounce package
 cream cheese,
 softened
1 8-ounce carton
 whipped topping
1 can cherry pie
 filling

Beat egg whites until stiff peaks form. Fold in next 4 ingredients. Spread ½ inch thick in well-greased muffin cups. Bake at 350 degrees for 10 minutes or until light brown. Cool in muffin cups. Loosen with knife; place on serving plate. Cream 2 teaspoons sugar, confectioners' sugar and cream cheese in mixer bowl until light and fluffy. Fold in whipped topping. Drop by spoonfuls onto muffins. Top with cherry pie filling. Yield: 24 servings.

Approx per serving: Cal 210, Prot 2.3 gr, Fat 10.4 gr,
Chol 10.5 mg, Carbo 27.9 gr, Sod 119.3 mg, Potas 53.0 mg.

Patricia A. Kaiser, Preceptor Beta Zeta
Chambersburg, Pennsylvania

Snowball Dessert

1 envelope
 unflavored
 gelatin
1 cup unsweetened
 pineapple juice
Juice of 1 lemon

½ cup sugar
1 16-ounce carton
 whipped topping
1 angel food cake
½ cup coconut

Soften gelatin in ¼ cup cold water in bowl. Add 1 cup boiling water, stirring until gelatin is dissolved. Add pineapple juice, lemon juice and sugar; mix well. Chill until partially set. Fold in half the whipped topping. Trim cake and tear into 1-inch pieces. Place in 9x13-inch dish. Pour gelatin mixture over cake. Chill until set. Spread with remaining whipped topping. Sprinkle with coconut. Cut into squares. Yield: 15 servings.

Approx per serving: Cal 273, Prot 4.3 gr, Fat 8.5 gr,
Chol 0.0 mg, Carbo 45.9 gr, Sod 149.1 mg, Potas 87.2 mg.

Mrs. J. R. Lunn, Gamma Alpha
Findlay, Ohio

Piña Colada Squares

4 envelopes unflavored
 gelatin
6 envelopes Sweet
 'N' Low
2½ cups unsweetened
 pineapple juice

1 cup vanilla ice
 milk
2 to 3 tablespoons
 flaked coconut
⅛ teaspoon rum
 extract

Soften gelatin with Sweet 'N' Low in pineapple juice in saucepan. Bring to a boil, stirring until gelatin is dissolved; remove from heat. Add remaining ingredients; mix well. Pour into 9x13-inch dish. Chill until firm. Cut into 1-inch squares. Yield: 72 squares.

Approx per square: Cal 102, Prot 2.5 gr, Fat 0.2 gr,
Chol 0.4 mg, Carbo 23.8 gr, Sod 81.9 mg, Potas 70.1 mg.

Nancy D. Alarcon, Xi Phi Theta
San Antonio, Texas

Raspberry Delight

¾ cup butter,
 softened
2½ cups
 confectioners'
 sugar
2 eggs

1 pint fresh
 raspberries
8 ounces whipping
 cream, whipped
8 ounces vanilla
 wafers, crushed

Cream butter and confectioners' sugar in mixer bowl until light and fluffy. Add eggs 1 at a time, beating well after each addition. Fold raspberries gently into whipped cream. Sprinkle half the crumbs in 7x11-inch dish. Layer creamed mixture and whipped cream over crumbs. Sprinkle with remaining crumbs. Chill for 2 hours or longer. Yield: 20 servings.

Approx per serving: Cal 228, Prot 1.7 gr, Fat 13.8 gr,
Chol 66.8 mg, Carbo 25.5 gr, Sod 123.0 mg, Potas 48.3 mg.

Connie Stevens, Beta Omega
Menomonie, Wisconsin

Fruit and Yogurt Dessert

½ apple, chopped
½ banana, sliced

⅓ cup lemon yogurt

Combine apple, banana and yogurt in bowl; mix gently. Spoon into dessert dish. Yield: 1 serving.

Approx per serving: Cal 112, Prot 0.9 gr, Fat 0.8 gr,
Chol 0.0 mg, Carbo 28.5 gr, Sod 1.7 mg, Potas 336.5 mg.
Nutritional information does not include lemon yogurt.

Gloria Smethers, Preceptor Laureate Kappa
Beatrice, Nebraska

Strawberries Cardinal

⅓ cup fresh squeezed
    orange juice
½ cup raspberries

1⅓ cups sliced
    strawberries

Combine orange juice and strawberries in bowl. Marinate for 1 to 4 hours. Purée raspberries with chopping blade in food processor. Press purée through fine sieve to remove seed. Drain strawberries. Spoon into dessert glasses. Top with raspberry sauce.
Yield: 4 servings.

Approx per serving: Cal 36, Prot 0.7 gr, Fat 0.4 gr,
Chol 0.0 mg, Carbo 8.4 gr, Sod 0.9 mg, Potas 148.0 mg.

Jolyne M. Dunn, Preceptor Theta
Jefferson City, Missouri

Strawberry Delight

2 small packages
    strawberry
    gelatin
2 10-ounce
    packages frozen
    strawberries

1 pint whipping
    cream, whipped
1 angel food cake,
    torn into large
    chunks

Dissolve gelatin in 2 cups boiling water in bowl. Add strawberries; stir until thawed. Fold in whipped cream. Fold cake into gelatin mixture. Spoon into mold. Chill until set. Unmold onto serving plate. Yield: 12 servings.

Approx per serving: Cal 404, Prot 6.7 gr, Fat 15.1 gr,
Chol 52.8 mg, Carbo 62.8 gr, Sod 227.1 mg, Potas 170.6 mg.

Elaine Murphy, Alpha Pi
Tacoma, Washington

Strawberry-Rhubarb Parfait

4 cups chopped
    fresh rhubarb
⅓ cup sugar
1 envelope
    unflavored
    gelatin
2 cups fresh
    strawberries

½ cup evaporated
    skim milk,
    chilled
½ cup whipped
    topping
1 tablespoon shaved
    semisweet
    chocolate

Combine rhubarb, sugar and ¼ cup water in saucepan. Simmer, covered, for 10 minutes or until rhubarb is tender. Drain liquid into small saucepan. Cool. Sprinkle gelatin over cooled liquid. Let stand for 5 minutes until softened. Heat for 3 minutes or until gelatin dissolves, stirring constantly. Cool. Reserve 4 strawberries. Combine remaining strawberries and rhubarb in blender container. Process until smooth. Beat evaporated milk in mixer bowl until stiff peaks form. Fold in fruit purée, whipped topping and gelatin mixture. Chill for 2 hours or longer. Spoon into dessert glasses. Top with strawberry half and shaved chocolate. Yield: 8 servings.

Approx per serving: Cal 71, Prot 1.4 gr, Fat 1.3 gr,
Chol 0.0 mg, Carbo 14.5 gr, Sod 3.5 mg, Potas 215.4 mg.
Nutritional information does not include evaporated skim milk.

Dolores Koelln, Laureate Beta
St. Paul, Minnesota

Strawberry Trifle

1 10-ounce pound
    cake
1 large package
    vanilla instant
    pudding mix

1 cup milk
1 cup sour cream
1 pint strawberries,
    sliced

Slice pound cake ¼ inch thick. Arrange over bottom and halfway up side of glass trifle bowl. Combine pudding mix, milk and sour cream in bowl. Beat by hand for 1 minute. Spread half the pudding over pound cake. Layer half the strawberries over pudding. Repeat layers. Chill for 2 hours or longer. Garnish with whipped topping and chopped nuts. Yield: 6 servings.

Approx per serving: Cal 443, Prot 6.4 gr, Fat 22.9 gr,
Chol 85.5 mg, Carbo 56.8 gr, Sod 216.9 mg, Potas 248.0 mg.

Janice Dallas, Xi Xi Sigma
Copperas Cove, Texas

Patsy's Whipped Topping

1 teaspoon unflavored
    gelatin
½ cup nonfat dry
    milk powder

3 tablespoons sugar
3 tablespoons oil

Chill small mixer bowl and beaters. Soften gelatin in 2 teaspoons water in small bowl. Add 3 tablespoons boiling water; stir until gelatin dissolves. Cool. Combine dry milk powder and ½ cup ice water in chilled bowl. Beat at high speed until stiff peaks form. Add sugar, oil and gelatin mixture gradually, beating constantly. Chill in freezer for 15 minutes. Chill in refrigerator until serving time. Stir before serving. Yield: 32 tablespoons.

Approx per tablespoon: Cal 19, Prot 0.4 gr, Fat 1.2 gr,
Chol 0.2 mg, Carbo 1.7 gr, Sod 5.7 mg, Potas 18.4 mg.

Patsy Quint, Laureate Omicron
Wichita, Kansas

Index

Microwave recipe page numbers are preceded by an M.

197